# FOLKTALES AND LITERATURE OF HIMALAYA

*Himalaya Past and Present Series*

# FOLKTALES AND LITERATURE OF HIMALAYA

*Editor*

***K. S. Gulia***

ISHA BOOKS
DELHI-110 009

**Folktales and Literature of Himalaya**


ISBN : 81-8205-419-2



Published in 2007 in India by
Isha Books, B-63, Ist Floor, New Gupta Colony,
Near DDA Market, Delhi-110009
Phone: 9212142040
E-mail: ishabooks@hotmail.com

*Laser Type setting by*: Tact Computer Graphics, Delhi
*Printed at*: Salasar Imaging System, Delhi

# Contents

# Introduction

## Kashmiri Literature

Kashmiri poets and prose writers were using Urdu or Punjabi as their medium when they wrote. Even at *mushairas*, poetry was recited in these two languages. Some time Hindi was also the medium of expression.

A poem written by Ghulam Ahmad Mahjoor was recited by some one to Rabindranath Tagore. Tagore appreciated the way the poet had expressed himself. It was a translation in English which was recited, and the story goes, was not done very well. But Tagore liked the way the poet had expressed himself. He asked about the poet and the language in which it had been originally written. When he was told that poet was a Kashmiri and poem was in Urdu, he retorted why a Kashmiri must write in Urdu when Kashmiri by itself was a very developed language, grammatically and expressively better than many other regional languages of India. His sentiments were conveyed to Mahjoor.

Around that time, Dr. Mohammed Iqbal visited Kashmir to attend a *mushaira*. He was surprised to note, like Tagore, that most of poetry was being recited in Urdu, Punjabi or Hindi. There, standing before the audience, he advised the poets, story writers, novelists and prose writers of Kashmir to try and write in Kashmiri. That, coupled with Tagore's sentiments, which were well known by then, gave a boost to the intellectuals. They started having a relook at what they had been doing and what future course they must adopt. Writing in Kashmiri had taken its first tentative step.

Babu Rabindranath was right. Much before the Aryans came to Kashmir, Shina languages of Indo-Iranian family were dominant in Kashmir. When the powerful had taken full control of Kashmir, Shina had been pushed aside and Sanskrit became the language. From about the 14th century, medieval Persian too started creeping into Kashmiri. With such foreign influences, Kashmiri boasts of peclutiarities like certain vowel and consonant sounds, which no other Indian language has. Kishtawari is the most popular dialect of Kashmiri.

Now some eighty years down the line, Kashmiri is trying to come into its own. There are poets, story writers, novelists, who have excelled. Their work is considered at par with the best that is being written in other Indian languages. Kashmiri writers have been bagging Sahitya Academy Awards. Now with consistent efforts of Kashmiri intelligentia, the language has been included in the 8th Schedule of the Constitution.

Kashmiri literary has a history of at least 2,500 years, going back to its glory days of Sanskrit. Early names include Patanjali, the author of the *Mahabhashya* commentary of Panini's grammar, suggested by some to have been the same to write the Hindu treatise known as the Yogasutra, and Dridhbala, who revised the Charaka Samhita of Ayurveda. In medieval times the great Hindu school of Kashmir Shaivism arose. Its great masters include Vasugupta (c. 800), Utpala (c. 925), Abhinavagupta and Kshemaraja. In the theory of aesthetics one can list the Anandavardhana and Abhinavagupta. The use of the Kashmiri language began with the poet Lalleshvari or Lal Ded (14th century), who wrote mystical verses. Another mystic of her time equally revered in Kashmir and popularly known as Nunda Reshi wrote powerful poetry like his senior Lal Ded. Later, came Habba Khatun (16th century) with her *lol* style. Other major names are Rupa Bhavani (1621-1721), Arnimal (d. 1800), Mahmud Gami (1765-1855), Rasul Mir (d. 1870), Paramananda (1791-1864). Also the Sufi poets like Shamas Fakir, Wahab Khar, Soch Kral, Samad Mir, and Ahad Zargar. Among modern poets are Ghulam Ahmad Mahjur (1885-1952), Abdul Ahad Azad (1903-1948), and Zinda Kaul (1884-1965). During 1950s, a number of well educated youth turned to Kashmiri writing, both poetry and prose, and enriched modern Kashmiri writing by leaps and bounds. Many Kashmiri men and women, who had their education in Kashmir and are now settled abroad, have been publishing newspaper to be circulated among Kashmiris in the countries where they are residing, trying to popularize the language.

## The Literary History of Kashmiri

The literary history of Kashmiri began in the $12^{th}$ century. Poetry is the key word, with writers experimenting with different forms of it in all ages. Down the ages, everywhere men have been in the forefront of poetry, prose and folklore. In Europe, women poets and writers were unheard of till the beginning of the nineteenth century, when Jane Austen burst on the scene with *Pride and Prejudice.* But such was the bias against woman at that time that her first work was under a pseudonym. That was not so in Kashmir Literature when Lal Ded in the $12^{th}$ century started writing verses, in Kashmiri. There was no Kashmiri male writer of any substance at that time, or before her who had written in Kahmiri. She was everybody's favourite – Lal Ded or Granny Lal. Her sensitivity and mysticism in *Vaakhs* appealed to each alike, scholar and peasant. Other works of this formative phase (till about 1555 AD), though not as brilliant as Lal Ded's are *Shrukhs* of Sheikh Noor-ud-din, Mahanay Prakash of Shiti Kantha, Banasura Katha of Bhatavatar and Sukhadukhacharitam of Ganaka Prashasta.

## The Flourishing of the Love Poetry

Love-poetry flourished in the next few centuries. Along with the mystical and esoteric verses perfected by Habib Ullah Navshohri (1555-1617) and Rupa Bhawani (1625-1720), a new kind of love poetry developed. This was the beautiful *lol* lyric, sung mostly by women. Habba Khatoon (1551-1606) and Aarnimal (late $18^{th}$ century) were the ruling ladies of this genre of mellifluous verses. Here is an example from the poetry of Habba Khatoon.

Although a garden jasmine I,
in the very prime of bloom,
yet waste I as the snow in June.
Come in the garden, Love,
Come and enjoy the jasmine bloom;
It blooms for you.

**Influence of Persian Literature**

Persian cast a big spell on Kahmiri in the late 18th century. Kashmiri literatures like Mahmud Gani and Waliullah Motoo (both mid-19th century) took to translating from Persian literature and folk lore and started writing *masnavis* (couplets expressing one emotion) and *ghazals* (romantic poetry set to music) in a big way. The legendary love tales of Laila and Majnu, Shirin and Farhad, Sohrab and Rustum, came to North Indian literature through Kashmiri scholars. There were many more such tales which a hundred later was looked up by story writers of the Indian film industry. Many of these tales have been made into films.

***Lila* poetry**

*Lila* poetry was another innovation where the poetry sang like a lover-devotee of the Creator's exubreance. Paramanand (1791-1885) excelled in this. There were others, like Prakash Ram, Maqbul Shah, Lachman Rama, Rasul Mir and Shams Faqir, who dealt said throwing light in their own way on contemporary problem. Songs and ghazals have always been a part of Kashmiri literary culture. The cult of the *maikhana* (liquor house) and *sharaab* (wine) in *ghazals*, popular in Urdu poetry too, was created in the 1890s and 1990s. The few decades of the 20th century saw a prolific writing of mystical and secular poetry, *ghazals*, *masnavis*, and *geets* (songs).

**The Beginning of Prose in Kashmir**

Prose appeared pretty late in Kashmiri, only in the beginning of the twentieth century. But there's really not much good Kashmiri prose, except for a few translations. It was also the time of great socio-political movements all over the country, which had their impact on modern poets like Ghulam Ahmed Mahjoor (1885-1952).

**Dogri**

The whole of Jammu Province south of Pir Panjal, some parts of Himachal Pradesh, viz. Kangra, Chamba, Kullu, Mandi, Suket, some parts of Punjab viz. Gurdaspur, Pathankot, Nurpur, Hoshiarpur and some parts of Pakistan, viz. Shakargarh tehsil of Sialkot comprise the area where Dogri is spoken. There are about five millions dogras in India at this time. It has a rich literature Dogri folk tales form a substantial part of it. There are over seven hundred Dogra folk tales which have been collected and printed so far. The Dogra tales provide a peep into the backyard of

Dogra culture. Here gods and goddesses assume human forms and join human beings to drive home some important truth or moral lesson. Anything is possible in this world to make believe but the values of enshrined in the tales are clear. Quite a few tales have a king or a prince as the main character, the reason being that Duggar was or long a land of rajas. There are also some interesting women-centered tales portraying their superior intelligence out-witting their men folk. British researcher on Dogri language, John Beams, include Dogri in the group of eleven Indian languages gives its area as lying between the Punjab and the valley of Kashmir. (*Outlines of Indian Philology*, p. 11). Dogri is a feminine form of a word Dogra which is a tribal name signifying the people of Duggar. Various views have expressed about the origin of the word Duggar from Dvigarta (Gauri Shankar, 1981), Durgaha (H.R. Divahar 1970), Dungar (Prashant, *Research Bi-annual* Vol. 1, pp. 7174) and Durga (Gauri Shankar 1981, Shivanath 1976). The last one corroborated by a Chamba copper plate inscription of the eleventh century (Vogll, 1911, p. 183) seems to be the most plausible.

**History of Dogri Language**

As Amir Khusru lived from 1253 to 1325 AD, the existence of Dogri language earlier to 13th century is proved. The earliest known mention of Dogri language is found in his list of Indian languages-Sindhi, Lahauri, Kashmiri, Dogri, Dhursamundari, Tilangi, Gujarati, Malbari, Gaudi Bengali, Awadhi and Dehalavi. Inscriptions dating from 12th century AD contain Dogri expressions (See *Dogri Inscriptions* by Shivnath (1976) pp. (52-55) and R.N. Shastri's *Dogri Shodh Sindha*, 1981 (pp. 40 ff) referring to some *sanads*, letters agreements and title deeds written in Takri script and Dogri language dating from 1750 AD to 1860 AD. The earliest extant Dogri work is *Rajauli*, a Dogri translation by Tehaldas from the original Persian work by Bali Ram. The work was translated for Raja Dhyan Singh of Kotla in the latter half of the 18th century AD (Gauri Shankar, *Sapta Sindha*. 1972), Rev. Carey mentioned Dogri in his list of Indian languages in 1916. A Dogri translation of the New Testament is said to have been published by Christian missionaries of Sirampur. A few pieces of Dogri poetry of Dattu of second half of 18th century and of Rudradatta, Ganga Ram and Lakkhu of the 19th century are available. Jyotishe Vishveshar translated *Lilavati*, a Sanskrit work on Mathematics into Dogri in 1873 AD. It was in the 20th century that Dogri writing showed a quick growth in various fields of poetry, prose, novels, short stories, plays, etc.

**Dialects**

Some English and Punjabi scholars describes Dogri as a dialect of Punjabi and Kandyali, but the veteran linguist Dr. Siddheshwar Verma has pointed out that Dogri is structually an independent (*Nameetana* Oct.-Dec. 1967) and not a dialect of any other language. Shivnath mentions seventeen dialects spoken in the area in Duggar. These are standard

Dogri, Kandyali, Kangri, Bhatiali, Sirmauri, Baghati, Kiunthali, Kului Gujari, Rambani, Pongli, Hoshiarpur Pahadi and Lahnda. Bhadrawahi, Rambani and Pongli have common features with Dogri and Kashmiri while Kangri, Hoshiarpur Pahadi and Lahnda have common features with Dogri and Punjabi. With the passage of time, other dialects spoken in the region have left their mark on spoken Dogri.

### Dogra Art, Literature and Music

The Dogra culture is descended from that of the *Indo-Aryans* who settled in and became the main population of India. Dogras are divided into castes on the same lines as *Hindus* in other parts of India, but have local variations.

Basohli, Ramnagar and Jasrota in the Jammu Region, are famous for the 'Pahari Style' of miniature painting. Dogra folk literature comprises of (a) Prose forms short stories, proverbs and riddle; (b) Verse from classified as under : 1. Ballads:- (a) Baran, (b) Kaakan, (c) Love ballads, (d) Devotional (e) those of women saints. 2. Lyrics:- They are vast and varied and difficult to mention e.g. love lyrics, ceremonial lyrics, dance lyrics etc.

Dogri folk songs too range from love to heroism and sacrifices. Ceremonial lyrics give analysis of human reaction to ceremonies. 'Biayian' are sung to celebrate the birth of the male child, indicating gender bias. Family lyrics pertain to household members such as mother, father, daughter-in-law, mother-in-law and their relationships. Contemporary Nepali Literature.

### Nepali Short Stories and Poems

While the natural splendor of Nepal has been celebrated in many books, very little of the substantial body of Nepali literature has appeared in English translation. Every story or poem provides vivid descriptions of life in Nepal. Despite state restrictions, poetry in Nepal remained the most vital and innovative genre, in which sentiments and opinions on contemporary social and political issues were frequently expressed. While the Nepali short story adapted its present form only during the early 1930s, it has rapidly developed to a surprisingly high degree of sophistication. These stories insights into the workings of Nepali society — into caste, agrarian relations, social changes, the status of women, and so on.

In the Kingdom in the Himalayas, tribal animism, Buddhism, and Hinduism live in harmony. In the folklore of Nepal, religious mask-dances with the sound of large barrel drums illustrate the age-old battle between good and evil. The panoramic scenario of the lofty Himalayas, its guardian deities, beautiful landscapes, lush green valleys and soothing climatic conditions have always been the source of inspiration to hard-working these hills. Numerous traditional dances, folk songs, much folklore, folk music and folk forms of theatres and oral tradition of the Nepalese and other tribals residing in different regions, mostly, in the north and the north-eastern parts, have made significant contributions to the enrichment of the cultural heritage of Nepal. Nature, mother earth and the enviroment have also had an influence on literature and culture from the ancient period. Nepali language and culture drew their inspiration from the Vedas, *Gita* and other sacred Hindu books.

We also hear a *gayen,* the itinerant singer of the Nepalese folk tradition, side-by-side with temple songs. A book on Nepali stories is like a multi-coloured lantern. The folktales of Nepal cover almost the entire spectrum of human emotions a and situations. Some of them have the mellow fregrance of love, while some others reek of hatred and jealousy. Some tales have ghosts and apparitions as their main characters, while in some others one will find people indulging in cannibalism. They reflect many local lifestyles, activities, beliefs, feelings, superstition, customs and inhibitions, as well as a deep faith in the supernatural. Several of these stories confirm the old theory of the German orientalist Max Muller about the migration of tales from country to country with changes of names and places. Variation of these stories can be found in distant countries. Kings and queen transforming themselves into birds; places vanishing into thin air; and birds coming to the rescue of men. The romantic ambience of the tales captivates the hearts of children and adults alike.

## Nepali Songs

The translation of the *Ramayana* into Nepali was done by the poet Bhanubhakta Acharya, who is considered the architect of the modern Nepali language. The *Mahabharata* was translated around 1901, and the *Gita* in 1935. Most of the songs, dances and folklore are linked with the nature and its gods. Epics and other sacred scriptures have a deep impact on the hill culture and social life, which has flowed in the history of mankind from generation to generation, mostly in the form of oral tradition. Only recently have the folk songs, folklore and other musical forms been made available in printed form.

No religious ceremony is complete without innovation and offerings to the goddess nature. After a harvest, the first grain is offered to the gods and goddesses of nature, and in some cases to the souls of dead forefathers. Animals and birds have a very significant role in festivals and ceremonies. During *Diwali,* the festival of light, every family in Nepali society offers *puja* and worships cows, dogs and crows.

When languages develop, they have to be taken notice of. With persistent efforts of the Nepali speaking people in India, which inhabit north Bengal as well as the State of Sikkim, Nepali language has been included in the 8th Schedule of our constitution. It has gathered momentum and importance in our national life.

# 1
# Folklore of Nepal

## The People

Whatever knowledge about the Gorkhas I have for the last quarter of a century tells me that they are among the friendliest people in the world. A people ostensibly free from evil propensities, they are God-fearing and truthful. Their hospitality is spontaneous and easily given. They make excellent soldiers and the world knows them as tenacious fighters.

In prehistoric times Nepal sheltered many tribes. The Kirats and the Nagas, who resided in the north and west of India prior to the influx of the Indo-Aryans, were slowly elbowed out to the eastern parts, to Nepal and Sikkim. History records that the Kirats subsequently became the rulers of Nepal and twenty-two dynasties ruled the country for ten thousand years. The Kirats hosted Emperor Ashoka when he visited Nepal in the third century B.C. A number of Indian princes sought shelter in Nepal to escape religious fanaticism whenever it exploded.

## China Factor

In the course of her chequered history, China has often overrun Tibet, forcing her people to seek sanctuary in Nepal. Nepal, then, is a conglomerate of disparate tribes and races living in different valleys, donning different clothes and speaking different languages and dialects. While the aborigin tribes, like the Bhoksas, Tharus and the Dhimals, reside mainly in the Terai regions, the Brahmins, Chhetris and Thakuris are found all over the country. The Gurungs live mainly on the southern slopes of the Annapurna ranges, in west and central Nepal. The Magars (also called Thapas), are in the southern slopes of the Dhaulagiri mountains. The Rais, Limbus and Sunwars are, in the main, the inhabitants of the eastern regions; the Sherpas and Tamangs live along the northern highlands, and the Newars have inhabitants of the valleys of Kathmandu and Pokhara.

The ethnic grouping of the people of Nepal is of no particular importance for the purpose of our present study. In a word, the present Nepalese are a mixture of the original inhabitants and the migrants from the north and south. One finds pure Tibetans near the Tibet border, and Indians in the

Terai region and the midlands. The rest of the areas are a mixture of the three—the degree varying from place to place. The major religions of Nepal are Hinduism and Buddhism. The elements of one intrude into the other so that it is not easy to differentiate them. Moreover, most deities are common to both religions. The people, as a rule, are religious and observe all traditional customs and rites.

The glorious cultural heritage of Nepal is manifest in the diverse social customs and hundreds of festivals, which are celebrated the year round in one part of the country or another. Innumerable temples decorate the landscape. So numerous, indeed, are the shrines that Nepal is referred to as the 'Kingdom of Gods' and 'The Land of Temples.' The most remarkable thing about Nepal is the total absence of violent religious strifes and racial conflicts on her soil.

**Religeous Tolerance**

Although most of the population is Hindu, there is no discrimination. This profound religious tolerance was noted and recorded by Huen Tsang, the seventh century Chinese traveller. In some Hindu and Buddhist temples, one even comes across portraits of Christ and Mahatma Gandhi. This splendid egalitarian spirit is evidently a reflection of the genetic excellence of the average Nepalese.

*The Magars:* The Magars, or Mangars as the tribe prefers to call itself, are one of the important tribes of central and western Nepal. It is said that the Magars settled down in Palpa seven to eight centuries ago and then fanned out to other areas of central and western Nepal. They had their own Raja, and an independent Magar State flourished till the nineteenth century. As their numbers grew and the pressure of population on land increased, the Magars spaced out towards the west and east of Palpa (within Nepal) and sprawled into Darjeeling District, Sikkim and Bhutan, where a one comes across members of this tribe in large numbers. They are now well-settled in the hill districts west of the Nepal valley, generally as far as Dailekh. Some Magars did settle in eastern Nepal where they constitute a minority.

*The Clans:* They are subdivided into seven clans, viz., Ale, Thapa, Burathoki or Bura, Gharti, Rana, Pun and Roka. Of these, the Rokas are the smallest and the Thapas the biggest clans. All clans, however, enjoy equality of social status and inter-clan marriages are normal. Their language, *Magar Kura,* is however, not spoken by the whole clans. It is spoken chiefly by the Ales, Ranas and the Thapas. Many Puns and Buras speak a dialect called *Kam Kura,* or *Pun Kura*, which has considerable local variations. The clan name serves as the surname for men, and they are addressed as such—Bal Bahadur Ale, Ram Parsad Burathoki, Man Bahadur Pun, Alekaman Gharti and so on. All Magar women, on the other hand, are called Magarni. This but a collective name not the clan name. The

Thapas are the largest clan in Nepal. They are widely spread over the entire country.

*The Puns:* The Puns have Mongolian looks. They are perhaps the simplest of all the Nepalese tribes and figure in many stories as simpletons. A typical Pun wears his hair long and greases them with ghee (clarified butter). The Puns are more localized than the other Magar clans, and mostly come from the districts of Char Hazar Parbat and Baglung along the river Kali up to Dana. The Burathokis bear a strong resemblance to the Puns. They are of big built and make excellent soldiers. The Magar Ranas are distinct from the Chettry Ranas. They are a big clan and are widely spread over the country. Their ancestors are believed to be the Chittaur Rajputs who migrated to Nepal during the early Muslim era in India.

*The Gurungs:* Most of the Gurungs hail from the high pasture lands of Lamjung. They mostly inhabit higher and relatively more northerly parts of central Nepal. They are also scattered in other parts of the country, particularly in eastern Nepal. For a newcomer it is rather difficult to differentiate a Gurung from a Magar by outer appearance and dress. All Gurungs, however, wear a thread necklace '*Rup*'. The men wear nine strands with nine knots, and the women, seven strands with seven knots. The Magars are mainly agriculturists. Whereas the Gurungs are predominantly shepherds and graziers.

The Gurungs comprise of two main clans: the Charjat and the Sorajat. The Charjat consists of four castes viz., the Ghales, Lamas, Lamchanes and Ghotanes. A Charjat Gurung considers himself a shade higher than the Sorajat, and the Ghale is regarded as the highest caste among the Gurungs. Over a period of times taboos have crept into their foods habits; some castes do not eat chicken whereas others do not touch mutton or pork. The Gurungs are both Hindus and Buddhists, and their customs contain elements of both. Their language is *Gurung Kura.* The dialects differ from one Gurung stronghold to another. All dialects however, have one common feature; they are all phonetically nasal. A Gurung woman, of any caste or clan, is called a Gurungseni. Whereas a Gurung describes himself (in *Gurung Kura*) as a Thammai or Gurum.

*The Thakuris:* The Thakurs, or Thakuris are the Rajput immigrants from India to Nepal. They claim royal descent and enjoy a comparatively higher social status by virtue of their birth. The present royal family of Nepal are the Thakurs of the Sahi clan. A number of privileges accrue to a Thakuri because of his birth. He receives a better education and occupies an important position in the army—as also in the civil service. Some important posts are also reserved for the Thakuris.

*Caste Hierarchy:* In the social hierarchy Thakuris are only next to the Brahmins. They are not restricted to any particular part, but are scattered fairly widely throughout the length and breadth of the country. Their lineaments are like those of the North Indians. Their major clans are

Chand, Mall, Khan, Sahi and Sen. And these (clans) are further sub-divided into hundreds of others. The prefix to a surname sometimes indicates the district from which the man comes. A Bhirkotya Mall is thus a Thakuri hailing from the village Bhirkot, irrespective of his present residence. As this is also a custom prevalent in some parts of India, the practice may well have been imported with the migration of the tribe to Nepal. The offspring of mistresses and concubines (of the Thakurs), are known as Khawas. They normally practice endogamy. A Thakur may marry a Thakurni girl of any clan other than his own. Thus a Chand may marry a Mall girl or vice versa. Like Hindu marriages in India or wherever the Hindu diaspara in. The marriages are also solemnized by the Brahmins.

*The Chhetris:* The Chhetris, another warrior class of Nepal also enjoy a high social status. Chhetri is a derivation of the Sanskrit word *Kshatriya*. The Chhetris are immigrants from India and regarded as members of the warrior classes. Although found in relatively greater numbers in the Kathmandu valley, they are widely scattered all over the country. They are orthodox Hindus and worship the cow. The sub-sects of the Chhetris are Basnet, Bhandari, Adhikari, Khatri and Karki. A Chhetri woman of any sub-sect is called a Chhetrini.

*The Tamangs:* Tamangs are, immigrants from Tibet. They are sometimes called Bhotias, a term normally applied to the Tibetans. In the eastern parts of the country, they are called Lamas and Murmis. A great number of Tamangs are also found in North Sikkim and the Darjeeling district of West Bengal. The Tamangs have a rich mythology and look upon themselves as the descendents of a cow who bore three sons. The Tamangs are the progeny of the youngest son.

*The Thakalis:* The Thakalis dwell in the area between Ghasa and Jomson along the river Kali. Because of the concentration of Thakalis in this area, the river is called Thak-Khola. The tribe has taken to trade and almost all the affluent traders all over Nepal are the Thakalis. They can be compared to the Marwaris of India. Their women are also proficient in business—a quality exclusively restricted to the Thakali women in Nepal. Many *bhattis* all over the country are run by Thakali ladies. The *bhattis* run by them are the cleanest, most well-managed and by far, the most popular.

*The Newars:* Newars are easily the shrewdest people in Nepal. They are another important business community in the country. They are believed to be the original inhabitants of the Kathmandu valley. A large number of them can speak English and Hindustani and have the potential of becoming good guides. The Newari women also run some *bhattis* along routes frequented by soldiers and tourists. The Newars eat beef. Orthodox Hindus, therefore, most of the time avoid eating with them. Their most significant contribution to the country is in the sphere of the arts, painting, sculpture and architecture. Most of the high quality *Tankas* have been painted by the Newars.

*Rais and Limbus:* The Rais and Limbus are dwellers of eastern Nepal and spill over in large numbers into Sikkim. They are the descendents of the Kirats, who were known for fashionable living. They were the first immigrants into Nepal. They are generally short tempered and any heated discussion with them, or criticism, ought to be avoided. The Rais and Limbus have their own peculiar customs and beliefs. Their custom of marriage is of particular interest. When a boy wants to marry a girl he is invited by the parents of the girl, to their house. Here he is required to sing a song, which is really a riddle. A girl's failure to reply, gets the boy his bride. Should she, however, solve the riddle, the boy goes back a rejected suitor. Dissimulations, of course, are always there in case the couple are in love—a clever girl feigns her inability to reply.

*The Sherpas:* The Sherpas are of Tibetan origin and inhabit the main trade routes between India and Nepal. They help carry loads for the wealthy traders and make excellent porters in the higher regions. They have their own language and practice the Tantric Lamaism of Tibet.

**Religion of Nepal**

The religion of the people varies from a rather orthodox Hinduism to Tantric Lamaism, including the worship of ghosts and goblins. These creatures often figure in their folktales. In their beliefs and superstitions they appear to be (almost) obsessed with giants. This fetish with size could perhaps, be traced to their encounters with the Yeti. Many scholars now believe that there was, in fact, an age when giants fraternized with men. It may be the memories of that era, which now shadows their superstitions.

In the remote areas, both polyandry and polygamy are practiced though these were officially banned a long time back. The marriage customs of the people vary from arranged marriages, like those of the Brahmins *(Bahuns* in Nepali), to the *rodighar* of the Gurungs. The *rodighars* are youth clubs where young boys and girls of a village meet and mix freely and choose their partners by a system of trial and error. There is an element of permissiveness in the love-life of the Sherpas and Lamas. Their attitude to divorce and widow remarriage is equally varied and diverse.

It is the folklore of this lovable people, living a free life and breathing the fresh Himalayan air, that this slim volume deals with.

## Nepal Khari ko Katha

**Nepal Valley: Its Legend**

Many millenia ago, there was sea where Nepal is today. With time and upheavals of nature. The sea recorded, leaving in its wake many lakes which are part of Nepalese landscape. One of the lakes was called

Nagtal, after the name of its presiding deity Nagraja Karkotak. The lake reflected the eternal snows of the Himalayas. Its shores were rich in flora and fauna. In short, it was an idyllic place. At about the time this lake came into existence, Rishi Vyas told the Pandavas that they were guilty of *Gotra hatya* from which they could be absolved only after a *darshan* of Shiva. The brothers went to the Himalayas and managed the briefest glimpse of the Lord, who quickly disappeared into the hills. The Pandavas ferreted him out and began to chase him. Shiva transformed himself into a buffalo and dashed up the hills. Bhim saw the divine beast near the present site of Kedarnath, in Uttar Pradesh province of India, and ran forward to catch it. The (divine) buffalo asked *Prithvi* for shelter and went underground. Bhim, however, grabbed hold of its hind parts. The head of the buffalo surfaced in Nepal and he came to be called *Pashupatinath,* or 'Lord of the animals.'

Nepal itself is known as *Pashupatinath bhumi,* or the land of Lord Pashupatinath. People started pouring in to pay homage to the Lord. But Nagtal lake became a hindrance for them. The lake was a favourite haunt of one *Asura* who troubled the pilgrims a great deal. Lord Vishnu then incarnated himself as a boar, dragged the *Asura* in the lake and killed him. He then siphoned off the water of the lake to form the river Bhagwatmati, or the river of Vishnu.

This sacred river is now called Bhagmati. The dry bed of the lake became the site of many towns which sprang up in due course to commemorate the advent of Shiva as Pashupatinath. The temple of the Lord is a consequence of the hard work of many generations who have been residing on the banks of sacred river Bhagmati. Architecturally, the temple is like a Pagoda, with a gilt roof and beautifully carved massive doors. It is the holiest of the Shiva temples in the sub-contiment.

According to a different Hindu version, during *Dwapar* age Nepal was ruled by the *Asuras.* An *Asur a* king called Mahindra, the son of Varnasur, dammed the Bhagmati river and turned it into a lake. He caught people who passed that way, drowned them in the lake and killed them. Terror-stricken men prayed to Lord Krishna to deliver them from the depradations of this *Asura.* The lord destroyed Mahindra, the *Asura* king, and reconverted the lake into the holy river. The valley again became habitable. To commemorate this event, a number of Krishna temples were constructed all over the country (the most famous of those was constructed by Raja Sidhi Nar Singh Mall in the sixteenth century. Events from the Hindu Epics, *Ramayana* and *Mahabharata,* were carved on the stone walls of this temple).

A colourful Buddhist legend says that lotus did not grow in the ancient lake, among other flower did. One day on *Chaitra-Purnima,* a Mahatma, called Vipaswi Buddha, passed that way and threw the root of a lotus in the lake. He told his followers, 'This root will grow into a plant. When the plant blossoms into a flower, *Swayambhu,* or the 'self-born' will be revealed here as flame. The water of the lake will drain away and leave behind a beautiful valley. Men will then move in to inhabit this valley.'

Many years passed. One day on *Ashwin-Purnima,* the lotus root blossomed into a flower. It had a heavenly beauty and an unearthly charm and reflected five hues of a flame. It was in fact *Swayambhu* or the self-born, revealing itself. The news spread far and wide and reached the ears of the Mahatma Sikhi Buddha. He came to Nagtal with a large number of his devotees and by way of obeissance made three *parikramas* around the lake. Sikhi Buddha then sat on the bank the lake for meditation and remained there for a number of years. At last he attained *moksha,* and his devotees interred his body in *Swayambhu lake.*

Many years lakes, another Mahatma, Vishambhu Buddha, arrived at the lake with his followers and meditated there for many years. When he attained *moksha,* he told his devotees that the lake would soon be replaced by a valley. At about this time Manjushri Buddha was residing in the north-eastern part of Tibet, and he came to Nagtal, in the wake of Vishambhu Buddha with his followers. On reaching there they completed the prescribed three *parikramas* round the lake. Then Manjushri went to the south bank and drawing his scimitar, cut a passage through the hills. Water gushed out through the new widened course.

### Lake to Valley

The drained lake was replaced by a valley through which flowed the River Bhagmati. Manjushri attained *moksha* and left his mantle in the hands of his devotee, Dharamkar, who became the first ruler of Nepal. The people established a village and named it Manjupatam in honour of Mahatma Manjushri. This village is now called Deopatam. The exact place where Manjushri Buddha made a passage through the hills is called Chovar, and it is situated eight kilometres south-west of Kathmandu. A deep gorge located there is believed to bear the indentation marks of Manjushri's scimitar. It offers an excellent panoramic view of the snow-clad Himalayas.

## Legend of Kathmandu

Thousands of years ago, the beautiful valley of Nepal was covered by a lake called Nagtal. The water was drained off through the kind intervention of Vishnu, the Lord of preservation, and the valley became habitable. Since nature bountiful, men converged into this beautiful land from far and wide. Soon the population swelled. The people, aware that the land was a gift of God, were noble and god-fearing. But it is in the nature of men that even the best of people are prone to petty misunderstandings and quarrels. As time passed some disputes naturally arose. There was, however, no one to administer justice. And as neither side relented, petty quarrels soon became serious conflicts. So the elders prayed to God to send them a Raja who could administer justice and settle their disputes. This wish was also granted. But a Raja must have a capital. Thus the seat of the Raja came to be called Kantipur or the dwelling place of authority.

### Period of Prosperity

Now with a fair arbiter to settle their disputes, the people had more time for prayers and hard work. This led to a period of tremendous prosperity and the coffers of the Raja were filled with gold. Centuries passed and the country became richer and richer. At last, during the reign of Shantikar, a golden temple was constructed. The place was very sacred. (It is said that rods of iron that happened to touch the temple walls were transformed into pure gold).

Lord Shiva, the god of destruction and procreation. Kedarkhand, a mountainous area to the west of Nepal was the abode of Lord. It was at this time that the Pandavas were advised by Rishi Vyas to proceed to the Himalayas for a *darshan* of Shiva to expiate the sin of *Gotra hatya*. The Pandavas went to Kedarkhand to be absolved of their transgression by the Lord of mountains. They got a glimpse of Shiva in the Nag Tibba ranges and set out in pursuit. Shiva, who did not wish to pardon the murderers easily became invisible at a place which came to be called *Gupta-kashi*, or the hiding place.

### The Holp Buffalo

Thereafter, Shiva assumed the form of a buffalo and fled to the higher hills. The Pandavas, privy to this change, followed close behind. Near the present site of Shri Kedarnath temple (still visited by many Nepalese), the divine buffalo dived to disappear into the ground. But Bhim, the mightiest of the Pandavas prevented the buffalo's escape by holding onto its tail. The Pandavas were given a *darshan* by Lord Shiva and absolved of their sins.

The head of the divine buffalo surfaced in the holy land of Nepal, in the heart of the capital town of Kantipur. The people were overjoyed at the appearance of Shiva and constructed a temple to in his honour. After the arrival of Pashupatinath, all the gods and goddesses began to come to Kantipur for a *darshan* of Shiva. When Kalpavriksha, the tree of heaven heard the praises of Pashupatinath, he assumed human form and came to Kantipur to pray to the lord. He joined a procession that was on its way to the temple of Shiva. But Mahadeva from whom nothing is hidden revealed this secret identity of Kalpavriksha to one of his devotees and told him that this was a marvellous opportunity of forcing Kalpavriksha to make his home in the capital.

**Kalpavriksha**

The devotee of Shiva recognized Kalpavriksha and caught hold of him. The tree of heaven tried hard to free himself, but Lord Shiva's had bestowed his devotee with magic powers. At last Kalpavriksha told him that he could not possibly leave the heavens—his absence would create chaos in Trilok—but he would grant the boon of providing his ganger. And in four days there arose a magnificent Sal tree in the centre of the city. From this the devotee of Shiva carved out a beautiful house which came to be called Kashtam and apam or Kathmando, literally meaning the House of Wood. As time passed, the name of Kantipur was changed to Kathmando. The town was built and rebuilt as the houses grew old and dilapidated but the temple of Shiva and the Kashtamandapam remained firm bearing all the vagaries of nature.

## Karunamaya: The Legend

Karunamaya, the god of mercy, was living in Tibet and had not yet migrated to Nepal. This is the story of that period. The country was in the grip of a severe and prolonged drought. Men and beasts were suffering greatly. The people did everything possible. They made sacrifices, performed *tantric* rituals and propitiated the gods and demons alike. But nothing helped. Finally, the *raj-purohit* (royal priest), Bandhu Datta, was consulted. The arrival of Karunamaya, the god of mercy, into Nepal, he advised, could alone save the situation. 'Where does he live? We shall go and fetch him,' said the people. 'You cannot reach him,' Bandhu Datta continued, the dwells in the land of demons. There are many rivers and obstacles in the way. Only men of true religion or men of means, like kings, can reach the place.' 'Let us go to the king,' said the people. 'No, that also will not do,' Bandhu Datta replied. 'No, you will have to seek out his father, the old king in his temple.' The present king will be of no help.

Many years ago, the old king Narender Dev had abdicated the throne in favour of his son Bir Dev.

**The Despot**

Whereas Narender Dev was a religious man, his son was a cruel treacherous despot. Many openly whispered that the twelve year drought was a continuance of the vileness of their ruler. Bad kings bring disasters to their subjects. The people went to the old king, Narender Dev, and begged him to accompany them to the abode of Karunamaya, the god of mercy. The king declined saying that as he had renounced the world, he was unaffected by suffering or joy. The men pleaded with him in the name of god and mercy, and the king relented. After due deliberations between Narender Dev and the *raj-purohit,* it was decided to include Nag Dev Karketak in the party. He would, it was felt, help overcome the water obstacles. A holy man of Patan was also included in the entourage, both to carry presents for Karunamaya and to appease the more troublesome demons. Nag Dev Karketak was approached and told of the mission. He demurred saying that because of his slow speed he would not be able to keep pace with the party.

### Miniature Form

Their problem, however, was resolved by persuading him to assume miniature form and be carried in the pocket of the priest. All preparations over, they set out at last on their long and arduous journey. Nag Dev Karketak helped across many obstacles, adding greatly to the speed of the party. He would assume forms of huge serpents and provide impromptu bridge over rivers, *nullahs* and ditches. With each successful crossing Karketak would re-enter the pocket of the priest. After a very long and tedious journey fought with risks, they reached the land of the demons. The god of mercy, Karunamaya was staying in a well-guarded palace. Ferocious demons on all sides prevented the party from reaching Karunamaya. When his mother, who was a she-demon, came to know the purpose of the mission from Nepal, she spread her bed in front of her son's door. She did not want her son to leave for this errand. She did not want the bisectors to meet Karunamaya.

Men were dying for lack of water. All the rivers and wells of Nepal had dried up completely. Time was running out and the party outside Karunamaya's palace was greatly distressed at its inability to reach the god of mercy. At last, Bandhu Datta undertook a severe penance and performed religious rituals; Karunamaya was obliged to appear before them. But there was another hurdle to cross. Had Karunamaya tried to step over mother's body he would have been afflicted with leprosy. He, therefore, transformed himself into a bee and flew to the place where the priest was performing the powerful rituals that had forced Karunamaya to out. He entered the utensil kept ready for him and Narender Dev promptly secured the lid. They were prevented from leaving by Karunamaya's mother who attacked them with her army of demons.

### Fight between Devas and Danavas

The priest Bandhu Datta called in the gods for help, and a fierce fight ensued between the *devas* and the *danavas*. The demons took to their heels, but Karunamaya's mother lingered on. Bandhu Datta explained her the reason for which they were taking Karunamaya away. She pleaded that Karunamaya be allowed to occasionally come back within a certain distance from where she could see him. To help Karunamaya, who was inside the utensil, find his way back, she gave some seeds to the party to throw as they went along. The trees that sprouted came to be called *deodar,* 'the timber of gods.'

**Journey to Nepal**

The party finally set out on their long journey back. When they entered the territory of Nepal, Bandhu Datta performed a unique *pooja* to which all the gods were invited. And they accompanied the procession all the way to Nepal. Brahma was at the head of the party on his chariot drawn by the royal swans, followed by Vayu, the ruler of winds, astride his fleet-footed stag. Above them all, rode Sun, on his chariot drawn by seven horses, dispelling darkness and bestowing warmth and brightness. Kubera, the god of wealth, spread riches along the route. Indra, the king of gods was in the centre riding *Airavata,* his four-tusked white elephant, holding a parasol aloft to shade the whole party.

As they were going along, one of the gods uttered the syllable *bhu.* Bandhu Datta immediately realized the significance of this utterance— that the place where *bhu* was intoned (by the god) was to be treated as the birth place of Karunamaya. Accordingly, the vessel in which Karunamaya was brought was enshrined in the temple that was built there. As the party went further, a discussion was held about the most suitable dwelling for Karunamaya. Each man clamoured to have the god reside in his town. As they arrived at Igatyag near Patan, people assembled in droves to welcome the god, and everyone agreed that the wish of the people should prevail. By popular will Karunamaya was installed at Patan. The drought disappeared, and prosperity came back to Nepal. From that day Karunamaya,* has been the *Ishtadeva* of Nepal.

## Legend of the New Year

Why should I keep this bit of worthless sand? Your powers of prophecy, after all, appear to have been taken away from you by the goddess. You have let me down this time, I want to throw this worthless sand in a dung heap' Raja Anand Mull said to his court astrologer, Sidhiwanth.

Why the prophecy has not come true has made me uneasy. I had meditated again and again and fully examined all aspects before advising you. Frankly, I suspect foul play,' replied Sidhiwanth, his face turning pale.

**'Nepal' – The Name**

This is a true story and dates back to the time when a new calendar was introduced in Nepal. The older people say that the event dates back

* The other names of Karunamaya are Banga Deo, Machhendranath and Swayambhu Nath.

to the year 879. The name 'Nepal' is, in fact, mentioned for the first time around this period. The country was then divided into two sister states ruled by two brothers. Jaya Deva Mull, the elder brother, had his capital at Kathmandu, and Anand Mull, the younger, had the seat of his government at Bhatgaon. Anand Mull had a court astrologer named Sidhiwanth, who was renowned for his gift of prophecy. It was said that he had received the blessings of Rishi Bhrigu on account of his devotion and prolonged *tapasya*. His predictions never backfired.

One day Sidhiwanth told Raja Anand Mull that at a particular time sand collected from the holy Bhagmati river would turn into gold. He had dreamt of huge heaps of gold. He had meditated on the significance of this dream he had consulted books on astrology and had theorically studied his dream. The Raja dispatched some men to bring the sand. The specified period passed, but the predicted transmutation did not occur. Sidhiwanth was non-plussed.

**Matter of Luck**

He consulted the scriptures again and concluded that there was indubiously some foul play. He told the Raja about his apprehensions and insisted that the book was correct. He said, 'I am certain that the sand was transformed into gold. It is, however, possible that the labourers employed to fetch it somehow heard of my prediction and hid the blessed sand somewhere. It is all a matter of luck. I will tell you of a mythological event to illustrate my point.' And Sidhiwanth narrated the oft-repeated story of a devotee of Shiva, who missed a great treasure because of ill luck.

Someone was reciting *Om namo Shivaye, Om namo Shivaye.* This Shiva and Parvati leash when they were taking a round of srishti. She asked Mahadeva to bless him with something. Shiva replied that he could not give his devotee anything more than what his luck would hold. But Parvati insisted. The devotee was an old man of eighty-five whose eyesight was failing. Shiva placed large heaps of gold, diamonds and jewels on the way for him to pick and stood behind a bush with Parvati to see what the devotee would take from the huge pile of wealth that he had left to the picked up.

At the same time that Lord Shiva had left the pile, a thought crossed the mind of the devotee. He knew his eyes were failing him, and it was likely that he would soon become completely blind. It was not out of place, therefore, to be prepared to face the dark and gloomy days ahead. Accordingly he tied a piece of cloth over his eyes to practise moving as a blind man. Feigning blindness he passed by the fabulous treasure kept for him by Shiva. He did touch the heap of diamonds without knowing what he had touched, or missed, and went his way. Sidhiwanth then concluded, 'I am sure, your majesty, something similar has happened to the gold that was.' 'No,' insisted the king emphatically, 'your prediction was wrong.'

**Shankadhar**

The Raja went away, and Sidhiwanth felt deeply humiliated. He set fire to his books of prophecies and fainted. Anand Mull ordered the useless sand thrown out. As he watched the disposal of sand his eyes were held by the glitter of gold, some of which was clinging to the baskets that contained the sand. He summoned the labourers and interrogated them. They told him that when they were returning with the sand, they met a man named Shankadhar, who was known to one of them. Out of courtesy Shankadhar invited them for dinner, which they were glad to accept. After many drinks and a hearty meal, Shankadhar asked them about their strange load, and told them that he required some sand for construction work. He requested them to leave their load with him and collect some more sand on their way. The labourers agreed, for they had eaten his salt. They unloaded the entire lot at his place except the few grains that still clung to the baskets.

**Magnanimity of Shankadhar**

Whilst Anand Mull was making these enquiries, a messenger came from Kathmandu with a message that a man named Shankadhar had been blessed with lot of gold. He had requested that all debts of the sister states be paid, and the gold utilized for the betterment of the masses. A similar request was sent to Jaya Deva Mull. The two states then combined to form a territory, and Jaya Deva commemorated this event by starting a new calendar. Even now the New Year's day is celebrated with prayers to the God who can turn sand into gold.

## Legend of Swayambhu Nath

**The Temple of Dew Drops**

It is said dew drops provided water for the construction of this beautiful temple of Shakya Muni. It is variously called the temple of Buddha of Shakya Muni, and the temple of dew drops.

The temple of Swayambhu Nath is located in the charming sylvan surroundings on a hillock about 250 feet high at a distance of about three kilometres, west of Kathmandu. It is one of the oldest and most glorious of Buddhist *chaityas* (*stupas*). The main *stupa* is a solid hemisphere of brick and earth supporting a lofty conical spire capped be a pinnacle of copper. On all four sides of the spire, are the all-seeing-eyes of Lord Buddha. The *stupa* is equally sacred to the Hindus and the Buddhists. Legend has it that the lotus of Buddha first blossomed at the exact spot where the shrine now stands. The large hemisphere of the *stupa* represents the *garbha,* or the seat of all creation.

The creation of the temple has its own story to tell. In olden times, a Raja constructed beautiful aqueducts over a spring at the junction of busy routes to commemorate his name. This was a common practice, and it was felt that the path to heaven (for the builder of these springs) would be made considerably easier by the blessings of thirsty men. The outlets were exquisitely designed and carved, dragon heads. However, at the opening ceremony, the Raja was dismayed to find that the aquaducts were dry. And the people who had thronged to see the inauguration of the spring, laughed out of the other sides of their mouths. The Raja was embarrassed and upset, and attributed this failure to the wrath of gods. The royal priests suggested human sacrifice as propitiation. The noble Raja sat deep in thought, and finally came to a solution. He called his son and said, 'Tomorrow morning, before the rise of the morning star, go to the spring of the dragons. You will find a man lying there. Sacrifice him by cutting off his head. Here is the sword.' The son nodded his head in consent and departed. Next morning, like a dutiful son he carried out his father's instructions. Curiosity, however, prompted him to see the sacrificed man. He was aghast to see that he had actually sacrificed his own father. The prince was overcome with grief and remorse and was also terrified by the wrath of gods.

**The Fast**

He fasted without food and water for many days, till he fell asleep with sheer exhaustion. The goddess Bajrajagini came in his dream and said, 'You have obeyed the orders of your father. Had you disobeyed, you would have been a sinner. By obeying him, you are still a sinner. To expiate your sins, you should construct a temple of the Shakya Muni.' This was wind of the goddess, what if it was a dream. He collected his courtiers and ordered the construction of a temple. The days of his trials were, however, not yet over. Soon after the construction was begun the kingdom was afflicted by a severe drought. The dry spell lasted for many years.

**Princely of Water**

The rivers, springs and the wells went dry. The countryside turned into a desert. Men had to go to far off mountains to fetch some water. There was no water to continue the construction of the temple. The prince devised a plan. He had many white sheets spread near the construction site at night to catch the morning dew. However minimal the amount, it helped accelerate the rate of construction. But even this was not the end of the prince's woes. One night, a demon came in the form of a bear and damaged the temple. This was repaired. But the following night, the construction was damaged again. They could not find out who was obing for many mights. They had to keep a rigid when finally they dicovered who was doing the mischeaf.

The erllain was chased away. The temple was completed, and it stands to this day. It is called 'The Temple of Dew Drops'. It is said that the sins of men are washed off" by a single visit to this shrine.

## Legend of the Kokla Pheasant

This is the true story of a heartless money lender, who charged his clients exorbitant rates of interest. The poorer the client, the greater the rate of interest. Many of them were unable to clear their debts and ended as his bonded labourers. He was also a congenital miser, who enjoyed the feel of money, the mounting figure more than the gains it could fetch for him. All his ill-gotten wealth was concealed under the ground. His greed grew with the years. The people, tired of his usury, prayed to the gods to deliver them from his excesses. Their cries of suffering at last reached the ears of the gods who decided to teach the usurer a lesson. Indra, lord of the clouds and thunder, sent devastating rains.

### The Deluge

The downpour was almost like the deluge when Vishnu had incarnated himself as a fish to save the world. The incessant rain caused a number of landslides. Unfortunately for the miser, the recur ring landslides pushed his buried treasure elsewhere. After the rains he dug at hundred and one places to look for his wealth, but there was no trace of the hoard. So great was his grief that he neither ate nor drank. He moved from hill to hill shouting, '*kata lukayo, kata lukayo*?' (Where have I hidden it? Where have I hidden it?) He died a miserable death. None volunteered to perform his last rites, and he was, therefore, barred from being born as a human being. He became the bird Kokla, and, still flies from hill to hill and tree shouting in agony, '*Kata lukayo*? *Kata lukayo*?'

Even now his agonized cries can be heard, '*kata lukayo, kata lukayo*?' (Where have I hidden it? Where have I hidden it?) What is worse is that no one comes to help him locate his lost treasure, nor even to sympathize with him. The bird warbles away, asking '*kata Lukayo*? *kata Lukayo*?' It is believed that if a man eats the meat of this bird, he loses his memory. In fact, the meat is given to an enemy by subterfuge, so that he loses his memory and wanders about shouting aimlessly, '*Kata lukayo, kata lukayo*?'

## Legend of Jeevan Amrit

Throughout the ages the one consuming desire of men has been to acquire the nectar of life to revive the dead. Short of that, men have been craving for power to be able to communicate with the dead. Bandhu Acharya of Gola was no exception.

The story goes that Bandhu Acharya spent a lot of time in the company of mendicants who were practitioners of *tantra*. In the course of time his *tantric* practices helped him to acquire many secrets and powers. He, however, had a consuming passion for mastery over life and death by the acquisition of the nectar of life. One day, as he sat meditating and performing the *tantric* rites, in the temple of the *Devi*, She appeared in person and said, 'Your devotion is deep and persistent, and the sincerity of your desire, beyond question. I will fulfil your cravings on the condition that you do what I ask you to do.' Bandhu agreed. Devi was pleased and said, 'All right. I want you to sacrifice the person now standing behind you at my altar?'

**The Sacrifice**

This indeed was a simple task. In those days, it was common practice to offer themselves as victims to sacrifice for the good of the king and his kingdom. Bandhu Acharya thought that the Devi had really been kind and asked for a minor an offering. Overjoyed, he looked back without the slightest hesitation, and found his only son standing behind him. There was, however, no going back on his word, and he sacrificed his son at the altar. The goddess was pleased and told him to go to the place where he would find the nectar of life. That nector Deer said would bring his son back to life. Full of hope, Bandhu Acharya carried the body of his son and put it in a box in his private room. He told his wife that he was leaving for some distant place on urgent business. He forbade her to enter his private apartment, or open the box in his absence. Then hurriedly packing some essentials he left for his uncle's house in Kathmandu.

His son wife had not seen their son that day. For many days she waited for the return of her only son. At last she become apprehensive about his safety. She could not keep her mind off her child and constantly worried about him. Something within, some uncanny intuition of a mother, told her that her son was in trouble and that her husband knew what had happened. One night she had a strange dream in which she saw her husband was carrying the dead body of their son. She got up with a start, went straight to the private apartment of Bandhu Acharya, and opened the box which he had forbidden her not to. To her horror, she found the dead body of her son. She wailed loud and long, waking up the neighbours, who came rushing to her house. In her agony, she went on cursing her husband, and her luck for having married such a man.

**The Rumour**

The rumour spread that there was foul play and the son had obviously been killed by the father who had lost his head. Soon, all the relatives reached her house. Her own relatives arrived from Kathmandu, from Gola came her husband's relations. Now, as is common, they eyed each other with suspicion and opinions differed on every conceivable matter. The men from Gola argued that they must wait for the boy's father, but the woman's relatives from Kathmandu disagreed to it. The boy was no more, they argued, and there was no need to create obstacles on his journey to heaven. His soul, they felt, must be wandering disconsolately and cursing the inconsiderate relatives. Bandhu must have gone mad, they were sure, there was no need to wait for him to perform the last rites. Bandhu's relatives, on the other hand, strongly felt that the father must be given a chance to have a last look at his son. The lady of the house favoured her own people, whose wish finally prevailed. The boy was assigned to the holy fire.

### False Hope

Bandhu Acharya came back with the nectar of life, full of hope that he would revive his only son and gain knowledge of the world beyond where his own son had been. Excited at this prospect, he went straight to the box. It was empty. The nectar was useless now. Bandhu was disgusted and went to his people at Gola and severely reprimanded them. On coming to know the insolence and high-headedness of his wife and her people, he decided not to go back to them. By the power of *tantra* he became invisible and was never seen again.

To this day the people of Gola stage a mock funeral every year to commemorate the story of Bandhu Acharya, and hurl vociferous curses on the people of Kathmandu. The moral this katha as wise people say is: why make this life miserable in the hope of getting the nector of life.

## The Mapa Guru of Kathmandu

Kathmandu is the holy city where the Kalpavriksha has contributed his wood for the construction of Kashtamandapam. It is the city where Pashupatinath dwells near the city is the altar of Mapa Guru. The residents of Kathmandu sacrifice a buffalo at this altar every year, and offer enormous quantities of cooked rice to fulfil their promise to the Guru. He, in turn, rids them of ghosts, goblins, spooks and witches. No demons can, therefore, ever bother the residents of Kathmandu.

Many centuries ago there lived a fabulously rich man in the city he had a son named Kesh Chander. Because of riches of his father he had grown up as a spelt child. The wealth that he inherited when his father died turned his head. He sacked all the old, faithful servants and employees who looked after his estate. He took to evil ways and consequently, fell on evil days. He drank heavily and spent most of his time in the company of women of easy virtue. The rest of his time was spent in gambling. As the old saying goes that a droplet taken each day will empty even a perennially full lake, his vast but limited, coffers were being gradually depleted and a day came when he became penniless. His friends, who were, and mostly are, lovers of fair weather, left him. Women, who swore undying love, pushed him out of their apartments, calling him mad. He was left only with his house, an ancestral property for many generations. On the hope that he would win his money back, he sold the house and gambled the money as a last resort to regaining his lost wealth. He lost, and became both homeless and penniless.

**The Sister**

Devoid of shelter and money and bereft of friends, he thought of his sister who lived in a far-off village. He reached her house in tatters. She welcomed him with open arms and provided him with food and a clean set of clothing. Partial comfort again revived his latent desire to get rich overnight. He wanted to make yet another splash at changing his fortunes. He had, however, no courage to borrow money from his sister. His desire to gamble, however, got better of him and he sold the costly utensils in which he was served food by his sister. But he lost the money again.

Evil habits die hard. He tried again and lost again. His sister soon discovered the cause of missing utensils and was terribly embarrassed. She admonished him in camera, and told him that his chicanery would make her lose face with her husband. Brothers were supposedly a source of pride for their sisters, could she take any in him? She now served him food on banana leaves. This reprimand chastized him and he left the house without touching his food, promising never to return. He felt hungry on the way. He had a single copper coin with which he bought some stale food. He then went straight to the Swayambhu Nath hill to pray. He kept his meagre food on a rock and closed his eyes for prayers.

**The Doves**

A flock of dhikur (doves), in the meantime, came and settled around the food. Amongst them was a pair of doves that lived in the temple of Pashupatinath. When Kesh Chander opened his eyes after his prayers, he saw the doves hungrily eyeing the food. Notwithstanding his own hunger and offered to doves his food. The doves of Pashupatinath were very pleased by his act of generosity and brought him gold equivalent to the weight of the food eaten by their flock. Kesh Chander wrapped the gold in a piece of cloth and set out for his town. The journey tired him and he sat down to rest under the shade of a banyan tree. Unfortunately, a notoriously blood-thirsty demon called Mapa had his dwelling on the same tree. Kesh Chander heard his grunts he told him that he was a very rich man, he would, if the agrees to sparel him his life, feed him a buffalo and lots of rice everyday. Mapa agreed and promised him that he in turn would keep Kesh Chander's residence free of ghosts and evil spirits.

### The Goddess was Pleased

Kesh Chander came back and rebought his house. He bought many plates of silver and gold and sent them to his sister, along with many other presents. This greatly pleased the goddess Lakshmi who bestowed him with greater and greater profits in his business. He gave large sums to various temples and fed the poor. His friends and women sought to cultivate him again but he had learnt his lesson.

After remaining everything that he lost his thoughts turned to Mapa Guru and the promise he had made. Everyday he would feed him a buffalo and lots of rice. He did this till the last day of Mapa Guru on earth. After his death, Kesh Chander built a temple in his honour. The people of Kathmandu still make the offering of a buffalo and rice once each year to commemorate the last day of Mapa Guru in Kathmandu.

## Themi ka Nag Devata

### The Serpent God of Themi

Hundreds of years ago, there lived a python in a *tal* near Bhatgaon. It lured people by displaying his *Kuberbhandar* and devoured them. Precious items like gold and jewels belonging to those who had been descoard would be seen floating over the water's surface, and unsuspecting wayfarers who entered the lake to recover the wealth would never come out again. Men prayed to the gods to rid them of this menace.

The news reached a mendicant of the neighbouring town of Themi, who decided to kill the *nag*. He came to the *tal* accompanied by a devotee. Before entering the water, he instructed his devotee to watch the surface. If he saw blood, it would mean that the python had been killed. If, on the contrary, milk floated on the surface it would simply imply that he had died. To enter the lake, the mendicant would have had to transform himself into a python. The mendicant had altarned the power to transform him into any human being. He was aware that by killing the *nag,* he would have been guilty of murder, and the power to change into any form at will would be taken away from him. So he handed over some rice (some accounts say it was *vibhuti)* to his devotee and asked him to sprinkle it over his body as soon as he came out of the lake. The mendicant then transformed himself into a *nag* and entered the *tal.*

### Magical Rice

Seeing the magic rice in his hand, the devotee became evilly ambitious. He fervently wished the *nag* would kill the mendicant as that would make him the sole possessor of the rice which could work miracles for him. He was saddended when he saw blood on the water's surface. What if he did not sprinkle rice on the python mendicant, he asked himself ?

And ran. The mendicant surfaced in the form of the *nag* and went after his devotee, requesting him to sprinkle the rice over his body. But the man was beyond caring. Unfortunately for him, he tripped and fell and the entire rice spilled on the ground. The *nag* bit him and he died instantly. The nag then came back to the *tal.* And ever since, people from far and wide, have been coming to worship the Nag-Devta of Themi. However, no man from Themi ever dares to come near the *tal.* The belief is that Nag-Devata is still there in the *tal.*

## Fair of the Thief

It is impossible to predict, with any degree of certitude, how a man will react to adversity: whether he will be snowed under and take to evil ways, or rise to heights of grandeur. 'My time has come. Go and get some money to meet any contingency that may arise. Also, buy a few clothes for the baby,' said a wife to her husband. He was a lotus-eater and never did anything more than the barest minimum. The idea of going out to look for work was unpleasant. Nevertheless he got up reluctantly and went to the jungle to cut wood. He took his bundle of wood to the bazar and sold it. Deciding that he would not need the axe again, he sold it to make some extra money. With his pocket fairly full, he happily turned homewards. On the way he crossed a *bhattiwali's shop,* where some men were carousing, gambling and making merry. The man thought, I am in luck. I am soon to be blessed with a child, I have earned by the dint of hard work, and I have been able to sell off my useless axe. If I gamble with this money now, I am sure to win. And he sat down at the gambling table. But he had run out of his quota of luck. He lost the entire sum, some on drinks and the rest in gambling. Cursing, he left for his village. Reaching home, he saw his wife in labour pains, and for the first time in his life, he suffered remorse. He "went back, set on to begging, borrowing or stealing to bring money somehow for his beloved spouse and for the infant who was yet to be born. What sins, he brooded, had the baby committed that he should be born to such a worthless father? The sun was setting, and soon the evening stars rose over the horizon. The birds were returning merrily to their nests for rest and repose. And he was moving away from home. He became sentimental and unable to contain himself, he burst into sobs. His loud weeping attracted a thief out on his nightly rounds. Learning of his plight, the thief told him to be calm and wait till he came back with his booty. The man waited almost all night. Just when he was beginning to despair, he heard a rustling noise nearby. The thief had come back with a bag stuffed with jewellery. Handing over the booty to him, the thief said, 'My friend, go back to your beloved wife. Who else is there to stand by her at this difficult time? Never gamble again and start some business. You have an innocent child to look after'. The man felt ashamed of himself and went back home. His wife had already delivered a son and he hurried to do the necessary shopping. In due course, he started his own business which happily flourished and his wealth multiplied by leaps and bounds. He often remembered his benefactor, the thief, and looked everywhere for him. But he could not be traced. To perpetuate his memory, the man opened a *dharamsala* in the thief's name. He also began an annual fair to synchronize with the day of his first meeting with a man who had a kind heart behind his questionable profession. The fair of the thief is still held in many villages.

## Chara ko Bhat

### The Bird's Breakfast

As happened every day at down, a bird rose early to search for her food. She found a nice pea in a field. She at once brought it with her and decided to have a hearty breakfast. She thought that as God had been particularly kind to her that day, it was better for her to have a bath, say her prayers and then have a feast. She flew off to the holy river for a bath. Her problem was where to keep the pea? If she left it on the ground either the ants would get it, or the other birds would take it. At last she kept the pea on the railing of a bridge and asked the carpenter, who was repairing it, to look after it. She then went to have a bath. After her return she asked the carpenter for the pea, but he just laughed and said, 'I am not your servant. Government pays me. I was ordered to repair a Government bridge. Your pea must have fallen off'. With this he went back to his work.

### The Despondent Bird

The bird didn't like this. She was heart-broken at the reply. She was apprehensive that as the other birds were already out, they must have finished off" all the grain. In any case, the farmers now would be guarding their stocks. She would have to go hungry. Whilst she was thinking this way, a policeman passed that way. She accosted him for help and said, 'Policeman! Policeman! please help a poor bird. I have lost my pea. A carpenter was repairing the bridge, 'I told him to look after it. He has either stolen it, or it has fallen off and I cannot recover it. I am very hungry and I just do not know where my pea has disappeared.' I do not know what to do.

The Policeman replied 'Oh, you arrogant bird, how dare you stop me like this? I have to maintain law and order for which I get paid and have some privileges. I am on my way to the house of an accused, who has promised me a sumptuous feast. What is it to me if you go hungry? I will have a meal.' And he went his way.

**Bad Luck!**

Having been admonished this way twice, she cursed her luck. After all, in this wicked world where was the need for a bath? She could have eaten her breakfast and then gone to the river. It was her own fault. Now she would have to go hungry. She was thus going her way, cursing her luck, when a police inspector happened that way. She stopped him and told him the whole story, 'Inspector, Inspector. Won't you help a poor lady. The carpenter lost my pea and your policeman refused to help. Will you please intervene and do something? Nobody is willing to help me!

The Inspector roared back and said, 'How dare you stop me? Can't you see I am going out? The minister is coming for a visit and I have to make all the arrangements. My promotion, which depends on his report, will be at stake. What is it to me if you have lost your pea? You can go to hell for all I care.' And he went his way.

The bird thought that she was in a land where people were selfish, self-centred and inconsiderate of other's problems. She would have to go hungry. She was musing thus when the minister came that way, riding on his horse. She stopped him and said, 'Minister! Minister! won't you help a poor lady? I have lost my pea and all the government servants who have passed so far have refused to help me. The carpenter lost it, the policeman was more keen on his feast, the police inspector was more worried about his promotion. No one has bothered to do anything about it so far.'

**The Understanding Minister**

The minister said, 'Much as I would like to help you my lady, I am sorry I have no time. The Raja will be coming this way and I have to see that all arrangements are made. I am really very sorry.' And he trolled away.

The bird was happy that, at least, someone had spoken to her in a civilized manner. The minister was probably busy. Otherwise, he would have helped her. Since he had a pressing business, what was the harm if he went his way? She was thinking like this, when the Raja came that side riding his elephant. She stopped him and said, 'Raja! Raja! you are the ruler. Won't you help a poor bird?'

She then told him the whole story. The carpenter had lost the pea, the policeman only shouted at her, the inspector roared and only the minister had some time to listen to her; but he had other work to which he had to give priority. She said, 'You are the King, won't you solve the problem of a lady?'

The King did not seem to appreciate the arrogance of a tiny bird, who had stopped him while he was on a visit to his people. He did not even care to reply. His bodyguard shouted at her, 'Get aside.' And the Raja ambled off on his elephant.

### Cursing the Luck

The bird was now sure that nothing could or would be done about the matter. She had approached the highest authority in the land and had been unsuccessful. Sitting on the railing of the bridge, she was contemplating on her bad luck. 'Why did I go for a bath at all in this heartless land? Surely doomsday is near at hand for this land of utter selfishness.' Thus sitting in a pensive mood, she suddenly saw an ant going around on her daily chores. She at once went to him and told him the whole story. At last she said, Ant! Ant! go and tell the elephant that he should make the Raja agree to my request, or I will eat you up.

The ant said, 'No, No, my lady, do not do that. I will go just now to the elephant and get the needful done,' and he ran to the elephant and spoke in his ear, 'You heard the bird request the king, and you also saw the rude way in which she was brushed aside by the arrogant bodyguard. I want you to persuade the king to help her otherwise I will give deadly sting on your nose.'

### Elephants Request

Thus threatened, the elephant addressed the Raja and said, 'I very much request you to listen to the bird, otherwise I will be bitten by the ant. And the pain may make me drop you and the fall may break your bones; you may even die.'

The king was surprised. An ant was forcing him to do what he had brushed aside. He, however, had no choice. What the bird was saying. He was terrified for his life. He at once summoned the minister and ordered him to look things had taken a strange turn. The minister left everything and ran to the inspector. He told him, 'So, you are the fellow who maintains law and order. Do you know the poor bird was ill-treated by the carpenter and your policeman did not solve her problem? Do something about it and make it snappy, or you may be deprived of your rank as well as your uniform.'

The Inspector went to the policeman and thundered at him. He, in turn, got hold of the carpenter and threatened him of dire consequences. The carpenter at once ran back and found the pea.

The bird had a sumptuous breakfast of pea that day.

## Bhagya ko Devi

### The Goddess of Luck

Long ago an old woman and her only some level in a certain village. They were very poor and lived from hand to mouth by doing menial jobs. At times, they were even compelled to beg. As the child grew and started understanding things, this state of things become more and more irksom and unacceptable. One day he asked his mother, 'Oh mother, why are we so poor?' And the mother replied, 'this is the will of the Almighty. It is a matter of fate'. The child was not satisfied with this reply. He told his mother that he would search for God and ask him who they were so poor. Saying this, he left his home and set out to the east. After a long and tiresome walk, he reached the outskirts of a jungle. He sat down under a huge tree to rest. As luck would have it, Shiva and Parvati came that way. Lord Mahadeva asked the child what he was doing in that dense jungle. The boy told him the whole story and explained his mission. He said that he was in search of God so that he could become rich. Mahadeva and Parvati were pleased with the child's firm determination. Parvati took pity on him and requested Mahadeva to give something to him. Mahadeva replied that the child could get only what fate had decreed for him. Should anything be given to him, the Lord said, 'it will not remain with him'. But Parvati insisted that something be given to the boy.

**The Gift**

Mahadeva could not song know to parvati gave him a gold-necklace. The boy was very pleased and set out for his home. Mid-way he developed a severe pain in his stomach. He kept the gold-necklace on the ground and went behind a bush to ease himself. Just then an eagle swooped down and flew away with the necklace. The child came home weeping, and narrated the whole story to his mother. His mother, however, did not believe him. Next day the child went again to the same place where he had met the kind couple. And Mahadeva repeated what he had told Parvati earlier: that having lost the necklace, the boy had come again to get one more, but that he still would not be able to retain it till his luck so desired. Parvati, however, pleaded his case again and asked Mahadeva to do something to remove his poverty. Mahadeva approached Brahma and requested him to help the child. Brahma gave a diamond ring to him. The boy started for his home beaming with joy.

**The Loss of Ring**

On the way, he felt thirsty. He searched for water and, at last, came to a lake. As he bent down to reach the water, the ring slipped from his pocket and fell into the lake. It was immediately swallowed by a fish. The child came back crying and narrated the whole incident to his mother. Next day he reached the same spot where he had met the celestial couple. Lord Mahadeva was struck by the child's determination. He spoke to Lord Brahma and then both went to Vishnu. Vishnu gave some diamonds to the child. Having been wisened by his earlier experiences, he went straight home. His mother had gone out begging. He hid the diamonds in a corner of his house and went out in search of his mother. In his absence, thieves came and took away the entire wealth. He knew was not a liar, that a kindly couple had bestowed on him on any rides which he could not hold. This made him better. He wept found that the diamonds had disappeared. His mother also lost her temper and reprimanded him for his aimless wanderings. He came home with his mother. There he –

**The Optimist**

The child had neither lost heart nor hope, and returned to the same spot the next day. Mahadeva thought to himself that in spite of repeated setbacks, the child had not lost his determination. He went to the goddess of luck and asked her to give something to the child. The Goddess gave him one copper coin and the child happily came back home and showed it to his mother. Luck had, at last, smiled on them. After a time, a fisherman came to sell his fish at their house. The boy wanted to eat fish and purchased one with his coin. When he cut the fish, he found the same ring that had slipped from his pocket many days ago as he had bent to drink water from the lake. He handed over the diamond ring to his mother. He then climbed the tree to fell some wood. There was an eagle's nest on the tree. The boy found his gold necklace in the nest. This was not all. As luck would have it, the thief who had stolen his wealth met with an accident. While he was suffering with his injuries, he saw a dream in which the gods ordered him to return the diamonds he had stolen from the child. The thief came the same day to his house and returned the diamonds.

And the widow and her son became very rich!

## Chueha Burhiya

**The Old Miser Woman**

Mother-in-law and daughter-in-law stories are the same the world over. They never seem to pull on well anywhere. This is one such story, that of a mother-in-law and her daughter-in-law, not different from any such stories.

**The Couple and their Son**

A couple had five sons. They married them to five pretty girls. At the time of every marriage, the woman would vociferously say that her daughter-in-law was like a daughter to her. They had no daughters of their own and this would fulfil an old desire. But soon, things turned out to be quite, quite different. The mother was jealous of her daughters-in-law. She felt that they were taking all the time and attention of her sons. She became openly hostile to her daughters-in-law. While she fed her sons with the choicest dishes, she gave only maize-bread to the daughters-in-law. They worked all day in the fields to grow fine quality rice, but that was not ever given them. Time went on and with it their resentment grew. One day the *kanchhi bahu* said, 'what is this life we are leading? The old hag is filling the stores with rice, but does not give us even a single grain. We work in the fields and help it grow, but never get to eat it. I think, it is rightfully ours. Why should we not take it?'

'I agree with you', said *sayenli.* 'But what can we do'? 'We can remove a little rice at a time, and bring it with us in the morning when we come to the field, or go to the jungle to collect wood. We can keep the same quantity of dried leaves in the ration bin,' said *kanchhi.*

**Fear of Exposure**

Full of pent-up resentment, they all agreed. The first day, they took some rice and ate it with relish in the jungle. They were worried lest the old woman discover their deceit. When this did not happen, they picked up courage and started taking more and more rice. This went on for quite some time till the rice bin was almost empty. It contained only dry leaves, with a thin layer of rice over them. Market-day was approaching, and this put the fear of God in their minds. The old hag would obviously blame them. They kept scratching their heads till the smart *kanchhi* came up with a plan.

**Demons and Ghosts**

'Let us mask our faces one night and shout like demons and ghosts. We can also say that although the old hag has hidden rice nothing can be concealed from us. We are going to eat all of it. It is rather good that she under-feeds her daughters-in-law and saves the rice for us. 'That should be a good method of killing two birds with one stone. The old woman may improve and the predicament we are in may be solved,' said *Kanchhi bahu.* 'Yes, I agree with my pretty and youngest sister,' said *jethi bahu.* All others agreed that they should put the plan into operation. Hence, they set about selecting there own masks. They all agreed that it would be a good method of killing two birds with one stone. Selecting their masks one night, they put their plan into operation. In the morning, they eagerly awaited the outcome. The mother-in-law got up with a slight fever and went straight to the store. Her worst fears were true. She called her daughters-in-law, 'Come my dear darlings, how are you all? You never sit with me,' she said to the girls.

They marvelled at this sudden change of heart. 'Did you hear any voices at night?' she enquired of *kanchhi.*

'No, mother-in-law. After doing hard and tedious work in paddy-fields, I was so tired that I slept like a log.'

'What is the use of working in the paddy-fields and storing rice for the demons?' questioned the old woman. 'What? What?' they all cried in chorus. 'You do not know, my children, I have been duly punished for my miserliness.'

From that day, *kanchhi* became the favourite of the house, and they all got affection from their mother-in-law.

## Na Ramaro Swasni

### The Unfaithful Wife

'Do not insist. It will make you unhappy. Go to sleep, and let me sleep,' said the sparrow to his wife. 'No, you must tell me. Who is this woman who has arrived so late, and why is she waiting so restlessly for the morning? While you fly around to far-off places, I sit on eggs. God alone knows where you go. For all I know, you must be having other wives in other places. You disappear for inordinately long periods,' she complained.

The sparrow was afraid that his wife would now relapse into that mood of doubt and despondency, which is characteristic of the female species. So he said, 'If you must insist, hear the story. It is not of the fickleness of man, but of a woman. But I do not even blame her. Her environment affected her so. In a land where polyandry is practised, how can you expect a woman to be happy with one husband?'

The she sparrow interrupted him with obvious irritation, Go on with your story and not be cynical.'

'Yes,' he continued. The woman who has taken shelter under our tree is the sister of the unlucky man who now faces a death sentence, because of the treachery of his wife. You know polyandry is prevalent in this valley. In that yonder village over the hill, there lived a man. Learned and well travelled that he was, he opposed this system. How could he tolerate his wife having more than one husband?

### The Custom

But that was custom in their society, and he was helpless. No woman came forward to marry him. So he prayed to the goddess that he be given the power to carve a woman out of his own body. The goddess came to him in his dream and told him to cut his body in two-halves: from one-half, he would be resurrected, while the other would take the form of a beautiful woman, whom he could marry. She, warned him to be careful and collect all the blood which was to come out of his body. It was to be an offering to Devi and offer it to the temple of *Devi*.

The man obeyed the goddess and did what he was told. To his great surprise, a beautiful woman took shape from the second-half of his body. He was so captivated by her feminine charms and so overpowered by passion, that he forgot to collect the blood and offer it to the *Devi*. While he made merry, the spilt blood turned into a snake and disappeared into a hole in the ground. This was no ordinary snake. He could transform himself into any form. He had also seen the beautiful woman and had been enamoured of her. One day he transformed himself into a handsome man and went to her house with presents of beautiful clothes and jewels.

**The New Suitor**

She had seen her friends live with more than one husband and secretly envied them. She fell an easy prey to the advances of the visitor and the snake became a regular visitor to her place. He would transform himself into a handsome man and go to her whenever her husband was away. She also became increasingly fond of her lover and nagged her husband persistently. She frequently managed to send him out on useless errands so that she could enjoy the company of her paramour more often. Gradually the very presence of the husband began to irritate her. She plotted with her lover to put an end to his life. The snake assured that it would not be a problem at all. He could easily sting him to death. She begged him to do that at the first available opportunity. The husband fully in love with his wife was not above that his wife was weaving a plot to kill him.

**The Opportunist**

One day the snake came to the house and concealed himself in a corner. He was waiting for an opportunity to strike. The man soon fell asleep, and the snake slithered towards him. The wife had feigned sleep but was wide awake. But fate *decreed* otherwise. As the snake was about to strike, the man was bitten by a bed bug. He got up with a start, and saw the snake. He drew out his *khukri* and cut the snake to pieces. The woman was inconsolable. She chided her husband severely, 'Don't you know that snakes are to be worshipped? Now I will have to expiate for your sin by visiting Kashi to perform the last rites of the snake.'

Credulous as the man was, he readily agreed. He was so much in love with his wife that he had failed to notice her growing coldness.

The woman cremated the body of the snake put the several head of the snake in a box she took it to Kashi. There she went to many *pandits* and *pujaris* and enquired about the possibility of bringing her paramour back in life. At last, a man who was an adept *tantric* told her that the only possible way was by sacrificing her husband. She readily agreed to do that. She was aware of the simplicity of this man and thought that she would easily achieve her objective. She had a locket made and put the head of the snake in it. She hung it around her neck and came back. On the way she kept thinking of a plan to kill her husband.

Days rolled on while she waited for the right opportunity. At last, she thought of a plan. She said to her husband, 'You are always so eager to go to sleep. Let us put some riddles to each other, and the one who fails to give the correct answer will have to grant the victor any wish. The husband agreed, and she asked question, 'Which is the thing dearest to me, and one that I never wish to part with?'

### Wrong Signal

The foolish husband thought that she meant him. In spite of many guesses, he failed. The lady had obviously meant the locket containing the head of the snake. At last the man gave up, and she told him that she wanted him to die to fulfil the terms of the agreement. He was taken aback, but he had no choice. However, he requested her to let him live for a few more days, so that he could see his only sister. He sent an urgent message to her; and the woman, who is now taking shelter under the tree is the sister of the unlucky man facing death.'

'You women,' said the sparrow to his wife, 'are always quick to blame men and eye them with suspicion. See what your sex is capable of ?'

On receiving her brother's message, his sister had set out at once. En route was a jungle she could not cross because of the darkness. So she chose a big banyan tree and took shelter under it for the night. She, waited patiently for the morning. She had the gift of understanding the language of the birds and beasts, and heard the dialogue of the sparrows. There were two sparrows who had their in the hut that women lived who had a snake as her paramour. From the location the birds were describing the girl could understand that the sparrows were talking of her brother and her sister-in-law. Hearing of the hopeless situation her brother was in, she got up and set out for his house. The dialogue of the sparrows had revealed the truth to her. She told him the whole story and exposed the wickedness of the faithless wife. When confronted like, the woman couldn't demp anything. The man snatched the mysterious locket from her neck, opened it and found the head of the snake. He put it in the fire, and cut off the nose and ears of his unfaithful wife.

He married another woman who had other husbands, as was the custom of the society, and they all lived happily ever after.

## Mo le Teenota Khanchhun

### I will Eat Three

And so they continue to roam about as wandering ghosts. Many times on dark cloudy nights their acrimonious debate can still be heard.

'I will have three and you have two,' the witch shouts at the top of her voice.

Then the ghost roars, 'No I deserve three and you can have two.'

And this endless debate goes on.

Long long ago, there lived an old couple in a village. They were ever-quarrelling. The neighbourhood were tired of their altercations. One day, the old man went to the market and bought five mangoes with the money that he earned that day. Hardly, had he entered the door of his house, when he started shouting, 'I will have three and you can have two. I worked throughout the day and earned some money. Since you are married to me, I have to share the hard earned food with you. O God! when will you take this old wreck back?'

**The Grumbles**

The old woman would not tolerate all this. She retorted, 'I keep working throughout the day like a machine. What do I get? You cannot even provide me with one square meal. Cursed be the day I married you. I will have three and you have two. I have no faith in you.' In any case, how do I know how many have you already eaten outside.

The fight went on late into the night, and almost till the time the morning star was due to rise. At last they were exhausted and the old man said, 'All right, let us arrive at some decision. One who speaks first will get two, and the one who does not talk will get three mangoes.'

**The Trick**

The old man thought that he had played an intelligent trick on his wife. His wife is as used to lengthy arguments whenever he was around. He was sure she would not be able to keep her mouth shut. He had misjudged her. He was not aware of the stubbornness of the fair sex! The couple maintained total silence till the sun was almost over their heads. The neighbours were surprised. They had her any voice since morning. They were not used to this quiet and peace in that house. At last they decided to investigate. Two or three daring couples of the neighbourhood picked up enough courage and entered the house. They were surprised to see the old couple hiding in different corners with their heads covered.

They called out them; none of them stirred. Thinking they were dead, the neighbours decided to take them to the cremation ground to perform their last rites. The old couple maintained complete, for none was ready to lose the extra mango. At last the procession reached the cremation ground. On route some people said that they were at last rid of the constant quarrels of the old couple. A few bright wits said that whilst the couple lived, no thieves could ever enter their street.

At the cremation ground they realised that they could not cremate both together. After some discussion, they decided to cremate the man first. The pyre was made ready and the man put on it. Fire was lighted, and the man now felt enough was enough and shouted out the unfairness of it all. Had they forgotten that ladies always come first. Hearing this, the old woman said gleefully, 'now I will have three and you have two.'

The old man said, 'If you were put on the fire first, you would have also yelled out. I will have three and you have two.'

Hearing this conversation, the people thought that the couple had become ghosts and wanted to eat five of them. Only they were undecided who would eat three. Thinking this, the men took to their heels. The old couple ran after them shouting at the top of their voices, 'I will have three.' 'I will have three.' The people panicked and fled as fast as they could.

The couple at last reached their home By that time mangoes had gone bad. They were long tired and exhausted. The man refused to work any more since they did not have any money, but could not buy food and they both starved to death. But now no one in the neighbour hard came forward to perform their last rites, they became ghosts, shouting to this day, 'I will have three, and you have two.'

## A Tale of Love

### The Couple

Once upon a time there lived a couple in a certain village. They had been married for more than twenty-five years, but God had not blessed them with a child. This state of barrenness was unbearable to the woman. She performed severe penances and followed the advice of all and sundry—any one at all who showed her the slightest ray of hope. Her desire, however, remained unfulfilled. The lady would spend many nights lying awake thinking of her unborn child. There were frequent altercations between husband and wife, and their married life became unhappy. Around that time some menducants visited her village and established their camp there. Many people went to them with their worries and requests. The mendicants seemed to have a host of remedies for all ailments, real and imagined, physical and mental. The woman thought it a good opportunity. She went to see them with her husband asked them to alleviate her suffering.

### The Mahatma who Listened

The Mahatma listened to her with great interest, nodding his head from time to time. Finally, he took pity on her and gave her a conch shell. He told her to put the shell in an earthen vessel with some aromatic herbs, and cover it with fresh earth. She should then sprinkle some water on it every day. She must follow this procedure for one week, after which she should remove the earth and, God willing, her desire would be fulfilled.

They were came home with great expectations. The couple very happy with this providential meeting with the holy men. The woman did exactly as the Mahatma had advised her to. She could hardly wait for the seventh day to pass and literally, kept counting every moment. As soon as the sun went down the horizon, she unearthed the conch shell. To her great and pleasant surprise, a beautiful male child was in the vessel. He gave her a sweet smile. He had perfect features and a petal-fresh complexion. The couple was overjoyed. They brought up the child with immense love and affection. They took great pains to see that he was given choicest foods, and provided with most expensive clothing and the best toys. He grew up to be a handsome man.

**The Visitor**

One day, the princess of that land happened to come to that village. She saw the boy and fell in love with him. In her heart, she had rowed that she would marry that boy. She told her mother about her wish. In due course, the boy was married to the princess. The marriage ceremony was performed with great pomp and show. Many kings and princes came to attend the marriage, and admired the good looks of the couple, and envied the good fortune of the king to have found such a handsome match for his daughter.

One day, the king was busy in the affairs of the state. His son-in-law was having a walk around the palace. Suddenly, a strong gale carried him off and he reached an unknown place. It was a beautiful and enchanting land. Many flowers were in bloom and a great many butterflies were displaying and fanning their rainbow colours in the sun. They all flew towards the young prince and carried him on their wings to the king of the land. The Raja was pleased to see him, fussing over him a great deal. The prince missed his wife and his parents who were at a loss to know the cause of his disappearance. At his new place, he had no dearth of luxuries but he was unhappy.

**The Unhappy Prince**

One day he went out for a walk where he met an old she-mouse. The old lady told him that she had a very beautiful house which was close at hand. The prince was looking tired after a walk and wanted some refreshments. She invited him for a drink. The prince agreed. The old lady asked him if he was married and, in fact, offered her own beautiful daughter to him. The prince told her the truth. The new proposal made him miss his wife all the more. He then came out of the hole. The she-mouse followed him for some distance with earnest requests to stay back and take her daughter for a second wife, he did not want another woman as a wife and ran away from there. At last, he reached a thick jungle, but he kept moving. He lost his way. The sun was about to set. He met a cuckoo who asked him where his house was and invited him to go with her to her dwelling. By now, the prince was fully resigned to his fate and readily agreed. The cuckoo made him ride on her back and flew with him to her exotic land. Her house was located in a beautiful garden with myriad flowers and luscious fruits. Many birds were chirping melodiously.

**The Beautiful Flower Plant**

The cuckoo lived in a beautiful palace with a lovely garden. She moved from tree to tree singing her best songs to amuse her guest. The young man noticed that there was a strange flower plant with a single flower of hiterto unseen, but matchless beauty. On investigation he came to know that a beautiful princess was residing in the flower. The cuckoo requested him to marry this 'princess of the flowers.' But he did not agree to the match saying that he was already married. The cuckoo and the princess kept on pressing him to agree to the proposal. He flatly refused. At this the princess who was hearing the dialogue changed her form, came out of the flower and appeared before him. He was surprised to her wife standing before him. She told him that she had created the entire world of magic by her mysterious power to test the fidelity of her husband. She said she felt to be the happiest woman in the world for what more could a woman desire than a faithful and loving husband.

The boy brought his old parents to the palace to live with them. They were the happiest family in the world.

## Rajkumari Sunkeshi

**The Golden Haired Princess**

This is the true story of a golden haired princess called Sunkeshi. She had seven brothers and was the only sister. Her parents, the Raja and Rani, loved her dearly. No sooner did she say anything, or make any wish, it was granted. God had given her abundant endowments by way of feminine charms; a petal fresh complexion, sparkling almond eyes, thin, seductive lips, flowing golden tresses which almost touched her knees, and an impressive figure. She was, beyond doubt, the most beautiful girl in the whole kingdom.

One day, she went for a bath to the river along with her friends. The young girls had a great time, splashing water and giggling away to glory. They played many games. They dived, jumped, and chased each other. And in these antics, one hair of the princess fell off and was washed away. When the loss of one hair of Sunkeshi was reported to the Raja and Rani, there was a consternation in the palace. A thorough search was launched in vain. The loss of a hair of a virgin has always been considered a bad omen. To cap it all, the hair under question was golden and belonged to the princess, the only daughter of the Raja. Hence something had to be done about it.

So without a thought to the consequences, the Raja announced that Sunkeshi would be married to any one who would find the golden hair. The mouths of many young men, princes and commoners, alike, watered at the idea. For a while it appeared that all tracks were leading to the river where many a search party spent a lot of time. The princes and Rajas came from far and wide and from the adjoining states, to find the golden hair and claim the hand of Sunkeshi in marriage. They all returned with heavy hearts. No one who tried had any luck. No one ever knows the whims and fancies of the goddess of luck. She is so inforedeable. She smiles on a beggar and makes him a king and a king into a pauper at one stroke.

**The Lost Golden Hair**

As she had ordained, one day the princes went for shikar. After a hot chase, they all converged on to the river for a swim. There was an overhanging branch of a tree which grazed the water of the river, the princes would climb it and dive into the water. By chance, the eye of one of the princes was held by a shining object on the branch. He went for a closer scrutiny. Lo and behold! it was the lost golden hair of Sunkeshi. At this discovery, the prince, both smiled and then wept. When the others asked him the cause of this strange behaviour, he said, My sister should be happy. But I am not happy. Without giving any thought to what he was saying, he took a row. What I am going to do now.

**King's Vow**

The prince was reluctant to bring the hair home. But others in his party know that it was he found the hair. The princes willy-nilly brought the hair home. As was expected, the discovery of the hair sent a wave of joy and intense sorrow in the palace. The hair was no doubt found, but because the vow of the Raja, the princess was now to be married to her own brother! Her own father was thus to become her father-in-law! It was unthinkable. How could there be conjugal relations between a brother and a sister? Out of the well into the deep sea! The king cried in anguish to the gods, but there was no way out. The kings of the past never broke their vows because of the fear that the reigning goddesses of the kingdom would desert them. The state would be subject to decay caused by severe droughts and terrible deluges, bringing untold misery to the subjects. The king was in a dilemma and consulted the royal priests.

After deep meditation, they all advised that the vow be honoured and that the princess married to the prince who found the hair. The king was resigned to his fate, and prepared himself to sacrifice his daughter for the sake of his subjects. So a day was fixed for the marriage. The princess was in a greater predicament. All young girls dream of happy lives with their husbands. The poor and the rich, alike, look forward to that day, and the princess was no exception. What a fate? The princess thought and thought and, on the appointed day, before the rise of the morning star left the palace and went into the jungle. There she climbed an old banyan tree and hid in the branches. Soon the people came to know of her disappearance. A thorough search was launched but, she was not found. The palace was agog at the strange turn of events. The search party at last reached that part of hte jungle where the princess was liding where a crow was cawing incessantly:

'of Luck you all see,
The princess hides in the tree.'

In the olden days, many men who mostly level near the jungles, could understand the language of the birds and beasts. The party thus came to know about the hideout of the princess, and reported it to her father. The king at once came and addressing the princess said:

'Alight alight oh daughter mine,
The wedding bells are soon to chime.'
And the princess replied:
'Alight I shall oh benevolent Raja,
But tell me first,
Are you my father
Or father-in-law?'

**King's Shame**

The king was put to great shame at this question. He took out his dagger and thrust it in his heart, dying instantly. Her brothers met the same fate; when she asked them if they were her brothers or brothers-in-law, their pride was hurt to such an extent that they preferred to die rather than answer that question. At last the prince to whom she was to be married said:

'Alight alight oh Sunkeshi,
The wedding time is soon to be.'
The princess said,
'Alight I shall oh prince,
But tell me first,
Are you my brother or my husband?'

At this strange question, the prince also committed suicide. Fortunately, the tree on which the princess was hiding was, in fact, a prince who had been under a curse for centuries and had been transformed into a tree. The curse was to be redeemed by the blood of eight persons. The drops of blood from the royal family released the curse, and the tree was transformed into a handsome prince. He at once asked for the hand of Sunkeshi in marriage. The princess inherited the kingdom of her father and they lived happily ever after. And the crow keeps on his incessant cawing even now,

'What fate ordains
Unchanged and firm
Like a rock it remains.'

## Yota Farsi ra Tisko Swasny

### A Pumpkin and His Wife

Once upon a time there lived an old couple in a village. They did not have any children. The woman would constantly grieve fate. She went over her to many temples to pray for a child. She would approach every mendicants who came to the village, and performed all the rituals suggested by them. Performing rituals turned out to beexpensive. Most of the meagre earnings of the old man were thus spent.

One day, the old lady was cursing her fate as usual. The maize had dried but she was feeling too lazy to put it in the storage bins. Whilst she was sitting in a pensive mood, she thought she heard that her days of worry were over; that God had heard her prayers and sent a child to look after her in her old age. She was surprised to hear this voice and turned her face to investigate. Lo and behold, there was a pumpkin rolling towards her. He told her that she could go in the hut and rest as he had come to look after them. The lady was overjoyed Pumpkin was their son.

After some time, she came to the pumpkin and told him that he should take lunch for his father who was working in the fields. The pumpkin got ready at once. He appeared to be a tireless worker. He reached the field where his father was working and, after introducing himself, gave him his food. That God had sent them a helping hand was a surprise for the old man but he was in wardly happy.

### Pumpkin's Love

Days passed and the old couple grew more and more fond of their adopted son. One day, the father and his strange child went out for a walk. The daughters of the landlord were also going for a ride on the same road. The pumpkin saw landlord's daughter Kanchhi and fell in love with her. He confided in his father about his desire to get married to the youngest daughter of the landlord. The father was reluctant, because not only was his status much below that of landlord, but his child also could not be considered really eligible. The pumpkin was, however, very insistent and would neither eat nor drink. The poor farmer was thus compelled to approach the landlord for the hand of his youngest daughter. Luck again played a part. That night Shiva and Parvati appeared in the dreams of the pumpkin's beloved and gave their blessings to the proposed marriage. Therefore, when the farmer came with the strange proposal, she readily agreed. The marriage took place with great pomp and show.

### The Flowering Tree

After the marriage, the girl served her husband and his parents with great devotion. The pumpkin, in turn, would do anything to keep her happy. One day, the newly-weds were going out for a walk. The birds were out on the tree branches adding to the melodious orchestra of nature. Flowers were in full bloom. The fancy of the girl was caught by a flowering tree. She requested her husband to get her a flower. The pumpkin got ready and started to climb. However, his foot slipped and he came crashing down. The pumpkin broke in two and out came a handsome prince! He told his wife that because of certain misdeeds, he was under a *shap.* He had been told that the effect of the curse would be over by the devotion of a wife with all the thirty-two virtues. She was thus his saviour. They happily went home and the prince told the entire matter to his foster parents. Therefore they were a happy family.

## Legend of Satota Didi Behani

### Seven Sisters

Said the father to his daughters, knowing fully in his heart of hearts that he was about to commit a breach of trust with his own flesh and blood. How wicked the circumstances can get and how badly men can get cornered? Isn't it unimaginable that a father should stoop so low as to scheme to desert his children heartlessly? But it is not always the circumstances alone that drive men to kill their conscience. Most of them take shelter under the pretext of adverse, circumstances to succumb to their own ill-nature. Oblivious of the evil designs of their father, the girls readily agreed. When their mother had died, the father was grief-stricken, had decided to devote his entire life to looking after his seven daughters. But time is a great healer. He soon fell for the charms of another lady and married again. To the people he explained that he was getting married so that his daughters could be looked after better. As was expected, the step-mother started ill-treating her step-daughters: all seven of them ranging from the ages of seven to seventeen. She make a plan to get rid of these step daughters and convinced her husband in such a way that he felt for his scheme.

They would scold the helpless girls endlessly, and made their lives absolutely miserable. The climax came when the mother got around their father and they both decided to get rid of them. So with the sole and ignoble aim of leaving them in the jungle at the mercy of wild beasts, he tried to lure them by promising to take them to the annual fair. Inwardly their father was sad that he was about to commit a breach of brist. Innocent as the girls were, they readily agreed. The cruel father delayed the departure in such a way that they started their journey well after mid-day. By evening, they reached the middle of the jungle and the father suggested that they take shelter for the night under the banyan tree. They all decided to get up early in the morning and go to the fair. The girls were very tired and soon fell sound asleep.

**The Hearless Father**

The father was just waiting for such an opportunity. He sealed their eyes with wax and returned home to the heartless woman.

When the girls got up the next morning, they called out to their father, but there was no reply. They also could not see anything. They cried their hearts out for this unexpected turn of events and bewailed loud and long. As luck would have it, the banyan tree was the dwelling place of the *Ban Devta*. He had witnessed the callous behaviour of the father. He took pity on the girls and addressed them thus, 'Don't worry my children, your eyes are dosed with wax only.' He gave them detailed instructions on how to reach the spring to wash their faces and regain their sight. *Jethi* led them to the spring. They washed their faces and were able to see again.

**Joy and Fear**

Their initial joy, however, was soon replaced by intense fear. They were in the middle of a thick jungle, alive with the calls of dreadful, wild animals. They had lost their way and could not go back. Thinking that their father had probably fallen a prey to some wild animal, they searched for him all over without luck. As they were wandering from place to place in search of their father, they were attracted by the lights of a house. Approaching nearer they discovered it to be a palace. They were in two minds whether to move in or go away. At last, curiosity got the better of them and they entered the palace. To their horror, they discovered that the house belonged to a giant who was dozing near a huge platter of food. They were very hungry and soon forgot about their fear and sat down to eat. The giant kept snoring heavily. The sisters had their fill and hid the remainder of the food behind a pillar. After that, they moved in the interior chambers of the palace. They hid in the corner of a room from where they could see the giant. After some time, the monster got up. He seemed to be very hungry. He was astonished to notice the disappearance of his food. He searched here and there and noticed the remnants of his lunch near the pillar. Unintelligent, idiots as the race of giants are, he reprimanded the pillar severely, 'So you are the one who has eaten my food. You will soon learn a lesson.' Saying this he hit the pillar hard, injuring his fists.

**Stupid Pillar**

The monster was now really in rage. How dare you hit me back? You stupid pillar. I will teach you a lesson.' And saying this he brought a huge staff and lashed out at the pillar with full force. The lifeless pillar broke down and a big block fell on the giant's head, killing him instantaneously. The girls were watching all this from a distance. They were trembling with fear. Seeing the giant dead, they slowly picked up courage and came out. With their entire might, they disposed off the giant's body. Now they were the sole owners of the palace. Their search revealed that the giant had a vast treasure of jewels and pearls which he had collected by killing his victims. He did not what to do with the gems. The storehouse was full of eatables. They had no dearth of anything and started living happily there was nothing which had to be brought from outside. Comfort and security again reminded them of their father. How they pined to be with him and look after him. Such was their love for their father.

### Hope of Peace

Their father had gone back home with the hope that his wife would be happy and there would be some peace in his life. This was not to be, because nagging is a habit, and habits die hard. She endlessly nagged him and at times, even said that if he could leave his own daughters in the jungle, how could she have any faith in him. 'Who am I? How do I know that in my old age, you won't forsake me? On my luck! Curse be on the day I married you.'

The man was sick of all this and went back to the jungle to search for the remains of his daughters. He searched hither and thither but to no avail. He was likewise attracted by the palace lights. Approaching it, he discovered that it belonged to his own daughters. They showered all their affection on him and told him to carry as much wealth as he wanted to silence the lashing tongue of their step-mother. He went back with many diamonds and jewels and told his wife, the entire story. 'Oh you stupid man,' said she, 'why did you not take more wealth from them? Will this last us long? When will you ever learn?' Chiding him thus she forced him to go back to where his daughters level.

He went and told his daughters the type of life he was leading. They told him that in that case, they would send a special present for their mother. They put venomous snakes and scorpions in a vessel and covered it tight. They told their father that this was meant for the step-mother who must open it alone in a room.

The women thought it was a treasure which her husband had brought for her. She opened the vessel and died a painful death. Daughters and their father thereafter lived peacefully.

## Shyal ra Chituwa

### The Jackal and the Tiger

In a certain jungle there lived a pair of tigers. They were newly-weds and madly in love with each other. They spent most of their time in the den. The tiger would even drag the kill to the den where both of them would eat together. This put a severe strain on scavangers like jackals and hyenas who were mainly dependent on the remnants of what the tiger preyed. Even the hyenas were able to look after themselves to some extent, but the jackals suffered a lot. Most of the members of the jackal community had a rather famished look.

It was because of back of food. One day they held a conference and asked their leader to do something. The wise old jackal reassured them and promised to solve their problem.

**The Visitor**

He visited the tiger's den when the tiger was out for hunting. He admonished the tigress severely and told her of the effects of confining her husband indoors. Lack of sunlight and fresh air had already weakened him so much that even he, a jackal, could beat him up. In fact, he had the gall to tell her, 'Let me see him, and I will give him at least three kicks.' In the evening the tiger came home with the kill. The tigress told him of the visit of the jackal. The tiger was greatly amused by it and brushed the incident aside by saying that the jackal must have lost his head. Next day, while the tiger was out, the jackal came again and repeated the threat, 'So you have not taken my advice,' he said to the tigress. 'Let me meet your husband. I will give him at least three kicks in his buttocks. I am powerful enough to teach him a good lesson.'

**The Repeated Threat**

The tigress again told the tiger what the jackal had said, but he did not take it seriously. On the following days, the head of the jackals again repeated the threat, and his tone became more and more harsh and overbearing as the days passed. At last the tigress became sick of it and wept before the tiger. Rid me this menace, otherwise I will have you and go to my parents' home.

The tiger flew into a rage at this blatant display of bad manners by a mere jackal. 'How dare this rascal bother my wife?' He decided to wait for the jackal the next day and teach him a good lesson. He could hardly sleep that night and came out many times to see if the morning star had risen. At last the day dawned. Sure enough, the jackal came roaring outside.

**The Clever Jackal**

The Jackal was very clever. He sensed the tiger was in. He did not come in near the tiger. He kept a safe distance. The tiger heard the jackal and rushed out to teach him a lesson. The jackal roared, 'If you have the guts, follow me.' The tiger charged at him with great speed and fury. The jackal was prepared for such an eventuality. He entered a cave which had an opening on both sides. The cave was so narrow in the middle that he could pass through easily but the tiger could not. The jackal quickly went across and came back from the opening on the other side.

The tiger was struggling in the middle. The jackal gave him three kicks in the back and said, 'See the result of depriving yourself of fresh air? Here take one, and another, and yet another.'

Thus beaten the tiger learnt his lesson, thereafter he started some portion of the hunt out there so that jackals could feed themselves. The food problem of the jackal family was solved forever.

## The Greedy Wood-cutter

Once upon a time, long long ago, there lived a woodcutter in a certain village. He was very hard working and honest. His work, however, required great physical exertion and the returns were meagre. He toiled all day long to eke out a living. He could barely make both ends meet, but dishonesty never came near him. His sole implement for living was an iron axe which he loved more dearly than a child. On non-working days, he would golden axe. At the same time he would keep on whispering endearing words to it.

As he used to do every day. He went to the Jungle for cutting wood. He had selected some dry branches of a banyan tree which were hanging over a pond. He went on cutting wood and caressing his axe from time to time. As luck would have it, his axe slipped from his hand and fell into the pond. Great was his shock and surprise. He almost jumped after the axe. How would he now cater for the needs of his family? They would all starve to death. He came down and tried to recover the axe. The water was too deep and he was a non-swimmer. Utterly helpless and non-plussed, he sat down on the bank and cried himself hoarse, '*O Jal Devta*, have pity on me and my children. What will I do now?'

*Jal Devta* heard his cries. He came out with a golden axe and said, 'Stop crying my child, here is your axe.'

### Silver and Iron Axe

The wood cutter eagerly looked at the axe but his look soon changed into a stare of despair. 'This is not my axe', he said, and started cursing his luck again. The water deity dived in and came out with a silver axe. He rejected that either. He wanted his own axe. The reaction of the wood cutter was no different even this time. *Jal Devta* dived again and surfaced with the iron axe. The wood cutter was beside himself with joy and snatched the axe from his hand. He hugged the axe and profusely thanked the deity.

The god was very pleased with him for his honesty, and gave him the gold and silver axes also as presents. Singing happily, the wood cutter came with his load of wood and three axes. En route he met a friend also a wood cutter who asked him how he had amassed so much wealth to have bought both a gold and silver axe. Simple and straightforward as he was, he related the whole story.

**The Stupid Friend**

His friend could hardly sleep that night. Next day he went to the same tree with branches overhanging the pond. He made it a point that his axe slipped from his hand. He then cried long and loud about his bad luck: how would he look after his family, etc. He was well aware that he had no family. He cried himself hoarse but the deity was obviously taking too long to appear. At last the deity did come out with a golden axe. On enquiry, the wood cutter said 'Yes, not only does this axe belong to me, I have also dropped silver axe and an iron axe in the water.'

*Jal Devta* laughed at him and said, "Is it that easy to cheats the god? Neither you had and silver or gold axes, nor are you married. Saying this *Jal Devta* disappeared.

## Greed for Gold

Once upon a time there lived a wealthy merchant in a certain village. He was very rich but was not satisfied what gods had given him. He wanted still more wealth. His only ambition was that he should be the wealthiest man in the whole world. One day a yogi came to his house. The seth looked after him with greatest solicitude care. The yogi was highly pleased and asked the seth to demand a boon. The seth said, 'I have just one desire. I want that whatever article I touch should turn into gold.'

The mendicant said, 'so be it,' and went his way—with the reminder that the boon would be effective from the following day. In his eager wait for the next day, the seth could not sleep the whole night. Whilst the morning star was still shining high in the sky, he got up and went for a walk. He wanted to brush his teeth with a *datun* (neem stalk). As soon as he touched the *datun,* it turned into gold. He was thrilled and decided to convert some more *datuns* into gold. Which made it impossible for him to clean his teeth. He decided to have a bath, but as soon as he touched the bucket, both the metal (of the bucket) and the water turned into gold.

**The Golden Touch**

He was feeling very hungry and wanted to have food but the food also turned into gold. Pained and harassed, he went to his wife to seek solace. One touch turned his wife into gold. This was too much and the seth cried in anguish. The boon was no more a boon, it had become a curse. Raising his hands to the heavens, he prayed to God for mercy. He was praying that he wanted to be reverted to what he was before the boon bestowed on him. The almighty heard his cry and the yogi came to that village again. The seth begged him to relieve him of his misery. This was granted. The seth had learnt his lesson. He distributed all his wealth amongst the poor. Thereafter he lived in peace and contentment till the last day of his life.

## The Wise Prince

Long time ago, there was a Raja who had six Ranis. It was at a time when people belived that only a son could perform a man's last retes. The Raja didn't have sons from his ranis. People, therefore, laid great stress on begetting sons. That is bad enough for don't we all know that daughters are more sincere to the parents than the sons? What was worse, many men made the birth of a son an excuse for lust and married a number of times.

One day, the Raja went out for shikar with his prime minister. On the way, they came to a well where some girls were filling water. The Raja saw a pretty wench and in no time at all fell in love with her. She indeed had all the feminine endowments, that would lure any man. The Raja came back to the palace, but he was very restless. His six Ranis fussed over him, but to no avail. At last the Raja called his prime minister and told him the cause of his restlessness, 'Mantri, I have a strong feeling that the girl whom I saw today at the well will bear me a son. I am sure that she is right woman for me.

### The Psychophant

The prime minister was a psychophant. He at once agreed. He said that he had had a dream the previous night that his excellency would meet the right girl at the well. The dream had come true. On Raja's command he then sent men to fetch the girl to the palace. In his lust, the Raja failed to notice that the girl had inverted feet and was in fact, a she demon, a witch, disguised as a beautiful woman. On reaching the palace, she showed great annoyance for the inconvenience caused to her. The Raja endearingly told her the cause and said that he wanted to make her his maharani. She declined saying that he already had six wives and moreover, she had no time for him. After great persuasion, she consented but on one condition. The Raja was blinded by his lust for the witch. He did not ask what her condition was for marrying him. He said he was prepared to agree to all her conditions. The wicked witch said that she wanted the six previous Ranis to be blinded and banished to the jungle. She also said that she would keep their eyes in safe custody. The Raja shuddered at the idea but he had already given his word. He had no choice. He sent all the six Ranis to the jungle where their eyes were gouged out then blinding them and brought to the new Rani. The marriage was then performed with great pomp and show.

### The Pregnant Rani

As luck would have it, the third Rani was "with a child when they were banished to the jungle. In due course of time, she gave birth to a son who was so handsome that all the birds and beasts of the jungle came to see him. The boy grew up to be an exceedingly intelligent and smart child. He was a favourite of all his mothers. The *Jethi Ama* supervised his bringing up with the greatest care. *Kanchhi Ama,* who by virtue of being youngest was the most energetic, travelled over great distance in the jungle to fetch luscious fruits for the boy. They all doted on him and fussed over him. He also loved all his mothers dearly.

The she demon did not bear any child to the Raja. But a demon that she cunning, she took the family priest in confidence and they both managed to cheat the Raja by telling him that she would bear him a son only after fourteen years of their married life.

**The Persistent Witch**

Time went on. The boy grew up and saw the six springs of his life. This was also the time when the witch came to know about his birth and was tortured lest she be discovered. She tried many methods of killing him but the boy was a beloved of the gods and was always saved. At last the she demon summoned him to the palace and made a great show of love and concern for him. She told him that she wanted to adopt him. The family priest was in complete league with her. Together they convinced the Raja that he should adopt the boy as their son because then, and then also, a son would be born to his Rani. As was their plan, the priest also advised that after the adoption, the child be sent to his maternal grandparents for a few years.

The Raja was by now only playing second fiddle to the cunning witch and agreed to all her suggestions. The she demon wrote a note for her brother, who was known far and wide for his ferocity and love of human flesh, and sent it along with the boy. In that she explained her whole situation, and asked him to eat up the boy as soon as his escorts turned their backs. After making elaborate arrangements she sent the boy to her brother with some of her trusted soldiers. The mothers of the boy, on the other hand, worried a great deal and were unable to bear his separation. They cried themselves hoarse till the *Ban Devta* himself appeared before them and reassured them of the safety of the boy.

The party escorting the boy entered the thick jungle where they felt tired and decided to rest awhile. As they dozed off, the *Ban Devta* took the note written by witch. He tore it and instead placed another in the packet of the soldier. In that note he had changed the message. Instead the note instructed the parents and brothers of the witch that the boy was her son and should be brought up with all care. After many days of travel, the party reached their destination. The boy was looked after well. As time passed, he became a great favourite with the entire colony of demons and came to know all their secrets. The demons taught their magical powers to the boy. They showed him their magic ash which, when thrown on a person, would burn him to cinder. He also came to know of the seemingly harmless pieces of firewood, which could be transformed into deadly snakes and who could bite a victim to death. He also saw the eyes of his mothers stored and preserved in a vessel.

### The Clever Boy

One day, when all the demons were out on their usual rounds, the boy thought that the time was ripe to finish them off and take the eyes to his mothers and revive their vision. When the demons returned, he threw the ash on them and released the snakes to kill them. He then lost no time in reaching his six mothers and gave them back their sight. Leaving them in the jungle, he went straight to the palace and told the whole story to the Raja, and burnt the she demon to ashes before his eyes. He summoned the priest and released the snakes to deal with him.

The Ranis were brought back to the palace. The Raja was full of shame at the untold sufferings brought on them by his lust. And they lived happily ever after.

## An Old but Lucky Jackal

### The Food Stocks

Once in a jungle there lived a very clever Jackal. As he grew old and infirm and became very weak, he could not perform any service to his kind, other jackals deserted him to die in peace. No member of his community would ever invite him to the left-overs of the tigers' prey. Even if he did manage to reach the prey, other members would scare him away saying, 'You have lived a full life *kaka,* now let your children eat.' He could barely make a living by catching a few mice and old pheasant. Occasionally, he feasted on carrion. He cursed his very existence and prayed to God to take him back. But how can one die till his days in the world are over? He came in front of tigers many times to provide them with a meal but the tiger would not oblige him. Thus life dragged on.

One day, a hunter came to that jungle with his bow and arrows. The jackal saw him and thought that this was his long awaited opportunity. He passed in front of the hunter to offer himself as a target. But the hunter ignored him. He had not come to kill jackals. What use are jackals any way? The flesh is unpalatable, and the skin is not too good. Oh, what a curse to be born as a jackal!

Soon a deer passed that way. The hunter shot his arrow at him at once, and hit the deer behind the ear, killing him instantaneously. The hunter cleaned the stomach out and tied up the carcass to carry it, when a boar happened to come that way. The hunter thought it was his lucky day and shot an arrow at him. But, as we know, the boar has a thick skin. The arrow only wounded him. He came straight for the hunter.

### The Fight

The hunter had been careless. He had allowed the boar to come close. The boar being at too close a range, the hunter could not manoeuvre himself into a position to shoot another arrow. So he took an arrow in his hand to fight the beast. The boar charged with all his fury. In the scuffle that followed, both the hunter and the boar were killed. That is not all. There was yet another casualty. In his blind range, the boar trampled over a young python which also died. Thus in quick succession, there were four deaths. The jackal was watching from a distance and very much wished that he was in place of the python to have been rid of his miserable existence. But soon hunger got the better of him. Seeing all the contestants and the delicious python dead at one stroke, he realized why God had not willed him to die yet. He had food for many days and not a soul in the vicinity to share with it.

### The Greed

As a first step, he decided to move the food stocks to safety. He mustered all the strength left in him and slowly dragged the bodies to his dwelling. He was almost exhausted by the effort. He wondered whom to eat first. Rather than satisfy his hunger, he started calculating the stock situation; that the boar would last one month, a deer so much more and so on. Life was, at last, worth living.

### The Stock

He was happy now. He had food stocks for more than a month. Though the meat would rot but hadn't he been living on carrion for many years. He just could not decide what to eat first. He suddenly remembered that there was yet another item that had the smell of food. He went back to the scene of the grim fight to investigate. Sure enough, the bow of the hunter had been made out of intestines that could be eaten. He decided to eat that and save the other items for the morrow. With this the old jackal bit at the taut guts. This released the tension of the bow which hit him on the head with a mighty force killing him there and then. Thus, he could enjoy what God had given him.

## Backbiters Beware!

After the death of his father, a prince lion he became the Raja of the jungle. He was kind and compassionate and never killed for sport. Since life has to feed on life and this is the inevitable way of nature, other animals of the jungle were very happy with their king.

Once it so happened that a hunter came to that jungle to catch the lion. He put a trap and luckily for him, the lion's foot got caught in it. He was a powerful animal and broke the trap. His foot was, however, badly injured. Poor fellow was confined to bed. His servants, the tigers and panthers provided him with the necessary food.

**The Unhappy Subjects**

His subjects were very unhappy at his injury. They thought it their duty to go and inquire after his health. One and all gathered at his door. The lion was pleased with his popularity. There was a pair of bisons among the lion's subjects, who had the bad habit of backbiting. With the result that they had strained relations with many denizens of the jungle, especially with one of the jackals. The reason was not far to seek. They were unhappy with the jackal because he never greeted them, which they thought was their due. Wherever they went, they spoke ill of the jackal.

**The Instigation**

The sickness of the lion afforded them a golden opportunity for instigating the lion against the jackal. They went to the lion and told him that they had heard the jackal talk ill of him. He was in fact, heard to say that it would have been better if the lion had been taken away by the shikari. The community would have got rid of his depredations. That was why the jackal had not even come to visit the king. Not only was it bad manners,' it was outright disloyalty. It was dangerous to let such a fellow live in the jungle. He would avail of the first opportunity to let down his king. The lion heard this and flew into a rage. He decided that as soon as he was well, he would seek out this traitor and put an end to his life.

The jackal also had some good friends. In any case, the bisons were not very popular because of their bad habit. The dwellers of the jungle had come to realize that their praises and censures should not be taken seriously. The friends of the jackal heard the bisons and fretted for his life. They went and related the entire conversation to him. The jackal thought that the bisons had overstepped all limits of decency. He decided to pay them back in the same coin. He smeared his paws and legs in mud and sprinkled dust on his body. Thus made up for the act, he went to the lion.

**The Good Friend!**

After salutations, he begged the lion's pardon for being late. He told him how worried he was at the unlucky affliction of his beloved king. The first thing he did was to pray for the good health and longevity of the king. He then went around the entire jungle to look for a particular herb which he knew was efficacious for injuries sustained from iron traps. But it obviously appeared that the all-devouring, greedy and reckless bisons had eaten all the plants. He then went in search of a veterinarian of the zoo, at a great risk to his own life. But what was his life, he was ready to lay down the lives of his entire family for the well-being of his noble king.

**The Remedy**

While he was there, the superintendent of the zoo happened to come to consult the doctor about the accidental injuries sustained by a pet lion. This rare coincidence was surely the result of his prayers! How else could one explain the coincidence. The doctor told the superintendent that the surest remedy for wounds sustained from steel was the application of the fat of a bison on the affected part. The superintendent of the zoo had then had a bison slaughtered, and the lion felt better with just one application of his fat on the wound. The point was well made. The lion ordered his tigers to fetch the bisons and kill them. The bisons paid with their lives for their scurrilous habit of backbiting.

**The Way of Luck**

'No, I want to buy the most wonderful thing in the world,' said the boy to his parents. 'After all, I am the one who has found the gold coin.'

One day, while a boy was making houses of mud and sand, his eyes were attracted by a shining object. Close scrutiny revealed that it was a gold coin. He pocketed it at once. He went straight home and showed the coin to his parents. The father said, 'Well done child; we will buy a sheep with it. From time to time, we shall sell the wool and thereby have a constant source of income.' 'No,' the mother said, 'we must not do that. I have never thought much of your sense of judgement. We must buy some food stuffs so that the family can feed well for some time at least.' 'No,' said the *Kanchha babu*. 'The food stuff will finish in no time and then we will be back to forced fasts!' Why not buy a few hens. They will lay eggs. We could eat some and get the others hatched. The process can go on indefinitely.' 'I am not going to agree to anything like that,' said the boy, 'I want to buy the most wonderful thing in the whole world. After all, I have found the coin.'

**The Bargain**

The boy, being the only child, and spoilt his will prevailed. So he went from shop to shop asking for the best and most wonderful thing in the world that the coin could buy for him. The shopkeepers jeered at him, 'There goes the spoilt child. He wants to buy the most wonderful thing when he is himself a wonder!' At last, the boy noticed a monkey performing his tricks in a shop.

'Would you sell that monkey to me for a gold coin?' asked the boy. 'Why not? In fact I will give you the monkey along with the chain, replied the shopkeeper.

The bargain was struck and the boy came home happily with his monkey to the great annoyance of his parents. Now they would have to feed one more mouth. His father and mother started arguing on who was responsible for spoiling him. The blame and counter-blame seemed to go on endlessly and it led to a quarrel.

As time passed, the monkey grew very naughty. He would jump from house to house creating a nuisance in the neighbourhood. One day he happened to jump over a wall and landed in the house of a giant. He spied around and was attracted by the glitter coming from a room. He peeped in through the ventilator and noticed the giant counting his diamonds, pearls and gold coins. He sneaked in and, as the giant went to fetch more from a box, he picked up some and ran off with the booty to the boy.

**The Suspicious Giant**

This process was repeated a number of times till the giant became suspicious. He came to know of the intruder and decided to teach him a lesson. He feigned sleep and as the monkey came again he caught him by the tail. The monkey was, however, prepared for such an eventuality. He blurted out, 'Uncle, I have come from a far distance to look you up. I was wanting to surprise you but, instead, you have surprised me.' You are my maternal uncle. Long back mother had told me about you. Even now she weeps at times when she remembers her late sister-in-law, who died leaving you a widower.' Then addressing him directly he said, 'Uncle, you are still young. Why don't you get married again?'

**A Bride for the Giant**

And without waiting for a reply he continued, 'That is what I have already done for you. I have located a beautiful bride and shown her some of your wealth, which I took without your permission. Anyway, it is all safe and will come back to you after the marriage. My would be aunt is bewitched by your jewels.'

The giant released his hold of the monkey and keenly asked him more details about his new-found sister and would be bride.

The monkey had fully satisfied his curiosity. He noticed the great eagerness of the giant for a second wife, and he said, 'Uncle, let me go now because my pretty aunt will be waiting for me. May I take a few gold coins so that she can get her bridal attire made?' Saying this he took up a few coins in both his hands and went away. The giant requested him to come again. This way, the monkey robbed the giant many times. He handed over all the wealth to the little boy. He disclosed the plan to the boy and told him to get a dummy girl made. Accordingly, the dummy of a beautiful giantess was made and attired in fine clothes.

### The Clever Monkey

At last the appointed day of marriage arrived. His gullibility, had made the giant part with more than half his wealth. On the day of the marriage, the monkey went to meet him and said, 'Uncle your days of loneliness do not seem to be over yet. The priests have predicted that you cannot meet your bride immediately and must wait for a few days till the evil phase of the stars is over. The bride will come to you but let her remain in her room without any disturbance. In case you are impatient and touch her, she will immediately be transformed into straw.'

When marriage ceremonies were performed, the girl was transported to her husband's house. She was put on a bed. The giant eyed her many times through the chinks and key holes. She remained absolutely motionless. This aroused his suspicion and he was desperate to investigate. Not able to contain himself any longer, he opened the room and shook his wife to wake her up. Lo and behold, she had turned into straw! He cried at the top of his voice at the loss of both his second wife and his wealth. The monkey was, indeed the most wonderful thing in the world that the boy could buy!

## Teenota Thug

### Three Cheats

This is the story of three friends who were cheats of the highest order. Naturally, they were, to use a pun, thick as thieves. None in the neighbourhood had escaped their deceit. Everyone without exception ran from their shadows. So quick-witted were they, however, that they always managed to find a fresh prey every day.

Once when they were passing the shop of a sweet-maker, sight of the sweets made their mouths water. Their plan was quickly hatched since they all thought alike. One went to the sweet-maker and addressed him thus, 'Dada, may your business prosper. I hope it will prosper like the sweet-maker of the village on the river bank who made offerings to the river-goddess. Oh, what a boost the goddess gave his business! Sales were so brisk that he had to employ twenty-two servants and helping hands in one week.'

### The Muttering

Then as though talking to himself, he muttered, 'Oh, what he was and what he has become now? What a palatial building he has made! If the goddess is kind even the impossible can become possible. I also want to make some offerings to her to change my circumstances for the better.' And then addressing the sweet-maker he continued, 'Let me quickly buy some, and, if you want, I will carry your offerings also to the goddess on your behalf.'

'No, no, we have no time for that. You buy some and let us go our way,' said the second thug who seemed to appear from nowhere.

'Do not be so inconsiderate,' said the third, 'you must do a good turn every day. The poor sweet-maker has no time. He cannot close the shop to go and make the offerings himself. If he closes, his customers will be disappointed. And, by the way, what way will the goddess Lakshmi enter the shop? What is the harm if we carry some sweets on his behalf as offerings to the goddess.'

'There is no time, why get late? If he cannot close the shop, is that any of our concern?' said the second thug.

'No brother, do not be in a hury,' intervened the shopkeeper. 'Just carry some sweets. Surely I am not so mean that I will charge you money for the sweets offered to the goddess.'

And making two packets, he quickly handed them over to the two thugs in spite of the loud protests of the third that they were unnecessarily getting late for the sake of the shopkeeper.

**The Gullikk Sweet-Maker**

As was expected, the sweet-maker did not charge them a single penny. Having deprived the sweet-maker of a sizable amount of sweets, they quickly made their way to a shady spot and set to making three equal shares. Some of the sweets were two of a kind and could not be shared equally. Thus after making three shares, a surplus of some sweets remained. After a lot of haggling, they decided that those sweets would go to the fellow who had the most beautiful dream that night. They consumed their shares and went to sleep, eager for the dreams and the sweets. Two of them got up very early but the third slept on. They woke him up for it was time to decide who was to get the remainder of the sweets. Their friend was still sleeping. The other started relating his dream. 'I had a lovely dream. I was invited by Indra, the ruler of heaven, for dinner. Whilst we drank nectar and ate the choicest dishes, all his charming Apsaras danced and served us. Oh, how beautiful? What a nice time I had! Surely there could not possibly be anything better than this?'

The third thug who had dozed off again was woken up. The second started relating his dream. He said, 'I was invited by Brahma, the creator himself. Indra was also one of the invitees to the party where I went. But I, being a personal guest of Brahma, had a superior place. Surely, my dream is better than yours. In fact nothing can possibly surpass the charm of this dream.' Addressing the third thug, he said, 'Now let us hear your dream so that we reach a decision on the remainder of the sweets.'

### The Clever One

The third thug who still had his eyes half closed dropped his head forward with a jerk as though he was overpowered by sleep, 'Oh, let me sleep. A demon bothered me the whole night and I have not had a wink of sleep. If you are my friends, be kind and let me sleep.'

He again pretended to doze of. But his friends would have none of that. So he started narrating his dream. 'A demon came in my dream and said that my flesh was saltish, and that he loved saltish flesh. Saying this, he almost ate me but I quickly grabbed the remainder of the sweets and put them in my mouth. Thus I managed to avert a disaster and save myself by the skin of my teeth. As soon as my flesh turned sweet, the demon left me. I must thank you, my dears, that you had left some sweets which came in handy. Otherwise, today you would be mourning my loss. Oh, what a nightmare! I could hardly sleep.' Saying this he again pretended to doze off. The two thugs at once opened the packet of sweets, but it was empty. Some time during the night their friend had surrecptitiously eaten the sweats!

## Mero Nani Roee Maryo

### Whilst My Child Cries

Once upon a time there lived two brothers in a certain village with their families. Both of them had a daughter each. They lived as a joint-family with complete understanding and accord. People gave examples of their family whenever they talked of the joy of togetherness. But mother luck has her own unpredictable ways. There was an epidemic, which killed both the elder brother and his wife. Their daughter became an orphan. The younger brother, however, did everything within his power to bring up the girl and keep her happy. Whenever he bought anything for his own daughter, he made it a point to buy the same for his niece. Many a time, the two girls, mistook the items belonging to the other as their own and staged mock fights.

### The Bickering

Thus there was a constant argument among the sisters over their belongings, specially over clothing and toys. The wife of the younger brother usually favoured Kanchhi, her own daughter, and came to resent the Jethi. The love of the uncle for his niece was also viewed with disapproval by the lady of the house. She naturally wanted everything for her own daughter and constantly nagged her husband about this. This led to nasty quarrels at times.

The husband, as is the fate of all members of the male community, at last had to give in. The matters became so bad that the lady of the house constantly hurled abuses on the helpless girl. She was virtually reduced to the state of a servant in the house. She was asked to do all menial jobs, including grazing the herd. We know that, animals are more responsive to love than men. One of the goats got very attached to the girl. She pitied her and constantly prayed to God to remove her sufferings. The girl used to share her meagre food with the goat, the goat also receprocated by giving her all her milk.

Luck plays in different ways. The generosity of the goat was noticed by Lord Ganesh who blessed her with magic powers. The goat thought that the first beneficiary of this magic power should be the poor little girl. So she took her to a quiet corner of the pasture and offered her some fine dishes for eating. The girl in turn gave her the loaf of chaff that her aunt had given to her. Time went on. The girl gained in health and beauty. Many messages started coming from far and wide for her hand in marriage.

The lady of the house thought it to be a good opportunity to get rid of her. She accepted an offer from a distant village. Jethi was married in a simple ceremony. At the house of her in-laws, she soon won the hearts of all by her good nature, and gentle manners.

**The Marriage of Jethi**

She would get up before the rising of the morning star and finish the household chores. Her old father-in-law and mother-in-law had little to do except to go to the temple and pray for the longevity and happiness of their son and daughter-in-law. She gave birth to a son who was as handsome and charming as his mother. As soon as the girl left her uncle's house, it fell on bad days. The crops were attacked by insects and eaten by mice. A number of cattle heads died of disease. The old couple started keeping ill-health. One day the family came to the village of their niece on some business and stayed with her. Seeing the love, respect and affluence enjoyed by the Jethi, the old aunt was besieged herself with jealousy.

**The Cunning Old Lady**

A preposterous idea crossed the mind of the cunning old lady: that she should replace the niece with her own daughter. Outwardly she showered all the love on Jethi and her child. She asked her why did she not invite Kanchhi to spend a few days with her? She could lend a helping hand to her and it would be a welcome change for both the sisters. It would not only provide some relief to her from the everyday household affairs but it would help Kanchhi learn house-keeping from her. The simple and unsuspecting girl readily agreed. After a few days, she received a message that Kanchhi would be coming the following day. The aunt had requested her to meet her near the old well outside the village. So she did. But what followed was not in the plan. Kanchhi threw her in the old well! She had obviously come prepared for the dastardly act. She had brought one set of clothes of Jethi, which her mother had stolen earlier. She quickly changed into those clothes and went straight home and masqueraded as Jethi. She successfully managed to befool everyone except the child, He would keep on howking.

Luck plays a big hand in a person's life. She knew swimming and did not die as expected by the wicked Kanchhi. She noticed an iron staircase to one side of the well. She came out and hid in the old hut near the well.

**The Intelligent Animals**

The horse, the cow, the goat and the dog these are intelligent animals. They felt the absence of the mishess. Kanchhi neither caressed them with love nor spoke to them as gently as Jethi used to. Jethi's heart was full of sorrow for the child. After all, she was the mother. She could hardly bear the separation from her son. As soon as it was dark, she stole into the house. The animals at once recognized the footsteps of their mistress. They threw endearing glances at her. She spoke to them and said:

'Oh dear cow, dear horse,
With you all, my happiness lies,
But my mind cannot rest,
Whilst my child cries.'

She went further and the dog came forward wagging its tail. She told him:

'Oh my dog, oh my pet;
With you all, my happiness lies,
But my mind cannot rest
Whilst my child cries.'

She then went to the child's cradle and suckled her son with all her love. After that, she put him back in the cradle and fed the animals. Before the rise of the morning star, she was back to her hide out.

Next night, she did the same thing again. However, the husband was already full of suspicion and had noticed how the child was suddenly quiet. He was, however, too lazy to investigate fully. The third night the same nocturnal round was completed by Jethi. Her husband was, however, awake and as soon as she got ready to leave, he caught her. Kanchhi tried to raise an alarm, branding Jethi a thief, but to no avail. She had been exposed. Her nose and ears were cut and she was sent back. The family then lived happily ever after.

## Dhikur ra Kauwa

### The Doves and the Crow

A Crow always ate the eggs of the doves who lived on the same tree. One day the dove said to the crow, 'At least, have the decency of cleaning your beak before you eat my eggs,' said the dove to the hungry crow. 'Have a look at your beak yourself; it is smeared with muck. The holy river is so near. Why don't you go there and clean it before you peck at my beautiful and delicate eggs?'

The crow was taken by this rebuke at this. The pair of doves were to lose their eggs in any case. Why should he not respect their sentiments. Thinking this, he agreed to their seemingly meaningless request. 'All right, all right. I will grant you that much,' said the crow. 'I am going to the river and will presently come back. And remember, no tricks with me. I am too clever for you. Don't try to the smart with you.'

'No sir, I am known for my simplicity and honesty,' said the mother dove, 'If luck ordains that you eat my eggs, let it be so. You have saved the life of my husband and we are indebted to you for that.' Hearing this, the crow flew off to the river with great expectations of an early return and a hearty feast writ large on his face.

The story is about a crow and a pair of doves who lived on an old banyan tree. Once it so happened that her husband was out in search of food whilst she sat hatching the eggs. He was busy collecting edible material for his wife, when a shikari spotted him. The cruel shikari was about to use his *gulel* when a crow noticed him and, out of sheer instinct, raised an alarm. The father dove heard it and flew off before the missile hurled at him, could hit his head and separate his body from his soul!

### The Saviour!

The cunning crow had noticed what happened. On returning home, he made no end of boasting to the doves about his gallant act of saving the life of the male dove. But for this friendly act, the mother dove would have starved to death in the nest or the eggs would have gone bad. In return for his presumed act of bravery and friendliness, he demanded to eat their eggs! That was the price the doves were required to pay for staying with a bad neighbour and ignoring the age-old saying of choosing one's neighbours with care. The doves had ignored these classic words of wisdom and were now required to learn their lesson hard way. Which mother would let that happen, but she was helpless. The only thing she demanded was that at least the beak be cleaned before her eggs were pecked at. Hope has an uncanny way of lingering on and on. She was waiting some merack to happen.

### The Request

The crow went to the river and said, 'River, river, I saved the life of the father dove. In return for this act of bravery, the mother dove has offered me a feast of her eggs, but she wants me to clean my beak before pecking at them. May I clean my beak in your water?'

The river had flown through ages and had witnessed the wickedness of many generations. He had acquired the power to see through the minds of all creatures. He quickly grasped the situation and said, 'No, do not dirty the entire water. Go and get a pot and take some water in it to clean your dirty beak.'

Hearing this, the crow flew off to the potter.

'Potter, potter,' said the crow, I saved the life of the father dove, for that act of bravery and good neighbourliness, the mother dove has offered me a feast of her eggs. She, however, is an obstructionist and having promised wants to go back on her words. She, therefore, wants me to clean my beak before eating the eggs. Please lend me a pot. The river wants me to some water in the pot.

### The Admonition

'No, no', said the potter, 'Do you take me for a fool to make that suggestion. If I keep lending pots like this, how will I ever make a living? I have a large family to look after. I am, however, ready to oblige you on one condition. My wife is sick and I need the horn of a deer for medicine. You keep flying to distant lands and are sure to know where a horn can be found. Get me one and come to claim the pot in exchange,' saying this the potter turned his face and busied himself in his work. The crow was now despairing but the hope of eating the succulent eggs of the dove made his mouth water. He was sure his friend would help him.

'Dog, dog, come with me,' said he, 'I will show you where the deer live. Kill one and have a feast. Only let me have the horn and some meat.' And he went on to explain the reason for his requirement of the horn.

'I will be glad to come with you, my dear, but don't you see I am too weak. I have not had a meal for days and have no strength to chase the fleet-footed deer. I can come with you but first get me some milk from the cow.' That will restore my dowdling energy.

The crow was by now sick of the ever growing chain, but now there was a fresh possibility of storing some meat for a rainy day, because the dog surely would not be able to eat the whole deer. And then he would enjoy the feast of the tasty eggs that would revive his youth. So he went to the cow.

### Milk for the Dog

'Cow, cow, give me some milk for the dog who will then kill the deer,' said he. 'The deer are your rivals in that they stealthily eat all the grass of the pastures and leave little for you. So here is a scheme beneficial to both of us. I need a deer's horn for the potter who will give me a pot, in which I will take some water from the river and clean my beak, after which the dove will let me eat her eggs.' And he told her the whole story of his agreement with the dove

'Don't try to be clever,' said the cow, 'Everyone says you are very cunning but I am no fool either. Why should I give you the milk without due compensation? First go and get me some grass.'

Saying this, the cow turned her face and ignored the crow. But the crow was not prepared to give up. He stole an old sickle from a house and went to cut the grass. But to his great dismay, he discovered that the sickle was badly rusted and blunt and was, therefore, unable to do the job. He had to sharpen it. He had no choice but to go to the blacksmith. The crow went to him and told him the whole story. He also promised him a share of the deer's meat. The blacksmith became quite ready to oblige. He put the sickle in the fire to remove the rust before honing it.

The crow impatiently watched the slow process and kept requesting him to hurry up. His persistent requests irked and irritated the blacksmith. He took the sickle out when it was red-hot and told the crow to take it. The wise crow was too hungry, and sick of the persistent delay. For once he forgot that haste makes waste. He at once grabbed the sickle in his beak, burning it badly. He cried with anguish and forgot all about the eggs. He decided to steal the eggs as is his normal habit and not take undue advantage of a situation. He had to fell his belly with whatever he could get.

The doves hatched the eggs in due course and brought up their family. To live in peace without any fear they moved to another tree.

## Satota Bhai ra Bahini

### A Girl and her Seven Brothers

We want your permission. We want to take out sister with in fo a few days. said the eldest brother. 'We want her to help us in the performance of the puja of Shri Satyanarayan. The priest has assured us that an offering of a lotus plucked by a lady, with all the thirty-two signs of virtue, will bring us good luck. The goddess Lakshmi will herself come and bless us.'

'Oh yes, by all mean,' said the husband of their sister. How could be suspect his brothers-in-law.

This is the story of a girl who had seven brothers, six of whom were married. Being the only daughter, she was a great favourite of her parents. The brothers also loved her deeply. Her parents never admonished her or beat her even with a stick of flowers. God had endowed her with all the feminine charms. She had a very sweet nature. She was ever ready to do the odd jobs for all and sundry, and was greatly delighted to be of service to others. It was said of her that she was incapable of harming anyone, even inadvertently.

When she came of age, her parents received messages for her hand in marriage from many noble young men. They selected their son-in-law with the greatest care and gave away their daughter in marriage. They missed their beloved daughter a lot but were happy in her happiness. They were, however, not as lucky with their sons as they were with their daughter. All of them, except the youngest, were given to leading easy, fruitless lives with little scruples. The parents worried a great deal on that account. Thinking, as most parents do, that marriage, and the consequent enhancement of responsibilities, would mend their ways, they married six of them to as good girls as possible.

Habits die hards. The marriages made little difference to the boys who remained as easy-going, selfish and self-centered as every. Since all living things must die, the parents breathed their last before the marriage of the youngest son was solemnized. The brothers inherited the entire wealth of their parents. For sometime, they lived in as much luxury as money could provide. In course of time, they came to their proverbial last penny. Like most vile men, they turned their attentions to the jewellery of their wives, and soon saw the last of that too.

**The Advice**

They became desparate. Rather than do something positive about their dwindling fortunes, they wanted an easy buck and went to a *tantric* pujari of great renown for advice. He advised them to sacrifice a woman, with all the thirty-two signs of virtue, to the deity of the village-pond and eat her flesh! That would bestow untold fortune on them. This advice from the pujari also made them part with what little money they possessed.

The brothers thought a lot about the woman with the requisite qualities among all their relatives and acquaintances, and agreed unanimously that there was none better than their own sister! After deep deliberations and heated discussions, they went to her place and asked her to accompany them to the village to perform the puja of Shri Satyanarayan. Allowing the advice of the pujari, she was required to pluck a few lotus flowers from the village-pond as offering for Shri Satyanarayan.

**The Treacharoud Brothers**

As all girls are, she too was greatly excited at this opportunity of going to her *maitighar,* and got ready to accompany her brothers. The brothers gave her a rousing welcome at the village, and held a feast in her honour. On the appointed day, all of them had an early bath and went with their sister to the pond. She looked all around in the pond but could not see a single lotus flower. The Jetha told her:

'Go in the water sister dear
Then you shall see the lotus clear.'

The helpless girl entered the pond and waded up to knee deep water but could not locate any lotus. Addressing her brothers, she said:

'The water is knee deep,
But no lotus I can see,
Which why should I go,
Oh dear brothers tell me.'

The *Sayenla* replied:

Go further and deeper, oh sister dear,
Then you will see the lotus clear.'

The unsuspecting girl was eager to make a success of the puja of her brothers. She moved deeper till the water reached her waist but could not locate any lotus. She turned to her brothers and shouted:

'The water is waist deep
But no lotus do I see,
Which why should I move,
Oh dear brothers tell me.'

The wicked and selfish brothers had already reconnoitered the deep parts of the pond. So the *Mayenla* said:

'Move right, oh sister dear,
Then you shall see the lotus clear.'

The sister moved up again till the water came upto her shoulders. She could, however, not see any lotus. Still she did not suspect any foul-play and asked her brothers:

'The water is up to the shoulders:
But no lotus I can see,
Which way should I go,
Oh dear brothers tell me.'

The *Kayenla* replied:

'To the lotus you are very near,
Move left, oh sister dear,
Then you shall see the lotus clear.'

The girl moved as directed and with one step the water reached her chin. She could barely keep her mouth and nose above water for breathing. Not able to see her brothers any longer she shouted at the top of her voice,

'The water is up to the chin,
But no lotus I can see,
Which way should I move,
Oh dear brothers tell me.'

The *Rayenla* replied:

'Move right, oh sister dear,
Then you shall see the lotus clear.'

**Sister's Love**

The love of the girl for her brothers was sincere. In her eagerness to help the brothers, moved as directed and stepped into the deepest part of the pond. She was drowned and soon her body surfaced. The wicked brothers did not even move their little fingers to help her. As soon as her body started to float, they took no time to recover it and cut it up into pieces. The *Kanchha,* who was the only unmarried brother, was full of remorse. He was however, not in a position to open his mouth. He did not eat his share of this flesh. Instead, he buried it underground.

Time went on. The human sacrifice made, by the heart less brothers made scant difference to the fortunes of the family. They remained as poor as ever and were virtually reduced to beggary, except the youngest brother who went to a far-off land and made a fortune. After some time a fine reed sprouted at the place where *Kanchha* had buried his sister's flesh. It was a plant of rare beauty and brought forth colourful flowers. One day, a musician passed that way and cut the reed. He did not notice that blood oozed out from the junction of the cut. He made a flute out of the reed. The flute gave out very melancholy and heart-rending notes.

**Voice from the Flute**

One day, at the end of his usual performance, the musician was surprised to hear a sweet feminine voice emanate from the flute:

'Beloved was I of my parents,
My husband loved me as his dear wife,
I was killed by my brother,
The youngest saved my life.'

The musician was suprised at this touching note and thought that the instrument was a magic-flute. He held performances at many place where great crowds gathered to hear him play the magic-flute. At last he reached the town where the husband of the girl lived. He played the flute before a large gathering. At the end, the following lyric came out from the flute:

'Beloved was I of Ama Rani,
My Babu Raja loved me dear,

My husband, loved me as his dear wife,
Killed was I by my cruel brothers,
The youngest saved my life.'

What happened was really surprising. At this last heart-rending note, warm saline tears flowed out of the flute.

The husband who was among the spectators, recognized the voice of his beloved wife. He offered one hundred and one gold coins to the musician for the flute but he refused. The bargain was at last struck at one thousand and one gold coins. The husband hugged the flute and took it home. There he put it to his lips before the idol of the *Devi.* Closing his eyes he played on the flute for hours on end. At last he opened his eyes and to his great and pleasant surprise, his lips were resting on the petal fresh cheeks of his wife! His love had revived her life.

The sister remembered to send some money to her brothers. After all, she was their sister.

## Yamraj sang Bhent

### Meeting with Yama

The snake bit his four friends who died unslantaneously. Gojay was struck dumb with awe at the gruesomeness death which occured before so cold-bloodedly before his eyes. A huge mass of wealth, in fact the veritable treasure of Kubera, the god of wealth, lay before him. After the death of the four robbers, he was undoubtedly the sole owner of this wealth. He was, however, too dazed by the quickness of events of the last few hours. At that moment the snake, transformed into Yama, addressed him thus, 'It is not your time yet Gojay. When it comes, it comes. And till it comes, none can harm you. You can walk on live ambers or swim the seven-seas full of monsters, and still no harm will come to you.' Gojay was taken aback and stood speechless.

### Gojay's Destiny

After some time he taxed his brain to say something, but his mind was a blank, and almost in a state of shock at the events that had passed before his eyes in such a quick succession. In any case, he was not a very quick-witted person and, in spite of thinking hard, he could not figure anything apt to say.

'It is your destiny. Take this wealth and enjoy the worldly pleasures. Your last moment on this earth will be after fourteen years and fourteen days. The place is that yonder tree,' said Yama, pointing towards a huge, lonely tree in the distance.

This is the true story of two bosom friends, Gojay and Chuppay. They were both simpletons and did menial jobs for all and sundry, to eke out a living. They keenly heard the tales of exploits of the men from their village who had travelled to distant lands and made fortunes. Those tales, true and false, many of them undoubtedly exaggerated, always kindled their imagination. One day, they decided that they too should move out and do something big. Accordingly, one fine morning they packed their meagre belongings and set out to the east in the direction of the rising sun. They decided that they would keep moving in the direction of the sun which would surely guide them to their coveted destination.

**The Last Meal**

They stuck to their plan. Walking till mid-day, they reached the outskirts of a thick jungle. They decided to rest a while and take their lunch. Their appetite had been sharpened by fatigue. Whilst they were relishing their meals, a crow, who was a messenger of Yama kept cawing:

'Take your last meal.
Take your last meal.'

Neither able to follow, nor, in any case, bothered about the meaning of the call, they enjoyed their frugal meal because they were very hungry. After the meal, they decided to relax awhile because the sun was overhead and could not guide their steps. As they lay back to recline, they were startled by a rustling sound coming from their rear. They had barely turned their faces, when a huge buffalo charged towards them, snorting angrily. They had no time to react. Soon the buffalos was on them. It straight came for Chuppay and, lifting him up on his horns, flung him to the ground, goring him and trampling the life out of his body. Gojay was terrified and went cold and numb with fright. He was now all alone. If he went back, people would demand to know the whereabouts of Chuppay, who had already departed on his last journey. If he moved ahead, he was alone and would not know where to go. 'What is left in this world anyway?' He thought and went towards the buffalo with the hope that, in its fury, it would also kill him.

**Buffalo the Neck**

It was not his time to die yet. The buffalo was now as meek as a pet goat. In spite of severe and profound provocations, the buffalo refused to be goaded. Gojay considered death, by drowning. He was about to set out for the river when the buffalo transformed himself into a snake and started moving in the direction of the sun. Gojay's curiosity got the better of him or, perhaps, some latent force guided him, and he followed the snake. The reptile led him to a deserted palace built on a mound in a clearance of the jungle. Gojay heard some voices and went inside the palace to investigate. He saw two robbers standing with drawn scimitars. There were piles of diamonds and gold coins near by. Hiding behind the pillar, Gojay listening whatever they said to each other.

'If we kill them, we can have all this wealth between two of us,' said one.

'Yes, we can settle in a distant town and start our lives afresh. Maybe, we can get married and rear our own families,' replied the other.

'Oh yes, with one stroke of luck, we can move out of this life of hide-and-seek, and constant danger and uncertainty. Remember, soon as they enter, thrust the scimitars in their backs, and cut off their throats while they are still under shock,' said the other.

Gojay listened with awe; he was soon to witness murders! He thought he would intervene and maybe lose his own useless life. The thought had hardly crossed his mind when two more robbers entered, and the two present (in the palace) pounced on them and killed them. Gojay again had no time to react and resigned himself to the events. The two robbers, their hands still smeared with fresh-blood, made two equal piles of the wealth and were about to depart when one noticed a packet of sweets brought by the other two. It had so transpired that while their two companions looked after the wealth, the other two had gone to buy eatables. And they were as unprincipled as the couple who waited at the palace. They had too planned to put an end to the lives of their companions is food.

They put poison in their food. As soon as the two murderers took the sweets, their bodies shook, with severe convulsions and, within minutes their souls left their bodies. Gojay was stunned and came out of his hiding place when the snake appeared as Yama to tell him of his own destiny before disappearing. Gojay amassed the wealth and went in the direction of the sun. By night fall, he reached a town. There he posed as a big trader from a distant country. He bought costly apartments and started living in style. His wealth soon attracted many friends and admirers. He became the headman of the town.

### Beginning of the End

Soon there were proposals for marriage and he was tied in wedlock to a pretty girl. In this happiness, he completely forgot of his tryst with Yama. Whenever he did remember, he jeered that for once, Yama was wrong. There was no chance whatever of his going back to the wilderness to keep his appointment. Thus the time passed. He enjoyed life to the brim. The goddess of luck was very kind and favoured him in every undertaking. His wealth multiplied day by day. His children grew up to be handsome and lovable. He took to the costly sport of hunting. It is a wonderful life he was living.

One day, he was out hunting when the earth was shaken by severe tremors. He saw the town where he lived engulfed by the mother earth in a cloud of smoke and dust. There could be no survivors. The horse on which he was riding fled in panic and took him to the very tree shown to him years ago by Yama.

'What is there to live for now? My wealth, my family, my friends are no more,' and for the first time in many years he thought of his friend Chuppay. Overpowered by disgust he kept his appointment with Yama. He went to same tree which had pointed to by Yama a long time ago and ended his life by alonging himself from the same tree.

## Yota Jivit Manchhi

### A Man & Yama

Once a mahout took his elephant to a pond in a forest for a drink. God Yama also happened to be there, and was astonished to see a small man handling a big elephant with such ease.

When the elephant had had its fill of water, the mahout took him back and tathered him. Yama went to the elephant and asked, 'O great elephant, you are as big as a mountain and seem to be mightier than anyone else, why then do you act and move like a subdued dog from place to place. Can you not thrash that small man and live with your tribe?'

The elephant replied, 'Yama, you are perfectly right but you have not experienced the wisdom and shrewdness of man. Men are always wise and they can control and drive any animal as, and when, and where, they want. You always deal with death and have not come across a clever, wise and living man, you do not knows how sharp mended men are.

### Brahmin in Yamlok

Lord Yama returned to *Yamlok*. One day he called his messengers (*Yamduts*) and ordered them to bring before him a man who was alive. The messengers obeyed him and caught hold of a man who was dozing on his cot. He was a Brahmin by caste. When he was being taken to the *Yamlok,* he woke up with a start. Seeing himself carried by the *Yamdoots,* he was little frightened and astonished. With folded hands he asked them, 'I am not dead yet. Where am I being taken to?'

The *Yamdoots* replied, 'We have been ordered by our Lord Yama to bring a living man for him. We are, therefore, taking you to him.' Hearing this, the Brahmin began to plan some strategy with which to bribe Yama. And in a flash he planned out his strategy. He took the pen and paper and wrote.

*Dear Yama,*

*My blessings. I have came to know that you desire to have a living man in Yamlok. The dictism rules of God in such case are very clear that only the dead can be taken there. As soon as I came to know that you had sent your* doots *to bring a man: who was still live. I incarnated myself as a Brahmin. Although I had known all about your plans. I decided against rebuking you in the presence of others. Kindly meet me at Vaikunth. I shall wait for you there. But remember, keep my message to yourself. Don't durelge it.*

*Yours Vishnu.*

### Face to Face with Yam

On reaching *Yamlok*, the *doots* produced the man before Yama. The Brahmin handed over the letter that he had written earlier. Yama read the letter and turned pale. He stood before the Brahmin trembling with apprehension, and ordered his *doots* to clear out of the room. The Brahmin, then ordered Yama to go to *Vaikunth*. Meanwhile he took Yama's sceptre and started to rule his land.

Yama on the other hand, appeared before Lord Vishnu in *Vaikunth*. The Lord was indeed, astonished to see Yama there and asked him the reason for his sudden appearance. Yama replied, 'Lord, I am here on your orders—those you gave in your human incarnation—and I beg of you to forgive me.' Vishnu was clearly puzzled and said so. On hearing Yama's explanation, the Lord burst out laughing and told Yama, 'Yama, your *doots* made the mistake of bringing a clever Brahmin to you, who tricked you and sent you here. Now, I hope, you are aware of what happens if you abduct a man who is not dead. Remember that I have ordained man to be the supreme creature on this earth. Now you go back and send that Brahmin back with due respect. And remember, don't this sort of thing again.

Yama felt peeved and returned to the *Yamlok*. He had come to understand that what the elephant had said the man was correct. He ordered his *doots* to take the Brahmin back with ceremony and respect.

## Batho ko Katha

### A Crook will remain a Crook

I am hungry. How can I go to work on an empty stomach? How can I walk with a badly repaired shoe?' thought Batho to himself. 'First things first. I should get my shoes repaired and have a hearty meal. Then only will I be fit to proceed further. And if I cannot provide myself with these minor amenities, how can I hope to make a future?' he concluded, and made a bee-line for the bazaar.

Batho, as his name indicates, was a crook. He lived in that yonder village near the river junction. He waged a constant battle of wits to make a living by unfair means. Basically, he was too lazy to engage himself in any active pursuits. He was a card-sharp and invariably won at gambling. Soon, however people stopped playing dice or cards with him. Perforce, he had to resort to other tricks.

**Poor Wife!**

His way of life had a built-in element of insecurity, his wife was sick of him and his tricks. She nagged him endlessly. Their house was alive with her curses I abuses and cries. As was expected, Batho turned a deaf eary to her. In fact he openly advised others that the best remedy for a nagging wife was to turn a deaf ear to her. His wife came to know of this and decided to precipitate matters further. 'You will either work to earn your living or get out,' she said one day with an air of finality.

'I would rather get out. When there is always a fool available to part company with his money for my sake, why should I work?' Batho retorted.

'All right, then there is no place for you in my house. Get out.' shrieked his wife.

Batho felt insulted for the first time at the tone of his wife which was grossly impolite. After all, she was dependent on him. She would learn her lesson in a few days and come after him. He put on his shoes and moved out. Searching his pockets, he discovered that he was penniless. He had however reached a point of no return. He was hungry and his first problem was food. He had no face or desire to return home. He decided to go to some far off place to make a fresh start. But for that he must have a good pair of shoes and his stomach full. Thinking this, Batho went to the bazaar but, the people of his village were wise to him, and difficult to fool. Before undertaking the repairs of his shoes the cobbler would demand, or at least hope to see, some money on his person. He did not want to waste time.

**The Trickster**

He set out for the next village on his route of exploits: Reaching there, he got his shoes repaired from the cobbler. Putting them on with confidence, he told him that he had no change and would presently comeback to give the repair charges to him after a glass of Jhamr-Ko-Jhol (rice beer) and refreshments. He took his fill at the shop. He told the shopkeeper that as the cobbler owed him money and he would just holler out and tell him to make the payment. Saying this he called out to the cobbler, 'The money,' and made some gestures and signals. Then he went to the sweetmakers shop, ordered lot of sweets, some for eating, and some to be packed. He told the shopkeeper that the *bhattiwali* had yet to return him his money, and he would ask her to make the payment to him. After that he exchanged some singals with the *bhattiwali*. The cobbler, the *bhattiwali* and the sweetmaker thought that they were to take their dues from the other. Giving the impression that he had a long distance to cover, Batho then departed post haste.

After finishing the job in hand, the cobbler came to claim his wages from the *bhattiwali*. Both of them together then went to the sweetmaker. They were all suspicious of each other, which led to a heated discussion among them. The confusion, allegations and dewels, attracted a number of people. This led to further altercation and confusion lasting a long time, till the arrival of the washermen. The washermen, poor devils, were themselves sent on a wild-goose chase by Batho.

On his way from the village, Batho saw some washermen on the river bank. They were washing many colourful and costly clothes. Batho took out his packet of sweets. He smacked his lips as he ate and muttered 'Oh I wish the good man would distribute sweets every day. Oh how tasty they are and how nice that they cost me nothing.' Saying this and words to this effect, he cotinued to make a show of his enormous pleasure. The washerman was impressed.

**Befooling the Washermen**

'Where did you get these sweets?' asked one of them. 'Oh I wish I could get some more. I get them free', replied Batho. 'But where did you get them?' the washerman repeated his question. 'There is a good man of religion in the last village. He is on a visit there. Oh, these sweets are so tasty.' Batho replied. 'Did he give you these sweets?' The washermen asked. 'Yes he is distributing them free.' Batho answered. 'Will he still be there?' the washermen asked. In the meantime, all the washermen had collected around Batho. 'Oh yes, if you rush, you will get them, otherwise, he may go to the next village,' Batho replied. 'Will you look after our clothes,' one of the washermen asked? 'For a short time only. I have other work to attend to,' Batho said.

Batho thus sent the washermen on a wild goose chase. When they left he decamped with some selected clothes. The washermen reached the village and saw the cobbler, the *bhattiwali* and the sweet-maker fighting. It took them some time to discover the cause of the squable and the culprit, who had caused this confusion. They told the quarrelling men that their query was enjoying sweets on the river bank. They all returned to catch him but he had disappeared with the clothes.

**His Next Victim**

Batho's next victim was a wealthy trader. From a distance he noticed a caravan coming back with laden porters and ponies. His scheme made, he quickly hung the clothes on a tree and started to water the tree. As the caravan passed by, each man asked him the cause of his strange behaviour. He shouted back that they had no business to disturb him and his wonderful tree. At last the trader came by, riding his horse. It was the traders curiortp that made him ask the question.

'Don't disturb me and my wonderful clothes-bearing tree, go your way,' replied Batho.

The merchant hesitated for a while and then asked him 'Would you like to sell it?' 'Batho pretended he had not heard the question. 'Would you sell this tree to me? the merchant asked again. 'Not if I have a choice. My daughter is getting married and I need some money. The tree has already borne some fine garments. I am watering it and soon it will bear me some more clothes. I will sell them to collect the money.' After a little pause he added, 'In any case, the price may be beyond your means.' 'At least let me know your price, the merchant asked eagerly. 'Three thousand Rupees. And I have been watering it for last two days. So the clothes borne by the tree so far will be mine,' replied Batho. He was in his clement.

The merchant was doubtful. He did not Batho to change his mind. He took out the money at once and handed it over to him. Batho collected the clothes and muttered to himself, 'Oh God what cursed luck that I have to part with my tree. But my duty to my daughter is greater than anything else. Oh, how helpless I am.' He then pocketed the money and went away in a haste. Enroute he met some more people whom he tricked one way or the other. Thus waging a constant battle of wits, he went to the capital town.

**The Fame**

He soon attracted the attention of the gentry by his expensive dress and extravagant ways. His fame spread. He was invited by many men of status for dinner and often joined them in gambling where he always won. At least he was invited by the Raja for a game of dice. Raja asked him what his name was. Quick-witted as he was, he said that his name was *'Kanchha Babu'*, which literally means paternal uncle (a father's younger brother). In the meantime, the washermen, merchant and other victims of his deceit were on his trail and reached the capital. They were told that the Raja was playing dice with the stranger. They straight went to the Raja's palace. The washermen recognized the costly dress that Batho was putting on as the one stolen from them. The merchant who knew the king well took courage and approached the players. Batho had seen them all but feigned unrecognition. The king introduced Batho as *Kanchha Babu,* meaning uncle. The merchant became afraid. How could he say the partneral uncle of the king was a cheat. He requested others not to say anything and they came back.

Batho won a lot of money from the king and came back home to his wife. The money he had brought had forced his wife to stop nagging him. By judicious use of money he always kept his pockets full.

## Souteli Ana

### The Step-mother

A woman is a repository of tender emotions, and gentle feelings. But what goes wrong with a step-mother? She stoops to any depth to harm her step-children.

In *Satyug,* there lived a very poor family under the shadow of the Gauri-Shanker mountains. It consisted of a brother, his sister, their father and a step-mother. The step-mother treated both the children with hatred and malice. Because of a shortage of cots, both the brother and sister slept in the same bed. In order to bring them to ignominy the step-mother played a heinous trick on them. She put a newly-hatched snake in a glass of water and gave it to the girl to drink. The girl unknowingly gulped the snake. Days passed by and the little snake started developing in her belly, making her waist swell in girth. The sister also became very weak because the snake devoured all the food that she took. The step-mother now thought of taking undue advantage of the situation. She called on the village headman and his council and told them of the incestuous relationship between the brother and the sister. The village headman and his Panchayat had no way of knowing what had happened. They were pronounced guilty and were asked to leave the village. declared both of them guilty and banished them from the village.

They took refuge in a dense forest. The jungle was full of fruit-bearing trees and many animals and birds. The boy would catch the animals in his snare and the girl would cook the choicest dishes. Thus they lived happily and kept praying to God to deliver them from loneliness. One day, the sister became unconscious. While attending his sister, the boy saw a snake coming out of her mouth. As soon as the reptile saw the boy, he slid back into the belly of the helpless girl. The brother thus discovered the real cause of his sister's pregnancy. He kept thinking of various ways of making his sister get rid of the menace.

### The Snake is Trapped

At last he went to the village and fetched a jar full of milk. And the next time his sister became unconscious, he put that milk-jar in front of her. The snake came out to drink the milk and entered the jar. The brother closed the lid at once and trapped the reptile. He then buried the jar. Rid of the burden the girl started regaining her health. On the day of the *Bhai-duj* festival, the girl went in search of flowers to make a garland for her brother. She reached the place where her brother had buried the snake. A beautiful flower was blooming there. The sister plucked the flower and made a pretty garland out of its petals. After applying the tilak, she held out her hands to garland her brother. He warned her not to garland him lest she should repent later. But his sister could not understand his reluctance and garlanded him.

Immediately the brother turned into a snake. The reptile went to the step-mother and bit her. She soon breathed her last. The sister ran after the snake with cries of 'brother, brother.' But alas! the snake glided inside a big hole. The sister waited there and wept for many days. She would neither eat nor drink. She prayed to Nag Karkotak to send her brother back from *nag-lok.* At least, Nag Karkotak came in the form of a serpent and asked her why she wept. The girl narrated the whole story to the serpent and concluded that if her brother was not returned, she would fast unto death. Nag Karkotak was moved by her devotion to her brother and said that he would try. He played on a Veena near the hole. After a long time, the snake came out of the hole and started to sway rythmically to the music. Nag Karkotak, then gave him back his human form. Thus the brother and the sister were reunited.

## Kharayo ra Tisko Mitra

### The Rabbit's Rain: Unreliable Friends

Once upon a time there lived a rabbit in a jungle. He was good natured and possessed a keen sense of humour. He was fond of company and could never stay alone. He had many friends and boasted a lot about his popularity. He entertained his friends lavishly. Because of this, not only did he almost always remain under debt, he also neglected his family to a great extent. Some elders of the community advised him from time to time, and cautioned him but to no avail. The rabbit always talked of his innumerable friends who, he bragged would do anything for him.

One day some wild dogs came to that jungle. Seeing a well-rabbit they pounced at him. As the leading dog was about to catch him and almost caught him. He, however, tripped over a fallen branch of a tree and fell down. This alerted the rabbit and he got sufficient time to escape. The dogs soon formed up again and chased him. Fortunately for the rabbit, he found one of his good friends, a horse, grazing on the way. He went straight to him and requested him for help. The horse replied that the dogs were also his friends and never bothered him, although they could collectively kill him. How could he favour one friend against another? Saying this, the horse bent his long neek and started grazing again. The rabbit ran fast and went straight to his friend, a crow. But the crow said that although he could help anyone in the air, how could he possibly come down to ground level to help him. The dogs would catch him in no time and make a good meal of him. By evening he would be fully digested. Morever, his wife had just hatched the eggs and needed his help to collect food for the young ones. How could come to his aid and leave his family to starve.

The rabbit looked back and saw that the dogs were almost on him. He ran with all his might. En route he came to the lake and asked another good friend, a tortoise, for help. The tortoise said that he had no objection in taking the rabbit to his underwater dwelling, but that would only drown him? In case he gave him a ride and kept afloat, the dogs who were good swimmers would be more than a match for him. Thus the rabbit was abandoned by all his dear friends and started running for his life.

At last the pursuers and the pursued reached the edge of the thickest part of the jungle. The rabbit ran hardest and dodged the dogs under the cover of bushes which had many times served as his shelter and his home. The dogs lost his scent and thereby, the opportunity to catch him. The rabbit then remembered what the elders had been telling him all the time. The best shelter you find is in your own home, and the best helping hands are your own.

## Chatur Shyal

**The Clever Jackal**

Why should you tell your friends what is in your mind? In fact that is the last thing you should ever think of. In case Chaturay Shyal had done that, his body would have mingled back with the elements and his soul would have been wandering around the universe!

A jackal called Chaturay Shyal was a dweller of the thick jungles in the Terai. Near his cave, there were many villages. Chaturay frequently helped himself to the choicest roosters and hens. At times he even devoured some kids. His wisdom was known far and wide. In his community, he was equated with Birbal of Akbar's court. He lived by a constant battle of wits. Whereas he would go and steal the chicken, it was mainly the other members of his community who were chased and beaten.

Once a poultry disease killed many birds. The villagers became alert about their meagre possessions and invariably kept some dogs. This created a sudden dearth of food for Chaturay. One day the sky was overcast with thick clouds, and there was a little nip in the air. Chaturay felt like eating a chicken. His mouth watered at the very idea. He quickly rigged up a plan and collected some of his followers. They went outside the village and, as coached and ordered by Chaturay, beg a shouting, 'Watch out, watch out, look at the skies'. The villagers came out of their homes and started scanning the skies. This gave Chaturay a golden opportunity, and he quickly snatched some healthy roosters and took them away. The villagers did not even know what had happened. This way, Chaturay managed to trick the villagers a number of times and enjoyed a hearty meal for many many days and would not have go out to hunt.

One day another member of his pack decided to play the same trick on the villagers. But every Jackal is not clever. He was, however, caught. After a thorough beating, he told the villagers that the real culprit was Chaturay. He also promised to help them in trapping Chaturay.

**The Trap**

Chaturay was not aware of this scheme and unknowingly walked into a trap. The villagers decided to torture him to death. They first dragged him on the hard stones and on a dry river-bed. This was decidedly painful. Chaturay, however, resorted to a trick. As he was being dragged with fury and force, he burst into a full-throated laughter, said 'Aha, how lucky I am! I myself had thought of killing the lice in my body rolling on these hard stones. I have to thank these villagers. They are helping me to get ride of nice.'

The villagers heard this and stopped dragging him on stones. Instead they dragged him on the grass. Chaturay protested and said, 'Why are you dragging me on the grass? Do you want the lice to suck my blood? God will punish you for this crime.'

The men were happy that their enemy was being tortured. After some time, they decided to hang him to death. Whilst the men were discussing this plan, Chaturay come to know of it. Seeing death staring him in the face, he quickly thought of a plan and addressed the men thus, 'So you want to kill me. It is better to lose one's life than one's freedom. But I hope you know that the life of a jackal is in the stomach? I myself want to get rid of this life of suffering. I don't want to live anymore. I have already lost my freedom?'

**A Lesson for the Thieves**

The villagers thought of teaching a lesson to the other thieves of the jungle, and hung Chaturay on a tree that was visible from the jungle. Chaturay feigned death. Night fell and the creatures of the wilds started moving around in search of food. As luck would have it, the sneak from Chaturay's pack (who had sold him out), passed that way Chaturay was looking for such an opportunity. He called him out from a distance and said, 'Oh thank you brother. It is because of your kindness that I am enjoying the swing. Take any place do as I hav been doing and feel how heavenly it is. The foolish fellow was taken in by this and requested Chatu-ray to change places for a while, so that he too could enjoy the swing. Chaturay came down and hung his companion. Thus he regained his freedom. No other Jackal in years could match his wits.

## Teenota Mitra ko Katha

### The Three Friends

It is luck which makes a foolish man look wise. Their deeds are looked at as acts of great wisdom! This is so well-illustrated by the story of three beggars who were fast friends. Each one of them had a physical deformity. One was blind, the second, a hunch-back, and the third, lame. They stayed together and by mutual co-operation, seemed to be doing quite well. Early in the morning, with the first ray of the sun, they set out from their home for begging. After the day's collections, they returned to their dwelling and shared their earnings. A deep-rooted bond of friendship developed between them—a bond that adversity alone can foster. They grew very fond of each other and if one came back late, the others fussed over him a lot. Since they had human love, their lives were a liliss.

As they did every day, they went out begging. As luck would have it, the blind man stepped on a sharp object. He felt with his fingers and picked up an iron-spike. Thinking that it might injure another fellowhuman, and not knowing any safe place to throw it, he brought it home for possible use. The lame man similarly tumbled over a hammer and brought it with him. The hunch-back saw a long iron rod and brought it home. That year, the rains were scanty and the crops all but failed. Many people started resenting the daily rounds of the beggars. Some even admonished them by calling them parasites. They grew sick of this trend and decided to leave the place to try their luck elsewhere. They collected some foodstuff and set out. After walking many miles, they came across a dense forest. They were apprehensive of losing their way in the jungle, and even of losing their lives to the dangerous animals residing there. They almost decided to go back.

### The Goat

As they were hesitating over their next move, they heard the bleating of a lonely goat which had probably been separated from the herd. They caught the goat and tied a rope around its neck. Assured of their meat supply for a few days, and considering it to be an omen of good-luck, they decided to proceed on their journey. They cautiously entered the jungle and moved on. After a few miles, they were attracted by a faint glimmer of light. They decided to investigate and immediately set out towards it. On nearing the source of the light, they discovered it to be coming from the windows of a beautiful palace. They approached it cautiously and circled around the palace to ascertain the presence of any other human beings. The blind man, whose hearing was the most acute, confirmed that the palace appeared to be unoccupied at that particular moment. So they decided to move in. They went into each room but met no one there.

They were hungry. The palace was beautifully furnished and the store was full of eatables. They sat down to a hearty meal. The goat was not used to seeing such a place and was missing the herd. Hence she kept bleating.

It was truly dismayed by the surrounding she found herself in. The palace actually was the property of a giant who was out visiting his friends and relatives in the neighbourhood. When he came back, he was surprised to see the doors locked from inside and heard the strange sounds of the bleating of the goat. His surprise slowly changed into feelings of mingled rage and fear when he thought that probably some demons had occupied his house. He went near the door and mustering enough courage shouted, 'Well, well, I can hear the odd sounds that you are producing. Either come out and leave my house, or let us fight it out.'

**The Stupid Giant**

There was no reply except the bleating which grew in volume—the goat had been terrified by the giant's shouts of rage. The rightful owner of the house was flabbergasted and said, 'All right, let me at least see how you can pinch my finger?'

He pushed one of his fingers through the key hole. The three friends were calmly looking for such an opportunity. They made good use of the iron-spike and pierced the finger of the giant with their combined strength. The giant cried in anguish and pulled his finger out. However, he could not give up his dwelling so easily. He decided to try yet another time. 'Yes, yes, I admit you fellows can produce a peculiar sound, and pierce my finger; but let me see if you have the power to give a blow on my hand.'

He then thrust his hand through the window bars. The friends gave a fierce blow with the hammer and the giant's hand went numb with pain. He gave a shrill cry and pulled his hand out. The giant, however, had not yet given up. He again roared, 'I will not go away till I have seen how you guys look.' He then tried to peep through the keyhole. The friends seized the opportunity and thrust the iron rod straight into his eyes, blinding him. The clever she giant.

The giant could not take any more of it and ran away from there. He reached his neighbourhood and panting hard, related the whole story. The giants listened with rapt attention. They however, thought it incredible that there were mightier beings on earth than they. An old giantess came and volunteered to accompany him to investigate. She was also foolish enough to try the same tests and got a similar treatment. Both of them, panicked and ran back. The community was eagerly awaiting their arrival.

By now all the giants had collected at a place. They asked for the cause of their flight and fright. After due deliberations, it was decided by the elders that all of them should go back together.

The friends had gained time. In the long interval between the disappearance of the two giants and the reappearance of the community, the friends had decided to have a meal. They slaughtered the goat and prepared all kinds of dishes and delicacies. They were preparing to satisfy their hunger when the giants reappeared. After loud consultations and discussions they decided to make a giant ladder with the giant standing the shoulders of the other to reach the roof. This way, they would approach their adversaries from a position of advantage. The owner of the house volunteered to bear the weight at the bottom saying that he would gladly bear all the weight, but inwardly happy that he would occupy the safest place.

### They saw Human Beings

They thought it over for some time and acted upon it. This way one of the giants reached high enough to peep into the house from the upper ventilators. He saw only human beings and exclaimed in delight that not only was there anything to fear, but there were sufficient grounds for rejoicing as their most delicious food had reached them! The other giants lower down in the ladder could barely believe this and asked him to investigate thoroughly before arriving at hasty conclusions. As luck would have it, the three friends were oblivious of the impending disaster and were hotly debating from which end they should start eating, from the upper end or lower end. Partial afflunce had, for first time, brought up this issue of protocol amongst them. As is customary, the eldest, or the man of highest social position sits to the extreme right or the upper end, which is considered a place of honour. However, it is normally the youngest, who eats first. So the friends were debating whether to start from the upper side that is the right, or the lower end, or the left. The blind man who had an extra loud voice was arguing that they should start from the lower end, that is from him. The giant who was the owner of the house and lowest in the ladder had already had enough. His eyes had suffered a grievous injury. All he heard was that the eating was to begin from the lower end! Once bitten twice shy! He eased out from the lowest position and ran off. The ladder of giants came crumbling down, one falling on the other. Most of them were killed and the others broke their limbs.

### The Booty

The three friends sitting inside were abhvious to all this. They were enjoying their dishes with great relish. Loud wails of the injured giants however attracted their attention and they decided to investigate.

They saw some giants dead and caught glimpses of others in flight. Soon it was all quiet. The friends decided to make good their escape. They ransacked the house for all the jewels and valuables and left at a fast pace. After walking many miles without pause or rest, they reached a village. The evening star had already risen. So they decided to spend the night in the village. But with wealth, greed had already raised its ugly head. The hunch-back and the lame man decided to get rid of the blind man and pocket his wealth. They caught a cobra and cooked its head for the blind man. At meal time, they served it to him with great expectations. But luck had planned a surprise for them. The poison of the snake slowly restored the sight of the blind man. As he noticed the pieces of snake in the food, in a flash in he knew what his friends were going to do to him. 'So you wanted to kill me', he said.

The friends were taken aback and were speechless for some time. Soon they regained their composure and said, 'We only wanted to cure you of blindness so that you could enjoy the wealth. The remedy was suggested by a vaid.'

The blind man was convinced, and the friends settled for the night. To hide their embarrassment, the hunch-back and lame man kept telling stories well into the small hours of the night. Next day they were woken by the crowing of the cocks and they resumed their journey. By night fall, they again reached a village and decided to spend the night there. Greed had, however, not yet left them alone. The lame man and the man who had miraculously regained his eye-sight, decided to put an end to the hunch-back and share his portion of the wealth. At night, while the hunch-back was snoring, they gave a severe blow at his hunch with a log. Luck again played its part well. Rather than breaking his back, the blow only cured his hunch and he got up fully restored. The two managed to convince him of their noble intentions, and the friends spent a comfortable night. Next, as you can now imagine, was the turn of the lame man. A herb poison which was chosen by the two friends to kill the lame man straightened his leg.

When they came back to village, people were surprised see them healthy, without any disability. When they were prosperous, it was inertable that they get married. They lived happily and there was never any acrimoney amongst them.

## Yota Ghamandi Bhyaguto

**The Frog who was very proud**

Where else can a frog live but in a jungle and near a pond. He was a bully and all the other frogs were afraid of him. He had three handsome grown-up sons. He was very proud of himself and his family. The young frogs went together to the jungle in search of food and play. The eldest wanted to explore the jungle alone but his father would not permit this. He would insist that all the brothers go together and chided the eldest for his eagerness to go alone. The more his father stopped him, greater was the curiosity of the frog to see the jungle alone. One day, whilst they were out for play, the young frog gave a slip to his brothers and went ahead. He kept moving farther and farther. At last he came across a sleeping elephant. With each breath, the elephant's stomach would distend and deflate with a great amount of noise. He was an object of great wonder for the frog, who thought that he had discovered an expanding and contracting mountain. He decided to dig in, and make his own house there, and rear a family. He chose a place and decided to dig it for building a house. No sooner did he try to bite what he thought was earth, the elephant got up with a roar.

### The Escape

It was an elephant he had bitten. This scared the young frog who started to tremble. Being too near, he could not make out what he was confronted with. As soon as he saw the strange animal moving he took to his heels and ran for his life. He arrived home panting hard. His father admonished him and asked him the cause of his panic. He related the whole incident. His father flew into a rage at his cowardice. How could an animal be bigger than him? The son told him of the huge belly of the animal. The frog expanded his belly fully and asked 'surely it can't be bigger than this.' The young frog replied that it was much bigger. The old frog drank a lot of water and again distended his belly, looking at his son. His son again shook his head in disagreement. The old frog was, however, not prepared to admit defeat. He again took some more water and expanded his belly some more.

He did not have any idea how much his belly could take. He continued taking more water till his belly burst and he died.

## Lato

### The Simpleton

Once upon a time, there lived an old woman in a certain village. She was very clever and mean and was ever ready to trick the community. People were sick of her unscrupulous pranks. She had only one child, a son. God always balances the cunning of one member of a family with the stupidity of another. Her son grew up, to be a simpleton. People called him Lato meaning an idiot. The boy came of age but no one came forward to offer the hand of his daughter in marriage to him.

The lady was worried the matter was great dishonour to her. Who will cook for him and her when she grew very old? How would the family name pass down?

She was puzzled. These thoughts constantly tortured her. Seeing the other old ladies of the community doting on their grand-children, she was at once filled with envy and jealousy. One day she told her son that since no one was ready to offer his daughter to him, he should himself try and do something about the matter. He could go, she said, and start looking for girl on his own.

'But how can I do that? Even if I fall in love, it is not necessary for the girl to fall in love with me, he said. That was too wise an answer for an idiot. The mother told him of an ingenious plan. He should go and sit near the village spring where all the young girls came to fill their pitchers. He should select a beautiful girl and throw flowers on her. In case he could not find flowers, even small pebbles would do. In case she happened to look at him, he should give a smile. If she smiled back, he should move forward and introduce himself. If this plan failed in the case of one girl, he should try it on another, and yet another till he succeeded. This way love would bloom in a few days. Seeing a good girl, he must not lose the opportunity to woo her.

Making all these plans, the boy went to pluck a rose and was pricked by a thorn. He cried out in pain. He remembered that the mother had also mentioned small pebbles. That might be a good idea, he thought and collected some stones and went to the spring with high hopes. Soon the daughter of the village headman came. Lato remembered his mother's advice that he should seize opportunity with both hands. How to do that was his first problem. He thought that his mother possibly meant that he should pick up a big stone with both his hands and throw it at the girl to attract her attention. And that is exactly what the poor idiot did. The stone hit the girl on her head and instantly killed her. Lato thought that she was playing the fool with him. He went to her and caressed her but she would not respond.

He was a simpleton. He thought she was being modest. He whispered in her ear that he was not going to leave her and that in fact he wanted to carry her to his home and marry her. His mind could not think of anything else. He lifted the body and brought it home. Seeing the dead body of the daughter of the village headman, frightened the old woman and she dreaded the outcome. She told his son to take the body back and bury it in the jungle. He should then go to his maternal uncle's place, and not come back till she called him. The boy took the body to the jungle and buried it. He forgot the instructions of his mother and rather than proceed to his maternal uncle's house, came back home. When he was near the house, he remembered her instructions. He was, however, very hungry and decided to have some food before setting out for the journey.

He decided to follow her mother's instruction and decided to set out in his journey. But being hungry, he decided to take some food. His mother had cooked some food and had gone out to fetch water. Lato thought that in the absence of his mother, God had cooked food for him. He started eating and shouting at the top of his voice, 'I am a great man. God has cooked my food! I have killed the daughter of the village headman and no one has even come to know of it.' His shouts reached the ears of the village headman, who was grief stricken. But he immediately went out to investigate the matter. He came to the old woman's house. On inquiry, Lato told him all that had happened.

In the meantime, the mother had made a different plan to cover up the murder. She caught a goat, killed it and took it to the exact spot where her son had buried the girl. She dug the girl out and buried the goat in her place. She had hardly finished the job when she heard voices approaching the site. The villagers accompanied by Lato and the headman came there and dug up the place again. To their surprise, they found a goat and there was no trace of the girl. Lato went mad with fright because he thought the goat to be a ghost. And the mother, who had been cunning and clever with everyone else lived a miserable life till her end came.

## Rajkumari Aboli

### The Silent Princess

'The princess blurted,' Oh, how tragically the faithful animal died. The strong had reached its climax and the princess who had stayed so long at last had blurted. As the story reached its climax, Aboli, the silent princess, lost control on her tongue and blurted out, 'Oh, what a tragic end to the life of such a faithful animal?'

After a pause, as though she was surprised at her own voice, she added, 'And that too for the sake of a faithless and heartless consort! How cruel a man can become?' 'But, my dear, it just proves how cunning the members of the fair sex can be,' said Dev Bhuj. 'In fact they can stoop to any degree to achieve the object of their hearts, or to avenge themselves of their adversaries?'

'No,' said Aboli. 'It just proves how foolish and grossly callous men-folk can become. After all, did the king have no regard for the faithfulness of the dog? Or was it that he lacked judgement? I feel he was a slave of his passions, and if men get blinded by their lust and agree to do anything to please the fair sex, why blame the women?' The news that she had spoken at last spread like wild fire. Her parents had already kept everything in readiness. A *jaimala* was brought and Aboli garlanded Dev Bhuj, accepting him as her husband.

Once upon a time, the Raja of a certain state had an only daughter. She was blessed with peerless charm and beauty. One day the Raja went out hunting and took his daughter with him. Fate had ordained that the horse carrying her panic at the sight of a tiger. She fell down. In the melee that followed, she was rescued by her escort, but she had suffered a serious shock, and she lost her voice. The Raja called in *vaids* from every corner of the state. They tried all the rare herbs and *aushadhis* (medicinal preparations) on her but to no avail. When Aboli did not utter a single word, the Raja performed many *yajnas* and *pujas* in all the temples, but the object of his worry still living like an incubus over his head. Time passed but the dictum that time was a great healer, sounded like a mockery. One may get reconciled to one's own sufferings, but not to the sufferings of a child. Since the princess did not speak for years, she came to be called Aboli, the silent princess. People even forgot that her real name was Geeta.

Aboli grew up to be a woman of immense feminine charms. Many Rajas and princes sent messages and earnest pleas for hand in marriage. The Raja had no means of ascertaining the wishes of his only daughter for she was still speechless. He was in a predicament. No one could understand or share his worry and suffering. He could neither give, his daughter in marriage without ascertaining her wishes nor keep her with him for ever. What was to be? The Raja spent many sleepless nights and grew pale with worry. At last the *Raj-Purohit* advised the Raja that he should hold a *Swayamvar* for her, and that she would marry anyone who succeeded in making her talk. That was, indeed clever advice. The Raja agreed that was the best course. And he announced his daughter's *Swayamvar* with the necessary condition. Many suitors came from far and wide to claim her hand in marriage. After many tries, bordering even on the ludicrous, all of them left heartbroken and unsuccessful. Finally a prince arrived. His name was Dev Bhuj, he came from a southern state, beyond the mountains and the jungles. He told the princess that he had come only to meet her and tell her of a true story and ask her for her opinion. He was not really very keen to marry her. This aroused the curiosity of the princess about this strange suitor. She became keen to hear the story for which Dev Bhuj had come from such a great distance to seek her opinion. Dev Bhuj, however, took leave of her for a couple of days to see the capital of her father and other places of interest in the kingdom. This enhanced the curiosity of Geeta all the more. At last, when the interest of the princess was fully aroused, Dev Bhuj started the story.

Many centuries ago, a king lived in a distant land who had a very charming wife. The king was madly in love with her and she fully reciprocated his affections. One day, the king thought of testing her love. He went for shikar and killed some deer. He soaked a few of his clothes in blood. He put the stained clothes on the saddle of his horse and asked one of his courtiers, who was known for his histrionic talents, to go to the queen and tell her that the king had been killed by a tiger. He did. The events then took an unforeseen turn as events some times do. As soon as the queen heard of the tragic death of her husband, she fell in a swoon and shock. After a day, the king came out of hidding to see the result of his scheme. He was shocked to learn of the sudden death of his beloved wife. He wept in bitter tears. It was already late in the evening when the funeral procession was taken to the cremation ground. The king was at the head of the procession and kept a steady wail of his misfortune.

As is the custom, the dead are not assigned to the flames after sunset. By the time the procession reached the cremation ground, the sun had already set. The body could be assigned to the fire only on the following day. So the Raja remained with the body of his beloved consort while all the others came back. At mid-night, Shiva and Parvati heard the loud wails of the man. Parvati asked Shiva about the cause of his misery. Mahadeva told her the entire story. Parvati was moved by the stark tragedy, and asked Shiva to revive the queen. Pashupatinath replied that was the realm of Yama, the god of death, and that he was unable to do anything without consulting him. Yama was accordingly summoned. Yama said that the lady was in fact due to die and whatever happened was in accordance with her destiny. The only way of the Rani reviving now was by some individual volunteering to forfeit a portion of his or her life for her. Parvati was sure that the Raja himself would be quite prepared to do that. Shiva and Parvati then went to the Raja who was oblivious of the consultations that had taken place among the gods, and was wailing a pitiably. Shiva told him of the method of resurrecting his queen and asked him if he was ready to give a little of his own life to the Rani. The Raja agreed at once. His wish was granted by Yama. The Rani woke up as a young girl of sixteen, at the prime of her youth, because she had shed as many years as the Raja had given her. The Raja on the other hand, grew into an old man! They were no longer a match for each other.

Marriage between the young and old is never a happy one, and the tragic consequences of such alliances are well known. The Rani soon got tired of the impotent advances of the old Raja. She developed illicit relations with a young and handsome courtier. The Raja was not aware of all this. He was mostly busy with the *vaids* and was hopelessly trying to regain a bit of his lost vigour. He had a faithful dog who seemed to resent the turn of events and the unbecoming behaviour of the Rani. Whenever the paramour of the young queen came to her bed-chamber, he created such a racket by barking that many times the lovers had to part company in haste and dismay. This aroused the wrath of the queen. She was however, unable to do anything about the matter. She had to employ all sorts of decoys to go to her lover. The couple became so sick of the vigilant dog. They started thinking of ways to get rid of him.

The old Raja did everything in his power to please her. He was madly in love with her as an old man can be. One day, the cunning lady got hold of an old cot and lay on crying, 'pain, pain.' The Raja went to the side of his ailing wife as soon as he came to know of her state and enquired the cause and the possible cure of her suffering. She told him that she had an attack of a chronic disease from which she had suffered when she was unmarried. It had become dormant for many years and had suddenly erupted. It was cured only when she had a bath with the blood of a dog. Saying this, she gave a cry of intense pain. The Raja asked her to tell him all that she wanted to. She haltingly said that he himself had a fat enough dog who could be killed!

At this juncture, Dev Bhuj told Aboli that the remainder story would be to told the following day. Aboli, however, at once spoke out saying, 'Oh tell me, tell me, what happened.'

Dev Bhuj was very smart. He replied that the Raja of course was foolish enough and murdered the dog and his faithless wife did manage to get rid of the obstacle in her way!

The news of Aboli regaining her speech spread at once. She was married to Dev Bhuj and they lived happily ever after.

## Bal ra Budhi

### Brain or Brawn

May it be a man or a giant, none can ever hope to win by brawn alone. It is intelligence that usually comes out victorious. And if that brain happens to be that of a woman, none can overcome her. Men and giants are far too gullible and fall an easy prey to feminine charms. Here was mighty giant, who had lurned and eaten many men, put to eternal sleep by a woman.

Once upon a time, in the remote past, when men and giants lived together in the world, there lived a basket-maker in a certain village. He would go early morning to the jungle to cut bamboos and nigalu (cane) to make baskets with. After the rainy season, he would first cut the bamboos on the fringes of the jungle and, as, the day passed, he would move deeper and deeper. One season a giant came to live in the jungle. He started luring men and children for his cooking-pot. One day, he saw the basket-maker and his mouth watered. He posed as the Ban Devta and lured the man saying,

'If you need a bamboo fine
come further, come further,
If elastic be need thine
come further, come further.'

The bamboo-maker thought that the god was pleased with him and moved further into the jungle. The gaint was waiting for just such an opportunity and grabbed him. He hypnotized him and in that senseless state, he asked him about his house and certain other essentials. His plan was to impersonate the basket-maker and gobble up his family.

He transformed himself as the basket-maker and went to his house. As usual, he had a wash and sat down to sort out the bamboos and the cane. Whilst he was busy doing this, he said to the basket-maker's wife, 'Tomorrow, I won't have to go to the jungle because I have enough material to work for a few days. My darling, cook the choicest dishes and let us make relax and make fun.'

The giant then set to cutting the material into suitable lengths for the baskets. The lady went to him and as usual offered to press his legs and feet. The giant declined for fear of discovery because giants always have their feet turned backwards. This aroused the suspicion of the lady. She was a shrewd woman and could smell a rat. She went to the imposter and insisted on lending him a helping hand. This way, she managed to steal a glance at his feet. She was horrified to see that the toes were reversed. She was worried about the safety and well-being of her husband. However, her immediate concern was to get rid of this menace. She cooked a great many dishes and put a sleep-inducing herb in the food.

**The Complacent Giant**

Nobody had ever cooked for the giant. He had not tasted so many delicacies earlier and he devoured the food before falling into a deep sleep. The lady got enough time to further her scheme. She opened the main hole in the room that led to the cattle-shed on the ground floor. Directly below the hole she kept a number of pointed-stones. Then she oiled some peas and spread them from the bed of the giant to the hole. After the effect of the herb was over, the giant got up and decided to make mince meat of the family. He got up grinding his teeth and unknowingly put his feet on the peas. He had a nasty slip and fell through the hole, head first. Falling on the pointed stones, his head was smashed and he died instantaneously.

**The Thieves**

The lady was lying awake just waiting for such an opportunity. She went down and cutting his body into pieces, put them into a wooden-box. Leaving the doors open, she returned to her bed to steal a few winks of sleep. 'Open doors attract thieves,' so goes an old saying. As luck would have it, a band of thieves happened to see the open door of the basket-maker's house. Coming closer, they noticed the wooden-box and were tempted to steal it. The wooden-box was too heavy to be moved by one man. They secured the box with sling ropes and, carrying it on bamboos staves, hurried out with their load. Taking it to the jungle as fast as their feet could carry them, they opened the box they got the fright of their lives when they the pieces of the belly of giant. They ran helter-skelter and never got together again. They never ever crusted that village.

The woodcutter's wife located her husband after a day's search. In due course, he regained his senses. The locality was thus rid of the menace of the giant as well as thieves for all times to come because of the courage and presence of mind shown by the wood-cutter's wife.

## Siru ki Bakhri

### The Blessed Goat

Mother luck must always have her way and no one can really predict her moods and fancies. There once lived in a village a man and his wife, who got a lovely daughter after many years of married life and prayers to various gods for a child. But as luck would have it, as soon as the daughter was born, the woman died. The man was heart-broken, but time is a great healer. Like many other men, he resorted to the age-old pretext of needing someone to look after the house and the child and married again. Soon they had another daughter and, as was expected, the step-mother started ill-treating the elder child whom she called Mainchha, Dhon-Cholecha and Siru, out of contempt. The innocent girl had no one to turn for help, and was resigned her existence till matters became really intolerable. She had been told by her father that there was a goat which was a favourite with her late mother. She would take the goat aside and weep in front of her. The step-mother would often give her bread cooked from chaff, which she shared with the goat.

### What the Goat Said

One day, the goat spoke to her and said, 'Do not worry. You bring the loaf given to you, and in exchange I will give you tasty food.' Thus when Siru took the herd out for grazing everyday her favourite goat would give her choicest dishes in exchange for her loaf. This went on for many days. Siru regained her lost health and started to grow into a beautiful girl. Her step-mother became very jealous and asked her own daughter to go and investigate the cause for this, because she suspected Siru to be either selling the milk or drinking it herself. Next day, younger sister insisted that she would accompany the elder when she took the herd out grazing. Siru was simple at heart and told the Kanchhi about her favourite goat. This way Siru also fed her younger sister. Cunning daughter of a cunning mother, Kanchhi hid some rice under her nails, and showing it to her mother she told her the whole story. The jealous lady lost no time in killing the goat. Siru was thus left friendless. One day she took the herd out grazing, when she noticed a tree laden with ripe and luscious fruit. She climbed the tree and started picking the best fruit.

**The Innocent Girl**

As luck would have it, a couple of giants passed that way. They requested her for some fruit. She asked them to spread their cloth on the ground on which she would throw the fruits. The giants said, 'Oh child, why do you not climb down a little and hand over the fruits yourself. Why spoil the ripe fruits by throwing them on the ground?' The innocent girl came down and was kidnapped by the giants. When she did not return that day, her step-mother was glad, and considered it a good riddance. The father did show some concern but was happy that he was now spared the constant nagging. There was no one to show concern about the little lost girl. The giants took her to their palace in the thick jungle and told her to wait while they went out on some important business. They promised to give her the choicest food after their return.

Dazed by these events, Siru sat down in a corner and waited for the giants. She was suddenly surprised by a strange voice calling her. She looked around and saw a mouse addressing her, by name, 'Siru, Siru, Your life is in danger. The giants will kill you. If you give me some bread, I will save you.' She thought that the poor rat was probably hungry and gave him some bread. The rat told her to collect all the wealth that she could carry and disappear before the giants came back. He also told her to keep throwing chilly-powder on the way to eliminate her scent. The giants would thus lose track of her.

**Stupid Girl Siru**

When Siru reached her home, the step-mother refused to open the door. Siru shouted that she had brought enormous wealth with her, which would help them live a comfortable life. Her mother asked her for details and was half dead with jealousy. Surely her own girl could get more wealth? She briefed her fully and told her to go to the fruit-tree the very next day. Sure enough, the giants came and kidnapped her in the same fashion as they did Siru. At the residence of the giants the rat came out to ask for bread from the girl, which she flatly refused. The giants came back in due course and ate her up, and left her skeleton hanging outside her house.

Next day, the mother got up with great hopes and expectations. She was irritated by the constant cries of a crow and threw a stone at him. The crow was a messenger of Yama. He told her about the skeleton of her daughter. The wicked woman died of shock. Siru and her father lived with ease and comfort for the rest of their days. And the man never married again.

## Shaitan lai Chinauti

### A Challenge to the Devil

The story goes that once during the time when the race of giants shared the Earth with men, there lived a king, in a far-off state to the north. He was a benevolent, just and kind-hearted ruler, ever-ready to make any sacrifice for the good of his subjects. He had one vice, he boasted that he did not consider any personal sacrifice big enough for his subjects, and that he cared a devil for personal comforts. One day the devil himself heard his boasts and decided to belittle him. As luck would have it, a very severe drought, broke out in the kingdom. Crops failed and the people craved for two square meals. As was customary and a common practice then, every man approached the king for help, some even openly blamed him. The royal priests were consulted. As the devil had willed, they predicted that the only remedy was the sacrifice of either the prince or the king; preferably the prince.

### The Poet

Now, the prince was married and had a young and lovely wife. He was out hunting at the time of the prediction. When he returned late in the evening he saw his young wife lying on a broken cot shouting, 'pain, pain.' Her eyes were red due to excessive, weeping. The prince consoled her and asked her the cause of her misery. She told him that she had come to know that there was an intrigue in the palace and that a plot had been thatched to murder them. Nothing short of the death of both of them would satisfy the blood lust of the scheming opponents, and suggested it. would be safe for the two of them to flee—even waiving aside the formality of meeting his parents.

### The Prince Escapes

The prince was so deeply in love with his young wife that he consented without demurring. They quickly packed some belongings and, while the king with a heavy heart awaited the prince at the dinner table, made good their escape with the help of some servants who had all been possessed by the devil. There was no choice except to sacrifice the king who gladly ascended the altar. The drought ended, and a new king was elected from among nobles. The prince and his wife fled to the jungle. The prince was not aware of the prediction of the priests. His wife had not given him any chance to find out details. They went deeper into the thick jungle, and kept moving in spite of the black darkness all around.

At last they were attracted by some lights at a distance. They groped their way towards the lights and reached there after some time. The prince went in first to reconnoiter before he let his beloved wife in. He went around the house and was attracted by a noise from a room. He was tip-toed in to investigate and saw a giant in the throes of deep sleep. Had he wanted, he could easily have thrust his scimitar in his heart, but he was prince and princes have a sense of honour. They do not kill a sleeping enemy. So he woke the giant up.

**The Reflections**

As luck would have it, the prince was still wearing his shikar dress, which contained shining metal plates for the chest and head. As they got ready for the dual, the giant saw his own distorted reflection in those glistening metal-plates. He thought that the prince was aided by many fearful giants. He surrendered without a fight. The prince locked him up in the rear room and, having eliminated the danger, called his beautiful wife in. They were now the owners of this palatial building with all its fabulous wealth. The prince had so far not had time to think of his beloved parents and kingdom. Now that he did, he suffered from feelings of nostalgia and remorse, but it was senseless to go back now. He could not go back, he knew.

Next morning, the prince instructed his wife not to open the room at the back, and went out hunting. He disguised himself as a merchant and wandered off to the state of his father. There he came to know all that had transpired. He was happy at the love of his charming wife who had helped save his life. So he returned to her with renewed love. One day when the prince was away, she opened the forbidden rear-room and saw the giant. He was a handsome giant and it took him little time to allay the fears of the young lady.

The giant was very clever. He persuaded her to play a game of dice. The lady always found it difficult to pass the time when her husband was away and gladly welcomed this change. Soon a love-affair developed between the giant and the princess. The prince was, of course, unaware of this development. He was too deeply in love with his wife to notice any change in her behaviour. His faithless wife, and the giant decided to kill him one day. The giant was pleased with scheme—he could make a splendid repast of the prince, and have the princess to make love to.

One night, as the prince was sleeping by her side, she put a noose around his neck and asked him if he had any last desire. The prince said that his heart was with the people of his state and should, therefore, be transported via the stream to his native land. The woman then strangled him to death. The giant relished the body of the dead prince but spared his heart, which he put in a boat rigged out of leaves and the bark of a tree. As luck would have it, the boat was pulled in by the fishermen. To their great surprise, they saw an infant smiling in the boat. The king of that land happened to be without child. He was told of the story of the child in the boat. He summoned the fishermen, and adopted the child, who was brought up as the future ruler of the state. In due course of time, the prince grew up and ascended the throne. As for his faithless wife, she became a shrew and the giant, fed up with her constant bickering her, did what giants do. He ate her as he had done to her husband.

## Na Bhane ko Katha

### This Tale could not be Completed

How true it is that a doubting mind knows no peace. Many a delicate human feeling is married by elements of doubt and unresolved misunderstandings. How prudent is the thought that where there are sound relationships and bonds of love, it is better to be cheated than to doubt without cause? It is on account of this element of an over-suspicious mind that a Raja lost one of his most faithful servants.

Once upon a time there was a Raja who ruled a kingdom south of the high Himalayas. He was very fond of hearing and narrating tales and stories. Every night, he invariably listened to and related some tales. Whilst relating the tale, however, he would generally get tire and go to sleep. The tale remained incomplete each time. This was a common occurrence, day after day, month after month. The incomplete tale got sick of this summary treatment. Either the Raja aught not to have begun, or else, having begun, he should have seen it to its final denouement. The Incomplete Tale had propitiated the goddess and had received the boon that anyone who did not complete her would be subject to any punitive action she considered fit. Thus armed with supernatural powers, the Incomplete Tale went to the palace and appeared in the dream of a faithful bodyguard of the Raja. She asked him to warn the Raja that he should either not begin her, or if he did, he must complete her. Otherwise she would be obliged to kill him because she could no longer bear to remain incomplete day after day.

### The Dream

The bodyguard was in fix-whether to till raja about his dream. At last he went to the Raja and told him his dream. The Raja frowned at this show of audaciousness, but did promise to complete the tale. But as we know, habits die hard. Indeed, they accompany a man to the cremation ground. So the Raja did try to complete the story that evening but dozed off again and soon fell fast asleep. And who dare disturb a king! So the Incomplete Tale flew into a rage and came to the dream of the faithful bodyguard again. 'Now listen,' she said, 'I am absolutely fed up and if the Raja does not complete me tomorrow, I will kill him and if you tell him about our second meeting, I will petrify you.' 'My dear story said,' the bodyguard, keep cool for just a few more days.'

The story had been impatient and would not listen. 'If you tell the Raja, you will be petrified into a stone. I will become a deadly needle and will get into the Raja's dinner. I will pierce his main artery and let him go to hell because he has illtreated me long enough, and I cannot stand this any longer. And if you tell him this, you will become a block of stone. If he does not die with the needle or the plan misfires, I have an alternative one handy. When he is tired and thirsty after the hunting trip, I will appear in the form of a spring of clear water and as soon as he comes to drink it, I will create an avalanche and bury him alive. And if you tell him this, you will lose your own life. If this second plan also fails, I am going to appear in the form of a shady tree just at the time when he is tired after a hunt and wanting to rest. As soon as he lies down, one huge branch will fall on him crushing him to death. And if you tell him this, you will be transformed into a stone. And if this plan also fails, I will come in the form of a snake and bite him and put him to eternal sleep with my venom. And if you tell him, you will be transformed into a stone and mingle back with earth for ever.' Saying this the tale disappeared.

The royal bodyguard became awake got up with a start. He was covered with cold sweat and was trembling through and through. He was very afraid. He was torn between the calls of duty and the fear of death. He thought to himself, 'I have eaten the salt of the Raja for many years and must save his life at any cost.' Thinking this, he started shadowing the king and volunteered to be on duty for twenty hours. The Raja, of course, respected his daily performance the next evening and left the tale incomplete.

**The Faithful Body Guard**

The following day, when he sat down to have his meals, the faithful bodyguard stopped him and said that he would like to get the food examined. Sure enough, a deadly needle was discovered from the food. One more day passed and the Raja again left the tale incomplete as usual. The next day, after attending to the important affairs of the state, the Raja decided to go for a shikar. After a hot chase in the burning sun and sultry weather, the Raja located a beautiful spring and wanted to have water. The bodyguard however took out a water bottle and told him of the danger of taking cold water after a hot chase. The Raja agreed and took the water from the bottle. They had only gone a little distance when the hill behind the spring came crashing down. At night fall the Raja again left the tale incomplete. The faithful bodyguard, however, again managed to save him by timely intervention. At last only one danger was left—that of the snake. So the bodyguard volunteered to stand guard in the bed chamber of the Raja. Sure enough, after some time, the snake appeared and was killed by the bodyguard.

**Fate of the Body Guard**

Now as luck would have it, a few drops of the blood splashed on the face of the sleeping queen. The bodyguard thought it to be an ill omen and tried to wipe out the blood from her face. Just at that time, the Raja got up and saw the bodyguard touching the cheeks of the queen. He flew into a rage at the obvious impudence of the bodyguard. Without giving him any time to explain, the Raja ordered that he be put to death. The deadly doubt would not let him ask even for an explanation. Now as is customary, the bodyguard was asked for a last wish before he was hanged. He asked for one last meeting with the Raja. To remove any doubt, he told the Raja of his meeting with the Incomplete Tale and was transformed into a stone as incomplete take had producted.

And the Raja repented, this all his life.

# 2
# Folk-Songs of Nepal

One of the richest aspects of Nepalese 'folklore' are the folk-songs with their high lyricism and exquisite composition. As we proceed, you will realize that there is a wide variety before you, some sweet and brimming with all the gentler emotions of life, some deeply appreciative of the good neighbourliness in which the Nepalese society lives, and some expressing the sheer joy of living. The imagery is as colourful as the alpine flowers of the Nepal highlands. Pangs of separation from the beloved and loved ones are expressed in emotionally charged couplets.

Amorous feelings are given expression with freedom and lack of restraint. The folk-songs, have, therefore, a great ability to stir the emotions. Most of the songs are accompanied by dancing.

Folk-songs form an essential part of the cultural activity in the interior of Nepal. Playing on the *Madal* and singing comes naturally to most Nepalese. There are many songs and dances in which both boys and girls take part, singly or in chorus, jointly or in separate groups, by far the most common form is that the girls sing and the *marunis* dance with the boys.

**Beyond Words**

The fairs, many of which are held all over the country the year round, offer a great opportunity for community singing and dancing. The whole atmosphere resonates with melodies and reflects the inner accord of the Nepalese people with nature. Unfortunately, the entire song and dance atmosphere cannot be captured in words, not even in the words of the vernacular; much less in translation. However, the readers will be able to form a fair idea of the people who sing those songs.

**Lahuray and Maruni**

Let us have a look at some of the most popular hits. The well-to-do society of Nepal has a martial background. It is, therefore, inevitable that many folk-songs have an army setting. The first song is sung by a soldier *Lahuray* and his beloved is usually represented by a *Maruni*. The song has great flexibility, many couplets are improvised as dance progresses. The song goes on.

Lahuray:........ *Mo to ho sena ko lahuray*
*Mo sang jachha ki sahi.*
Maruni:........ *Chhi tista sena ko lahuray*
*Timi sang jandai na sahi*
*Timi sang gayo bhani*
*Khutta dukhi janu bhayen.*
Lahuray:........ *Oh liai diyun la sena ko gari*
*Mo sang janchha kih sahi*
Maruni:........ *Timi sang gayu bhani*
*Bhuko mari janu bhayan.*
Lahuray:........ *Oh liai diyan la*
*Ration ko bori, mo sang . . .*
Soldier:........ Oh fair dame,
I am a soldier from the army
Come with me, come with me.
Maruni:........ You are a soldier no doubt,
but you are not smart
I shan't come with you
You go to distant lands
If I accompany you
My feet will get sore by constant marches
No, I won't come with you.
Soldier:........ Oh fair dame, come with me
You won't have to walk For I'll take you in an army vehicle
I am a soldier, come with me, come with me.
Maruni:........ You are a soldier no doubt
but you are not smart,
I won't come with you.
If I come with you
I'll die of hunger
Oh I won't, I won't come with you.
Soldier :........ I'll get you a bag of army rations
Oh, come, Oh come with me.

**The Ruses**

And the song goes on and on with many excuses of the beloved like where will I get the medicines, clothes, etc. The boy keeps on replying and pleading a soldier in the army is always comfortable because he gets every factuly.

In the fairs, and, in the evening sing-song sessions most of the songs start with the following rather meaningless lines. They are meant as an invitation for all to come and join in the sing-song.

*Khane chamal chhaina*
*Launchhan sarangiko tantil!*
There is no rice to eat
But the notes of sarangi are still sweet.

The next song talks of the peasant community, happy at the sight of lush-fields and still complaining of lack of rest.

*Kati ramro mero yo pangre goru*
*Kati ramru mero hal*
*Kati ramro mero ubjani bali*
*Ramro chha mihinetko phal.*
*Dharti amai, dharti babai*
*Yasbata paunchhu anna*
*Pyaro ma garchhu, sanman garchhu*
*Dharti amai, dhanya!*
*Umer bitaen jotaima maile*
*Aena sukhko din*
*Jiu burho mero, man burho mero*
*Sukh chhaina ekai chhin!*
How good are my bridled oxen
How nice is my plough
How sweet are my ripe crops
And sweet is the fruit of labou.
Earth is my mother, Earth is my father
From her I get my food
I love you, I honour you
Oh Mother Earth, I thank you.
An age I have passed in ploughing
The day of rest has not come
My body is old, my mind is old,
Not a moment's rest is there.

The next song is sung at the marriage of a girl.

*Na ro na ro cheli timi maiti timro ghar hoina*
*Phool jasto timro joban aba timi hamro hoina.*
*Na ro na ro . . .*
*Ankha bhori ansoo parne, aama baba rundai janes*
*Dhoka nira bhar ra baini,*
*Ansoo poonchdai bida garne.*
*Bas bas cheli bhandai, saheli le laijane,*
*Saheli le laijane . . . Na ro na ro . . .*
*Sawan Bhadon runa lagyo cheli timro bidai ma*
*Kathai bhari bhandai aako chorana parne maiti ghar lai.*
*Cheli timro karmai esto bhandai jao cphoo lai bhandai jao.*

Oh my daughter sweet,
Do not weep.
The parent's home is not your permanent home.
You have bloomed like a flower
And now you are not ours!
With brimming eyes,
The parents move forward
To bid her farewell.
Her brothers and sisters are at the door,
To bed farewell.
Her friends have also arrived,
To bed her farewell
Even the rains have started weeping now,
For you are leaving us for ever.
My daughter go now,
May God be with you,
Weep not my daughter,
The parents' home,
Is not your permanent home. A song for Lahuray.

**'Lahuray'**

The next song has a touching theme with a very high lyrical quality. It is sung for *'Lahuray'*, who has formal the quletary service and going away on duty.

*Na jao chhari yo desh,*
*Aama lai ruaye ra.*
*Na birsa-janme ko hoan,*
*Aaphdo lai chhakaye ra.*
*Dhoi deo dukh aama ko,*
*Pasina le bagaye ra.*
*Chookao dudh ko bhara*
*Mehnat le kamaye ra.*
*Na jao. . . .*
*Na par aama ko chliati,*
*Cheya cheya turkraye ra.*
*Uthao desh ko jhanda, Swarga lai choowaye ra.*
Don't go, leaving your motherland,
Whilst your mother weeps.
Go if you must,
But don't forget your birthplace.
Go if you must,
But wash your mother's pangs of separation,
with your hard toil and sweat,
Pay her debt with your hard labour.

Do not forget your mother,
And your birth place,
Raise thy country's flag
To touch the very heaven.

And these verses express the villager's simple idea of love, linked with the landscape of Nepal and the Himalayas:

*Himalai chuli tyo paribata*
*Hiun kaile jaminchhal?*
Bageko pani ureko chitta
Kailan gai thaminchhal
*Bagaincha bhari phala re phula*
*Chheu chheuma karela*
*Ankha chhan tunra junkiri jasta*
*Jimkaune parela*
*Sun jesto Nepal ke ramra dekhchha*
*Swarga chha sansarma*
*Sun jasto premke jun jasto dekhchha*
*Mayako sansarma*
On the distant Himalayan peaks
When will the snow gather?
The running stream and the fickle mind
Where will they come to rest?
The garden is full of fruit and flowers
And the vegetables grow everywhere
Your beautiful eyes and lovely eyelashes
Are pretty like the fire flies.
How lovely is my golden Nepal
Like heaven on this Earth
My sweetheart is pretty like the moon
And sweet is the world with love.

In the following song the pangs of separation are uppermost. In this song a more plamtive note creeps.

*Himalai chuli ke yati ramro*
*Surpako kanchuli*
*Yo pap manma biraha chalyo*
*Na bajau bansari.*
How fine it is, the Himalayan peak
like the skin of a snake
This separation has filled my heart with sorrow
Oh do not play the flute.
*Shirko sindur launa bhaujyu*
*Hamra dajyu ai ra puge, Nepali jyanma:*
*Tyatiko jhaljhalko ke manchhyau nani ....*

*kaile ra aunthe ti timra dajyu, ranaima pareka?*
Put sindur on your hair, oh sister-in-law
My brother has come back to our beloved Nepal:
Don't taunt me like this oh little brother,
Will he ever come from the far off battlefield?

This song expresses the fickle-mindedness of a young damsel in the process of falling in love. Should she or should she not go with her lover?

*Kali pari dai kati ramro, dhak topi,*
*Kadai ma galbandi.*
*Sanu sanu gai kobachhi, hath ma linchh lahuri*
*Yo dali ma rassa chhaina, kina ghumchha mauri*
*Kali pari dai kati. . .*
*Sir ma laune sir ko topi, khutta ma laune jutta*
*Mero man ta do man bhayo eta jam ki uta*
*Kali pari dai kati. . ..*
How handsome is he
One who resides in that yonder valley
With a muffler on his shoulders,
And a slanting cap on his head.
How charming he looks,
The calves are very young,
There are no honey bearing flowers,
On the branches of these trees
Why are you hovering here oh bees,
How handsome is he.
His head covered with a cap, and shoes on his feet
My heart is unable to decide
To go with him or not to go.

On returning to his village after two years of service, a young Nepali lad spends the evening with village girls in a famous. After two year service in the army or any where else, the young man returns home. The sperds the evening the village damsals.

sing-song called *jhaore.*
*Taruni: Aba bheena na jao Lahuray*
*Nepal lai ma painchha jaagira*
*Lahuray: Jana sali chhore ra timi laa*
*Nepal ma paaone chhoon jagira*
*Barajooko dhoori mooni*
*Bhainsi lukne dhoolo*
*Masita gayo bhane*
*Bhagya hola thoolo*
*Taruni: Man pare ko khaunla plunla*
*Na pare ko khan na*

*Esta kura na garo bheena*
*Kasai sitta janna*
*Lahuray: Eso bhaye ao sali*
*Dimla sunko baala*
*Aru sita gayo bhane*
*Toki dimla gaala*
*Taruni: Sunko baala dimla bhanne*
*Ahile hoina cohile*
*Timi sitta janna bheena*
*Talu rahi chha khooile*
*Girl:* Do not go abroad my brother-in-law
You will get service in Nepal
*Boy:* I will find a job in Nepal. I will not go abroad, my darling
Promise to marry me, my love
It will brighten your future.
*Girl:* We will make merry,
To our heart's desire,
I will not I swear, I will not go with anyone else.
*Boy:* Then come and be my darling
I will give you a golden ring,
If you run away with someone else
I will cut your throat.
*Girl:* Your promise to give me a golden ring
It's long overdue
I can't be your sweetheart
For there is no hair on your head.
And this again has the eternal theme of love.
*Keta: Herana kanchhi paharai ma lalupote sabai phulyo*
*Keti: La hai kanchha sabai tipi malai lagai deona*
*Keta: Kahi jharchhan cheeso jharna*
*Kahi phulchhan phoola*
*phoola ko jasto chokho preeti*
*Mero man ma rakha*
*Herana kanchhi. . .*
*Keti: Kahin dekhchhan denra kanra*
*Kahi dekhchhan khojla,*
*Preeti lagaon aja kanchha*
*Kati ramro hola*
*Herana kanchha. . .*
*Keta: Sa ra ra hawa chalyo*
*Aja paharai man*
*Hu ru ra jeeban bityo*
*Kanchi ko samjha nai ma*
*Herana kanchhi. . .*

*Keti: Danra wari ghaam lagyo*
*Danra pari paani*
*Maya preeti lagai jaon hai*
*Bitaon jindgani*
*Herana kanchha . . .*

Boy: Oh my sweetheart, The valley is ablaze! The red flowers are blooming!

Girl: Oh my darling, get me all the flowers,
Boy: Here flows the cold stream
There blossom the flowers
My love is pure like a flower,
Keep it in your heart.
Girl: Oh sweetheart, the red flowers are blooming,
The valley is ablaze!
This lovely landscape,
Where valleys and rivers alternate,
Let us make love today
How sweet will it be my love,
Oh my darling, get me all the flowers.
Boy: A strong wind blows
Today in the valley,
The days are passing
with my darling.
See my love, the red flowers are blooming,
The valley is ablaze!
Girl: The sun is shining on this side of the valley
The rain is falling on that side of the valley
(Behold the beauty of nature)
Let us live together,
Oh my darling, get me all those flowers.

The next one is again an army song it is a very flexible song. At the some time it is very popular. The man and the *marunis* go on improvising couplets as the song progresses; reverting back to the original opening stanzas from time to time.

*Oh dhalki dhalki na hintnu hola*
*Yo kali ma jieu jane ber chhaina*
Do not, oh do not walk with a swagger
It does not take long to lose one's youth.
*Timi ta jai jao Bombai sahar me*
*Nargis bhaye ra*
*Timi lai bhetnu, mo nishchai aunchhun*
*Rajkapur bhave ra Sayenli, yo kali. . .*
You go to Bombay and become Nargis,
To meet you I sure will come as Raj Kapur
Oh sweety, do not walk with a swagger,
For it takes no time to lose one's youth
*India ko Raja le, Kashmir ko dhawa ma*

*Urai layayo rail ko hawa ma*
The Government of India
Has sent us to Kashmir
On the fastest moving train.
Don't walk with a swagger,
It does not take long
To lose one's life.

And whenever the soldiers go, they blame the girls of the place for winking at them and teasing them.

*Kara ma kara, kamarai khayo,*
*Chhala ko peti le*
*Hero na daju bhai gijaunchha mo lai*
*Yo shahar ko keti le*
*Aju to mo le bhat ee ra khayo*
*Tihun to karela,*
*Yo shahar ko keti, Chinnunn jaune,*
*Jham kaunchha parela.*
My leather belt is so tight,
It has eaten into my waist,
And to top it all
The girls of this place tease me.
I have eaten rice today,
With the vegetable of bitter gourd
The girls of this place
Wink at me even though I do not know them!

And the couplets go on endlessly; added at will and improvised: The song occasionally reverts back to:

*Dhalki dhalki na hintnu hola*
*Yo kalima jiu jane ber chhaina*

And now the most popular folk-song, a favourite of the young and old alike, more so when they have had an overdoze of *rakshi!* Holding each other by the waists or shoulders, more to support each other, actually men and women go on singing with a stress on the last syllable stretching it long like an elastic band.

*Kanth ma laune kanth phula a a a. . .*
*Aise he raja le bechi khayo o o o. . .*
*Aise he raja ko asha mo lai chhaina,*
*Gai jaunla maite ko desh ma*
The lovely necklace that I had,
Has been sold by this heartless man,
I have no hopes on him,
I will go to my parent's home.

And the blames go on adding. You have to hear it to believe. It is very difficult to narrate the tune or describe it musical rotations. Boys and *marunis,* holding each other by the waists, go on swirling and trying to stretch the last syllable longer and longer with each breath! *Phula a a a.* ... and *khayo o o o. . .*

And in this very class of short odes, now an all time favourite, which most of you may have heard some time or the other:

*Nainitalo, Nainitalo*
*Ghumi ayo rela,*
*Ankh na laune kalo kajal*
*Bulbula ma tela; Nainitalo*
*Naini talo, Naini talo.*
Oh sweety, come with me,
I'll take you to Nainital,
I will give you a ride on the train
I will buy you kajal for your eyes
And perfumed oil for your hair.
Oh sweety, come with me,
I will take you to Nainital.

## Some Selected Proverbs

Proverbs and folklore make a very important aspect of a people's life. The proverbs represent the village wiseacres and provide an index to the thoughts, and norms of the common man who, in fact, is the most important subject of study for a proper evaluation of the folklore.

Here, in this chapter, I present some selected proverbs. My aim is to prove to my readers that the Nepalese language is as flexible and easily adaptable to different thoughts and shades of meaning as any other language of the world. Semantics as in the other developed languages, is also an essential part of the Nepalese dialects.

The proverbs will be given in Roman, generally followed by their literal meanings. After that, Indian as well as English equivalents will be given where possible. It goes without saying, however, that it is not the literal meaning of the proverbs that matters. Nor can equivalents always represent the entire meaning of the proverbs which are full of high-voltage, human experience and packed with the wisdom of ages. Do not, therefore, go for the mere meanings, but think of the values and attitudes of the people who use them.

*1. Andha deshma ankha chimlaonu, langra deshma khutta khumchiaonu.*

In the country of the blind, act as a blind man and when. amongst the lame people, walk with a limp.

*Jaisa desh, waisa bhesh.* When in Rome, do as the Romans do.

*2. Aago tapnu muhra ko, kura sunnu burha ko*

Enjoy the heat of a fog, and, heed the advice of the elders.

*3. Indra ko aghari swarga ko biyan.*

To describe the heaven in front of Indra (The king of heaven). *'Ulte baans Bareilly ko'*, 'To carry coal to New-Castle.'

*4. Ishwar ko drishti ma sabhai barabar.*

All men are equal in the eyes of God.

*5. Ekant basa, jhagra na jhamela.*

When you stay alone, you are free from quarrels and misunderstandings.

*6. Kusangat bhanda ekant asal.*

It is better to stay alone than to have bad company.

*7. Karodhi lai sukh kahan.*

A man with a bad temper has no peace.

*8. Sabhai bhanda pachhi aune, manjha ma sutnu khojne.*

Last to arrive but desires the best bed.

First deserve, then desire.

*9. Sadhu sant bhukai mare, luchha khanchhan kheer.*

The saints die of hunger, the corrupt enjoy sweet-dishes.

This lyrical proverb is used to criticize mismanagement of the Government.

*10. Gheo na tel, paka buri sel,*

Why boast. You have neither ghee nor oil and you say you have the choicest dishes!

*Thotha Chana, baje Ghana.*

An empty vessel makes much noise.

*11.Unnati ko sathma avanati chha.*

Ups and downs are a part of life.

*12. Kukur jasto guni ra jawai jasto baiguni kohi hundaina.*

No one is as faithful as a dog and as unfaithful as a son-in-law.

*13. Kut peet lee bhut pani bhagchha.*

A good thrashing will even scare away the ghosts. With sincere effort and hard work, any problem can be solved.

*14. Keti kasti chha, bolnu na parne*

*Keta kasto chha, bhannu na pane.*

*Miyan biwi razi to kya kare ga kazi. This os tje substance of song.*

*15. Chara lai sunko pinjra bhanda jangalai piyaro.*

For a bird, living in the free air of the jungle is better than life in a golden cage.

*16. Jahan shanti ko bas, tahan prabhu ko bas.*

God resides at a peaceful place.

*17. Hulmul ma jeo jogaunu, anikal ma beo jogaunu.*

Save thyself in a mob and save the seedlings during famine.

*18. Aath ana ko lenden, rupaiya ko khan pin.*

When you possess only eight annas, how, can you make a budget for one rupee.

*Apni chadar dekh kar paaon phailao.*

Cut your coat according to your cloth.

*19. Aphai boksi aphai dhami.*

You are your own ghost, and your own sorcerer. Or in other words; You are your own best friend and your worst enemy.

*20. Kaamko bairi alchi, bhudhi ko bairi ris*

*Bal ko bairi bega, sabhko bairi kangal.*

Laziness is an enemy of hard work. Bad temper of wisdom. Pride is the enemy of strength, and poverty the enemy of all.

*21. Jahan kangal, uhi chandal.*

Hunger leads to crime.

22. Jo ropchha, tehi paunchha.

As you sow, so shall you reap. *Jo boe ga, wohi kaate ga.*

*23. Pake ko bans terho hundaina.*

The fully grown bamboo can't be bent. Old habits don't change.

*24. Bhera bhera sang, bakhra bakhra sang.*

The sheep move with sheep and goats with goats. Birds of a feather fly together.

*25. Sukh bhognu jana sangha, dukh bhognu manasangha.*

Share your happiness with others, your grief alone.

*26. Man changa ta loti ma ganga.*

When your heart is guileless, your Ganga is in your pitcher. (You live a clean life, you don't have to go to Ganga to wash your sins). This is the motto of the song.

*27. Germ kapra le matra jogi hundaina.*

One can't become a saint by donning saffron clothes;

*28. Ghamand phulchha, tarah phaldaina*

Pride may flower for a while, but does not bear fruit. Pride hath a fall. *Garur ka sar neecha.*

*29. Arka lai khane ko khalta ma aphai parchha.*

When you dig pits for others, you yourself fall in them.

*Kar bura, ho bura.*

*30. Nango rukh ma kohi basdaina.*

None takes shelter under a leafless tree.

*31. Akbari sunlai kasi launu pardaina.*

The gold from Vikramaditya's era needs no scrutiny, or in other words, the truth need not be verified.

*32. Arule tapai bhanos na bhanos aphai mapai.*

Self praise is no recommendation.

*33. Arko ko aas, nitya upwas.*

Keeps yourself otherwise you will achieve no thing. *Apne hath, Jagannath.*

*34. Aye babu ko, gaye sahu ko.*

Easy come, easy go. *Male-e-mufat, dil-e-bcreham,*

*35. Aphno kaj mahakaj.*

God helps those who help themselves.

*36. Avashayakta, avishkar ko janni ho.*

Necessity is the mother of invention. *Zarurat eejad ki maa hai.*

*37. Imanat chha ta, sab thok chha.*

Honesty is the best policy.

*38.* Ghat phute gamer lute.

If you quarrel amongst yourselves someone elso will take advantage. In Hindi, this has an excellent rendering in *Ghar ka bhedi Lanka dhaye.*

*39. Biralo gayo musa ko raj.*

When the cat is away, the mice can play.

*40. Thorai bolne aphno bhed kholdaina.*

Less talk has less danger of exposing yourself. If speech is silver, silence is gold.

*41. Jhinja le murho polchha, lahrale pahro tanchha.*

Even a spark of fire can burn a log, and the movement of a small stone can cause a landslide.

*42. Chucha ko dhan lucha le khanchha.*

The wealth of a miser is squandered by the vagabonds.

## Folk Songs

The richest face of the Nepalese "Folk Lore" are the folk songs of the land with a high lyrical quality and exquisite composition. As we proceed, you will realise that there is a wide variety before you, some sweet and brimming with all the gentler emotions of life, some deeply appreciative of the good neighbourliness in which the Nepalese society lives and some expressing the sheer joy of living. The imagery is as colourful as the alpine flowers of Nepal highlands. Pangs of separation from the beloved and loved ones are expressed in emotionally charged couplets. Amorous feelings are given expression with freedom and lack of restraint. The folk songs as is generally human, have a great ability to stir the emotions. Most of the songs are accompanied by dancing. Folk songs form an essential part of the cultural activity in the interior of Nepal.

Playing on *madal* and singing come naturally to most of the Nepalese people. Where as there are many songs and dances in which both boys as well as girls take part singly or in chorus, jointly or in separate groups, by far the most common form is that the girls sing and *marunis* (boys dressed as girls) dance with the boys. The fairs, many of which are held all over the country and the year round offer a great opportunity for community singing and dancing. The melodies and their essence.

The whole atmosphere resonates with the melodies and reflects the inner accord of the Nepalese with mother Nature. Unfortunately, the entire atmosphere of a song and dance cannot be captured in words, not even in the words of the vernacular, much less in a translation. However, the readers will be able to form a fair idea of the singers and their culture, and that is what we are out to achieve.

Let us now glance through some of the most popular hits. The well-to-do society of Nepal has an army background. It is, therefore, inevitable that many folk songs have an army setting. The first song is sung by a soldier *(lahuray)* and his beloved usually represented by a *maruni*. It has great flexibility and many couplets are added on the spot as the song and dance progress.

**Song One**

Lahuray *Mo to ho sena ko lahuray*
*Mo sang janchha ki sahi*

Maruni *Chhi tista sena ko lahuray*
*Timi sang jandai na sahi*
*Timi sang gayo bhani*
*Khutta dukhi janu bhayen.*

Lahuray *Oh liai diyun las sena ko gari*
*Mo sang janchha kih sahi.*

Maruni *Timi sang gayo bhani*
*bhuko mari janu bhayen.*

Lahuray *Oh liai diyun la*
*Ration ko bori, mo sang...*

Soldier Oh fare dame,
I am a soldier from the army
Come with me, come with me.

Maruni You are a soldier no doubt,
But you are not smart
I shan't come with you
You go to distant lands
If I accompany you
My feet will get sore by constant marches
No, I won't come with you.

Soldier Oh fair dame, come with me
You won't have to walk
For I'll take you in an army vehicle
I am a soldier, come with me, come with me.

Maruni You are a soldier no doubt
But you are not smart
I won't come with you
If I come with you

|  |  |
|---|---|
|  | I'll die of hunger<br>Oh I won't, I won't come with you. |
| Soldier | I'll get you a bag of army rations,<br>Oh come, Oh come with me. |

The song goes on and on. Beloved asks where she will get the comforts of life, and the boy replying that all sorts of comforts are provided to a soldier in the army.

**Invitation to a sing song**

When the sing song sessions start in the evening, songs have no apparent meaning. It is in fact an invitation to one and all to come and join. At the fair, the mode of beckoning in the same.

*Khane chamal chhaina*
*Launchhan sarangiko tanti.*

There is no rice to eat
But the notes of sarangi are still sweet.

**Song Two**

The next song talks of the peasant community, happy at the sight of lush fields and still complaining of lack of rest.

*Kati ramro mero yo pangre goru*
*Kati ramro mero hal*
*Kati ramro mero ubjani bali*
*Ramro chha mehenat ko phal.*
*Dharti amia, dharti babai*
*Yashata paunchhu anna*
*Pyaro ma garchhu, sanman garchhu*
*Dharti amai, dhanya*!
*Umer bitaen jotaima maile*
*Aena sukh ko din*
*Jiu burho mero, man burho mero*
*Sukh chhaina ekai chhin*!

How good are my bridled oxen
How nice is my plough
How sweet are my ripe crops
Sweet is the fruit of labour
Earth is my mother, Earth is my father
From her I get my food
I love you I honour you
Oh Mother Earth, I thank you
An age I have passed in ploughing

The day of rest has not come
My body is old, my mind is old
Not a moment's rest is there.

**Song Three**

The following song is sung when a daughter's marriage takes place. It is almost a Suhag like it is sang in northern India.

*Na ro na ro cheli timi maiti timro ghar hoina*
*Phool jasto timro joban aba timi hamro hoina.*
*Na ro na ro...............*
*Ankha bhari ansoo parne, aama baba rundai janes*
*Dhoka nira bhar na baini,*
*Ansoo poonchdai bida garne.*
*Bas bad cheli bhanadai, saheli le laijane,*
*Saheli le laijane..... na ro na ro ......*
*Sawan bhadon runal lagyo cheli timro bidai ma*
*Kathai bhari bhandai aako chhorana parne maiti ghar lai.*
*Cheli timro karmai esto bhandai jao aphoo lai bhandai jao.*

Oh my daughter sweet,
Do not weep.
The parents home is not your permanent home.
You have bloomed like a flower
And now you are not ours!
With brimming eyes,
The parents move forward
To bid her farewell.
Her brothers and sisters are at the door,
To bid farewell
Her friends have also arrived,
To bid her farewell.
Even the rains have started weeping now,
For you are leaving us for ever.
My daughter-go now,
May God be with you,
Weep not my daughter,
The parents home,
Is not your permanent home.

**Song Four**

This song is sung for 'Lahuray', a newly enrolled youth who is going abroad on military service. It song has a touching theme with a very high lyrical quality.

*Na jao chhari you desak,*
*Aama lai ruaye ra.*

*Na brisa janme ko thaon,*
*Aaphoo lai chhakaye ra.*

*Dhoi deo dukh aama ko,*
*Pasina le bagaye ra.*
*Chookao dudh ko bhara,*
*Mehnat le kamaye ra.*

*Na jao.........*
*Na par aama ko chhati*
*Cheya cheya turkraye ra.*
*Uthao desh ko jhanda,*
*Swarga lai choowaye ra.*
Don't go, leaving your motherland,
Whilst your mother weeps.
Go if you must,
But don't forget your birth place.

Go if you must,
But wash your mother's pangs of separation,
With your hard toil and sweat,
With your hard labour, pay her debt.

Do not forget your mother,
And your birth place,
Raise thy country's flag
To touch the very heaven.

**Song Five**

Nepal and the Himalayas have a beautiful landscape. The verses express the villager's simple idea of love for the land.

*Himalai chuli tyo paribata*
*Hiun kaile jamincha?*
*Bageko pani ureko chitta*
*Kahan gai thaminchha?*
*Bagaincha bhari phala ra phula*
*Chheu chheuma karela*
*Ankha chhan timra junkiri jasta*
*Jimkaune parela*
*Sun jasto Nepal kati ramro dekhchha*
*Swarga chha sansar ma*
*Sun jasto premke jun jasto dekhchha*
*Mayako sansarma*

On the distant Himalayan peaks
When will the snow gather?

The running stream and the fickle mind
Where will they come to rest?
The garden is full of fruit and flowers
And here and there the vegetables grow
Your beautiful eyes and lovely eyelashes
Are pretty like the fire flies.
How lovely is my golden Nepal
Like heaven on this Earth
My sweetheart is pretty like the moon
And sweet is the world with love.

**Song Six**

Which the pangs of separation are uppermost in the following song. As the song propesses, it become more plaintive.

*Himalai chuli ke yati ramro*
*Sarapa ko kanchuli*
*Yo pap manma biraha chalyo*
*Na bajau bansari.*

How fine it is, the Himalayan peak
Like the skin of a snake
This separation has filled my heart with sorrow
Oh do not play the flute.

*Shirko sindur launa bhaujyu*
*Hamra dajyu ai ra puge, Nepali jyanma:*
*Tyatiko jhalijhalko ke manchhyau nani*
*Kaile ra aunthe ti timra dajyu, ranaima pareka?*

Put sindur on your hair, oh sister-in-law
My brother has come back to our beloved Nepal:
Don't taunt me like this, oh little brother,
Will he ever come, from the far off battlefield?

**Song Seven**

'Should I or should I not go with my lover?' This song expresses the fickle-mindedness of a young damsel about falling in love.

*Kali parii dai kati ramro, dhak topi,*
*Kadai ma galbandi.*
*Sanu sanu gaiko bachhi, hath ma linchh lahuri*
*Yo dali ma rasa chhaina, kina ghumchha mauri*
*Kali pari dai kati...*
*Sir ma laune sir ko topi khutta ma laune jutta*
*Mero man ta do man bhayo eta jam ki uta*
*Kali paridai kati...*

How handsome is he
One who resides in that yonder valley
With a muffler on his shoulders,
And a slanting cap on his head.
How charming he looks,
The calves are very young,
There are no honey bearing flowers,
On the branches of these trees
Why are you hovering here oh bees,
How handsome is he.
His head covered with a cap, and shoes on his feet
My heart is unable to decide
To go with him or not to go.

**Song Eight**

Jhaore in a famous song of Nepal. It is sang when on return to his village after two years of service, a young Nepali lad spends the evening with village girls.

Taruni *Aba bheena na jao Lahuray*
*Nepal lai ma painchha jaagira*

Lahuray *Jana sai chhore ra timi laa*
*Nepal ma paaone chhoon jagira*
*Barajooko dhoori mooni*
*Bhainsi lukne dhoolo*
*Masita gayo bhane*
*Bhagya hola thoolo*

Taruni *Man pare ko khaunla piunla*
*Na pare ko khan na*
Esta kura no garo bheena
*Kasai sitta janna*

Lahuray *Eso bhaye so sali*
*Dimla sunko baala*
*Aru sita gayo bhane*
*Toki dimla gaala*

Taruni *Sunko baala dimla bhanne*
*Ahile hoina cohile*
*Timi sitta janna bheena*
*Talu rahi chha khoile*

Girl Do not go abroad my brother-in-law
You will get service in Nepal

Boy I will not go abroad, my darling
I will find a job in Nepal
Promise me to marry me, my love
It will brighten your future.

Girl We will make merry,
To our hearts desire,
I will not, I swear,
I will not go with any one else.

Boy Then, come and be my darling
I will give you a golden ring,
If you run away with some one else
I will cut your throat.

Girl Your promise to give me a golden ring
Is long over due
I can't be your sweet heart
For there is no hair on your head.

**Song Nine**

The eternal theme of love is very clear in this song.

Keta ***Herana kanchhi paharai ma lalupote sabai*** *phulyo*

Keti *La lai kanchha sabai tipi malai lagai deona*

Keta *Kahi jharchhan cheeso jharna*
*Kahi phulchhan phoola*
*Phoola ko jasto chokho preeti*
*Mero man ma rakha*
*Herana kanchhi*

Keti *Kahin dekhchhan danra kanra*
*Kahi dekhchhan khola*
*Preeti lagaon aja kanchha*
*Kati ramro hola*
*Herana kanchha*...........

Keta *Sa ra ra hawa chhalyo*
*Aja paharai man*
*Hu ru ra jeeban bityo*
*Kanchi ko samjha nai ma*
*Herana kanchhi*...........

| | |
|---|---|
| Keti | *Danra pari paani*<br>*Maya preeti lagai jaon hai*<br>*Bitaon jindgani*<br>*Herana kanchha...........* |
| Boy | Oh sweet heart, the red flowers are blooming!<br>The valley is ablaze!! |
| Girl | Oh my darling, get me all the flowers. |
| Boy | Here flows the cold stream<br>There bloom the flowers<br>My love is pure like a flower and the clear like the water of the stream,<br>Keep it in your heart. |
| Girl | Oh sweet heart, the red flowers are blooming,<br>The valley is ablaze with flowers red!<br>This lovely landscape,<br>Where valleys and rivers alternate,<br>Let us make love today<br>How sweet will it be my love,<br>Oh my darling, get me all the flowers. |
| Boy | A strong wind blows,<br>Today in the valley,<br>The days are passing,<br>With my darling<br>See my love, the red flowers are blooming,<br>The valley is ablaze!! |
| Girl | The Sun in shining on this side of the valley<br>The rain is falling on that side of the valley<br>(Behold the beauty of nature)<br>Let us live together,<br>Oh my darling, get me all those flowers. |

**Song Ten**

The next song is again an army song and not only the most popular but by far the most flexible. The men and *marunis* go back and forth it on the couplets and go on adding new ones at will reverting back to the original opening stanzas from time to time.

*Oh dhalki dhalki na hintnu hola*
*Yo kali ma jieu jane ber chhaina.*

Do not, oh do not walk with a swank
It does not take long to loose one's youth.

*Timi ta jai jao Bombai sahar ma .*
*Nargis bhaye ra*
*Timi lai bhetnu, mo nishchai aunchhun*
*Raj Kapur bhaye ra Sayenli, yo kali..........*

(From the era of Nargis-Raj Kapur pair of Indian films, the soldiers added this couplet. As the song progresses, it passes from Rajesh Khanna-Dimple to Govinda-Karishma).

You go to Bombay and become Nargis,
To meet you I sure will come as Raj Kapur
Oh sweety, do not walk with a swank,
For it takes no time to loose one's youth.

*India ko Raja le, Kashmir ko dhawa ma*
*Urai layayo rail ko hawa ma*

(From the era of first and subsequent aggressions on Kashmir by Pakistan, the soldier's serving there have added this couplet).

The Government of India
Has sent us to Kashmir
On the fastest moving train.
Don't walk with a swank,
It does not take long
To loose one's youth.

(And whenever the soldiers go, they put a blame on the girls of the place that they wink at them and tease them).

*Kara ma kara, kamarai khayo,*
*Chhala ko peti le*
*Hero na daju bhai gijaunchha mo lai*
*Yo shahar ko keti le*
*Aju to mo le bhat ee ra khayo*
*Tihun to karela,*
*Yo shahar ko keti, Chinnun na janne,*
*Jham kaunchha parela.*

"My leather belt is so tight,
It has eaten into my waist,
And to top it all
The girls of this place tease me.*

* Here they added the name of the place.

I have eaten rice today,
With the vegetable of karela (bitter gourd)
The girls of this place
Wink at me even though I don't know them!

And the couplets go on endlessly; added at will and extempore. The song occasionally reverts back to:

*Dhalki dhalki na hintnu hola*
*Yo kali na jiu jane ber chhaina.*

**Song Eleven**

And this is the most popular song, a favourite of the young and old alike, more so when they have had an overdose of *raksti*! Holding each other by waists or shoulders, more to support each other, men and women go on singing in long streched breaths.

*Kanth ma laune kanth phula a a a...........*
*Aise he raja le bechi khayo o o o...........*

*Aise he raja ko asha mo lai chhaina,*
*Gai jaunla maite ko desh ma...........*

The lovely necklace that I had,
Has been sold by this heartless man,
I have no hopes on him,
I will go to my parents home.

And the blames go on and on.
You have to hear to believe.

Boys and *marunis*, holding each other by waists, go on swirling and trying to draw longer and longer breath, at Phula a a a................and khayo o o o.................

**Song Twelve**

And in this very class of short odes now an all time favourite which most of you might have heard at some time or another,

*"Naini talo, Naini talo*
*Ghumi ayo rela, a Ankh na laune kalo kajal*
*Bulbula ma tela; Naini talo*
*Naini talo, Naini talo."*

Oh sweety, come with me,
I'll take you to Nainital,
I will give you a ride on the train

> I will buy you *kajal* for your eyes
> And scented oil for your hair,
> Oh sweety, come with me,
> I will take you to Nainital.

There is "a pleasure in the pathless woods" that no pleasure of the centres of modern civilization, how so ever well developed, can offer. Let us trek around and go to places which give as much pleasure as the land and people of Nepal.

# 3
# Eight Kashmiri Poems

## ANONYMOUS

Over the centuries many anonymous poems, which do not bear any title in the original, have been selected from various manuscripts hymns of the "sufiana music", which used them to illustrate various melismas. Some of these poems have reached us through oral tradition because in these times there was no way there could be western down.

Free from constraints of the conventions of form and diction, these simple poems are a spontaneous expression of the very throb of life as lived by the unknown multitudes engaged in their ordinary strife. If one looks deeply the duction and manners is in will be sea as that of the middle ages.

**4. He is Set in his Ways**

Away, away flew the bulbul,
And made it's nest in a remote thicket.
My love is having a boat-trip in the Dal;
He is given to trifles with strangers,
Oh could he return but once to me,
I would offer him chalices of wine;
I would prostrate at his feet;
And with my scarf wipe off his sweat.

*Bulbuly Ool Vyoor,* 18th century

**5. Plaintive Calls**

My golden love, my pearly love,
Hear my calls, my plaintive calls!
Once you went to sport in the king's yard;
The princess chose you and you were sold,
Sold you were and strung on a thread;
Strung on a thread and worn round the neck,
Worn round the neck and shining so bright;
Hear my calls, my plaintive calls!

*Naad Laayay*, 18th century

**6. A Ruthful Bride**

The moon is climbing, the basil is bedewed;
O moon, come down to see the hapless ones.

Those who have their brothers are often visited,
One who has none then pries and peeps,
O moon, come down to the hapless ones.
Those who have their fathers are visited often,
One who has none then pries and peeps,
O moon, come down to the hapless ones.

*Vasyi Zoonyii,* 18th century

**7. A Father to his Daughter**

Basil of the garden, sweet as candy,
My little daughter, my life is for you.
Blessed am I to have you as my daughter,
Roses from the beds your father has watered,
I shall cull and adorn your tresses;
You are a slender twig, my blood is for you.
Your mother bears a goblet full of attar,
To sprinkle on your swanlike neck.
You come to dwell with your brother in my house,
My little daughter, my life is for you.

*Mool Ti Kuur,* 18th century

**8. A Secret Excursion**

Come, my friends and companions, let's go to the Dal.
There we shall swim and wash ourselves.
There we shall find a smiling lotus;
The fruit of the lotus is sweet to eat.
Let's not let our parents know.
Childhood is the time to revel and rove.

*Dal Seel,* 18th century

**1. Nostalgia**

I made nosegays of jasmine in the garden,
And went to the bazar after six long months,
There I met my dear father;
He took me to his attic.
There he made a cushion for me to sit on;
He lit a lamp and placed it in the cranny,
He opened a book and read it to me;

Softly I began to reveal my heart,
Silently I began to shed big tears;
Fondly he placed his hand on my head.
"My daughter, you return to your in-laws", he said;
"The house of your husband is now your abode.
Your father's house to you is of no avail."

A mother's house is the royal house;
A brother's house is just a hope.

*Hyiyay Me Gundy Kery,* 18th century

**2. Consolation to a Bride**

Let me console you and then with full abandon
Adorn you there under the cherry tree.
O my pretty emerald, I shall wrap you in fine cottons.
Your father's sisters lull you in their arms,
And your mother Narcissus sings full-throated;
I have got your necklaces and coronets worth thousands.
Nothing but your love has brought me here;
I shall always hold your cares dear;
Lo, your mother's brother is also come to your solace.
I shall adorn you there under the cherry tree.

*Peerthoo Gyilaasi Kuliney Tal,* 18th century

**3. The Water-fowl's Chores**

"Where away, O water-fowl?"
"I am on my way to the field."
"Wherefore, O water-fowl?"
"To hatch my eggs."
"How many do you have?"
"Fifty and one."
"Can you give me one?"
"But I have got none."

*Gyilyi Kun,* 18th century *Tr.* by Shafi Shauq Marsiya

**Mulla Hakim Azim**

O my merciful God, free my heart and broaden my bosom;
For it is overburdened with sins.
My soul is like a caged bird.
Teach me to sing of the tragedy of Karbala.

*Marsiya,* 18th-19th century *Tr.* by Naji Munawar

# 4

# Medieval Kashmiri Literature (Shafi Shauq)

**Phase I Kashmiri Literature in the Making (1100-1300)**

Poetry is the major component of Kashmiri literature which is deeply influenced by the native form of the Shaivite philosophy, and its stylistic maturity makes one believe that this early poetry, although fragmentary, must have been the culmination of centuries-old creative activity. Unfortunately the nature of this ancient poetry cannot be known as the ravages of the turbulent centuries have left nothing of it for the present-day reader. We can safely assume that there must have existed a body of literature, inchoate and rudimentary, for several hundred years before the advent of the Aryans from North India. The aborigines, called Nagas, and the new settlers from Dardistan (the mountainous region extending from lat. 30° S to lat. 40° N and from long. 70° W to long. 78° E), gave the Kashmiri language its unique syntactic structure this structure could not have existed or would have gone into obhirion without their imaginative reconstruction of the life they lived, without fictionalising the facts that constituted their reality.

**The Pishachas**

The Dard Aryans, sometimes known by the derogatory name Pishachas in old Sanskrit texts, came to the valley several centuries before the advent of the Indo-Aryan Brahmins, and eventually established a culture of their own. The Dards were, as they presently are in Gilgit, Dras, Astor, Baltistan, Chitral, Honza, Kafaristan and the adjoining areas, inveterately tough and hardy, living in the most arduous climate. The archeological findings from Burzahom, in the vicinity of Srinagar, reveal that the Dard Aryans in the Neolithic Age had developed a culture that was determined by the unique ecological conditions rather than any sublime urge. It is the period roughly between 2500 and 1500 B.C. and during the same period the Brahmin Aryans from the plains of India migrated to the valley, partly for finding relief from the scorching heat and partly for the mysterious kind of terrain in the Himalayas inspiring a meditative soul.

Brahmins who had myrated. They possessed a respectably old and fecund tradition of learning, literature and wisdom and having found a congenial and pleasant dwelling place, the new settlers continued their scholarly and literary occupation in their Vedic and Sanskrit and, later on in the Apabhramsha. The great Sanskrit classics like the Puranas, the *granthas,* various chronicles, collections of tales such as *Kathasaritsagar,* amply reveal that the valley was inhabited by a people of great ideas and aspirations, centuries before the Christian era.

**The inspiration**

The zeal of the Brahmins which they showed in learning the scriptures must have inspired the natives too, with whom they lived quite harmoniously, and, consequently, the vernacular could not remain impervious to intellectual and creative activities. Unfortunately, nothing of the literature in the is vernacular of that era is to be found anywhere and we are left staring in the darkness of the well of oblivion.

It is, however, safe to conjecture that several play-songs, riddles, magic-chants, wailing rhymes, hunting slogans and the like, still a part of folk-memory, are reminiscent of that forgotten race of people, who were successively over-run by the non-native peoples and yet survived to leave behind their offspring. Such rudiments of folk-literature had an organic relation with the people's mundane strife and, as such, could not be stamped out by the elite literature of the rulers, and continued to form the strength of the cultural fabric that holds Kashmiris together as a distinct people with a distinct identity. This amorphous body of literature has, nevertheless, undergone radical changes in its phonological character though the underlying structure has remained.

It can however be said for certain that by or before the medieval times, the vernacular too must have evolved a tradition of what may be called, "elite literature."

**Preserving the Literature**

The men of learning must have begun to think that this literature, too, is worth preservation and we find the first signs of this realisation in the Sanskrit classics of the 9th and 10th centuries. It was characterised by perfunctoriness and technical virtuosity vis-a-vis the spontaneity and suppleness of the popular form. It survived chiefly in the intellectual quarter; some philosophers of the time, writing in Sanskrit, have recorded a few fragments in their spiritual and aesthetic treatises. The earliest specimens of this poetry, scantily scattered in various Sanskrit texts, have been quoted to elaborate and amplify various arguments concerning the principles of Shaivism like *pati, pasha* and *pashu,* or *para, apara,* and *parapara,* or *nara, shakti,* and *shiva.* Here is a *vakh* (Sanskrit: *vakiani,* a stanza of four hemistichs) of unknown authorship:

ascetic endurance removes darkness,
and illuminates with the light of truth;
one is liberated from the pother of mind,
and thus one realises one's true self.

### Chumi Pad

*Chumi pad* which were in the nature of instructions quatrains were composed by some of those ascetics who believed in rigorous discipline and efficacy of self-mortification in attaining salvation, and who engaged themselves in preaching noble ideas to a meliorate the moral disposition of the people. Popularly known as *chumi mety,* they maintained a conscious distance from the worldly strife to study its contingencies and incongruities without abhorring those who were in the thick of it.

### Trika

The rhyme, rhythm and the facile four-line stanza form of these pithy verses, hardly, intelligible now to a non-specialised reader, were quite easy to consign to memory and recite while propagating or discussing the ideas of the local Shaivism called *Trika.* Kashmiri Shaivamat was used by Kashmiri poets without considering the sophistications of its tripartite division into three schools: Agama, Spanda, and Pratyabhijna; they rather produced a poetic synthesis of the quintessential principles of all the three, as we see in the later poetry of the 14th century. It was a period of ideas as two diverse faiths, viz. Shaivamat and Islam had come into an intimate contact and the ordinary people sought a harmony in the kernel ideas without a sense of coercion.

The native people could not be ignored by the learned scholars and preachers of both the religions who spoke in their unique registers of faith; they realised this constraint and began using the vernacular, although underdeveloped, as a viable medium to have rapport with the commonality. Kshemindra Vyasa says in his *Alamkara* (dated 1050) that he advised contemporary poets to write in their mother tongue. He also refers to a poetic assembly in which a renowned poet recited his composition in the Deshbhasha:

Then stood up the Guru. He was inebriate and recited some of his verses in his mother-tongue.

By that time there was certainly a very respectable tradition of writing in Kashmiri, and the philosophers and aestheticians of the time writing in the lingua franca, could not dismiss it as a futile exercise. The first complete poetic work extant in Kashmiri is the *Maha-naya Praka-sh of* Sati Kantha (12th-13th century). There is hardly anything for certain to say about the author except that he lived near Pampore and that he wrote *Maha-naya Praka-sha* in response to King Sangram Singh's request.

The commentary written by some unknown Sanskrit scholar, included in the original MS, reveals that Sati Kantha was affiliated to the *Udyana pitha,* the school which preached Abhinavgupta's (11th century) Pratyabhijna, a doctrine of Kashmiri Shaivamat closely related to the school of Vedanta founded by Shankaracharya who visited Kashmir in the early years of the 9th century.

**Pratyabhijna**

The motif of the Pratyabhijna philosophy was self-recognition, an excruciatingly painful pursuit to attain salvation in the life lived by the individual. Sati Kantha wrote the poem while looking forward to the court for audience and appreciation and not to the commoners, yet he claims to have written it in the common speech of the common people: *"sarva goharam deshbha-sha."* His scholastic mannerisms and deliberate deviation from the common idiom have made the work almost unintelligible for the present-day readers. Many later day scholars wondered about its obscurity. It was found taht it is also due to the complexities of the underlying thought which is rather beyond the ken of the modern reader. The poem is a series of independent stanzas conveying discrete ideas; the common theme alone works as a linchpin to hold them together and compensates for the lack of progression.

**Maha-naya Praksha-sha**

*Mahanaya Praka-sha* comprises ninety-two *shlokas,* each *shl-oka* consisting of two lines of two hemistichs each. The four segments can fall into any of the six possible rhyme-schemes: *abab, acab, abca, aaba, aaaa* or *abba.* In rhythm and metre, the *shloka* or *va-kh* of the *Mahanaya Prakasha* closely resembles the *doha* in Sanskirt, Hindi and other North-Indian languages; it is a qualitative rhythm and each hemistich has four stresses. Grierson's remark that "this is not paralleled by any similar metric system in Persian and Northern India" needs further investigation.

Each *va-kh* in the MS of the *Maha-naya Praka-sha* has been interpreted by some anonymous commentator as a poetic version of one or the other basic principle of Shaivamat. But it is the poet's skill to transform these principles into suitable images that matters:

Kisi is a deity of the highest rank,
she devours voraciously even Bhairava,
with your humility, and ascetic reclusion,
you, too, could attain such power.

The Lord deserves your service and love,
for He emerged as the first vibration;
indivisibly united forever with Shakti
the seed that gives birth to the universe.

Blood and wine form two discrete drops
but a gale of wind mingles them together,

> 't', 'r', and 'h', are different sounds;
> by combination they give rise to meaning.

**Maha-naya Praka-sha**

Like other thinkers of the Pratyabhijna school, the leitmotif of the *Maha-naya Praka-sha* is also self-recognition, which is possible through an awakened *chid* or consciousness. When a *sadhaka* brings about motion in one's *chid,* a purposeful process sets in: *chitta* (sensual preception) become *chiti* (consciousness), which then acquires the next evolutionary stage *chetna.* This is the ultimate purpose and fruit of the spiritual quest or its *chida-nanda-labh* (the resulting spiritual bliss), and the seeker achieves a sort of lordship, Shivata or Maheshvarya:

> Unified *chid* is a meandering brook,
> every moment changing its direction and running.
> Incorporeal consciousness is the door to God,
> as immutable as the crow's eye.

Sati Kantha seems to have been deeply conscious of his poetic enterprise to communicate his personal mystic experience and he has expressed satisfaction with his success:

> Here, in this world, I purified my soul,
> I, Sati Kanth, reached and conquered the sky,
> in doing so, I excelled many a great man,
> and attained the pinnacle of success.

**Kashmiri Language Character**

This was the Apabrahmsha character of the Kashmiri language in the 12th and 13th centuries, popular with elite Brahmins, whereas the speech of the ordinary people was open to all manner of influence. It was the time when Kashmiri culture was in intimate contact with Central Asian culture, and Islamic faith and Sufism were gaining ground. Several crafts and occupations of Central Asia like *qualinbafi* (carpet weaving), *shaw sazi* (shawl weaving), *gabbaduzi* (gabba embroidery), *namda sazi* (felt making), *vazivan* (a unique dishpreparation), papier-mache etc. were being adopted as means of earning a livelihood.

At the same time as a corollary of this cultural renovation, the lexis of the language was getting drastically reshaped through borrowings and replacements. Besides need, prestige motive also played an important role in the making of the language. In the language of the *chumi pad* and the *Maha-naya Prakasha* only a few grammatical particles and affixes are observably different from Sanskrit; it does not reflect the true nature of the live language of that time, neither at the phonological level nor at the morphological level. It is unbelievable that the language could develop within a short span of one hundred years a unique system of vowels, particularly the high-central and the mid-central vowels, palatalization, six cases with distinct morphs for the ergative, dative, genitive and ablative and, of course, the intricate verbal concord, and several other features such as we find in the later compositions. The void Unfortunately, there is a big void between the compositions discussed above and the *va-khs* of Lal Dyad, the greatest name of the 14th century. It is safe to believe that the *vakh* continued to be the most popular form of poetry with a design to instruct and persuade. A few *va-khs* of one Siddh Mol have been preserved as a part of his colloquy with Lal Dyad. It is said that Siddh Mol was none but Shri Kantha, a descendant of Sati Kantha; he wrote a Sanskrit text, *B-alb-odhani ny-asa*. His *va-khs* are full of wisdom like the one given below:

> No light is as good as the light of your eyes,
> no place of pilgrimage is as sacred as are your knees;
> no friend is as reliable as your own pocket,
> no comfort is as pleasant as your quilt.

**The Spoken Language**

This was the Kashmiri language spoken actually by the real people who lived seven hundred years ago and was used by the poets who looked forward to the common, unschooled and unsophisticated audience for appreciation. This language is syntactically altogether different from all other Indo-Aryan, Dardic and Iranian languages; it has a unique phonological character, but like other Indian regional language which were evotring about the same time, is lexically dependent on Sanskrit.

**Phase II: Poetry for the People (1300-1550)**

The real history of Kashmiri literature begins with Lala Dyad, a woman gifted with extraordinary power of expression, representing the culmination of centuries-old tradition of poetry in the vernacular now inaccessible to us. Lal's life is shrouded in legends of an indeterminate kind, and, as such, she emerges as an archetypal figure of an affectionate and protecting mother; she is popularly called "Dyad" or grandma. Her poetry contains all those elements, such as esotericism, humanistic mysticism, obliqueness of expression and reliance on the spoken idiom, which flourished in the later ages.

The chroniclers of her time were mainly preoccupied with the glamour of court life; they simply ignored saying much about her, notwithstanding the important role she played in the cultural life of the 14th century kashmir. She was, however, panegyrised in befitting words by her immediate, successor and disciple, namely, Nund Ryosh, who professed with pride to have received instruction from her:

Lala of Padmanpore,
who quaffed *amrita,*
resides in our bosom; she is the avatara;
God bestow on me the virtues she has had.

**Lal Dyad**

It would not be vain to presume that the 'Oracle-Woman' who met the famous Muslim conquerer Sultan Shahab-ud-Din in the jungle and prognosticated success in his war, was none other than Lal Dyad, as the later historians have recorded. However, among the historians, Baba Ali Raina (16th century) was the first to mention her name and record various myths associated with the legendary woman. In his Persian chronicle, *Tazkiratul Arifin,* he calls her Lal Moj (i.e., Lala, the mother) and Rabia Sani (Rabia of her day). Out of all the legends recounted invariably by all other historians, emerges the hazy profile of a great woman who influenced the 14th century life.

It was a poor Pandit family Lal Dyad was born in the early fourteenth century. She was named Lala. In her tender age, she was married to a country yokel who was too blunt to understand her meditative nature. There are several interesting legends about the torments she had to face at her in-laws. Having no interest in the drudgery of life, she could not keep herself wrapped up in the responsibilities of married life, and eventually abandoned her home, and sought guidance and instruction from all the reverend saints of the time; she finally chose the spiritual path that befitted her unique mode of thought. She wandered from village to village, mixed with people to have an intimate feeling of the agonies of life, and taught them how to attain the joy of enlightenment without actual renunciation. The legend says that she walked in the nude as she deemed clothing a superfluous social obligation and slavery to custom, which she abhorred. But her clear and simple instruction about dress and diet, and the deep social consciousness, revealed in her poetry, do not support this legend. She always favoured the middle path in every aspect of life:

Wear such clothes as save you from cold;
eat such food as saves you from hunger.

That is why I began roaming about in the nude" implies a metaphorical negation of the material barrier of the body between the soul and the ultimate. This is off-quoted in kashmiri folk songs even today.

**Tumultoous Times**

Kashmir was in the throes of the plunder and carnage unleashed by a Tartar war-monger named Hilakoo or Dalchu. She was born during that period. Islam had established its basic institution of worship and propagation, and the king of the time, Renchan, a Tibetan prince who had fled his homeland, embraced Islam. This set the stage for the Sultanship in Kashmir which actually started in 1342 when Sultan Shamas-ud-Din Shahmir possessed the throne after marrying the widow of Renchan, called Kota Rani. We find vivid glimpses of the turbulent society in some of Lala's verses, albeit she kept herself away from the political turmoils that surrounded her.

> Behold a wise man dying of hunger
> as an autumnal leaf shed from the bough;
> and behold the oaf lashing his cook,
> I languish to break the fetters of my delusion.
>
> The fans, the canopy, the chariot, the throne,
> the revelry, the dancing, and the cushioned swings;
> have everything and yet you are not safe,
> it cannot allay your dread of death.

In the 14th century two disparate streams of faith, Islam and Shaivism, coalesced on the basis of the rudimentary elements of humanism common to them. Her poetry very clearly reflects that intellectual milieu of the fourteenth century. Islam reached the people of Kashmir through the sufi teachings of great sufis who visited Kashmir and developed rapport with the native saints and scholars. However, Lal Dyad had a strong affinity with the Pratyabhijana of Trika which originated in Kashmir and was expounded by various philosophers in various ages, like Somananda (9th century), Utpaldeva (10th century) and Abhinavagupta (11th century). It is a monistic thought, influenced by the philosophy of Shankaracharya who is believed to have visited Kashmir in the early part of the 9th century.

**Poetry of Lal Dyad**

Her poetry is unsurpassed in harmonising the depth of thought with feeling. Each stanza or *vakh,* consisting of four lines, presents a vivid suggestive image, essentially dynamic, which becomes a correlative of some of the other state of the awakened soul. Her philosophy deals with the threefold principle of Truth, i.e. Nara, Shakti and Shiva, making it easy for a non-specialised reader to understand the meaning of the individual being in the world and the individual's place in society and the cosmos. It aims at awakening the latent faculties of the soul, slackened by ritual and unquestioned acceptance of dogma, so that it is able to take a spontaneous leap to the Real which is manifest in everything and, first of all, in the inquiring self. Shiva's energy, namely Shakti, is present in every form of material existence and needs to be perceived without discriminating between the inferior and the superior, the low and the high, the artificial fabrications of an unenlightened consciousness.

### Unto Lord Shiva

By knowing Shiva, one is able to negate one's state of nothingness to affirm real being Though it makes no difference to Shiva whether known or not, but it is a question of the being or non-being of a human soul:

> I got rid of the void of nothingness
> I was dumbfounded and agape,
> it was a recognition of my true self,
> as a lotus blooms out of the aquatic weed.

In this absolute communion with Shiva, the intent inquisitor gains all the powers of Shiva or, as Somananda says, becomes an incarnation of Shiva: *bhavati siva-mayatma sarvabhave sarvah.* At this stage of attainment, all sorts of ritualistic worship and ceremony become gratuitous: *pujakah pujanam pujyam iti sarvam shivah sthitah.* Lal Dyad expresses this experience beautifully in several *vakhs.* The recognition of the inalienability of the human soul and the creator, and hence the recognition of the destination of the pilgrimage within the self of the seeker, is the leitmotif of *Lal-vakh:*

> Mind is the garden and faith the gardener,
> present to Him the flowers of devotion,
> bathe Him in the water of awareness,
> Shankara is awakened by the mantra of silence.
>
> I, Lala, pined away in the quest,
> finally, I strove and found Him near;
> I yearned to see Him, but the door was latched,
> the desire was intense, I sat there in hope

### Conflects with Brahmins

She vehemently vies with the brahmins on the issues of icon-worship and ridiculed the idea of gaining bliss and redemption after death. She believes that man's body is not uncalled-for and wanton, but the true abode of God and needs all care and comfort. Like Brihaspati, she believes that our body originated from the four elements, and what makes it unique is the heightened awareness, not separate from the body. There is no liberation after death; it is possible only within the stipulated life-span by subjecting the sensual existence to the awakened consciousness:

With sincere intent, seek Him in your body,
this body is another name of the Real;
consecrate it through purgation of your craving,
within the body lie fire and light.

She, however, at the same time preaches a conscious distancing from allurements of the material world, which she considers a tricky snare laid to capture the soul. She calls it a wilderness where one gets lost, and if one really desires to escape this "losing", the only way open is to get lost in losing oneself to lose losing; the guiding principle is love:

I, Lala, lulled my love in my bosom,
and died before I was dead;
I lost by losing myself in losing,
and regained myself in the fount of truth,
Quite merrily, I attained the truth.
and thus realised my true being.

**Poetry: Her Own Experience**

Although Lala's poetry is perfectly in consonance with the *Pratyabhijna* system of Kashmir Shaivism, it is essentially the personal experience of an individual in spiritual journey. Her philosophy works through fresh imagery and unconventional metaphor and attains timelessness and independence from the philosophical systems. Her perception of the dynamics of creation in the macrocosm and its reflection in the microcosm helps her build dramatic situations, which translate the transcendental into sensuous images that are replete with the energy of creation:

The lake too brimming to contain a grain,
assuaging the thirst of all beings;
the bear, the jackal, the rhino and the water-elephant
born, or not born, fall into the lake.

Fleeing in the azure the steed of mind,
covers a million miles in one wink,
when the reins of consciousness bridle its direction,
the wheels of breath and soul are controlled.

Lal Dyad, also known as Lal Yogeshvari or Lalisvari or Lal Arifa, died around 1390, and there is a common belief that she was buried near a mosque at Bijbihara. But it is also said that she changed into a flame and dissipated in the air. She is said to have offered her breast to Nund Ryosh to suck, when he was born and refused to suckle milk from his own mother; he was born in 1378.

**Effects of Poetry of Nund Ryosh**

Nund Ryosh, venerated by the titles like Sheikhul Aalam, Sheikh Noorud Din and Sahzanand, was incontrovertibly the first versatile poet of the language who used poetry as an effective instrument to reshape the life-patterns of I4th-15th century Kashmir. He chose the unsophisticated diction of the common man and used it with subtlety, flexibil, and dexterously to make it a viable literary language to encompass and communicate varieties of human nature and also its contingencies.

His cryptic verses, impregnated with an intimate awareness of life, laid down the substratum in which the unique individuality of Kashmiri people is firmly rooted, notwithstanding the catastrophic social upheavals which many a time brought the people to the verge of annihilation. He was one of the few poets who enjoyed tremendous popularity and reverence even during his life-time and whose works were preserved with admiration and adoration, so much so that Kashmiri Muslims often call his poetry "Keesur Quran" (Quran in Kashmiri). Similarly, Kashmiri Hindus' devotion to the great saint-poet is amply revealed by his title Sahzanand (one who has attained the ultimate truth).

Nund Rishi's eminence can be appreciated with reference to the moment and the milieu; all the constraints, conflicts, hopes, and disillusionments of the age are faithfully reflected in full depth and colour in it. Although the whole of the experiential content of his poetry is subdued to the mood of the dominant message that man's existence in this world is nothing but a short spell of forgetfulness or a continuous falling into the abyss and that it can be rendered meaningful and worth living only by an acute consciousness of the fall and by a conscious effort for redemption, his poetry at the same time reveals the hopes and joys of simple living and also the villainies of the exploiters and bigots who masqueraded as the defenders of virtue.

**The Rebel Against Rooted Customs**

He was very senscture to bigotry. He rebelled against unquestioned loyalty to custom and, in a quizzical manner, castigated the "mullas" and "gurus" of the time for their hypocrisy, peacockishness, vainglory and vacuity:

> Gather the food of oblation and glut to your fill,
> go to mooch and wander from door to door;
> when the hen of the Mulla ate the grains got free;
> it too crowed when people were going to bed.
>
> Gorgeous are the temple-tassels of the mullas' caps
> what a vainglorious and puffed gait they walk,
> wearing embroidered shoes and wreaths,
> bearing their begging-bowls under their arms!

He abhorred religious intolerance, exclusiveness, the politics of hatred and fanaticism that was threatening to disintegrate the social fabric.

> All men are scions of the same parents,
> why then, O God, you taught them hatred?
> May all Musalmans and Hindus
> Learn to love their God.

**Nund Ryosh and his Ideas**

His simple but revolutionary ideas of human brotherhood and love were immediately popular among the masses and thus posed a threat to the politics of division and exclusion. A contemporary historian, Jone Raj, refers to Nund Rishi's arrest during Sultan Ali Shah's rule:

> The greatest teacher among the Muslims is Molvi Noor-ud- Din. He was arrested for being a rebel.

It may be reiterated that Nund Ryosh was popular among Muslims by the name of Noor-ud-Din, and there is no other person of that period known by this name.

He was born in a weaver's family in the village of Kaimuh in 1377. His father, Salar Sanz or Salar-ud-Din after his conversion, had married a widow from village Khih (near Kulgam) after having lost his first wife who had given him two sons, Shush and Gandur. The chroniclers have related his pedigree to the ruling Sanz family of Kishtawar, both on the side of his father and on that of his mother. There is a long poem of unknown authorship about the pedigree of Nund Ryosh, with Nund Ryosh as the narrator. Nund, meaning "beautiful" was later on named Noor-ud-Din when he attained enlightenment after a long period of renunciation and self-mortification.

**The Saint Poet**

He was married and had a son and a daughter, but he could not shoulder the responsibilities of his family life and so devoted his life to the service of suffering mankind. There are many legends about the intrigues of the bigots and the feudal lords to try his continence by luring him to sensual pleasures, but they failed in every ploy. Even the charming dancer Yaavan Mets had to abandon her lascivious vocation and become a true disciple of the saint-poet. It was his popularity that drew the reverend preacher of Islam from Iran, Mir Muhammad Hamadani, to visit him at Tsar where he resided and, being deeply impressed by his thought, awarded him the famous Khati Irshad, a pronouncement wherein the saint-poet was designated as "Alamdari Kashmir", the Standard-Bearer of Kashmir.

Nund visited every nook and corner of the valley and established a number of institutions of Rishism which were run by his disciples, namely, Baba Nasar-ud-Din of Tsar, Baba Bam-ud-Din of Bomzoo, Baba Zain-ud-Din of Aish Mauqam, Baba Noor-ud-Din of Water Hel, Shama Bibi of Poshkar, Bahat Dyad of Zolus, and Shangi Bibi of Vitsarnag. The shrines of all these saints are still visited by Kashmiris in large numbers. The pilgrim's journey ended in 1438 when he was sojourning in the upland of Rahkay (near the town Tsar) under the shadow of a *brimij* tree. His body was taken to Tsar where it was laid to rest with full state honours; the funeral was attended by Prince Shahi Khan, later known as Sultan Zainul Aabidin Badshah.

**The Popularity is in Tact**

Nund Ryosh is the only Kashmiri poet whose popularity and respect has remained unabated both among the plebs and the court circles, throughout the centuries and, even now he is the most respected name in Kashmir. He is the only poet whose name figured on a coin issued by Ata Muhammad Khan in 1809. His death was mourned by several poets in beautiful elegies, and a number of *manqabats* or eulogies have been written on him. Sheikh Noor-ud-Din wrote short poems, usually quatrains, commonly known as *shruk* or pithy wise sayings, each expressing one kernel idea or concept of mysticism and the philosophy of plain living. A *shruk* is clustered around one image, mostly pastoral and agrarian, subdued to the mood of the message. In its form and prosody it is not different from the *vakh* but for the lexical items borrowed from Persian. He also composed lyrical poems which are predominantly didactic, nevertheless with the strength of metaphor. His verses are often quizzical, castigating the absurdities of individual disposition and disturbing the established notions about human nature. He exposes man's pretentions and the erratic ways of the world, silhouetted against the unfathomable void of death. The undercurrent of humour and irony, however, attenuates the bitterness and awe. Here is an allegory of man in the world:

> The fiery and wild flames of the world,
> a pomegranate bloom, I hankered for;
> Satan set my load of rushes on fire,
> I, a thief, lost my way to cross the river.

**Redemption of Man**

He envisions man's being-in-the-world as an inexorable falling into a fathomless abyss and the meaning of living as a continuous groping in the dark in search of a support for his redemption.

Underneath your feet is the abyss, and you dance;
tell me, my dear, what keeps you lax,
You leave behind all that you collect,
how then do you, relish and digest your food?

Some of his verses are faithful adaptations of the verses of the Quran. He also versified various religious obligations in a language easy to consign to memory.

Nund Ryosh was the precursor of the *sufi* tradition of Kashmiri poetry which reached its ripeness in the 19th century. Sufism of Islamic mysticism had much in agreement with Shaivism and the native cult of asceticism, known as *ryesut* which preached self-abnegation and a severe abstemious way of living. His death was mourned by his disciples and a few elegies of that period have come down to us through oral tradition. The events of his life and various anecdotes related to him have been recorded by a number of scholars and historians in successive centuries, and a large number of copies transcribed on old home-made Kashmiri paper are still available in various private and public libraries. The most authentic of these biographical narratives, commonly known as *nurnamas* and *rishinamas,* are: *risinamas amber* (MS 1808), *Nurnama* by Nasib-ud-Din Ghazi (MS 1621), *Nurnama* by Baba Kamal (1785) and *Nurnama* by Baba Khalil (MS 17th century).

Nund Ryosh had several female disciples like Shange Bibi, Bahat Dyad and Shama Bibi. There is a tantalizing fragment of an elegy on the death of the saint-poet by Shama Bibi : It is a prognant discriptioni of the saint poet:

Nunda Sanz has left for the empyrean,
our Nund Sanz is rapt in the empyrean;
Nunda was the only true Rishi,
we shall now see him in our native abode,
how and where shall I find him in this alien world?
His cloak, pattens, and wand are left here.
Can anybody attain in a thousand years
what he attained in his life-time?
No other rishi looked as graceful as he did;
O Rishi, your maid-disciples are wailing for you;
I find you always near, close to my bosom;
the evening has set in and how shall I reach you?
Nund Sanzhas left for the empyrean.

The fairly elaborate musical setting of such an elegiac lyric indicates that the tradition of lyrical poetry in Kashmiri had by that time attained maturity, and the refrain was accepted as a formal constraint which could guide as well as restrain the poet's emotion. The 15th century lyrics reveal a good amount of variety of didactic, devotional, mystic, and anecdotal poetry.

**Nund Ryosh's Life as other Poets Saw**

A number of anonymous poets have treated in dramatic fashion various incidents in Nund Ryosh's life and various miracles have been ascribed to him. The poets have written various forms of colloquies between the saint and other and scholars and also his kins to evoke sorrow and admiration for the saint's abjuration of his intimate relations and worldly pleasures when he renounced the world to embrace the suffering of reclusion. Most of these biographical poems unevil him as a sequestered hermit absorbed in passive meditation, oblivious the active role he played in the social, cultural and political life of the time.

**Baba Nasar-ud-Din**

Baba Nasar-ud-Din was the life-long companion of Nund Ryosh who, as the legend goes, carried him piggyback in a canebasket when he was decrepit in his old age. Nasar's quatrains, though only a few, are full of poetic wisdom and remarkable for succinctness:

These very arms and these very legs,
provide you with what you ask them for,
when these limbs are finally wearied,
who is there to ask for and who is there to give?

He died in 1451 and was buried at Tsar beside his preceptor. There is a long dialogue in verse of unknown authorship extant, in which Nund Ryosh is shown in conversation with a learned brahmin of the time, namely, Bum Saad. The poem reveals to the modern reader how pliant and viable the *vakh* form was for the expression of imaginative flights as well as for discursive argumentation, made savoury and lively by the skilful use of alliteration and other sound patterns.

Fire makes the sky fanciful;
tell me how many days are there?
How many worlds did He populate?
What is the number of constellations?

**Respite from Religious Descord**

Shahi Khan, who ascended the throne in 1419 and assumed the title Sultan Zainul Aabidin, ruled for over fifty years and gave the people a long respite from arson, plunder and religious discord. Peace and prosperity forged a feeling of well-being among the commonality who also began to partake in constructive activities.

Peace and prosperiting brought in its wake leisurely class of scholars, poets, and chroniclers also appeared who wrote in various classical styles in Persian, the official language. Several works were translated from Persian into Sanskrit and vice versa. The contemporary historian, Srivara, wrote in his *Rajtarangini:*

*Rajtarangini*

"Learning, like the kalpa plant, shot into many branches, thrived by means of scholarship, and bore heavenly fruits. There was not a branch of learning or arts or literature or fine arts which did not become celebrated in the world during the reign of King Srijaina....Holding that a man can receive instruction only in the language which he knows, and not in other languages, the king caused translation of various Shastras to be made by those who knew Samskrita, the vernaculars, and Persian. Even Yavanas can comprehend mineralogy, chemistry, and *kalpa* if studied in their own language. The king caused *Dasavatara* and *Rajtarangini,* the book of kings, in the Samskrita language, to be rendered into Persian. In the same way the *melecchas* read the *Vrihatkathasara,* the *samhita,* the *puranas,* and other books in their own language."

**Sultan the Poet**

The Sultan was a great scholar, he had command over several languages. There is a macaronic lyric in manuscript form ascribed to him, which contains one couplet in Kashmiri too:

The slender waist and delicate body are the passion's garden, and pleasure's foliage, the simplicity of fancy: the majestic height is a pillar to the zenith and the basis of the nadir.

Zainal Aabidin's pen-name was Qutab. He died in 1474.

Avtar Bat's *Banasur a vada Katha* is the only extant complete composition of the period. The poem, narrative in nature, is hardly intelligible to a common reader because the poet wrote it for the elite and gentry and not for the unschooled commonage, called *melecchas* by the high-brow scholars. The long poem is a lyrical rendering of the amorous affair of Banasur's daughter, Usha and Krishna's son, Anirudh, as the story occurs in the *Harvans purana.* Avatar Bat's adroit use of fresh imagery with a local colour is commendable, but his strict adherence to the stylistic contrivances popular in Sanskrit makes the poem extremely difficult for the lay audience. However, the musical beauty of the poem is accessible not even to those who do not grasp the meaning the musical is beauty is very clear:

> Usha, reclined on the cushioned bed, is as bright as the full moon of the month of Vaishakha.
> He enjoys her inmaculate body and as an oriole takes flight
> in the sky after savouring the blossoming bush.

**Zenivilasa**

Avatar Bat also wrote a long poem "Zenivilasa" to highlight and praise the king's efforts for the betterment of his people, but unfortunately no copy of the poem has been traced so far. What we know about the life of Avatar Bat is nothing more than the fact that he lived in Sultan Zainul Aabidin's time at Shalipore of Lar Pargana in Kashmir. He completed his *Banasura vada Katha* in 1446, as stated by him in the poem:

> Zainul Aabidin was the king of Kashmir and he had completed the twenty-sixth year of his rule when the poem was written.

Srivara, the famous historian of the Badshah's period, might possibly have translated Valmiki's *Visist Brahama Darshan* into Kashmiri. He wrote in his *Rajtaranjgini:*

> The king heard me recite the *Visist Brahma Darshana,* composed by Valmiki which is known as the way to salvation; and when he heard the annotations pervaded by feeling of tranquillity, he remembered them even in his dreams even as a lover remembers the gestures of his beloved.

Two are too other names mentioned in Srivara's *Rajtarangini,* who were associated with the court and had got the king's appreciation for having written in the vernacular, also deserve mention. Pandit Athasoma composed a biography of the king and, similarly, Yodh Bat wrote a play, "pure like a mirror", entitled, *Jainaprakasha,* in which he glorified the king for his unflinching efforts for the social, economic, and cultural upliftment of the people. However, the writings of these two authors are not available.

**Pandit Ganga Prasast**

Pandit Ganga Prasast was a reputed poet of the period but the only poem of his now extant is sufficient to reveal his erudition and craft. His long poem, "Muhmaya tsaryath," composed during the years between 1372 and 1384, that is Sultan Hassan Shah's reign, expresses the extraordinary mystic experience of an idealist who is profoundly distressed by social and moral corruption and has failed to convince people of the futility of materialistic strife and man's wilful plunge into the vortex of life, and finally suggests various ways of attaining spiritual elevation by total resignation and detachment. He has discussed several intricacies of astrology, yoga therapy and the *sastaras* while explaining man's condition in the world. The diction is again far-off and misty for the present-day reader:

> His fame makes Indra tremble and the moon wane;
> Hassan Shah in his tender age does his best for the well-being of his people.

The text of the poem *Muhmaya tsaryath* or *Swakh-dwakh muhmayazal tsaryath* is still in its manuscript form. Efforts have been made consistantly to study this poem.

**Beginning of Marsiya**

Shams-ud-Din Iraqi started Shiah system around 1450. It is then that the tradition of veriting elegics on the martyrs of the Karbala were started. The *marsiyas* written in Kashmiri followed the folk-forms of poetry, but they did not show adherence to any prosodic pattern and sacrificed every formal constraint of poetry to the spontaneity and intensity of the sentiment. A number of such *marsiyas* have been preserved by the learned scholars of the Shiah community who always considered them as the most important aspect of the identity of their community. There is hardly anything known for certain about the authors of these texts. Mir Syed Hassan is one of the earliest *marsiya*-writers who used lyricism to aggrandize the rueful and melancholic strain. His diction reflects the true nature of the 14th century Kashmiri, when Persian words pertaining to the matters of faith were finding place in common spoken Kashmiri;

> Lord, you are the giver, you are our home and hearth,
> You alone are beautiful, unsurpassed;
> I am thin air, how can I praise you?
> I, Latif, cannot comprehend your greatness;
> absolve me of all my sins.
> I could not pray five times a day,
> O God, I failed to carry out your command,
> how can I be saved in the world to come?
> Their [the martyrs] love is my sole earning;
> they attained their greatness in their submission,
> eschewed all pleasures and tastes.

Mir. Syed Hassan (Latif) died in 1411.

The *marsiyas*, although in fragments, of other poets are valuable for present day readers and scholars to understand the nature of 14th century Kashmiri. Here is another excerpt:

> Come, you sisters, let us bewail the slain brothers, one by one. Let us go bare-footed to Karbala in the last hour of the night and ask our brothers not to recline there on the roadside, but return home.

**End of Cultural Tradition**

Badshah Zain-ul-Aabidin region was a relatively peaceful era in kashmir. He died in 1474, his death the age of peace and prosperity came to an end; and a long winter for civil war and bloodshed was unleashed by successive treacheries in the court, which left no tradition of culture, art and literature rooted in the soil. A barren era of a hundred years in the history of the people reflects nothing but a passive suffering aided by several devastating natural calamities. Among Badshah's immediate successors, according to Srivara, only Hassan Shah had a penchant for fine arts:The king was versed in Sanskrit verses. but was fond of the vernacular songs...with a sweet voice he sang many high-tuned songs of unparalleled music and in many tunes, to the delight his courtiers and general popular.

Babar already was in ascendency in the plains of north India and he had his designs on kashmir but in power struggle that followed the demise of the king, the Chak dynasty surreptitiously emerged as a rival force to power. The Chaks, who were Dards by origin, remained staunch Shias and managed to beat down their Sunni rivals like Domas and Magres. In 1527, the Mughal emperor Babar invaded Kashmir for the first time, but it was because of the prudence and astuteness of a Chak, namely, Kaji Chak, that the Mughals had to suffer a defeat. He made the Mughals retreat another time in 1528 when they had practically conquered the valley with the help of a few local men of influence. In 1533 Mirza Haider Duglat launched a strong attack on Kashmir, and since the people were effete as a result of a severe famine, he succeeded in vanquishing the valley.

**The Chaks**

After a very short period of subjugation, the Chaks again made him flee the land, but in 1541 Mirza Haider Duglat sought the help from the Mughals and achieved complete success. However, a descendent of Shahmirs Nazuk Shah, was made the ruler to act as a puppet king. He could not, however, ingratiate himself with the Chaks, despite his best efforts, and finally his rag-bag rule tumbled, leaving the throne to his brother Abrahim Shah. He, too, could not withstand the manoeuverings of the Chaks, and finally, the Chaks occupied the throne in 1553 when Ghazi Chak arbitrarily grabbed the crown from the last heir of the Shahmirs, namely Habib Shah, and became the king in all the thirty five year that he ruled he had a constant pressure from the Mughals the Mughals had not given up their efforts on kashmir. The impending danger from the Mughals continued to fuddle his effort to bring peace to the fatigued folks.

**The Literary Observers**

The poets of this long nightmarish period are remembered not as genuine poets of any remarkable talent, but just literary aberration. There is, however, a considerable bulk of lyrical poetry of unknown authorship that represents the ordinary people engaged in various tellurian activities, but who kept walled up in their hearts a thousand modest but unattainable desires which gave colour and savour to their life, otherwise an abomination. The short fragments of secular lyrics, preserved in folk-memory, are gilded with unusual beauty of phrase and simile. They have a magical evocation, combining strong erotic element with mystic visions. They tantalize, particularly when the speaker or the central character of the lyric is a prematurely married girl, truthfully yearning to return to her parental home, and there, reunite with her childhood lover. These lyrics are immortal mainly because of their melisma that is available only to the natives, yet the poignancy and simplicity of passion is perceptible even in translation:

> My golden love, my pearly dear,
> hear me, O hear my plaintive calls;
> you went to frolic in the Raja's yard,
> the princess chose you, you were sold,
> sold you were and noosed on the thread,
> noosed on the thread and worn round the neck,
> worn round the neck, you shine so bright,
> but hear me, O hear my plaintive calls.

These song are written with the consideration of the demands of the 'sufiana' music. There are songs which mainly depend on the play of sounds the professional singers of this particular kind of 'sufi' poetry are generally versed in the unique tunes associated with such songs.

> O friend, what befell my Love? He has been never with me since he left. I shiver like an autumnal leaf. Since then, since then, since then...

**Vatsun**

The suppleness, spontaneity of expression, freedom of pattern and reliance on love-sentiment makes this form of the most popular form of Kashmiri poetry even today. This form of lyric appropriate for folk-songs is the *vatsun,* a native genre without any particular pattern of versification and rhyme-scheme; nevertheless, in most of the *vatsuns* the refrain comes after the third line in each four-line stanza.

There are such lines in this type of folk-poetry as are unsurpassed in their beauty and charm and primordial pathos:

> You are a poppy blooming at the precipice, I cannot endure
> your separation. Come, you take the staff and
> I shall carry a bowl, and we shall gad about freely.

There are stones and broken splinters that way, come this way to me, O sunshine.

## Life Cycles in Song

Kashmiri folk-songs, Birth, childhood, marriage, sowing, harvesting, and various rituals and festivals these are the kashmiri folk. Songs variegated in phrase and sentiment, are associated with the life in action. They reflect the people's repressed propensities, subconscious drives, attitudes to the changing natural phenomena, and the social relations in the medieval ages; the true history of the Kashmiri people is beautifully and most faithfully recorded in the folk-songs of the land.

## Phase III: The Surge of Lyrics: (1550-1700)

Zoon or Habba Khatoon is incontrovertibly the paragon of medieval poetry. She was the beloved queen of Sultan Yousuf Shah Chak. Her poetry is the apotheosis of eroto-mystic lyricism, characterised by the beauty of simplicity, naturalness of passion, mellifluousness, pathos, and rhythm. Her poetry strikes an artistic balance between craft and ease, and the result is that her poetry is simultaneously studied as well as spontaneous. She imbibed the sense of control and adroit rhythm from the classical Persian *ghazal*, popular at the court, but at the same time she did not let technique destroy the fidelity of emotion and expression. The autobiographical element is preponderant in all her songs, which acquire force when read or heard in relation to the pathetic legends shrouding her real person.

## Life of Habba Khatoon

The historians of the 16th century are totally reticent about account of her life. There is more than one account of her life, and one has to depend on the popular legends. The most popular story goes that she was the daughter of one Abidy Rather of Tsandhar and her original name was Zoon. She was married in her tender age to an illiterate rustic, Aziz Lone. One day, while she was culling saffron and singing to herself at an upland of Pampore, Sultan Yousuf Shah, who was on his pleasure saunter, saw her and heard her song. He was bewitched by her beauty and voice, and hence, got her divorced from her husband and made her queen. She got an opportunity to excel in music in the court where there were great masters. But when Yousuf Shah was arrested by Akbar at Delhi, she abandoned everything and loitered aimlessly from village to village. She was buried at Pantchokh, near Srinagar. However, it has been revealed quite recently that when Yousuf Shah was exiled to Bisok in Bihar, he requested the Mughal Emperor to get his beloved wife also there because he was almost mad on account of her separation.

He expressed his pang in the following couplet: In the longing for that paragon of beauty in Kashmir, my two eyes are two lakes of tears like Tarsar and Mansar.

Habba Khatoon was sent to the exiled king and there she was buried beside her husband after her death.

Contrary to this interesting story, there are a few verses scattered in her own poetry which suggest that she was the daughter of a nobleman, Syed-ul-Bahar of Srinagar and that her first lover was one Kamal.

There are hardly a score of her songs available, but one is amazed to observe the variety of themes and patterns of versification in these scanty songs. She sings with such a profound poignance and intensity as make her personal alienation the alienation of all mankind seeking fulfilment in reunion with the Ultimate.

> I am the earth and you are the sky,
> You are the veil to cover the secret;
> I am the dainty and you are the guest,
> Come and possess my pomegranate bloom.
>
> The summer is gradually fading away,
> I fear my amaranths may also wilt;
> Come, O Bulbul, come but now,
> Come and possess my pomegranate bloom.

**Her Poetry**

She here and there communicates obliquely the tidings of the human soul during a creative impulse, giving them "a name and local habitation". The freshness and musical movement of the lyric intact, The mythopoetic element of the following short poem is simply bewitching:

> The elves come down
> to frolic with us;
> the fish of the Wular lake,
> swim up the stream,
> to enjoy the waters of the Sindh,
> but return all thirsting.
>
> The sleepy muses of Indra
> sing within my soul,
> wearied at the spinning wheel.
>
> I got an iota of youth,
> he came to take me back,
> my eyes were half-dreaming.
>
> The fairies of the sky,
> descended to the Kowsar lake,
> to enjoy its fresh water;
> they bathed and flew back.

The bees of the hinterland,
visited the downs of Pampore,
to savour the saffron blossom;
they are tired while gathering nectar.

Habba's friends are wild,
they often keep her vexed;
they are fiercer than fire.

**Childhood in Her Poetry**

Childhood recurs very often in Zoon's poetry. Treatment of the theme however is not of philosophical meditation, as that of the mystic poets generally is; she rather dreamily reconstructs the days of bliss, evoking pathos and an intense sense of loss. She uses quite appropriate melancholic tunes and pensive rhythms that conform to the moments of abandon and rapture of rustic girls engrossed in simple and routine chores. She eschews statements and conclusions; she rather revives the moment with its innate freshness of feeling. The rustic backdrop of her poetry is purely elemental;

Come friends, let us go to cull jasmine,
There is no coming back after death,
I am waiting for my love to come,
O my love, rapt in flowers, come.

Come, friends, let us go to fetch water,
The whole world is in deep slumber,
I am here pining for his word of love,
O my love, rapt in flowers, come.

**The Longing**

There is a quintessential passion to revolt against the medieval restrictions. This is unmistable in her lyrics. The lover in her songs is unmistakably an immaculate virgin who, in defiance to hostile norms, desires a passive surrender and unrestrained reaching out towards her love and this attitude becomes a happy flowering of feminine longing:

Nightly I unlatched the door for you,
　　Hoping you come in a while;
There is no bar and why do you flinch?
　　What has made you scorn me?

The last hour's moon was bright,
He wildly came and possessed me;
Oh, he is pert to behave that way.

Once he met me at my aunt's house,
Decked I was in gold and silver;
It pricked, it pained, oh cruel of him,
All my necklaces were torn asunder.

Zoon chose the language of the commonality which is the only language fit for the lyrics that spring from a transported soul no doubt she was well versel with the customs of court, and its alture and etiquette. Her diction is free from the extraliterary mannerisms of scholarship and is warm with the throb of life. Although she had a smattering of the classical Iranian music, and it is also said that she introduced a new *raga* in the *sufiana* music, called "*rast* Kashmiri", yet she did not give up her rustic idiom. There is a compact pattern of rustic images and words related to village life.

By agreeing to Chak rule (1553-1586) the local lords had tried to bring peace and tranqueliting to kashmir which was ravaged by political turmoils and natural calamities, and that too under the imminent danger of the mighty expansionist Mughal empire. By defying the Mughal coercion and defending their sovereignty, the brave Chaks, particularly Yousuf Shah and Yaquoob Shah, had fostered a sense of self-respect among the Kashmiris who had lost all hope and courage. Nevertheless, the Chaks, too, failed to put an end to the state of anarchy, and when the Shia-Sunni riots brought the whole people to the verge of total annihilation, some very respectable personages solicited Mughal intervention.

**Treaching of Akbar**

Akbar invited Yousuf Shah to Delhi to discuss terms of peace, but there he was arrested; and with the help of formidable force under the command of Mirza Qasim, Akbar finally realised the Mughal designs that had failed several times since the time of Babar. In 1585, though Babur and lotus Humayun had treel their best to suljuate kashmir Yaquoob Shah Chak, the son of Yousuf Shah Chak, was defeated, and thus the Mughal rule in Kashmir started. After Zoon, there is hardly any poet of stature in the vicious years of turbulance and misery. The poets of the period are known merely for some fragments of their devotional lyrics to bridge the gap in the history of Kashmiri literature. Sheikh Daud Khaki (1521-85) was a celebrated scholar and poet in Persian. One solitary devotional lyric in Kashmiri has been attributed to him:

My words fail me to utter my affliction,
O Sheikh Noor-ud-Din, I need your help.

Khwaja Habibullah Nowshehri (1555-1617), perhaps the most esteemed name in *sufiana* music, is known for his devotional lyrics and his unorthodox and eloquent approbation of the redeeming effects of music, which, according to him, seduces man to spiritual transport and divine revelation.

> *Santoor, dahar* and other forms of music,
> which have no place in Islamic legislation,
> are the only assets of an ardent lover,
> let us go to the festival and revel.

The *marsiya* is the only literary form that flourished in the Chak period and several specimens of it have been preserved by various Shia scholars who remained conscious of the significance of their literary heritage. Mir Muhammad Ja'afar, Abdul Hakim Salih, Muhammad Hayat, Baba Muhammad Javid, Khwaja Akbar, Hasy Bat Nadim, Syed Abdullah Shah, Khwaja Abas, Mir Muhammad Ali, Syed Salih Ridwi, and Syed Sharit-ud-Din Ridwi are some of the best known *marsiya* writers of the time, revered and sung till date. But, unfortunately, no booaraply of any of them is found anywhere.

### The Mughal Rule

Before the Mughal anexel kashmir. Style was the order of the day. After it became a part of Mughal empire, the people had a respite from the Shia-Sunni discord and once more the men of imagination began to seek fresh inspiration. The Mughal rule could not elevate the local people from abject misery and could not reassemble their shattered national dignity; nevertheless, the period of peace and tranquility and the Mughals', ceaseless engagement in garden-laying and architecture made the people rather indifferent to their agony and political subjugation. The court became a rendezvous of Persian poets, historians and scholars; a veritable *Iran-i-saghir* (Iran in miniature), but Kashmiri remained relegated to the position of the vernacular of the submerged people.

Meanwhile, in 1698, Khwaja Noor-ud-Din of Bijapur succeeded in taking the Holy Hair of Prophet Muhammad to Kashmir which was housed in a shrine at Hazratbal in Srinagar. This incident of tremendous importance in the history of the people is referred to by Mehmood Gami, a famous Kashmiri poet of the time in the following couplet:

> Kashmir attained honour and glory by the Holy Hair, and is now
> another Madina by virtue of Muhammad's relic.

The advent of the Holy Relic was, besides being a milestone in the socio-political life of the people, a catalyst to accelerate religious zeal which was naturally reflected in Kashmiri literature.

### Sahib Koul

Before dealing with the Islamic devotional and 'sufi' poetry of the 18th century, the present survey needs to mention two important poets of the period who wrote in a different strain; Sahib Koul and Rwapi Dyad, who do not stand in any group. Sahib Koul was born at Habba

Kadal in Srinagar and received sound training in Sanskrit language and literature. His year of birth is not known and it is said that he died in 1676. Many of his works, mostly in Sanskrit, have been preserved, *Kalpa vraksha* and *Shrikastava* in Sanskrit, and *Zanam tsaryath* and *Shrikrisnavatara lila* in Kashmiri are deemed worthy of acclamation. His poetic talent found its full expression in his long lyrical narrative *Shrikrisnavatara lila.* It is an adaptation of the tenth *sakanda* of the Bhagvat Purana in which Lord Krishna's life has been portrayed in melodious and short three-line stanzas, each ending in a devotional refrain. The narrative has been plied with a dance rhythm with the help of musically potent words, and fresh images are drawn from the poet's keen observation and intimate communion with the objective world. The poem done in one metre, shows Sahib Koul's prowess to keep even the extravagance of music subservient to the intoxicating swing of the narrative. For instance, take this stanza from the fifteenth part, "The Rasa Dance" is in itself a revelation :

> The herd-damsels impassionedly followed him;
> forgetting all their chores, they ran;
> they yearned to hug their god of love,
> "posy and posy shall I offer him lotuses".

His 'Zanam tsaryath' is a long metaphysical poem, in which man's journey: from birth to death has been delineated allegorically.

**Rwapi Dyad**

Rwapi Dyad, like her spiritual preceptor Lal Dyad of the 14th century, composed pithy and epigrammatic quatrains, which were easily transmitted to folk memory and thus preserved. She could not achieve complete mastery on the *vakh* form although she tried to imitate fastidiously the style and philosophy of Lal Dyad, whom she adored:

> I seek protection at the feet of goddess Lal.

She sacrificed the beauty of expression and form to message; perhaps she had written this way, or oral tradition perhaps distorted her to quite some extent. Her philosophical resolution of the conflicts and sufferings of life was, within the framework of Kashmir Shaivism, the simultaneity of detachment and purposeful engagement, as well as coordination of the intuitive mind and the rational mind. She offered an avowedly subjective course to be maintained defiantly against the adverse forces of evil. The latent source of bliss within every human being has much to give, provided the seeker remains obstinately engrossed in its contemplation:

> One who undertakes self-scrutiny,
> Scoffs at none, will not be scoffed at;

and remains rapt in Hara's hope,
is sure to encounter one's true self.

Rwapi Dyad, also known as Rwapi Bhavani, was born around 1621 at Safa Kadal in Srinagar. Her father, too, was a reputed scholar. She was married to a thickheaded person, and at her in-laws' she suffered much affliction. She renounced family life and wandered aimlessly. People thronged around her wherever she went, and they called her "Alkeshvari" because she kept her hair loose. She had renounced the world.

She had had a short sojourn at Manigam and then went to Lar where she stayed in a shack built for her by her devotees at thè cool and pleasant stream-side of Shahkwal. Among the eminent people who visited her to seek her blessings, were the famous Persian scholar Sah Sadiq Qalander and the Mughal Sobidar Ali Mardan Khan. She returned to Srinagar in the last phase of her life and died in 1721. Shah Sadiq Qalander wrote the chronogram:

Alak, the avatara and the knower of Truth,
mingled with the elements;
she took a flight to the Empyrean,
for her good heart was close to His mercy.

**Advent of Abdali**

When Ahmed Shah Abdali attacked India, the first region he took control of was kashmir. He installed his first governor in 1752. The Afghan rule which lasted for over seven decades, has been recorded and remembered by Kashmiris as a protracted nightmare, as in misery and despondency it outdid all other periods of peonage. The Afghan rule continued to suppress people's imaginative faculties and creative impulse as there was only one concern, i.e., to keep life going. A few poets, who excelled in Persian, the official language of the masters, wrote casually a few short lyrics in Kashmiri, only to display their skill in using the classical Persian *ghazal* form in their mother-tongue. However, the experiment broadened the horizons of Kashmiri poetry which had remained confined to the rustic folk melisma.

The *ghazal,* apart from its alternate rhyme scheme, is characterised by rigorous loyalty to the classical prosodic norms, depth of thought and feeling, compactness of form, and flexibility to be used for all manner of themes, and, as such, it was a bold departure from the *vatsan* tradition. Nevertheless, the *ghazal* of the period could not be elevated to the perfection of the form for which it is popular. Its couplets could not be used as autonomous units with discrete and context-free images, and akin to the native *vatsan* it remained subservient to music, rather than subduing music to meaning.

**Faqir and Shahabadi**

The first two poets, known to have used the *ghazal* form, are Syed Muhammad Hadi Fakhir and Sa'dullah Shahabadi.

Fakhir (?-1780) was a scholar and *marsiya* writer who got his primary instruction from Ata Ullah Huma. According to Mohi-ud-Din Miskin, the author of the famous history *Tarikhi Kabir,* Fakhir was a prolific writer in Persian and Kashmiri. His idiom is highly Persianised but the flow and music compensate the loss in appeal:

> I saw my love, bedecked full like the shining moon,
> with face shimmering, hair unlocked, rambling in rapture.
> Fakhir, yearning for her cypress-shaped ardent body,
> is crazy with his attire torn from the collar to the hem.

Fakhir is also known for his *na't* which is a distinct form of verse devoted to panegyrising the person of Prophet Muhammed in the most sublime, prim and decorous diction. Fakhir's *na't* is an unstinted encomium for the Holy Prophet. He is the first poet to adopt the popular lays of wedding-songs for the *nat:*

> Your face is my Qibla, your brows are the arches:
> why should not I always bow to you?
> Your visage is glistening and the omen of goodness,
> the bonnie mole is the Black Stone in the Ka'bah
> The avenue to you leads to the Ka'bah:
> Why should not I always bow to you?

Sa'dullah Shahabadi, author of the famous history of Kashmir in Persian, *Bagi Sulaiman,* must have written in Kashmiri quite adroitly and with a conscious purpose and method, but his poetry has not survived. His only *ghazal* amply reveals his proficiency and masterly handling of the message and moral within the scope of poetry.

**Arnyi Maal**

Arnyi Maal, the spouse of a court-poet and dignitary of the Afghan period, namely, Bhawani Das Kachru Niku, is the most popular woman poet after Habba Khatoon Zoon. She was deserted by her husband in the prime of her youth and as such she spent the whole of her remaining life wailing for her lover. Her lyrics have become a part of Kashmiri *sufiana* music and only a few of them have been identified. Her songs are serenely melancholic:

> All for my love have I filled the cups,
> friend, go and call him in;

how unmindfully he scampers like a buck,
I am all prayers for him;
through lush meads and sloping mountains,
friends go and call him in.

Arnyi Maal died in distress in 1800, before her husband realised his folly. It is said that Niku, too, wrote in Kashmiri.

**Other Poets**

Three more names belonging to this period figure in various chronicles: Syed Islam Shah Azad (1818-66) of Khanyar, Srinagar; Jum, a woman-poet who lived near Jama Masjid, Srinagar; and Nund Dar (Kathyhol, Biroh, 1774). Nund Dar must have been a gifted poet as is revealed through his *marsiya,* entitled *Dolikyi sar* because it was sung by the professional singers on the rhythm of a *doliky,* a small drum. It is divided into seven stanzas according to various stages of a complete *marsiya.* The poem, unlike other *marsiyas* of the time, is well integrated according to the unique metre used. The *doliky* has been personified and it relates its story of coming into being, but the narrative becomes an allegory of the whole creation. The poet successfully commands words, images, and music to his intended meaning:

The woodcutter mercilessly felled me down,
he carved my inner substance out,
he skilfully turned me into a drum,
my hollow self began to sound aloud,
I became a victim of Satan's scheme,
thus I was pushed out from my tranquility
brought to the market and put to shame.
Listen to what my word says:
the word is but an ignis fatuus.

The intended meanings of poet come out adrortly in words, the images he weaves and his musie.

One of the seven stanzas is exclusively devoted to lament the assassination of Hazrat Imam Hassan and Hazrat Imam Hussain, the grandchildren of Prophet Muhammed.

**Phase IV: The Rise of the Romances (1750-1850)**

In the later part of the 18th century, there was a group of poets who were as familiar with Persian as with their mother-tongue. It was the result of a long tradition of education in Persian in various Pir and Akhun families, who held education as their monopoly, sharing it with the commoners, with some zeal, only at the level of the recitation of the Holy Quran. They knew and drew on the poetry of Iranian poets, particularly of the classical period. *Mathnavi* was the most important genre that was borrowed from the language of the non-native rulers. It is essentially a narrative form of the long poem written in rhymed couplets; descriptive and exhortative poems written in the couplet form are also included in this genre.

The famous Persian *mathnavi* writers like *Rudaki* (?-952), Farid-ud-Din Attar (?-1229), Maulana Jal-al-ud-Din Rum (1208-73) and Firdausi (?-1020), provided them with the models of *mathnavi,* employed for various subjects, mostly mystic allegories, and courtly love.

**Baba Kamal**

Baba Kamal was one of the first Kashmiri poets to get inspiration from Persian *mathnavi.* Although rhymed couplet was used even before him by Sheikh Nur-ud-Din, Baba Kamal was one of the first few poets to understand the other requirement of the *mathnavi,* that 7is, its thematic progression. He and his contemporaries, to experiment in the genre, also borrowed from Persian the particular metres, especially *bahri hazaj* appropriate for this form of poetry.

Kamal's only *mathnavi* is *Quisa-i-Habhab* or the story of Habhab in which he narrates an incident from Islamic history to show how Islam was accepted by the non-believers in the early period of its development. Kamal has also written a long lyrical narrative poem, *Vafat Nama-i-Anhazrat,* in which the passing away of the Holy Prophet has been mourned. The poem has been very popular for the profundity of grief, exuberance of devotional sentiment and the ease and simplicity of the poetic rendering of the *sirat* (the Holy Prophet's biography). He also wrote short lyrics which sound the from the folk-songs of the time.

Baba Kamal was the custodian of the famous shrine at Tsar, as he has stated it himself:

> The kohl in Kamal's eyes is
> the dust of Nur-ud-Din's door.

He is also famous for writing *Rishi nama* in which he recorded the *vakhs* of Lal Dyad and *shruky* of Sheikh Nur-ud-Din. He died in 1840.

Mir Abdullah Baihaqi found *mathnavis* a convenient medium to write Islamic injunctions and *hadith* (sacred sayings of the Prophet) in the interest of the common people. His two short *mathnavis* are *Aqaid* and *Vaga'i.* Baihaqi lived in Srinagar and died in 1785.

Abidy Pala wrote a short allegorical *mathnavi* in the same period; it bears a chronogram, according to which it was written in 1786.

**Sufi Poetry of Kashmir**

Islamic mysticism found its adequate creative expression in Kashmiri Sufi poetry, which deals with various aspects of *tasawuf,* which developed side by side with Islam as a mystic philosophy deeply influenced by Greek philosophy, Zoroastrianism and even Hindu Vedanta. Sufism, like all other varieties of mysticism affiliated to various religions, is concerned with the kernel concepts of love, which is not an unquestioned passion or infatuation but an individual's ardent desire, based on pure reason, to near God.

The sufis believe that the whole creation is an epiphany, as God has declared the motive of the creation: "I was a hidden treasure and I desired to be known, so that I made the creation that I might be known." The basic sufi teachings had pervaded Kashmiri poetry even in the 14th century, but they found their full expression in the 18th century, under the direct influence of Persian sufi poetry. With its increasing appeal to the masses, sufism was established as an important social force, which emphasised a way of life demanding utmost continence, piety, and asceticism. The sufi leaders and the trained initiates organised themselves into a network of hospice-like institutions called *takyias*, where they imparted into themselves a sort of rigorous training in self-mortification and found refuge and speritial peace

**Muumin Seeb**

The first sufi poet in Kashmiri who started instructing disciples in the *sufi* way of life and the art of poetry, the medium of the sufi ideas was Muumin Seeb. He was born at Byabgam in Pulwom sometime in the fifth decade of the 18th century and died in the early part of the 19th century. Nothing is known about his life except that he was the teacher of some important sufi poets like Swachi Kral, Karam Buland and Mahmud Gami. His main contribution to Kashmiri poetry is his only *mathnavi, Kesur mantig-u ttayyar*, which is an adaptation of the famous Persian classic by Faridu Din Attar. It is an allegorical poem in which all the birds gather round their companion hoopoe, known for his wisdom and foresight, and reveal their pangs to him. All of them have a common yearning, that is, to see the fabulous bird, called Simurg. The hoopoe appreciates their intense longing and leads them in their difficult journey to the abode of the Simurg. The journey has seven stages, viz. desire, love, recognition, absolution, unity, wonder and annihilation.

**The Seckess of the Truth**

The journey was not an easy one. In the excruciatingly trying and perilous journey most of the birds perish and only thirty of them, effete and burned out, succeed in attaining their destination and behold the mysterious Simurg whose effulgence bewilders them. When they come out of their trance, to their amazement they discover the Simurg in their own forms. The poem, thus, ends in a summary statement that the travails met by the birds in their quest for the prototype bird symbolise the painful experience that a seeker of the Truth undergoes in his spiritual journey from the world of illusions to the world of revelation. The poem has its appeal in the imaginary situations and the various interlocutions among the birds about their intensity of desire and the reality of the Simurg. The poem, however, loses much of the possible beauty by the poet's straying out of the familiar landscape and relying on abstract settings without any sense data.

Here is, for instance, the description of the vale of wonder:

> As I entered the sixth valley in the journey,
> A lion I was, but trembled like a jackal;
> only those can understand me who are frozen in wonder,
> the elephant becomes a mosquito with debility;
> one who is drowned in wonder
> is struck with showers of arrows;
> feels always transfixed in a vortex,
> in constant dread of utter wreck;
> whether on the bank or in the river,
> one is oblivious of the river, bank,
> and of one's head and feet.

Muumin's shorter lyrics are full of sermonising, only the musical quality makes them poetry:

> Step from the without into the within,
> there you can anchor your faith;
> there alone you shall behold the magnate;
> what is there that you have attained otherwise.
> Drink your own blood to quench your thirst,
> or burn your blood in the lamp,
> in the light you shall see your friend,
> you have to eat the flesh of your own body.

Swachi Kral, Karam Buland and Shah Gafur are the three important poets who formed a group after Muumin Seeb. Swachi Kral was of course the most original poet who abhorred the shibboleths of sufi poetry and sought concrete images for his mystic concepts; the search resulted in a fresh idiom distinctly different from the hackneyed;

> A magnificent mansion amidst the ocean,
> wherein is seated the emperor,
> there is neither day nor night,
> the world you have is but a phantasm.

Swachi Kral lived at Yinder in Pulwom but later on fled the village for some unknown reason. However, his grave is located near his native village and the epitaph bears his date of death, that is, November 29, 1854. His father, Arif Kral, was a popular poet but only one song ascribed to him has been preserved. Karam Buland lived at Tsivydor in Byiru, but in his youth he migrated to the village Henzgond in Wahthor where he married in the family of the Bands or professional actors of folk-theatre. His songs are popular among peasants who sing them while deweeding their rice-fields. There are serene

allusions to various legends of remote ages which make the toiling peasants unmindful of their fatigue and the summer heat.

> Majnoon was a true lover,
> he tramped through the Najd,
> Laila went there to see him;
> O love, I shall ferret for you among the flowers.

Karam Buland died in or around 1844.

Shah Gafur wrote musical songs which are highly erudite, replete with Islamic and Shaivite allusions not easely found other verses:

> The whole universe came into being, out of what abode?
> Out of "la" (nothing), emerged "ilallah"
> (nothing is without God).
> "myim" (the letter representing Muhammed) and "alif"
> (representing Allah) are inseparable.
> Why should not a lover lay down his life to it?
>
> Seek, Brahma, Vishnu and Maheshvar.
> Your body as well as your soul belong to them;
> you will be nowhere if they are away from you.
> Hence you seek him through your meditation.

Shia-Sunni strife took its toll. Though the *marsiya* flourished in the Chak period, but the bulk of it was destroyed in the Mughal period and also in the Afghan period as many of the repositories of old manuscripts were burnt in the Shia-Sunni quarrels. However, the fragments that have survived amply reveal how the *marsiya* writers chiefly relied upon the language of common speech and employed natural utterances to arouse and stir pathos and grief. Mir Muhammed Ja'far, Abdul Hamid Salih, Muhamed Hayat, Baba Muhammed Javid of Hassanabad, Hasy Bat Nadim of Gund, Syed Salih Ridwi of Haigam, Syed Sharif-ud-Din Ridwi of Ahmadpore, Magam Mirza Jaza Ullah of Rajpore, Mir Muhammed Abas of Vyos, Kugam, Muhammed Aazim of Dob Shadipore, Syed Amir-ud-Din of Daulatabad are some of the names out of the galaxy of *marsiya* writers of the 17th and 18th centuries.

The major portion of the Arab and Iranian legend, myth, and history had reached Kashmir, and had started assaulting local legend myth and history which sank into oblivion. Kashmiris accepted the Arab and Iranian import as their won. Kashmiri literature was, however, enriched by several Persian genres like the *na't, mangabat, jangnama* (heroic stories of battles), *bazmiah mathnavi* (a romantic *mathnavi), ghazal, sarapa* (a poem describing a person cap-a-pie), *qasidah* (a panegyric), *rubaii* a quatrain with a unique metre), and *mustazad* (an incremental poem) which became quite popular with the poets writing in the vernacular. However, the popularity of these non-native genres did not obliterate the old endemic genres like the *vakh, vatsun, lyila* and *tsaryath.* Tasawuf of Islamic mysticism was the preponderant influence and the shaping force of much of Kashmiri poetry hundreds of Sufi terms have got transfused into the language.

## Departure from Tradition

Mahmud Gami in the one poet who well represents this enthusiastic eclecticism and perfection of synthesis. He not only introduced the new forms but also brought them to a state of consummation which his contemporaries and successors wished to attain. His poetry is, on the one hand, the epitome of the lyrical poetry akin to folk-poetry, and on the other hand, a daring but pleasant departure from the worn-out tradition of didactic and instructive poetry. Mahmud is the only poet after Nund Ryosh (Sheikh Noor-ud-Din) whose works have been preserved in a large number of manuscripts, found in all corners of the valley and whose songs have been sung by the best singers of every age as well as by the folks in their moments of merriment or dejection. His greatness was acknowledged in his own life-time by his contemporaries; for instance, Wali Ullah Mattoo:

> Outstanding among the Kashmiris is one name.
> Mahmud Garni, unexcelled in his time,
> I was exhilarated to see him at Shahabad,
> He was the supreme master in his craft.

## Mahmud Gammi

Mahmud, born in 1765 at Arvadir (now Mahmudabad), in a scholarly family and assumed the humble profession of teaching Arabic and Persian. Mahmud had had equal proficiency in Arabic and Persian in his childhood and began composing religious poems like *na't* and *manquibat* in Persian. The legend goes that he started writing in his mother-tongue when his son, S'ah Sultan, died in his tender age; the grief was too profound to know any formal style. However, the opinion is not credible as, according to his own statement, he composed his *mathnavi Sheereen Khusraw* when he was 26, i.e., is in 1785. And an old manuscript reveals that he started writing in Kashmiri with the *na't.*

He was also a good sermoner and achieved much fame in the valley. The snobbish urban Maulvis pejoratively called him "Gami", i.e., a rustic, but he did not feel snubbed by this name and retained it as it rhymed with the great masters of the *na't* in. Persian, viz. Nizami and Jami, who had inspired him. He was famous as a bard, a scholar, a *dervish* and sometimes a prankish philanderer. A number of anecdotes, some of them obscene, are associated with his name, a part of folk-memory.

Mahmud's style is unique in the whole range of eight hundred years' poetry. Mahmud's main output consists of *mathnavis* and love-songs, but his creative urge, inventive zeal and imagination are found uniformly in all types of his poetry. Its force and uniqueness lie in his skillful combination of familiarity and loftiness, but the skill never becomes obtrusively apparent to draw readers' attention to the verbal artifice. Although he consciously follows the foreign models, he relies chiefly on the latent musical potential of everyday speech, and on his own feelings for inspiration; it was his poetic credo.

Mahmud wrote hundreds of lyrics, and many of them are excellent. In all his lyrics, the intensity of feeling springs from his despondent awareness of the vanishing past, the past of his community and the past of his individual being. The individual yearnings, aspirations and deprivations get more intensified when given vent against the background of yore:

Little by little, I shall make a bed of garden basil for him;
I shall wash my body in the water perfumed by saffron, camphor, and musk;
Come, my friend, and sit under the shade of the conopying *chinars*,
Do not leave me to my foes taunts, I am a hapless dame.

Let the oriole go to ask the crow,
Where have gone the men of passion?
To whom shall I reveal my fate's afflictions?
I had a dream in the nether-world,
In the dream, I vanished into a naught,
Then, at the springside, a lightning overtook me.

**Mystic Connotations**

Though he was very inventure Mahmud could not totally escape from the constraints of Kashmiri love poetry; he, too, retained the female voice of the *vatsun*. The effeminate tone and epicene expressions, such as we find in *git* forms of other North Indian languages, perhaps befit the mystic connotations. Human condition is depicted, in all forms of mysticism from pre-Socratic times to the present day, an immanence composed of a single element, that is, the intelligence or the creative principle *(nafas al-Rahman* or the breath of the compassionate in the Quran) and the predicament of the human beings is its alienation from that Essence; it always craves for gnosis through the reunion. The love pervading all the songs of Mahmud is simultaneously the physical love and the mystical longing for the absolute. He is a *sufi* poet, par excellence.

> Out of love, the Lover breathed into the bubble,
> the same breath made the bubble merge with water;
> what then perished and what did abide?
> O the gaysome one, what made you forgetful?

**His Style**

When Mahmud wanted to write a mathnaivs instead of translating the text, he chose a plot of his taste and then employed all his lyrical genius to construct a narrative that he sustained and artfully modulated. His *mathnavis,* generally based on the love-theme, have the scope of interpretation in terms of *wahdat al-wajud* (the doctrine of the unity of being). Mahmud wrote ten *mathnavis,* all the ten are based on Persian models.

His first *mathnavi* is *Shirin Khusrau* (1785). It is an adaptation of an Iranian legend about Khusrau, who gives his heart to Shirin when a friend of his presents a verbal picture of Shirin to him. He is love-sick and, in order to save him, a portrait of Khusrau is kept hanging in Shirin's garden. When she catches sight of the portrait she, too, is swayed by the amorous surge. After much travail, the two lovers get married. But after a short time, Khusrau marries a second time and Shirin is loved by a sculptor, named Farhad. In order to try Farhad's love, he is asked to dig out a runnel of milk out of barren rocks, an ordeal in which Farhad succeeds. Khusrau, being jealous, sends a wrong message to the woebegone Farhad that his beloved is dead. Farhad, unable to bear the shock, strikes his head with his own hammer and kills himself. Khusrau remarries Shirin but to his utter ruin his son from his other spouse falls in love with Shirin and kills him. Shirin too, eventually commits suicide. Notwithstanding the complications in the plot, Mahmud successfully sustains the drift of the narrative. He has used beautiful similes to delineate Shirin's visage and the backdrop of events:

> The mole on the cheek, red as a pomegranate petal,
> is like a black pepper burning in a blaze.
> The darkness is illumined when she smiles.
> Applause is merited by the pearly bands.

**His Unique Style**

Mahmud's second *mathnavi* is Sheikh San'an, which he wrote in his youth and was much circulated in manuscripts, soon after its composition.

The poem, worked out in a unique metre of six syllables, is based on a story from Farid-ud-Din Attar's *Mantig-u-ttayar.* A reverend saint of the Iranian city Balakh Sheikh San'an dreams, prostrating before an icon. In order to know the implications of the dream, he sets out to Rome where he falls in love with a princess of the land, who happens to be a fire-worshipper. After much affliction, he prays for absolution and ruefully returns to his country. But the princess of Rome also hankers after him and moves to Balakh, where the two get wedded.

*Yusuf-Zulaikha* is most popular mathnavi of Mahmud which is based on the 11th *sura* of the *Quran* which has been called *Ahsan al-qasas,* that is, the most beautiful of all stories. The poet was also stimulated to write the *mathnavi* after reading Jami's (1414-93) Persian version. Aziz Ullah Hqani (1864-1927) has acknowledged the fact in his tribute to Mahmud that work remain unexcelled. The theme has been dealt with name other poets but none came at par with Mahmud's and mathnavi.

Karl Freidrich Burkhard, the famous orientalist, was moved by the poem and he translated it into German and published it along with the original text. Not too far back, Kashmiri women deemed it to be their virtue to memorise the whole poem and sing it on occasions of festivity. The popularity of the poem lies in Mahmud's subtle treatment of human relations, deep pathos, quaint pastoral setting, simple language, but above all the flexibility of metre, varying according to the dominant emotion of the situations. The mellow songs interspersed in the poem also considerably add to its charm. The smooth flow is also enlivened by various interlocutions and ironic treatments. The landscape is indeterminate, but made quite familiar and plausible:

> For the whole day he shall ramble about at the hill-side,
> and make posies of highland-flowers,
> he shall remain savouring, as much as he likes,
> goat's milk, butter and ghee.

**No Sermons on Morality**

Mahmud has conveyed the essential part of the original story and has avoided unnecessary digressions and moralising. The handsome son of Yoqoob, namely, Yousuf, dreams the sun and stars descending from the spheres to lie at his feet. The dream, narrated by him to his father, is interpretted as a prognostication of his attaining the status of a prophet. His step-brothers become jealous, they take him on a picnic and, in the wilderness, throw him into an abyss. They tell their father that Yousuf was devoured by wolves. However, a band of merchants rescue Yousuf and take him to their land where he is sold to the king of Egypt, Aziz. The young wife of Aziz, Zulaikha, who had dreamed of him, recognises him. Having given her heart to him, she entices him to have carnal intimacy with her. As Yousuf does not succumb to her voluptuous escapades, the truant wife gets angry and complains to her husband that Yousuf tried to molest her. Yousuf is arrested and tortured. After some time, Yousuf pleases Aziz by interpreting a dream he has had and is freed. Meanwhile, he happens to see one of his step-brothers who informs him that their father has lost his sight. Yousuf sends one of his garments to his father, by the touch of which his sight is restored. His step-brothers feel remorse and call Yousuf back. Zulaikha's husband dies and she is married to Yousuf. The story ends with Yousuf's death and Zulaikha's lament. The elegy on the death of Yousuf is certainly the best elegy in Kashmiri.

*Lel-Majnum* is yet another famous long poem of Mahmud. It is a lyrical adaptation of Nizami's Persian poem. Mahmud not only abridged it but also gave it a new cultural context by placing the character and events against the background of Kashmiri customs and rituals. Instead of using the monotonous couplet form, he contrived the narrative in *waniwun,* the popular form of marriage songs and in *vatsuns*. The poem is unique for its ingenious form and ingenuous expression. The poem is still very popular among the professional folk-singers.

Mahmud's other shorter narrative poems are: *Harun Rashid, Yak Hikayat, Pompiry Nami, Mansur Nami'* and *Pehely Nami*, which are rich in poetry and Sufi thought, but could not gain much popularity. Mahmud established *mathnavi* firmly as a distinct genre in Kashmiri and set forth models for the poets to come Mahmud died in 1855.

Among the poets who started writing before the close of the 18th century are: Baba Khalil, Pir Ali Sah, Walli Ullah Mot, Zarif Sah, and Aziz Khan.

**Baba Khalil**

Baba Khalil is mainly famous for writing a *Nur Nama* in Persian, his contribution to Kashmiri poetry is his only *mathnavi,* entitled *Qisa-i-Hazrat Sam'un*. The poem is based on an anecdote from Islamic history and is written mainly to castigate women for their frailty. The poet's misogyny finds vituperous expression in several couplets. The poem lacks originality of ideas and imagination, and there is hardly any merit in the use of words. Baba Khalil was one of the disciples of Baba Nasib-ud-Din Ghazi and lived at Chivdora.

Pir Ali Shah also lived at Chivdora. He is the author of one of the most popular *mathnavis in* Kashmiri *Kadij Nama*. Although biographical in nature, the poem is a brilliant poetical exercise in combining facts with imagination and merging grief with devotion. Originally aimed at writing an elegy on the death of Hazrat Khadija, the poem deals with the most crucial stage in Prophet Muhammad's life. Hazrat Khadija, who had married twice before her marriage with the Holy Prophet, has had far-reaching influence on the latter's life and as such on the whole history of Islam.

Pir Ali Shah quite ably, and that too within the ambit of poetry, depicts the harmonious relations between the Holy Prophet and Hazrat Khadija for over twenty-five years, though she was fifteen years senior to him.

The Pir's primary intention in the *mathnavi* is to portray a woman who is a paragon of all virtues and noble disposition and for this primary motive, he chose a language which is mellifluous, made more appealing by the devotional songs in the style of marriage lays, interspersed in the text. The Holy Prophet's love as an affectionate husband and Khadijah's response guided by virtue and piety, all is admirably captured by the poet. Pir Ali Shah was the grandson of a much revered saint, Hazrat Syed Simnani, and remained associated with the circle of the disciples of Baba Nasib-ud-Din Ghazi. He went on a pilgrimage to Mecca in 1858, and died soon after his return. His shrine at hivdora is the centre of an annual festival.

**Wali Ullah Mot**

Wali Ullah Mot is famous for his *mathnavi, Himal Negyray* which is based on a native myth about the tragic love-story of Himal, a rustic dame of Balapore, and Negyray, the serpent-prince of the netherworld. The poem derives its force and efficacy from the engrossing myth which can be interpreted in more than one way: in psychological terms as the relationship between the id and the ego; in anthropological terms as the reconciliation between the Naga aborigines of the valley and the Dard Aryans from the Central Asia; and at the aesthetic level as the relationship between illusion and reality.

The poet has succeeded in sustaining the dream like mise-en-scene for the supernatural characters and events to seem probable. A village Pandit, vexed by his peevish wife, reclines at a river-bank and, keeping his bag under his pillow, has a sweet snooze. On awakening, he stretches and decides to return home. When he bends to lift his bag, he is awe-struck to find a big serpent coiled inside the bag. He soon overcomes his dread and closes the mouth of the bag, and with an evil design to get his wicked wife bitten by the serpent, sets out for his home. When he is home, he call's his wife and asks her to find a gift for her in the bag. He goes out and shuts the door to be sure that he gets rid of his wife. After a while, he re-enters the room.

**Negyray, the Prince**

He is bewildered to see a handsome lad conversing with his wife. The lad tells them that he is Negyray, the prince of *Talpatal* (the netherworld). The Pandit couple, who had craved for years to have a son, adopt Negyray as their son. Negyray grows into a charming youth, secretly marries a serpent-princess of Talpatal, but does not forsake the Pandit and his wife. One day while rambling solitarily, he meets a country dame, named Himal. She at once falls in love with him and Negyray is also captivated by the charm of Himal. Negyray forgets everything about his past, marries Himal. They live a peaceful life at Balipur (Shopian).

Negyray's first wife somehow comes to know about her hushand's infidelity. She comes over to Himal and informs her about Negyray's serpent-character and about their marriage. Himal does not believe in the story, but the serpent-princess asks her to prepare a puddle of milk and urge Negyray to have a dip in it. Himal does all that she has been asked to do, and despite Negyray's entreaties, she compels him to plunge into the puddle of milk. As soon as he steps into the puddle, he disappears and reaches Talpatal, where he is reunited with his first wife. The rueful Himal seeks the help of a hermit and manages to reach Talpatal and ferrets out her lover. They are reconciled, but when Negyray's serpent-consort knows about it, rivalry starts. Himal gets Negyray's two serpent-sons killed, and in requital, she too is bitten to death. Negyray, being much agonised, takes her carcass to the upper world, and knowing that art of resurrecting, keeps it hanging on a tree. After forty days she comes back to life.

A trader living nearby descries her there and falls in love with her. On his entreaties, she promises to espouse him but after forty days, as she expects her serpent-lover to come back to her. The trader waits for forty days, and when the stipulated time expires, he goes to her chamber where he is stunned to see her in deep slumber and a big serpent is coiled round her waist. He at once takes out his sword and dismembers the body of the snake. Himal wakes up and is almost petrified to see the gory scene. She at last requests the trader to prepare a pyre for the slain Negyray. The pyre is made and ignited and when it is all aflame, Himal, in her utter agony, abruptly plunges into the blaze and is reunited with her lover in the form of ashes.

Wali Ullah also translated two Persian *mathnavis*: *Cahal Israr Ran Zaruriyati Din* of Hazrat Amir Kabir, but no copy of the two works is available. Besides the three *mathnavis,* he wrote several mystic songs and *na'ts.*

Wali Ullah lived at Wuhan in Badgam and died in 1858 at Madina while on his pilgrimage.

Aziz Khan was Wali Ullah Mot's teacher and his name will figure in the literary history of the language for his two beautiful songs that have been incorporated in Wali Ullah Mot's Himal Negyray. Perhaps the rest of his poetry has not survived; otherwise he would have been one of the major poets in Kashmiri. Wali Ullah Mot writes about him:

> Aziz Ullah Khan was a bird of love,
> his verses could kindle our soul.

Zarif Shah, too, is associated with Wali Ullah Mot for writing twenty-three songs for *Himal Negyray,* and was senior to him. He lived at Safapore and died in 1866. He used to visit Ponch region annually and died while crossing the mountains. He was quite proficient in writing *na't* in the *wanwun* or marriage song style. Some of his songs are found scattered here and there in old manuscripts. Wali Ullah Mot has eulogised him and has acknowledged him as one of his teachers.

The tradition founded by the above-mentioned poets flourished in the 19th century in all directions and several major poets, like Maqbool Sah Kralarari (1802-77), Maqbool Amritsary Prakas Bat Kurygemy (?-1875), Rasul Mir (1860-1890) and Parmanand (1794-1879) contributed significantly to Kashmiri literature as the well-built literary language was now available to them. Their literary output, mainly in the genres of *mathnavi, vatsan, ghazal* and *lila,* became the most esteemed literary heritage of the Kashmiri people.

## Kashmiri Prose

Kashmiri prose could not, however, be unfolded to meet the diverse demands of Kashmiri writers, or we may say that Kashmiri writers did not feel the need to use it because their demands were not so diverse. Persian, Sanskrit and later on Urdu remained the languages of the court, religious institutions and the government offices.

Throughout the medieval period, all the biographies, chronicles, and religious books continued to be written in the non-native languages, either for the prestige motive or for the sense of inferiority forged by the persistent non-native rule. An oral tradition of Kashmiri prose was, nevertheless, always there, particularly in various forms of homilies which had developed a variety of styles and was transferred from generation to generation of the men of the pulpit, as they could not use any other language to have intimate rapport with the illiterate plebs.

## Regidity of Style

The styles of all the sermons remained rigid as all the *muftis* and *vazkhans* always prefer to deliver the sermons in their original form to sound more authentic. No attempt has been made to collect and record this live tradition of Kashmiri prose. A few scanty manuscripts of various sermons are, however, still traceable.

It goes to the credit of the *marsiya* writers to have used poetic prose, although fixed in style, to mourn the death of the martyrs of the Karbala. They painstakingly preserved their heritage, and luckily a large number of such manuscripts are extent in various learned Shia families. Since the tradition of these MSS goes beyond the 14th century, they are of much importance to the philologists as well as literary historians.

The prose used in these *marsiyas* is monochromatic, unidirectional and highly charged with intense feelings of the same tenor. The alliteration and rhyme-words play an important role in their structure which obeys the norms of *nadb* (an encomium for the dead), *daqiq* (abstruse prose) and *muqaffa* (rhymed prose). The ornately florid alliterative prose, embellished with hackneyed similes and apostrophes is consistently found in all these *marsiyas* of the known writers as well as in the apocryphal ones. The *marsiyas* of various periods have already been dealt with, although cursorily in the preceding survey.

**Folk-Drama**

*Pethir* one more dependable access to the prose literature of the medieval age is the folk-drama, known as *bandi pethir.* A body of such farcical plays had been preserved through oral tradition. Some of these plays are *Vatal Pethir* scavengers' drama), *Buhiry Pethir* (grocer' drama), *Gwaseny Pethir* (hermits' drama), *Razi Pethir* (the kings' drama) and *Dirzi Pethir* (the Dards' drama). The professional practitioners of the drama considered it an anathema to deviate from the original style of the play acquired by one generation of them from the preceding generation. A clue to the origin of these plays is found in the *Vatal Pethir:*

> Fool: Hey, when has your drama come?
>
> Chief Vatal: O my life to you ! Harsh Dev was the king, Warsh Dev was his minister, Abihor was his fool and Dayi Dyut was the chief actor.

The dialogue clearly indicates the 14th century origin of the drama; Raja Harsh ruled in the early years of the 14th century. All these *pethirs* are essentially bawdy pantomimes aimed at castigating the targets for their incongruities, and provoking a mirth of the simplest and elementary nature. In a burlesque manner, the characters, highly exaggerated, are drawn from the ranks as well as the sundry professionals.

**The Style**

The *pethir* works through clowning, buffoonery, lampoon, and wild dances. The *pethir is* made more interesting by the intermittent songs supported by *swarnay* (Sahnai) and *dol* (drum). It is an open stage drama in which sometimes the spectators also partake. Some words are deliberately distorted; the physical actions are exaggerated, the situations are absurd, the jokes are stale and the scenes end in surprises and disclosures: all is aimed at provoking hee-haws and making the men of rank and respect ludicrously hapless. The *pethir* was in fact people's protest against oppression and, at the same time, a sort of defence mechanism of the submerged populace to provide them with momentary respite from the tyranny of the alien rulers and, in a way, avenge them for their implacable atrocities. In some of the *pethirs,* for instance, *Buhiry pethir,* the foibles and vices of common people are also unveiled. The *pethir* was, therefore, an unsophisticated medium of education, which taught through laughter. Kashmiri folk-theatre has been a strong fabric of Kashmiri culture which helped its continuity through the ages.

Kashmiri folk-tales remained consistent in their style and were repeated in their origional form from generation to generation—the ultimate distinctive characteristic of creative literature it was like folk-theatre *italic/band pethir*. Though it is not possible to determine the date of their composition, it is safe to believe that the tales represent the form of the language that it assumed after the 14th century when Persian lexical items filled a large number of slots in the lexis of Kashmiri and also replaced a large number of words of Sanskritic origin.

## The Story Teller

The adept narrator of the tales, called *delviligor* (the story-teller), was usually a professional entertainer, who displayed his art, especially during the dull wintry season of total inertness. When invited to a feast, he would come along with his apprentices, carrying the stringed instrument *sarang* and a *not* or pitcher and recite tales to beguile the long and bleak winter nights. Some of these folk-tales, in their untarnished style, were collected and published for the first time by Aurel Stein (1862-1943) under the title *Hatim's Tales*, as the narrator's name was Hatim Tilwony. These tales surely represent the prose literature of the medieval period.

## The Tradition of Kashmiri Literature

Thought the traditions of Kashmiri literature were established before 1800, these were finally accepted by the writers of the 19th century who expanded them and also carried them to the verge of flatulence and, in some aspects, turgidity and pleonasm. The themes of courtly love: battles, meaninglessness of worldly life, craving for reunion with the nonchalant beloved, and delineation of love's beauty, became obsessions with poets and fixtures in the 19th century poetry. Only those poets could attain success who struggled against these time-worn cliches. It was really very difficult for the creative writers to come out of the overwhelming influence of the major writers of the 18th century, particularly Mahmud Gami.

# 5
# Medieval Dogri Literature

## Geographical Background

The landman called Duggar spreads over the Himalayan and Shivalik ranges and covers some slices of the Indo-Gangetic plain in the south between the Jhelum and the Yamuna rivers. It is the land of mountains and mists in the higher ranges of freshwater streams, grassy meadows in the lower hills and of arid to fertile soil in the plains. Politically it lies between Kashmir beyond the Banihal Pass and the Punjab and embraces the Jammu region of the Jammu and Kashmir State, Himachal Pradesh up to Sirmur, some part of northern Punjab, i.e. district of Hoshiarpur, Gurdaspur (India) and Sialkot, Gujarat and Jhelum in Pakistan.

The deep rivers and seasonal streams have broken impregnable rocks and created deep ridges. Geologists, geographers, anthropologists and historians have stated that the early man settled here and lived in caves along with his gods.

## Mother Goddess

The early tribal society practised matriarchy and the image of the creator of this world was attributed to the divine female, the mother-goddess or *mata.* Mother-goddess still dwells in the deep caves right upon the high mountains, whether it is the Vaishno Mata near Jammu or the Pingala-Mata in district Udhampur. There are many temples of the female duty spread over Himachal Pradeh also. Many such caves lie in upper Shivaliks and there is a lot of literature created in praise of Mother-goddess during the era when man was a food-gatherer. Later when man became a food-producer and started hunting and domesticating animals, Mother-goddess was offered sacrifice of animals outside the cave on the top of hillocks, and thus Mother-goddess came out of the cave. There are songs known as *karakas* in Dogri folk literature which testify to this phenomenon.

## Emergence of Male God

At a later stage patriarchy took over the concept of a male-god emerged. We now find Shiva-Shankara-Ruddra or Luddra in Dogri, who had also once dwelt in the caves of Shiva-Khoshi in Riasi (Udhampur district) of Sumerta area. Village Sharada (Sararh) of Kathua district, has also a deep cave of Lord Shiva.

Later it is believed Ruddra-Mahadeva left this cave and came to dwell on the snow-topped high snowcapped peak of Mani-Mahesha in the Chamba district of Himachal Pradesh. When snow melts in the rainy season, in the day of Shravana Purnima, pilgrims from all over Duggar visit it. Many such peaks are situated in the Himalayas all over Duggar. Besides Shakti and Shiva worship, tree worship also started side by side.

**Nature Worship**

Even in the present age, there is tree worship in Duggar. Peepal and Amala trees are worshipped and special *yajnas* are performed. Tulasi is a sacred plant grown in every Dogra Brahmin family. It is watered daily and a special festival is held *Tulasi Vivah* (marriage of Tulasi) on Probodhani Ekadashi which generally falls in the month of October. Then came Naga-worship which is prevalent to this day in the interior region.

According to Naga mythology, Basuki or Vasuki Naga had nine sons and few daughters. There are two types of wood-carved temples in Duggar, the Naga gods and Nagins (female Naga gods) and Naga images at waterfounts, springs, tanks, etc. Many of the nine Naga gods generally have their abodes in deep water, where people go to worship on different occasions or festivals. Some communities perform the hair-shaving ceremony of their male children at such places and they consider some Naga gods as their family deity.

**Bherha-Indra Fight**

At the advent of the Aryans there were clashes between the Nagas and the Aryans. Bhairha (Bherha) Naga fought a war with Lord Indra. At a later stage Bhairha had driven Aryan King Sudasa of Bharata tribe to go across the Yamuna river, but afterwards he was allowed by Bhairha Naga to enter the area around the Parushani (Ravi) river. During the battle of 'Ten Kings' on the stream of Parushani river, Bharata king Sudasa was promised help by Bhairha Naga, but Bhairha Naga forces were destroyed by Lord Indra by creating a storm.

Dogra traditions tell us that afterward there was no clash between Naga tribes and Aryan tribes and Aryans adopted Naga worship and Brahmins got priesthood in the performance of Naga worship.

At a later stage Nagas were dominated by another clan led by Gugga Chohan (Cohan) who is also called Raja Mandlik. There are *karakas* of Raja Mandlik and also 'bars' in Dogri and other languages about his exploits. It is said by some scholars that, after the advent of Gujjars in the Punjab, the Naga clans were driven to the hilly areas and the people changed their castes. They are nowadays found among goldsmiths, tailors, dyers and weavers, etc.

We find small Gujjar principalities in some parts of Himalayas and Shivaliks up to the end of 10th century and a few in the beginning of the 11th century. The kingdoms of Gujjars were shattered by Yamani-Turks—Gaznavies and later by Gouries. Khaljis swept away all Gujjar kingdoms at the end of the 13th century.

**Emergence of Shaka Dynasty**

During the 7th century B.C., Shakas had entered the Himalayas. Two clans of Shakas, i.e. Anasi (according to Chinese) and Kashas (Khasas of Dogri) had already settled before the advent of Kushanas in the early 1st century A.D. Thakkassr or Takkars had also their settlements between the Himalayas and the upper Shivaliks, who are said to have given to the Dogri language its new script, i.e. Takari. Kashas were successful in establishing their small principalities in the valley of 'Anasa' (Chinese Ananasi), a tributary of Chandra Bhaga and had their influence up to Manavar Tawi of Rajouri, which was attacked by the Tughlaqs in early 14th century. These people are nowadays found in the Himalayas and they worship Naga gods, Shiva-Shakti, Varuna and even Lord Vishnu. In the meantime Rajputs too entered Duggar, i.e. in Kandi belt and Shivalik hill between the 10th and 11th century and established their small principalities.

**The Islamic Attacks**

In early 11th century, Katoch Rajputs of Nagarkote-Kangrha were weakened by the raids of Mahmud Gaznavi, but Chamba principality was flourishing. A general of Chamba, a legendary warrior, Raja Bhadra Deva attacked small principalities in the south-west of Chamba. Bhairhla, a town in the mid-Himalayas, was captured and named Bhadrawah. He swept all the small principalities of the remaining Gujjars called Ranas and established his kingdom of Bandhralta (modern Ramnagar of district Udhampur), which remained up to early 19th century. With the advent of Bandhralas and their capital at Bandhralta the cult of Natha-Pantha started flourishing, which created a new trend in Dogri literature.

Mohammad Gouri was a very shrewd warrior. He defeated the Turks by allying himself with Raja Vijya Deva of Jammu in 1181, after establishing a fortress in Sialkot (ancient Sakala of Madrad Desh, a Dogra town). During this period Muslim Sufis from Kashmir and Punjab visited Duggar too and the impact of Sufism on Dogri *bars* started.

A warrior clan called Khokhar or Gakkharh, is said to have killed Muhammad Gouri in 1206. In 1221 Jalal-ud-Din Mongabarni, the last Shah of Khwarazm or Khiva, was driven to Punjab by Chingez Khan and sought asylum in the dominions of Iltutmish, but he was refused. The Shah-

Mangabarni entered into an alliance with the Khokhars, defeated Nasir-ud-Din Qubacha of Muttan, raided Sindh and northern Gujarat and went away to Persia. Up to the period of the Tughlaqs, the Khokhars had established themselves in the Shivaliks and had their capital in Talwarha on the western bank of Chandra-Bhaga in modern Riasi of district Udhampur. Tilak Chand or Raja Tilak Khokhar was once heard of rebelling against the central rule of Muhammad-bin-Tughlaq and was forced to abdicate in favour of his son. But the Khokhars grew powerful during the period of Firoz Shah Tughlaq.

**Invasion by Timur**

In 1398 Amir Timur invaded India. He found Jasarath Khokhar to be a full-fledged master of the Shivaliks from Jhelum to Sirmur occupying Lahore, and had erected many forts in the Shivaliks, the famous one was in modern Ramkote of Kathua district on Dhar-Udhampur Road, where there was a clash with the armies of Timur in 1399.

After the death of Amir Timur, Jasarath Khokhar again became powerful and kept even Punjab in his grip for some time. The Khokhars remained a terror for Delhi Sultanate. Bahlal Lodhi succeeded in dominating them. Later they helped the Mughals in 1526, but they were divided and Islam Shah Sur crushed them and demolished their forts in the Shivaliks, and drove them across the Jhelum. Khokhars had their influence for about two centuries in Duggar. Our folk literature does not say more about the Khokhars, though their impact upon Dogra culture cannot be forgotten. However there is a Dogri *mantra* which tells us about the death of Jasarath.

**Skirmishes and Alignments**

Duggar remained independent, but divided into small states, some fighting one another, and some aligning themselves against Mughals who had established their power in India by 1526. In the 18th century we find a mention of two important Rajas of Duggar, i.e. Raja Ranjit Deva of Jammu and Raja Sansar Chand of Kangarha. There were other Rajas like those of Guler and Nurpur, Chamba and Basohli, Mandi, Bilaspur and Kullu in Himachal Pradesh and Bandhralta, Bhaderwah and Kishtwarh in Jammu region. Some of them patronised talent, be it in literature or painting, and also valour on the battlefield. The Paharhi school of painting developed in the courts of some of these Rajas. Some of them had encouraged scholarship. These States were twenty-two in number; eleven were to the east of Ravi river and eleven to the west of it; they have been referred to as the "Panjab Hill States" by historians.

**Dogri Language**

This is a brief historical survey of the land of Dogras, which we knew through our cultural and religious traditions. As the area remained scattered and under small principalities, a systematic history has not been written yet. The language of Duggar is Dogri. The first reference to Duggar as a land is found in the writings of Baba Farid, a Sufi saint, and the first reference to Dogri language is found in the Nuh-Sipehr, a *mathnavi* of Amir Khusru-Dehlavi in the early 13th century. We have an earlier instance of 1168-69, i.e., Chamba's specimen of Dogri language carved on the stone of a water-spring. Most of the linguists try to prove the development of modern Indian languages through a zig-zag process of struggle in which Sanskrit plays a major role.

After long years of research the Dogri scholars have created a formula for such a development through Sanskrit, Prakrit, and Apabhramsha, and very easily they prove the development of any language in India applying this formula.

**Development of Dogri**

In the development of Dogri language our Dogra scholars too apply the same formula and very easily try to pull Dogri language towards Sanskrit. They take the root of Dogri language towards Shourseni Prakrit, filling the gap of Apahbramsha with the supposition of Duggarha or Duggada Apabhramsha, which has never appeared in the history of Dogri language.

The development of a language is not that simple. There is the influence of other Prakrits in Dogri. Paishachi and Pali Prakrits have also influenced Dogri, even Dogri pronouns. Dogri language is very ancient and it has its own history of development. It was the language of some tribes who dwelt in the Shivalik Valley. They may be Naga people or some other aboriginal tribes. They were brave people and could not be cowed down by the Aryans. In the Indo-Gangetic plains, the Aryans were successful in sweeping out the local tribes and drove them towards the south, and there might be the domination of Vedic 'Sanskrit' over the remnants, but so far as the Himalayas and the Shivalik belt are concerned, the local tribes gave Aryans a tough fight. They could never be driven out and thus they kept their culture alive and even influenced the newcomers in the Indo-Gangetic plains, who developed trade relations with them.

**Words, Syntax and Grammar**

Dogri language has its own system of sounds. It has adopted the sounds of other languages, but after adding a slight change to them, thus the number of sounds in it went on increasing and at present there are 84 to 86 sounds in Dogri language. In this way Dogri has piled a lot of vocabulary and it is moving towards a new development. There is a lot of syncopation in it. We see two or three words joined together making a new single word, but here the word shrinks too, keeping the time factor in consideration.

When the sound system, words and syntax have separate rules the grammar also is different. The system of *karakas* (cases) is a bit different and the number of *karakas* is a bit larger than in Hindi and Sanskrit. In syntax the *karaka* is changed according to the agreement of gender (as in Hindi) but also of number (unlike Hindi). Along with suffix and prefix, there is infix too in Dogri, which we can find only in the Munda group of language in India.

Whenever a *karaka* joins with a noun or pronoun or even with an adjective, it mixes and mingles so deep, that the *karaka* loses its own shape. Sometimes the vowel sound of a *karaka* remains behind. It is owing to the special nature of syncopation in Dogri. The kinds of noun in Dogri are seven (as in Persian and unlike Hindi). The shades of pronouns can be transformed to noun, adjective and verb. The syntactic system in Dogri too is slightly different. Owing to syncopation, the absorption of the *karaka* in the noun make the sentence too short. Owing to nasalization, there is agreement between the helping verb and the noun.

**Use of Negative**

Whenever a negative is used in a sentence, the helping verb, which comes at the end of the sentence as in Hindi and Punjabi, mixes with the negative at the initial stage and never comes at the end of the sentence. Moreover Dogri seems to be a tonal language. In Dogri we find Semitic and Hemitic influences in some cases, when there is aspiration in dental consonants, i.e., 't' changes into 'th'. For instance 'Bharata' is 'Paratha' in Dogri. Sometimes 'a' indicates feminine gender while 'a' or 'aa' indicates masculine gender.

The area of Dogri is very vast and so there are many dialects in it. Mainly there are two dialects: one spoken in Kangarha and other in Jammu. The Jammu dialect has been so much influenced by Panjabi, that George A. Grierson had mistaken Jammu Dogri as a dialect of Panjabi, while he named central Dogri of Shivalik as Paharhi and separated it from Jammu town. An now the literature of 1100 to 1800 belongs mostly to Kangarha dialect of the Shivalik Valley.

It has two scripts—one is Dogre, or old Dogri script, and the other is Jakari. The latter is used in Chamba Himachal Pradesh while Dogre or old script is used in the vast area of Jammu and Kashmir. Old records are found in both the scripts. Dogre has its own character and differs from Devanagari, which is syllabic, while Jakari is alphabetic, like Roman script. Occasionally Devanagari was also used and Persian script too. At present Devanagari is used for Dogri. In the University, colleges and schools, Persian script is also allowed though it is now not that much in vogue.

**Dogri Literature**

Although Dogri was the official language in Duggar and the Dogra kings corresponded with each other in Dogri in the 17th century, there was no development of a literary tradition in Dogri under their patronage. On the other hand, a multi-lingual literary tradition came into being. Sanskrit being used as the language for serious scholarly writing on Dharma-Shastras, *jyotish,* medicine, etc. Braj Bhasha was used for literary compositions of *kavya* type and Dogri for light compositions like songs, *bhajans,* etc. even panegyrics and verse narratives of valour, the exploits of heroes like *Bar* of Gugga. No serious efforts have been made to preserve and catalogue this literary heritage. Dogri compositions in particular became part of the rich folklore—numerous varieties of songs, *bars, karakas.* A rich repertoire of folk-literature—folk songs, folktales, riddles, proverbs also developed. There were no names tagged to the composers or writers. It is also not possible to arrange individual pieces in a chronological order at this stage.

## Religious and Secular Literature

There are two types of literature in Dogri—religious and secular—Religious literature can be divided and brought under various sects and religions. For example, there are *mantras* created by Siddhas and Natha Jogis, which go up from the 7th to 15th century in Duggar. These *mantras* are preserved by the Jogi and Sarsali sects, which have been kept just like Shruti-Sahitya. The language and sounds are very old, which are not prevalent in Dogri today.

These *mantras* were learnt by heart and passed on from one generation to another. These were treated as most sacred and secret by the Jogis and Sarsalis and they do not tell them to the members of the other families, lest they should become impure and lose their power. The *mantras* of the Siddhas are of one kind. Their language sounds vulgar but they have a symbolic meaning. These are used for releasing a person from a ghost or vampire, etc. The *mantras* of the Jogis, who adopted Islam, are of another kind. They have some Islamic tint and are generally used to release a person from the clutches of a ghost, vampire, etc.

All these *mantras* are found in free verse and only a few are in metre. These are in praise of a god or goddess, whether Naga god, Shakti goddess, Lord Indra or some Natha Guru. The poetry is very rich and beautiful and very lyrical when set to music.

### *Karakas*

*Karakas* are songs sung in praise of some god or goddess. It is a very old genre of Dogri poetry, marked by rhyme and rhythm. It is sung to the accompaniment of a drum. Every god has his own *karaka* and it is preserved by the Gardis, a special caste of Jogis who beat the drum and sing.

Gods have been put in three categories Naga-Devata, Jogi-Devata and Shaheed-Devatal. All these *devatas* are further divided into male and female. Shaheed-Devata is one who is considered martyr after death and has a *dehari* or small temple erected for him. The language of the *karakas* is very flexible and it has been changed during the passage of time by the singers, but the theme is there and it has some historical information in it.

A Dogri poet considers his Mother-goddess as supreme and all the gods are in her service. The moon, the sun, Lord Indra, the Param-Jote and Vayu (the god of wind) are serving his Mother-goddess. The Dogri poet has his own conception of the universe and the earth created by Mother-goddess. She emerges carrying *pial-loka,* arrives in *mash-loka* and then the world is created. For in-stance,

> *Pial-Loka* stands on your head,
> And then you arrive in *Mash-Loka.*
> Arrives in *Mash-Loka,* my mother,
> And the world got created.

There are countless *karakas* in Dogri language in praise of Basuki-Naga and his nine sons, but the *karaka* consecrated to Bhairha Naga has special poetic beauty and carries historical information, as already discussed. Moreover it has resemblance with the Rig Vedic *mantra* in which Lord Indra attacked Bhairha Naga, creating such storm and thunder when he was going to help Bharata King Sudasa against an alliance of ten kings on the bank of the Ravi.

**Jammu and Himachal Karaka**

There are also *karakas* of Raja Mandlik or Gugga Chohan. The Dogri version of the *karaka* sung in Himachal Pradesh is a bit lengthier than the version sung in Jammu. These *karakas* tell us about the hostility of the Naga clan against Raja Mandlik, who killed all the Nagas and became the supreme power. There are *karakas* of Shaheed-Devata in every part of the Dogri region. The *karaka* of Baba Jitto and Bua Bhagan relates the tale of exploitation of the peasantry by the feudal lords and the resistance of the peasantry against feudal lords. There are many versions of the *karaka* of Baba Jitto, and these have a rich poetic beauty, where *karuna rasa* prevails in the entire work.

***Bar***

*Bars* are songs of *vir rasa,* sung in praise of the chivalry of a warrior. Though Raja Mandlik is a *devata* yet there is a *bar* in his praise in Himachal Pradesh. Dogri *bars* have been composed in praise of kings during the period of Turko-Afghan invasions, in which they fought. Some *bars* are also found in praise of Sufi peers in Dogri. As *karakas* are sung by *Gardis, bars* are sung by *darehs,* generally Muslims.

### *Bhakh*

*Bhakh* is a very beautiful and charming genre in Dogri literature as well as Dogri music. These are in free verse, as well as in *chhandas.* Love lyrics are also sung in *bhakh* style. At least six singers can perform a *bhakh* and every singer has a particular part to play in the performance of a *bhakh.* The art of performing a *bhakh* is very difficult and subtle, as it employs Dogri classical music.

The exact meaning of *bhakh* has been a matter of discussion among modern Dogra scholars. When a man stands atop the Shivalik or a Himalayan peak, he would be captivated by the beauty of snow-clad mountains in the north and the charming sounds of the flow of the rivers, while in the south a plain created by these rivers by their struggle for millions of years, looks beautiful in the silvery mist during the day time. His voice reacts when it smashes against the hills and creates an echo, a charming sound called *bhakh* in Dogri; a particular kind of music in Dogri. In Dogri, *bhakh* means a quick reply, reaction, or echo. The sound waves created by *bhakh* travel in all directions, but are stopped by the rivers and high mountains and thus, it is limited to an area. The *bhakhs* differ from area to area. There are dozens of *bhakhs* between Chandra Bhaga and Ravi in the Himalayan range and in the Shivalik and Kandi areas. Any poem or song can be sung in all the *bhakhs,* but the charm of each is different.

### *Ceetrhu (Gitrhu) or Lyrics*

These songs are saturated with romantic feelings and are generally sung to the accompaniment of a small drum called *dholak.* These can be used for dance too. There are thousands of such songs which tell us the tale of the past. There are longer poems too, which relate some romantic tale or other rich in poetic characteristics. *Kunju-Chenchlo, Glimoo, Roohlan Di Koohl, Channa,* etc. are famous love tales created by our anonymous poets.

Many types of lyrics are sung at the time of marriage. These are of two kinds: those for the bride and for the bride groom, called *suhag* and *ghorhi* respectively. Musically these are of two types; some are sung like *bhakh* in which no instrument is used and others are sung alongwith drum and a pebble. Such *bhakhs* are called single *bhakhs,* having a single round or twist in it and are generally sung in towns by old women, but village matrimonial (*bhakhs ghorhis* and *suhags*) are general *bhakhs* sung by women in the classical manner.

Besides long, medium and short *bhakhs,* there are *trorhakas* in Dogri lyrical poetry, which are sung just like *bhakhs,* but its note is broken once during its performance for a second's jerk-like pause and then started again and thus its duration is very lengthy, say up to the completion of a *bhakh*. These are in rhyme or *chhandas* and even in free verse.

### Variety of Song

There are also children's songs, play songs, festival songs, harvesting songs of the peasantry songs for the plantation of paddy, songs for the weeding of maize and paddy, songs for the husking of rice or even for carrying of load, i.e. dragging a log of wood or other heavy objects, or carrying of palanquins. For every occasion there are particular songs in Duggar, be it the funeral procession of an old man or woman, for the festival of Navratras, for the doll-wedding of children, festival of Lohri celebrated on the 29th of Posha in Vikrami era, i.e. 13 January.

### Lohri Songs

*Lohri* songs are of two types—of girls and boys. There are many such songs, which have preserved old language and phraseology, now incomprehensible. For instance, there is a *lohri* song sung by male children which refers to an attack on Delhi by some raider, who later looted and ran back. In this song, one child leads singing a full line while others respond saying *herani*. The meaning of *herani* is not known; or perhaps it means *Heirani* (O, Queen) and it is used in many other songs as a response by the group of children. Village folks say that the meaning of *herani* is *hei-hirani* or she-deer while deer songs are sung at night during the *Lohri* festival in the villages. Here are some songs of male children.

### Herani

A dagger for cutting, brothers,
A dagger for cutting.
*Herani*
Murderers had come.
*Herani.*
They had shot nine hundred arrows.
*Herani.*
I begged for one arrow.
*Herani.*
I told the name of my elder brother.
*Herani.*
Elder brother was a *begari* labourer.
*Herani.*
While the younger one was a horse rider.
*Herani.*
First fort was in front of Dilli.
*Herani.*

First attack was on Bhadro 9th.
*Herani.*
The first attack was torn.
*Herani.*
And took the sheet of cloth and escaped.
*Herani.*

There is an other *Lohri* song where the children respond saying *'herani'*.

Multicoloured brothers.
Multicoloured.
*Herani.*
The trousers of an old woman was hung on a Simbal tree.
*Herani.*
Ghuggu Rana was also on the Simbal tree.
*Herani.*
Sounded the Chhajja in front of the old woman.
*Herani.*
In front of Chhajja were Jattu and Pattu.
*Herani.*
Jattu and Pattu were burnt (alive).
*Herani.*
Mother-cow helped in getting *Mukti.*
*Herani.*

This song tells us about a scene after a battle where Ghuggu Rana, a Gujjar chieftain, was hanged on a Simbal tree. Women were raped and their trousers were flung on the same tree of Simbal, which is a tall tree. A drum-like sound was created on the *Chhajja* in front of the old women. Two men, Jattu and Pattu, were burnt alive. When a group of children don't get any reward from a house after singing the *Lohri* songs, they sing this song standing at a distance in a teasing manner. They are generally chased away or beaten by the housewives. This song is considered vulgar.

**Bhakti: The Religious Trend**

The religious texts, have come down by word of mouth and appear to belong to the period prior to 1800. These embrace *karakas* in praise of Naga Devatas, different forms of Shakti as enshrined in palaces like Vaishno Devi, Jawalamukhi, and the *mantras* of Natha Pantha preserved in the families of Jogis. A chain of such *mantras* recited by a Sarsali (a caste among the Jogis), expert in stopping or diverting rain or hailstorm is recorded here:

(i) Move, move,
O, cloud,
The chariot of Indra;
The god of rain.
Move like
The hurling speed of a potter's wheel,
Water in the streams,
Milk in the cows.
And you move,
O Chariot cloud,
With the *sat* of Sita,
With the confidence and control of mind of Lachhman, the Jati.
With the energy and
Power of Hanuman,
Move, O, You,
With the arrow of Bheron
Shouts and roars,
Afterwards be raised.
O Chariot cloud
Leave my boundary,
Leave my sin.
And go to basin.
Leave destroying corn,
And eat *banasa*
Climb upon the hillocks,
Make Dham-Dham.
Wet and soft.
Bhagti of mine.
The power of the gurus
The word of Ishwara Mahandeva.
The water moves down the neck.
And,
May Hanuman raise a shout,
Victory to God,
Victory to Mother-Goddess.
Victory to Mahandeva,
Victory to Parvati, the Mother,
Victory to Ganapati Ganesha.
Victory to the Cow, the Mother.

There is another chain of *mantras*, which refers to the name of three Nath-gurus. In the previous *mantra*, there is no mention of any Natha Guru of Siddha, except for the word 'Guru'. Let us examine this chain too:

**(ii)** Rose in the lower belt,
A good fine *badali*
*Jagis* caught it.
And threw it on the mountain high,
Trident of Beli,
Trident of Kenthar-Natha
Chambe-Natha in the shape of Maya
Agnakund, Bhoot-Patal,
Roaring Dakani,
Let Guru Gorakh Nathani save us.

**(iii)** The sky roars.
Making a hurling sound.
The Sarasali roars
Down the sky. On the earth.
Who created Sarsal ?
Who earned it?
God created. Gorakh earned it.
Chandika in the right hand,
Daggar in the left hand.
My dagger is very fast and brisk.
Some iron smith has made it:
Made it in seven blazes of fire.
Made it on the first Sunday of the month.
Sarsal started uttering Gorakh-Kundali,
A dark and dusky shower has arrived,
A peacock has swallowed it,
Whose thorn,
What it acts. Whose it eats. Yellow roof
Hanuman is sitting on the yellow roof.
And Hanuman roars and shouts.

This is now the standard literature in Dogri. There are other *karakas* which have been composed for certain Jogis.

***Sufism***: During the medieval period, particularly in the 14th and 15th centuries Duggar saw the influx of a number of Sufi saints, called *peers* locally. When they expired *'peer khanas'* were established on their graves, which Hindus and Muslims visited as their devotees. Lands were donated to such *peerkhanas* by the local rajas. In some places wrestling matches were organised in the name of certain *peers*. Some *karakas* and *bars* were composed celebrating these *peers*. Besides *karakas* and *bars*, there are also *mantras* lying with Muslim Jogis and Fakir. Fakir is a sort of sect among Muslims like Jogi. They use such *mantras* to cure people suffering from various diseases and pains. Those who cure people with the help of the *mantras* are called *parhina* by both Hindus and Muslims. Such *mantras* are called *kalami.* The language of such *mantras* is very tough and in many cases quite incomprehensible. There is no mention of any *sufi* or *peer* in such *mantras,* but in the end there is a mention of some prophet, like Suleiman or Fatima. A *mantra* of this type runs as follows:

Orha Kakorha,
Flinch the tooth of entire Daines.
Our nailed does not injure:
And Jati would take it with him.
If it goes ahead,
I shall nail ahead.
If it goes back,
I shall nail back.
If it goes right side,
I shall nail right side.
If it goes left side,
I shall nail left side.
After nailing I shall control it.
If it attacks.
It would blast and die.
The tree of *ak.*
The branch of him,
O Jogan,
Let your birth be in the third *patal.*
Let Suleiman be sought.

**Bajigir**

Bajigirs a nomadic tribe, who are mostly Muslims use this *mantra.* The word 'Orha-Kakorha' which is incomprehensible here is used by a nomad Hindu tribe called Kouru, who hunt snakes, lizards, mongoose and foxes. Kakorha or Kakorhi is the name of a Naga god and also of a snake.

***Rama Bhakti and Krishna Bhakti***

Such types of bhakti is not traceable in Dogri poetry up to the end of the 17th century, but Ramayana, Mahabharata, and *Krishan Lila* are found in Dogri folktales too, though the version varies from place to place. In the poetic form *Ramaini* (Rameni) and *Pandveni* are used in rituals by some sects of Natha-Pantha, who call themselves Bhagats. These people are called Megha and are superior among all the Harijan castes. Though themselves Harijans (in Jammu and Kashmir) they worship all gods and icons with full purity like Brahmans and they consider all Harijans untouchables. These people are the remnants of Naga and these people have their resemblance with the Meghas of Meghalaya or Tripura State, whom R.C. Majumdar considers the remnants of Nagas.

People in Duggar perform a *yajna* called *gusettana*, i.e. Goushedana which is a non-Aryan *yajna*. In this *yajna*, cow sacrifice was heard, but with the passage of time, in *gusettana* a symbol of an animal (perhaps cow) is made of corn flour called *Kodra* and sweet *bagani*, a drink is made of it to be served in the *yajna* is maintained. The *yajna* is performed at night and the recitation of devotional songs goes on all night along with special old-type musical instruments. The head-priest is an old man called *Guru* or *Gora*. He initiates the recitation, called *masadhe*, with a *bhajan* and then starts telling the tales of these epics in verse and prose. Other religious tales regarding Natha-Pantha are also told in this way. Thus *Rameni* and *Pandveni* are sung which are from Ramayana and Mahabharata.

### Influence of Bhakti Movement

The reform movement of Bhagat Kabir had a great deal of influence and there are hundreds of couplets like *dohas* and *kundalis* in Dogri which have become proverbs for daily use.

### Chivalry in Dogri Literature

The Dogras remained professional fighters and thus there has been much literature which tells us of their valour. In Dogri there remained a tradition of composing *bars* in praise of certain heroes. In Himachal Pradesh the *bar* of Raja Mandlik is very famous and later the *bars* were composed and sung by *darehs* in praise of feudal lords. There are many *bars* in praise of Jasarotia kings and Jumoval kings. Here is an extract of a *bar* in praise of Bandhrals, who had established their kingdom Bandhralta in Jammu region in 1020 A.D. which is now Ramnagar town in Udhampur District.

### Samana Banj

The boundary of Bandhrals.
They have killed Mankotias
And their widows are weeping
Please give me my *guddanu*,
To dig *talda* to eat.

Here in this couplet the poet is relating the plight of Mankotia kings after their defeat at the hands of Bandhrals and the condition became so bad that there was nothing to eat and thus wild roots had become the food of the royal servants.

Manak Chand (1565) was a court poet of Raja of Kangarha, who had written a chivalrous poem in praise of Raja Rup Chand (1360-88) of Nagarkote Kangarha. The poem is only of four lines, yet it tells us about the chivalry of Raja Rup Chand.

Later, Gambhir Rai (1650), a court poet of the Raja of Nurpur, a small hill-state during the period of Jehangir, wrote a *bar* in praise of Raja Jagat Singh.

**Romance in Dogri Literature**

The folk songers of Dogri have preserved the tradition of Bhakh and Geetrhu. This poetry was never down but was handed eraly generation to generation.

**(i)** The waist of Malatu is so slim,
That it is a bean of *karangal* tree
I sit and watch in the front,
And you climb on the hilly track
The snake bites in the month of May-June,
And the venom spreads.
Who may treat you my dear?
Who may uproot the herb?
Your husband treats you, my dear,
And your brother-in-law uproots the herb
The waist of Malatu is so slim....

**(ii)** In the shade of the mango tree,
In the shade of the parapet,
Your name may be carved,
We shall leave and depart.
You would remain behind.
And you would repent.
But O my dear sparrow,
The time shall never come back in our hands.

**(iii)** My moon rose on the hillock of Rajauri.
O dear, be a bird and meet clandestinely.
How shall we meet, O my dear life,
There is much lovesickness, my dear life.
My moon rose on the hillock of Riasi,
Much lovesickness is there, my life, and much pensiveness.
My moon rose on the temples of Jammu,
The lips laugh, yet the mind shivers inside.
My moon rose on the Chhownies of Jammu,
We shall depart, O my life and the memory of our sweet talk will remain.

O dear, I embroider a complex flower on the white sheet.
Your promise was for four days, but it is now the thirteenth month.

There are many lyrics in Dogri in which we find naked descriptions of romance, but the folk-singers sing such songs freely.

Besides these we find many other sorts of songs in Dogri. Elegies have been composed on the death of kings. Humorous and satirical poems have also been found. Moreover, there are anti-untouchability satirical songs in Dogri. For instance:

O Pandit, think before drinking the water,
The tortoise and the crocodile give birth in water.
Where does their placenta go?

## Prose Writings

Dogri prose that has passed into Dogri folk literature consists of numerous folk-tales. About two dozen collections of these tales have been published. And surely some of the tales must have been composed by some people well before the 19th century. The tales of Natha-Pantha are very interesting, which have not yet been collected. In the process of narration they must have undergone changes. It is not possible to assign to them any authorship or any date. Not much effort has been made to locate old texts. *Ekadashi Mahatam,* a book in Deva-Shesha script, has been found in a temple of Hoshiarpur (Punjab) by a Panjabi scholar, who deemed it a book in old Panjabi, which is purely Dogri language. This book belongs to the 12th century.

## *Rajavali Rajouli*

An important text that has been discovered is *Rajavali* or *Rajouli,* a translation of a Persian work of Vanmali Das Mukhlispuri alias Bali Ram Gosain, written during the period of Shah Jahan of Delhi. It was translated around 1785-87 into Dogri by Tehal Das, who was in the service of Raja Dhian Singh of Kotla. It is a beautiful specimen of 18th century prose in Dogri. The translation is so well done by Tehal Das, that it looks like an original work in Dogri. His selection of words and phrases is admirable. Though he remained a Braj-bhasha poet, as a few couplets in Braj-bhasha are found with *Mangala-Charan* of *Rajavali.* If however he needed any Persian or Sanskrit word, he fully used his knack of its *Dogrikaran,* i.e. the transformation of foreign words into Dogri.

## Dogri Poetry from 1100-1800: An Overview

This is a period of upheaval throughout India, as, the Central Asian tribals were continuously raiding the country. There were such raids up to the advent of the British. There are said to be four phases in Indian literature, Vir Gatha Kal, the Bhakti Kal, Riti Kal, i.e. age of Romanticism, and the age of patriotism. In Dogri we have these types but the periods are a little different. We find Bhakti, Vir Gatha, Romanticism and anti-feudalist trends. Duggar never remained directly under the British and feudal oppression was great, so we have some *karakas* of Baba Jitto and Bua Bhagan and other lyrical poetry, which we can consider anti-feudalist. In the other parts of India, feudal oppression was the same and there might be anti-feudalist literature, which critics have not yet analysed. Roughly in Dogri we divide these phases according to the availability of the literature, whether in oral or in written form. Dogri scholars and critics are of opinion, that "till very recent times Dogra land has had a multiple literary tradition with Sanskrit as the language of scholarship-treatise on Shastras, Jyotish, etc., Braj-bhasha for literary creation like *kavyas*, e.g. Datt Kavi, Tehal Das, Kanshi Ram and others and Dogri for light diversion and emotional expression, which did not get recorded and was appropriated by Dogri folk tradition—folk songs, *gathas*, etc.

It is impossible to determine their authorship and chronology. Richness of folk literature but, as we have already discussed, of these trealise Dogri folk-literature is a rich treasure-house. The Dogri poets never left any event unnoticed or unrecorded. There are lengthy versions of Dogri *karakas* and *bars,* which our folks have preserved. It requires hard toil to ascertain their authorship and date. Vedas too have been picked up and recorded in the 14th century by Sayan and Madhav. In this selection there are some specimens of the literature of Natha-Jogis in Duggar. The poem "The Jogans" is a *mantra* composed by a Jogi who seems to be a disciple of Guru Balak Nath, in whose period he lived. The language used is of an area which is between District Chamba of Himachal Pradesh and the Kathua and Doda districts of Jammu.

"The Chariot Cloud" seems to be composed in the area of Bhandhratta kingdom beyond Upper Shivalik, as its language consists of words of this area along with a few words of Pothohari, which might be used in the 14th century and preserved in Shivalik area and some places bearing such names. The period assigned to it is after the death of Jasarath Khokhar.

The first recorded poem of four lines is considered to have been written by Manak Chand (1565), a court poet of the Raja of Kangarha in praise of Raja Rup Chand of Kangarha (1360-88). Gambhir Rai, a court poet of Raja of Nurpur, Himachal Pradesh (1650) composed a *bar* in praise of Raja Jagat Singh. Gambhir Chand was a poet of Bhaderwahi whose work in a few lines is available and has been published.

The other recorded poems were composed by the Queen of Raja of Guler (Himachal Pradesh), Vikram Singh (1662-75). One is in praise of Raja Vikram Singh and the other is in praise of the Queen, Rani Durga

Devi. There is a *bhakh* song composed after the death of Raja Hari Dev of Jammu (1650-86) which is very popular among Dogri folk-singers.

**Influence of Lord Krishna through Poetry**

Then comes the turn of Maya Das (1720-1802), Raghbir Das and Sham Das, devotees of Lord Krishna. Maya Das went to Uttar Pradesh to learn the art of *Ras-Lila* and played *Krishna-Lila.* His longer poem *Baran-Mah* (twelve months) is also very famous, where the poet narrates Ramayana, but at present only passages for eight months are available. Raghbir Das, a disciple of Maya Das, used to daily write a poem in Dogri but we could have only two devotional songs of his. We could not discover any of Sham Das, the disciple of Raghbir Das, and hence the grand disciple of Maya Das.

When Maya Das was composing devotional songs, his contemporary Dattu or Datta Kavi or Devi Ditta in the countryside (1723-1811) was writing lyrics in Dogri. He was born in Bhaddu, a small state of Bhadwal Rajput and served in the patronage of Bhaddu as well as Basohli state, both are now in District Kathua. Later Dattu became the court-poet of the Jammu king Raja Ranjit Deva. He was a great Sanskrit scholar and a poet of Braj-bhasha. His books are:

1. *Vir Vilas,* an epic in Braj-bhasha, where the poet inserts Dogri words here and there.
2. *Baran-Mah* in Braj-bhasha, which gives a description of the seasons.
3. *Datta Sangraha,* an anthology of different poems.
4. *Bhup Viyoga,* at the death of Raja Bhupati of Bilawer state, now in Kathua district.
5. *Amrit Viyoga,* at the death of Raja Amrit Pal of Basohli state.
6. *Kamal Netra Stotra,* a very famous and beautiful devotional song in praise of Lord Krishna in Braj-bhasha, which has been sung in the temples.
7. *Braj Raj Panchasika,* a long descriptive poem in Braj-Bhasha where the poet describes the attack of Prince Braj Raj Deva on Raja Ghumand Chand Katoch of Kangarha for his usurping Pathiar; a part of Chamba State. Dattu was also accompanying the prince on his campaign. Braj Raj Panchasika contains two *kavittas* (eight line poems in Dogri). One is in the Kangarha dialect and other is in Jammu dialect.
8. *Raghu Chandrika* (Braj-bhasha)
9. *Krishna Mahima Stotra* (Braj-bhasha)
10. *Krishna Shatika* (Sanskrit)
11. *Sayan Panchak* (Sanskrit)
12. *Ritu Vani* (Braj Bhasha)
13. *Gopi Viyoga* (Braj-bhasha)

Only one love lyric of Kavi Dattu is now available in Dogri language—"Advise me, O Devi Ditta," which is a very famous folk song in Duggar. It reveals that he has written many such lyrics in Dogri, which have gone into the folklore. Some Dogri scholars are of the opinion that this lyric is a piece of some longer poem by Dattu.

**Influence of Braj Bhasha**

In the tradition of Dattu we find two other poets, Shiv Ram and Rudra Datt. Shiv Ram was the nephew of Dattu who was also a poet of Braja-Bhasha, but we find only an eight-line *pada* of Shiv Ram in Dogri, which shows the influence of Braj-Bhasha on it.

Rudra Datt, the son of Shiv Ram was a contemporary of Maharaja Ranbir Singh. He remained a court-poet of Jammu Darbar, but later he left Jammu and went to Kangarha and then to Guler State. He wrote in both the dialects—Jammu dialect as well as Kangarha dialect. His period is after 1800 so we have not included his poetry here. These poets are from the middle class and of the towns, while Kavi-Lakkhu, a people's poet, is from the peasantry. There is no written record of his date of birth and death available at present, but it is said that he was living in the village Baguna in Samba Tehsil of Jammu District, when Raja Ranjit Deva was ruling in Jammu. Some say that he was born during 1775-80 and others say that he was a contemporary of Raja Gaje Singh 1687. He was from the caste of ironsmiths, who did carpentry too. Kavi Lakkhu is a people's poet and is quite famous for his riddles in Dogri, which are known throughout Duggar. There are many proverbs and tales about the life of Kavi Lakkhu prevalent among the country-folks. For instance:

**Sikkha Tarkhanaki Buddhi,**
**Chhe Puthian Te Ikka Siddhi**

It is an interesting tale about Kavi Lakkhu, that his father-in-law put a condition before marriage that, if he could give seven right blows upon a log of wood by his axe, he would get the bride, otherwise not. Lakkhu was in a fix how to do it, as seven strikes at a stretch at the right spot was difficult for him. It is said that his father-in-law was smoking pipe inside, and Lakkhu was out with an axe and a log of wood. His betrothed wife came outside with the excuse of fetching water and uttered the above couplet:-

**Learn the knack of a carpenter,**
**Six with the opposite and seventh right.**

Lakkhu was not so dull-headed as not to understand; first he struck on the log of wood with the opposite side of the axe and the seventh strike he gave from the right side of the axe on the same spot. That was really a clever riddle.

The riddles of Lakkhu seem to be short poems saturated with *shlesha-alankar* and have been used by the country folk, who might have made -slight changes in the language too. There is a special quality in the riddles of Lakkhu, which tell us also about the time, place and situation in which he had uttered the riddle. We could collect only two poems of Lakkhu—one is a love poem and the other a poem for children.

# 6

# Medieval Kashmiri Literature (Shafi Shauq)

## Kashmiri Literature in the Making (1100-1300)

Kashmiri literature began with poetry which is deeply influenced by the native form of the Shaivite philosophy, and its stylistic maturity makes one believe that this early poetry, although fragmentary, must have been the culmination of centuries-old creative activity. Unfortunately the nature of this ancient poetry cannot be known as the ravages of the turbulent centuries have left nothing of it for the present-day reader. We can safely assume that there must have existed a body of literature, inchoate and rudimentary, for several hundred years before the advent of the Aryans from North India. The aborigines, called Nagas, and the new settlers from Dardistan (the mountainous region extending from lat. 30° S to lat. 40° N and from long. 70° W to long. 78° E), who gave the Kashmiri language its unique syntactic structure, could not have existed without their imaginative reconstruction of the life they lived, without fictionalising the facts that constituted their reality.

## The Dard Aryans

The Dard Aryans, sometimes known by the derogatory name Pishachas in old Sanskrit texts, came to the valley several centuries before the advent of the Indo-Aryan Brahmins, and eventually established a culture of their own. The Dards were, as they presently are in Gilgit, Dras, Astor, Baltistan, Chitral, Honza, Kafaristan and the adjoining areas, inveterately tough and hardy, living in the most arduous climate. The archeological findings from Burzahom, in the vicinity of Srinagar, reveal that the Dard Aryans in the Neolithic Age had developed a culture that was determined by the unique ecological conditions rather than any sublime urge. It is the period roughly between 2500 and 1500 B.C.

During the same period the Brahmin Aryans from the plains of India migrated to the valley, partly for finding relief from the scorching heat and partly for the mysterious kind of terrain in the Himalayas inspiring a meditative soul. They possessed a respectably old and fecund tradition of learning, literature and wisdom and having found a congenial and pleasant dwelling place, the new settlers continued their scholarly and literary occupation in their Vedic and Sanskrit and, later on in the Apabhramsha.

**Vidyapati**

Vidyapati was an equally great poet of other worldly matters, as even in his own days he was described by Abul Fazl (c. 1598) as famous both for his *nachari* (Shiva hymns) and *tirhutis* (songs of the passion of love).

In this regard it is appropriate to refer to Vidyapati's dramatic work called *Gorakshavijaya* (The victory of Guru Gorakhanatha, c. 1415). The theme of the play is the redemption of Gorakhanatha from a life of carnal pleasures. Moreover, in some profound personal poems Vidyapati clearly regrets having passed many years of his life singing of earthly joys and that youthfulness is something transient and should be seen as such.

**Contemporaries of Vidyapati**

The contemporaries of Vidyapati were numerous. Their works are often camouflaged in anthologies of music as illustrations of musical notes and metres. The most important of them are the one now know as *Bhashagita Sangraha* though earlier mistakenly called Kamsanarayana's *Padavali* (c. 1620) and Lochana's *Ragatarangini* (The Waves of Melodies, 1670).

Among those who are definitely Vidyapati's close contemporaries, the most prominent was Amritakar (c. 1400-82). He was a statesman. Vidyapati himself has written in praise of his qualities. Vishnupuri (c. 1425-1500), the illustrious devotional poet, Bhanu (c. 1440-1500), Kumar Gajasingha (c. 1449), Kaviraj Bhikhari Mishra and Dashavadhan Thakur are the other prominent poets. As the number of their poems is meagre, one can only observe that they followed the Master but none could claim equality with him.

Two groups of poets, however, deserve to be noticed. The first consists of those who were patronised by the rulers of a small kingdom in the Nepalese district of Morang. The other group formed a distinguished circle around the last ruler of the ruling dynasty of Oinivars, King Lakshminath, alias Kamsanarayana (c. 1503-27). He was inspired by Hussain Shah (1493-1519), the great medieval patron of poetry and learning in Bengal. His son Nasarat Shah (1519-31) attacked Mithila and brought the Oinivar dynasty to an end. He had, however attracted a number of poets and writers. The best of them was Govinda Thakur (c. 1529) who could in many ways excel the master, yet cannot be described as very much distinct from the Vidyapati tradition.

### Influence of Vidyapati (c. 1527-1700)

Slowly and slowly the influence of Vidyapati spread for and wide. In Mithila there grew up a tradition of singers in the courts of contemporary rulers. But the vogue of Vidyapati's lyrics spread in the neighbouring lands where they made greater contributions in other distinct ways as well. There were numerous poets who openly imitated Vidyapati's lyrics. Most of them were also masters of music, who mostly treated literature as an accompaniment of music. Another characteristic that marked their work was the desire to make their craftsmanship more important than their subject matter. Often they would write love songs and yet easily take up as their subject the "divine" Vaishnava hymns comprising the love sports of Krishna and his lady friends, hymns of Shiva, Shakti and Ganga and occasional lyrics like *barahmasa, uchiti, samadauni,* etc. Among those who excelled in ornamentation and sophistication there were three eminent poets: Chatura Chaturbhuja (c. 1589-1604), Lochana (c. 1681-1702) and Govindadas (c. 1663-70). All of them reveal a greater interest in the use of various niceties of *alankarashastra* (science of poetical ornamentation).

Thus, Govindadas used "all the simple and complex figures of speech and other devices known in Sanskrit rhetoric. His great achievement was metrical perfection added to musical resonance and rhythmic movement". He loved alliteration and assonance so much that sometimes there is hardly any originality or remarkableness in the thought content. Though only the external is apparent in his poems, it cannot be denied that the poet's power of describing the amorous sentiment and the colourful imagination were of a very high order... The music of his rhythms and the sonorous diction of his language, full of *tatsam* (Sanskritized) words and forms, compensate for everything. The poet modelled his songs after Vidyapati.... He has written on the psychological aspect and on all different topics of the love poetry of Radha and Krishna... Musical word painting was his *forte.*

Nevertheless, in the depiction of the passion and the disappointment of love and its intensity, he has really very few equals.

(*History of Brajbuli Literature,* pp. 109, 134)

One can, however, see that this was a deterioration due to the super abundance of decoration at the cost of poetic insight. It was perhaps a revolt against this tendency that led to a breakaway later in the poetry of Nandipati and Manbodh.

### Depth of Feeling in Poetry

Indeed, even in the work of some important poets like *Chatura* Chaturbhuja, one can see the tendency towards simplicity and depth of feeling. Chaturbhuja was very much like Amritkar, a statesman who was in touch with the Mughal emperors, and perhaps that is why he called himself *Chatura* (the wise). His hymns are addressed both to Shiva and Krishna. He can write in both styles—learned and Sanskritized as well as easy and simple.

Lochana was the famous writer of a great work on music. He did not write very fine Maithili poetry as his interest was more in music than in poetry which made him famous. He, however, thought of his own poems as equal to those of Vidyapati himself. Strangely enough Lochana and Govindadas became first known as Bengali; Chaturbhuja had actually written in Bengali also. It seems that by this time the exchange and interaction of Maithili and Bengali had reached its peak.

### The Long Lasting Tradition

The Vidyapati tradition in Mithila did not die out by 1700, it continued till quite recently. But it was more imitative than distinguished, and as such it became more interested in dramatic poetry than in lyric poetry. For this reason the new poetry led by Manbodh in the 18th century and the Kirtaniya drama made a new kind of poetry popular, even though the declining, decadent poetry of the Vidyapati tradition continued till Harkhanath (1847-98). Nevertheless, outside dramatic poetry, one may notice a few popular poets of the Vidyapati tradition: Umapati (c. 1600-76), Ramdas (c. 1623-68), Bhanjan (c. 1704-60), Nidhi, the famous writer of *Langani* or narrative songs of love (c. 1739), Ramapati (c. 1744), Keshava (c. 1761), Shripati, Mahipati and Jayananda. Verily every great poet in Mithila down the ages has paid a tribute to Vidyapati. He has been much imitated in his songs of love.

### Vidyapati in Neighbouring Regions

#### Brajavati

Vidyapati exercised no less powerful influence outside Mithila than in Mithila. Bengali scholars who came from Bengal for higher studies in Sanskrit went back with the songs of Vidyapati on their lips. The script of Maithili and that of his vernacular were very much alike and they were inspired by the great achievements. Consequently, Vidyapati's poems became as popular in Bengal as in Mithila. It is said Lord Chaitanya (1480-1533) was particularly attracted by the violent passion of love delineated in these sweet songs and he read in them the strivings of a devout soul for the grace of the Supreme God.

*Shrimad Bhagavata* and *Gita Govinda* had already paved the way for such interpretation of love songs of Krishna and the Gopis. Lord Chaitanya's learned disciples developed a system of Vaishnava philosophy in which human love became the replica of devout love for God. Consequently

Vidyapati's lyrics were taken as sacred to the Vaishnavas as the songs of Solomon are to devout Christians. This factor has even today endeared Vaishnava poetry to the modern Christians as well.

Vidyapati's songs filled the hearts of the Bengali men and women with such ardour that they began imitating the language and the contents of Vidyapati's poems. They have a special admiration for his songs. Gradually there emerged from such efforts a vast literature and a hybrid language as well. In course of time Vidyapati and his poems were naturalized as Bengali literature. The language of Braj (Braj-bhasha), the birthplace of Lord Krishna, was also mixed and together a new Vaishnava vernacular came to be known as Brajbuli or Brajavali language.

The cult of Chaitanya spread far and wide in Orissa and Assam as well. Moreover the songs of Vidyapati were the earliest vernacular poetic endeavour in the whole of Eastern India. It, therefore, also worked as the vernacular model for the writers of these regions. Among the eminent poets of Brajabuli Jnanadas, Govindadas Kaviraj, Balaramadas, Narottamadas and Rayashekhara may be mentioned.

In recent years there was a revival of Brajabuli in Bengal. Bankim Chandra Chatterji and even Rabindranath Tagore wrote Brajabuli poems. The fact of the matter was that Vidyapati fired the youthful imagination of these masters and they indeed tried their hand at writing in it as if that would give them their early training in writing poetry.

Vidyapati's fame in Bengal grew on two grounds. First, that he was probably an old Bengali classic, and second, that he was a great "Vaishnava singer". Bankim and Rabindranath respected him in the first manner; Chaitanya and subsequent Vaishnavas in the second. Through Bengal, Vidyapati's influence spread to Orissa and Assam.

## Vidyapati's Influence

***In Orissa*:** Ramanand Rai met Chaitanyadeva on the bank of Godavari in 1511-12 and recited his Brajabuli poems. Other important poets of Orissa influenced by Vidyapati's poems were Champati Ray and King Pratapamalladeva (1504-32).

***In Assam*:** The first great poet who introduced Maithili was Shankardeva (c. 1449-1568). His earliest contact with Maithili speakers was during a pilgrimage of 12 years (1481-93) when he went to Varahakshetra. He is said to have met one Jagdish Mishra, who was a disciple of Vishnupuri, a famous Maithili devotee, well-versed in *Shrimad Bhagavata*. He wrote in Brajabuli many hymns called *baragita* noble hymns and several dramas. Madhavadeva, Ramcharan Thakur and Purushottam Thakur were other important of Brajabuli hymns and dramas.

***In Nepal* :-** During these years for quite some time there was disturbance in Mithila till the House of Khandwa established what later (by 1860) became the Darbhanga Raj. Naturally, therefore, the talented artists and poets went away to neighbouring places, chiefly the kingdom of Nepal. Poets and dramatists as well as musical experts and actors and dancers sought refuge in the secluded courts of Nepal. The Islamic injunction against these arts in particular made them mightily afraid of remaining unprotected, whereas the Hindu courts were devoutly interested in pursuing these arts. Moreover, the rulers of Nepal invited able men to organise the administration and laws of the country. There were also many Maithila matrimonial alliances in the Nepalese royal families. Above all intercourse between, Nepal and Mithila because of geogrphic proxemty have for quite a long time been very ultimate and close trade and commerce, traffic and business. For these reasons the peoples of the two countries had been very close to each other since time immemorial. Moreover, the Maithili-speaking areas inside Nepal make it imperative for the Nepalese to patronize Maithili scholars. This is the reason why Maithili literature in medieval times (from 1600 to 1800) mainly flourished in the Nepalese kingdom. Their influence came to an end in 1768 when the Gurkha king of Garhwal, Prithvi Narayan Shah, conquered the kingdom of Nepal.

The Nepalese courts were strongholds of many languages. Maithili, Bengali and Newari were equally popular. Maithili, Drama was the most developed activity. Poetry outside drama was, however, equally cultivated under the Malla kings. Many of them were themselves poets and a few of them even got poems in Maithili inscribed on stones or temples the most respectable place.

The Nepalese poets were innovators but they invariably drew inspiration from the Vidyapati tradition. They wrote lyrics according to their requirements—devotional on all the ten incarnations of Vishnu, like Jayadeva's *Gita Govinda,* as well as on Ganesha, Surya, Chandrama, Bhimsena, Bhairava, besides the traditional themes of Radha-Krishna and Hara-Gauri. They were not a part of the Vaishnava Movement of Bengal and cannot be considered apart from the mainstream of Maithili pan-Indian Bhakti movement. Among secular themes the poems were written on the various topics of daily interest along with panegyrics and elegies of high quality.

**Distinguished Poets of Nepal**

The best of the poet's of Nepal were Jyotirmalla (1613-33). Jagatprakashamalla (1644-72), Bhupatindramalla (1695-1722), Pratapamalla (1639-89), and the saintly Siddhi Narasimhamalla (1626-57) were the best poets of Nepal. The most distinguished of them was perhaps Jagatprakashamalla who patronised many poets of eminence. Out of them Chandrashekhara Singh and Jagatachandra wrote some of the finest poems of this period. Jagatprakashamalla and Chandrashekhara were close relations and loved each other intensely. Upon the death of Chandrashekhara Singh, Jagatprakashamalla wrote an elegy of fifty long stanzas called

*Gitapanchakam* which can easily claim to be the best single poem written in Nepal. In depth of sentiment and in the deft and artistic use of all the faculties of the language the poem is unique. Ordinarily the poetic excellence of Nepalese poets may not be great, but this poem is different and the difference is easily marked.

The poems of the Nepalese writers are a legion but most of them are still lying unpublished in scores of anthologies of music in the libraries of Nepal. It is, indeed, obvious that the influence of Vidyapati was more creative and inspired a greater number of Maithili poets in Nepal during this period than even in Mithila.

**Contribution Drama**

Later medieval Maithili literature excelled in the field of drama. This is more remarkable in view of the fact that while in the whole of northern India, drama had died out, it flourished in Maithili and some of the greatest contributions were made to literature in this genre. Several factors led to this unprecedented success of drama. The first was the opposition to the drama and the art of acting in India from the Muslim conquerors on religious grounds. They regarded them as blasphemy. They encouraged scholarship, philosophy and religion, but did not patronize these.

Somehow in the secluded principalities in the marshy lands of Mithila and the jungles and hills of Nepal, the conquerors could not penetrate deep enough. Therefore, from all over the plains upon the massive destruction of Nalanda and Vikramashila monasteries by Muhammad Bin Bhakhtiyar Khilji by the end of the 12th century, they drove the creative artists away while they marched on to the province of Bengal.

Secondly, the Maithili-speaking people were in a stronghold of social seclusion by virtue of their attempts to safeguard their integrity through their codes of conduct. *Maithilia Nibandhas* (Digests and Manuals) were compiled on every aspect of social life which consolidated Hindu society outside the influence of Islam.

Thirdly, Mithila had high traditions of scholarship which established its prestige as the leader of indigenous learning in the whole of Eastern India. It also turned to the cultivation of art and literature, more for recreation and delight than for scholarship. In this regard the interest created by the South Indian rulers from Karnataka (1097-1324) in musical arts developed with the passage of time. The Oinivara Dynasty (1353-1527) continued the patronage. When the persistent Muslim inroads destroyed the Maithili courts, and drove Maithili musicians away to places of safety in the hills and jungles of Nepal, the centre of patronage shifted to the Nepalese courts of Malla kings. Later when the House of Khandwala was established in Mithila from 1556, the patronage of musicians especially in the field of acting was revived.

It was thus that Shubhankar Thakur's (1588-1619) *Shrihastamuktavali* was written on the movements and suggestions of the hand in dancing. Last but not the least, the bold declaration for using the regional vernacular in Sanskrit draines by Jyotirishvara and Vidyapati and the consummate skill the vernacular songs of Vidyapati made it possible to evolve a new vernacular stage in Maithili, the like of which was not seen anywhere else in Northern India.

**Kirtaniya Drama of Mithila**

Sanskrit drama had become stilted, devoid of any popular appeal. The edifice of the vernacular drama in Northern India was built on the ashes of the Sanskrit drama. To fill that void vernacular drama started gaining ascendancy The Islamic opposition to drama gave it a final death-blow. The dramatic activity took refuge in distant and secluded places. Nevertheless the form and the framework of the vernacular drama were taken from Sanskrit drama. In the beginning, the native folk tradition of recitation and impersonation of characters appear to have been prevalent. Vidyapati's songs were sung strictly according to their musical values. Earlier, Jyotirishwar had described elaborately the various kinds of musical melodies, dances and actions on the stage.

**Influence of Maithili**

The word *kirtaniya* was not known in the early days, for Jyotirishwara does not mention it. But the tradition of the stage was present even when Sanskrit plays were written like Shankar Mishra's *Gitadigambara.* It is not exactly known when and how Maithili began to be introduced into the Sanskrit plays. But obviously the need to be intelligible to the audience extensively on the stage must have brought into vogue the Maithili elements.

The aim of the dramatist is casually mentioned in a play by Umapati Upadhyaya (1580-1644). That a new vernacular drama was put on the stage is clear from the story of a Maithili expert in acting in Vidyapati's *Purushapariksha* (The Test of Man). It is described that the drama was performed on the stage and the actor was so thoroughly adept in his art that while he was trying to present his excellence in the knowledge of drama he impersonated Rama in Bhavabhuti's Sanskrit play *Uttararamacharitra* so well that he actually experienced the acute pleasure of meeting Sita and died in a fit of ecstasy.

The fact, however, is significant that the first Maithili drama, Jyotirishwar's *Dhurttasamagama,* is available in two versions—one in Sanskrit and the other a vernacular adaptation, obviously to give the speeches in Sanskrit plays in the common man's idiom like Prakrit and Apabhramsha or for translating Sanskrit and Prakrit passages into Maithili. The *nandi* (benedictory verse) is in Maithili and frequently the Maithili adaptation is in itself complete. In other words, Jyotirishwar presentation was not a duplication, rather the Maithili version is an innovation.

The earliest extant full-fledged drama in the new manner began with the purpose of satirising Buddhist monks. The play *Dhurttasamagama* (c. 1326) was intended to be a farce and it aimed to expose the corruption in society. So also is the second great play written by Vidyapati (1340-1448) *Gorakshavijaya* (The Redemption of Guru Gorakhnath, c. 1415). It negated worldly pleasures and exhorted to uphold the superiority of the path of salvation.

The subsequent plays, however, justified the name *kirtaniya* for the plays in Maithili. Of them the most important was Umapati's (1580-1640) play *Parijataharan* (The Abduction of Parijat Flower, c. 1620). It dramatises the well-known Pauranic exploit of Lord Krishna. It is, therefore, truly a *kirtan.* (praise of God), the drama is a *kirtaniya* drama. But it must be remembered that it is not the Bengali type of *kirtan.* Indeed, there is a tradition that Umapati was a true devotee of Lord Krishna, and he used to sing and dance before his idol in his home. Therefore the intention of making his play intelligible to the lowest classes which he gives towards the end of the play is rightly served by the presence of translated vernacular passages.

**Umapati's Later Plays**

In later years Umapati's play was shorn of its learned appendages—Sanskrit and Prakrit passages—and a skeleton vernacular version alone used to be exhibited as an early model of the *kirtaniya* play. Indeed the stock characters of a *kirtaniya* play came to be named after the kind of characters who appeared in this play. Other important plays on the life and deeds of Krishna which were incorporated as *kirtaniya* plays were: Devananda's (1640-1730) *Ushaharan* (The Abduction of Usha, c. 1700), Nandipati's (1710-90) *Shrikrishnakelimala* (The Garland of the Sports of Lord Krishna, c. 1740) and Rampati's (1720-92) and *Rukminiharan* (The Abduction of Rukmini, 1745).

Kavi Lal's (c. 1720-80) work *kirtaniya* plays in praise of Lord Shiva. One of these *Gauriswayamvar* (The Marriage of Gauri, c. 1755) became very populars. It uses Sanskrit and Prakrit sparingly and is actually regarded as a model of the later *kirtaniya* drama, par excellence. Other important plays on Shiva are Shivadatta's (1785-1845) *Gauriparinaya* (c.1810) and Kanharam's (1800-60) elaborate play *Gauriswayamvara* (The Marriage of Gauri, 1842). These eminently successful plays on Lord Krishna and Lord Shiva justified the appellation *kirtaniya* for the drama of Mithila.

Of course, there were many plays on other themes of an instructive and inspiring nature, such as, Govinda's (1430-1510) play on the Nala, the Gambler, *Karna* Jayanand's on King Rukmangada, and Chanda Jha's on Rama.

The *kirtaniya* was basically a rural drama. It was generally performed in the night. The stage was usually a simple platform and the audience was never more than the inhabitants of a village. The formal outward format was that of the Sanskrit drama. After a prayer the *sutradhar* (manager) used to make his appearance. His costumes were a *jama* (blouse), a *nima* (a scarf like napkin) and a *payjama* (trousers). He used to wear a pair of *padukas* or wooden, sandals. He covered himself with a wrapper (cotton, silken or woollen according as the weather was) and a turban-like local headdress called *satha pag*. He had in his hand a small rod called *phulahatha* (flower-stick). He was generally accompanied by his wife, and it was his duty to introduce the patron. He took pride in making a display of scholarship and knowledge of "learned" things, usually in broken Sanskrit-Prakrit.

**Composition of Cast**

The number of actors at any time did not exceed seven or nine. The dramatis personae were announced in an entrance song *(Pravesh gita)* though often entrance song for each character was also given. The *nayaka* (hero), the *nayika* (heroine), two or three *sakhis* (friends of the heroine), *narada* (a negotiator) and the *vipata (vidushak,* or buffoon) formed the stock character of a *kirtaniya* party (called *Jamati* group). The stage directions and speeches in prose continued to be given for a long time in Sanskrit. For the rest, the dialogues were carried on in Maithili songs or couplets. If any action was to be shown on the stage such as Parvati's penance or a battle, generally a description of it was sung on the stage. Men or boys usually impersonated women. There used to be stage versions of the play which the actors committed to memory. Rehearsal or training was common, particularly the orchestra was trained in the *naradiya* form of musical instruments.

*Kirtaniya* performance was mainly for entertainment-cum-*kirtan* (praise) of some kind. Besides music, vocal and instrumental, there was the fun of the *vipata,* and the display of crude improvisations like Garuda (the bird vehicle of Vishnu), Mayura (peacock—the vehicle of Karttikeya), and Airavata (the divine elephant-vehicle of Indra) and the symbolical gesticulations of the actors, to please the spectators.

*Kirtaniya* performers got a chance to excel in singing Maithili songs of traditional melodies like *mana* (persuasion of the lover or the beloved), *tirahuti* (various states of love), *nachari* (hymns of Shiva), etc. On the whole, the *kirtaniya* drama of Mithila was a glorious achievement of medieval Maithili literature. It accelerated the pace of simplifying the Vidyapati tradition of literary affectation in style and embellishment and paved the way for the emergence of long narrative poems. In itself it created a taste of the dramatic and musical arts. Moreover, it contributed to the popularity and development of Maithili language and literature century after century.

**Rise of Maithili Drama in Nepal**

The pinnacle of medieval Maithili drama was the evolution of a tradition of vernacular drama in Nepal. Its source of popularity was the highly sophisticated courtly patronage of music and dancing. Their literary quality as well as their professional attainments as a performing art mark them out as a class of writing by themselves.

The *kirtaniya* drama had emerged in Mithila as an attempt to bring up a new kind of drama at a time when the Muslim rulers in the whole of Northern India were threatening to eradicate it on account of their religious prejudice. Twice the Muslim inroads disrupted the peaceful existence of the Hindu courts of Mithila; first, in about 1324 when Maharaja Harasinha was routed and fled to Nepal, and second in about 1527 when Lakshminath alias Kamsanarayana was defeated by the Muslim rulers of Bengal. Even earlier in about 1100, the depredations of Mohammed-Bin-Bakhtiyar, and those of Ijjudin Tughlak and several others had been responsible for driving away Maithili writers and scholars to Nepalese courts.

For quite some time the territory of Nepal was ruled by Harasimhadeva (1296-1324) and his descendants. There were some matrimonial alliances between them and the Malla rulers of Nepal. Following these events the love for drama in Maithili found a place in the courts of Nepal. In the beginning Sanskrit dramas were written under Jayasthitimalla (1380-94). But later after the death of Yakahamalla in about 1474, Maithili drama began to be written and staged at Bhatgaon, Kathmandu and Lalitpur.

Maithili dramas under the rulers of Bhatgaon were most numerous. Even as early as 1533 we learn that Maithili dramas had begun to be written. They were all inspired directly by Jayadeva and Vidyapati; Jagajjyotirmalla (c. 1618-33) got Maithili works on the art of music prepared. The best play which was written under him was *Muditakuvalayashva* (1626). It was indeed in every way a fully developed drama with prose and poetry and various dramatic situations of powerful emotions. Another very popular play *Haragaurivivaha* was in the *kirtaniya* tradition and displayed another variety of drama—colloquial, energetic and eclectic. These plays had the benefits of being written primarily by a talented Maithili dramatist Vamshamani Jha.

After Jagajjyotirmalla, the Maithili drama was naturalized in Bhatgaon and a large number of them were written and staged. A repertory had developed by the time and almost every year on the occasion of some festival or important occasion in the realm a new play was staged or an old one was revived.

Jagatprakashamalla (1644-73) had the credit of getting ready a dozen such plays written and performed. His son Jitamitramalladeva (1673-96) was an equally enthusiastic patron of Maithili drama. But gradually he began to patronise dramas in other languages as well. Bengali dramas in particular came to be written and staged for the first time.

# 7

# Medieval Dogri Literature: THE SPIRITS

### A Jogi

In this *mantra,* the poet describes two types of *jogans* who are friends and foes of human beings. Nine Nathas kindle fire, and Guru Balak Natha, a learned scholar, binds evil spirits with a raw thread.

*Om Namo*
Like a kite,
In the sky
The *jogan* dwells;
The *jogan,* hard of hearing,
Binds with her spell.
Bloody lips,
Ears without rings,
Dark and dusky
With large breasts,
And broad teeth.
*Atthar Kali,* most horrible,
Flying along
With three hundred *jogans.*
The wicked *jogan*
Makes rounds in the sky,
But nine Nathas[1]
Prepared *dhoonl*[2]
And kindled fire.
Bala[3] Jogi,
A learned scholar,
Of Narad Giani,
Binds it

1. Gurus of the Natha Sect
2. The fire of hermits, always burning
3. Guru Balak Natha Temple of Guru Balak Nath is in Himachal Pradesh

With a raw thread,
And three handfuls
of water.

Seven types of corns.
Black goat
Breaks her fast,
Of sweet *babbrun*[1]
Black *jogan* always teases,
Gentle *jogan* always laughs.
Hanuman gave a shout,
And saved her.
Eat *dakani*[2]
Keep your breast forward,
Keep your back behind.
If thrown or sent away,
Go to your place and house.

From *Jogan,* 15th century *Tr.* by Desh Bandhu Dogra "Nutan"

## Chariot Cloud

**A Jogi**

Here in this *mantra,* which is a part of a chain of *mantras,* the *jogi* requests the Chariot Clouds, over which Lord Indra, the god of rains rides, to stop roaring and not to create hailstorms. Here the *jogi* also mentions the death of Jassa (Jasarath Khokhar) across Mahan Luddra river.

The ploughmen start tying ploughs,
The *khettarpals*[1] are wet,
The goats and hens are swallowed by 460 *jogans*
And Jassa[2] is killed across Mahan Luddra river.
Millions of forts surrounded by sea-like ditches.
See, the picket of Hanuman is coming closer.
Warrior Hanuman raises a shout:
"Chariot Cloud:
Leave, leave, please leave,
All our four sides."
Shouts and roars:
"Afterwards be raised,
Chariot Cloud!
Leave my boundary.

---

1. Area under a *satrap* or governor.
2. A Dogra hero of the 14th-15th century.

Thus,
Go across my boundary,
Leave destroying corns,
And eat the vegetation
(Of jungles),
Climb upon the hills high,
The dusky hills,
The shadow of blackness,
Make *dham-dham*[3]
Wet and soft".

From *Ratha Badala,* 15th century *Tr.* by Desh Bandhu Dogra "Nutan"

## Raja Rup Chand and the Siege of Kangra

*Manak Chand*

Manak Chand (Manak Chand, 16th century) was a court poet of the Rajas of Kangra, formerly a Punjab hill state, now part of Himachal Pradesh. He is known for his rhapsodies in praise of his patrons and their ancestors. Little is known about his life or his works. Only a fragment of his rhapsody on Raja Rup Chand of Kangra (1360-88) is preserved in the *Kangra District Gazetteer.*

The poem describes the siege of Kangra by Feroz Shah Tughlaq, the Sultan of Delhi, and the Raja's surrender:

Rup Chandra went forth
To meet the Sultan, Lord of Delhi.
He bowed low, down to his feet,
And on his back the Sultan put his hand.

[Untitled], 16th century *Tr.* by Shivanath

## In Praise of Raja Jagat Singh

*Gambhir Rai*

Gambhir Rai (Gambhir Rae, 17th century) was a court poet of the Rajas of Nurpur, a small hill state, now part of Himachal Pradesh. He composed and recited rhapsodies describing the valorous exploits of Raja Jagat Singh of Nurpur (d. 1646), who had been a favourite of the Mughal Emperor Jehangir Raja Jagat Singh had named his state after Queen Nur Jahan.

The poem is written in a high flown style akin to the Dogri folk-ballad form called *bar*:

3. Ail directions.
4. A dish offered to the gods.
5. A female demon.

Jagata, the Raja,
A devotee, king, son of Basdev,
Conquered the country beyond the Indus,
Led his forces to the ocean,
Pitched his camp in the snow country,
Pointed his guns towards the sky.
Thus he came to be renowned as Jagata.

From *Prashasti*, 17th century *Tr.* by Shivanath

## Two Poems

### The Queen of Raja Vikram Singh

The following two poems written by the queen of Raja Vikram Singh (17th century) were recorded by the late Raja Baldev Singh of Guler, now in Himachal Pradesh, as songs, *Gitiyan* in the local dialect. The first is written in praise of Raja Vikram Singh (1662-75) and the second in praise of her mother-in-law, the queen-mother Durga Dei.

### 1. Raja Vikram Singh

Vikram Singh,
The beloved son of Kalyan Dei,
Verily like the moon;
Blessed you are indeed:
Your face is graceful and lovely;
You are like Lord Krishna,
Stately like a branch of Chamba.

### 2. Queen Durga Dei

Praise to you,
O Queen Durga Dei!
Your mind is one with Krishna.
You have fed the cows on grass.
You have hung nests
Under the window shade,
Where there is cool water
And thick shade,
Where the birds
Roost with ease.

From *Gitiyan*, 17th century *Tr.* by Desh Bandhu Dogra "Nutan"

### The Song

This is a *bhakh*, a group-song in Dogri classical music, popular in the countryside. It was written by an unknown court poet on the death of Hari Deva, King of Jammu. The song is generally sung by a group of women or children.

The bees fly away but the hives remain;
Who cares for the hives?
Long live King Harideva,
Who cares for the hives!
Hermits leave but the hermitages remain;
Who cares for the hermitages?
Long live King Harideva,
Who cares for the hermitages!
Water flows away but the rivers remain;
Who cares for the rivers?
Long live King Harideva,
Who cares for the rivers!
Husbands die but the wives remain;
Who cares for the wives?
Long live King Harideva,
Who cares for the wives!
Brothers die but the sisters remain;
Who cares for the sisters?
Long live King Harideva,
Who cares for the sisters!
Kings die but the subjects remain;
Who cares for the subjects?
Long live King Harideva,
Who cares for the subjects!

From *Bhakh,* 17th century *Tr.* by Desh Bandhu Dogra "Nutan"

**The Birth of Kusha**

An episode from the Ramayana which is told in a Gusettana *yajna* runs like this:

On hear say Lord Rama had consigned Mother Sita to exile. She was living in the hermitage of Rishi Valmiki, basically a Shudra scavenger. Mother Sita gave birth to a male child. One day she went to fetch water from a spring, situated at a distance from the hermitage. Mother Sita saw monkeys jumping and leaping upon the trees. She saw some mother-monkeys carrying their offspring on their back or clinging to their breasts. Mother Sita was afraid that their offspring might fall, but they did not actually do so.

Mother Sita scolded the mother monkeys saying, "You foolish she-monkeys! Why are you carrying your babies with you instead of keeping them in the house? If they fall and die, your husbands would flay you alive." One of the mother-monkeys responded, "O woman! You don't understand that I can feed my baby without letting him weep. If my baby falls down and dies, I would know and tell my husband. You have not brought your baby with you, and if any animal takes your baby away in your absence, what would you tell your husband?"

Hearing the reply Mother Sita became frightened. She left the pitcher of water there and then ran to bring her baby with her. In her absence, when Rishi Valmiki could not find the baby, he became perplexed and thought that he himself was absorbed in deep meditation and some animal might have taken the child away. He took some *kusha* grass and made a child out of that, by the power of his *mantras.* When Mother Sita returned, she was surprised to find another child taking after her own child. In this way she got another child named Kusha.

From *Ramayana* [date uncertain] *Tr.* by Desh Bandhu Dogra "Nutan"

**Birth of Shri Krishna**

Here in Duggar, village-folks have a different version of the birth of Lord Krishna. According to this folktale, Lord Krishna is the grandson of the Naga King Uggarsen (Ugrasen). They tell this tale as follows:

One day, Raja Uggarsen was out an inspection of his kingdom—A Rakshasa entered his palace in the guise of Raja Uggarsen and made all his five queens pregnant and left. All the queens gave birth to children one by one, i.e., Kans, the king, Fiddu, a barber and an assistant of Raja Kans, Kuchharh-Dhubba, a washer man, who washed the clothes of Kans, the king of Mathura, and Channu Chamar, a cobbler who made shoes for Raja Kans. The last was a girl named Devaki, who lived with her parents in Patal Loka.

In due course Raja Kans started ruling over Mathura. A serpent assuming the body of a human being used to visit daily the Darbar of Raja Kans (a serpent reaches the age of one hundred years, he can assume the body according to his choice). As barbers are supposed to be very cunning and clever, Fiddu the barber recognised the serpent and told Kans about him. Raja Kans asked how he could know. The barber replied that human beings have lines on their hands and fingers while his fingers are plain, and if he is burnt alive, he must leave his "Mani" after him, as, such serpents keep a "Mani" on their heads.

The serpent was also very clever. He smelt the intrigue of the barber. He left the Darbar at once, but the soldiers of Raja Kans followed him. They blocked all the paths leading to Yamuna, so that the serpent may not jump into it. There was a hermit named Vasudeva, who lived on the bank of Yamuna, in a small cottage. The serpent went into the cottage and begged Vasudeva for shelter who hid him in his "Kamandal" of water. The soldiers reached there and searched, but could not discover the serpent anywhere. They asked the hermit to vacate the cottage, as they would burn it. Vasudeva came out along with his "Kamandal" and they set the cottage ablaze.

The serpent requested Vasudev to take him to the middle of Yamuna and put him there. Vasudeva went into the water and when he reached the middle of Yamuna, he was pushed by the serpent and was taken to Patal Loka, where his father Naga Uggarsen was ruling. Vasudeva asked the serpent why he had dragged him from Prithvi Loka to Patal Loka. The serpent said, his life was saved and so he wanted to thank him. He advised Vasudeva that his father Uggarsen was a great king having the wealth of the three worlds, but the most valuable object was his younger sister Devaki. His father would ask him (Vasudeva) to demand whatever he liked from him, then he should ask Uggarsen to bestow upon him his daughter Devaki.

**Marriage of Devaki**

Vasudeva married Devaki. He sought permission from Uggarsen to go to Prithvi Lok. The serpent had also advised Devaki to demand only the thumb of his right hand from her father Uggarsen, when he would ask her to demand anything at the time of departure. When Devaki was weeping at the time of departure, she was asked by her father Uggarsen to demand anything she wanted and she demanded the thumb of his right hand without demanding any dowry. She got the thumb of the right hand of her father.

The couple came to Prithvi Lok, Devaki being the most handsome lady of the three worlds. Devaki took the thumb which she had got from her father and worshipped it just like a god in full veneration. She requested the "thumb" to erect a fine palace for them on the bank of the Yamuna in Mathura, which would be so huge and flawless, that no palace in the three worlds may compete with it.

The palace was erected along with all facilities in it. The news spread all over the world that a couple had arrived in Mathura, who was so healthy, wealthy and fine, that neither the god of wealth nor any heavenly being could compare with them. As Raja Kans was very ambitious, he wanted to see the couple. He had the couple invited to his palace for a courtesy call. Devaki sent Vasudeva to the royal palace to meet Raja Kans. She decorated her husband in a royal manner and sent many presents of pearls, diamonds and other costly things with him. She asked him to invite Raja Kans and his coterie to a feast.

When Raja Kans and his coterie along with all his servants and his army reached the palace of Devaki, they were astonished to see the richly-decorated palace, which they had never seen on the earth. The servants and the waiters were decorated with precious pearls and gold.

When Devaki came to greet Kans, he was wonderstruck to see her beauty. She was wearing such fine dress and costly jewellery that Raja Kans could not dare to look at her face. When she next came to serve them meals in the dining hall, she had changed her dress and make-up.

She had got arranged hundreds of fine and tasty dishes and served them herself. Fiddu, the barber, was very cunning; when Devaki served them with curd, Fiddu mischievously sprinkled a drop of curd on her foot. Devaki did not notice it.

Every time Devaki entered the dining hall along with her maid-servants in different dresses and make-up, Raja Kans asked Fiddu, the barber, how many wives Vasudeva had. Fiddu replied that there was only one, but every time she changed her appearance with her make-up, costumes and jewellery. Raja Kans could not agree, but Fiddu the cunning barber asked him to look at her foot where he had sprinkled curd, when she was serving for the first time. The water in the curd dried, but the white curd had left its impression on her foot. Fiddu made it clear that she was changing her dress, but did not care to wash her foot.

When all the dishes were served, Devaki came before them and requested with folded hands, "My brothers, we are too poor to serve you according to your status; kindly take this simple meal. Kans was ashamed to hear it, as Devaki had become his sister to whom he would have to give due respect and honour.

Later when Raja Kans was told by a prophecy, that he would be killed by his sister's son, he thought that he had no sister, but Fiddu the barber reminded him of Devaki.

From *Mahabharata* [date uncertain] *Tr.* by Desh Bandhu Dogra "Nutan"

**Bhairha Naga**

**Anonymous:** Bhairha Naga is the most widely worshipped Naga-God in Duggar. A *karaka* celebrates his prowess thus:

First son of Basuka Naga,
Named Bhairha (Bherha)
First job given by Baba Bhairha (Bherha),
And flew the Tawi[1]
From the high mountains.
Waves upon waves,
The water rose and hurled.
And the clouds,
Thundered and roared.
Swift storm, hurricane created.
Showering hailstones,
And rain stormed.
Baba Bhairha (Bherha) arrived.
The greeting songs are sung.

From *Karaka of Bhairha Naga* [date uncertain] *Tr.* by Desh Bandhu Dogra "Nutan"

**Mother Goddess**

The *karaka* often recited in praise of Aad Shakti (Adi Shakti) Mahamaya, dwelling on the top of upper Shivalik at Chountrah in Udhampur District, relates as follows:

O Mother-Goddess!
In which divine house were you born?
Which god has worshipped you?

Born in the house of Param Jote,
And the three worlds have worshipped me.

Which god cooks your meals?
Which god fetches you water?
The sun and the moon keep my kitchen,
And Indra fetches me water.

Which god decorates your bed?
Which god keeps fanning you?

Param Jote spreads my bed,
The god of wind keeps fanning me.

From *Aad Shakti* [date uncertain] *Tr.* by Desh Bandhu Dogra "Nutan"

**Two Poems**

**Maya Dasa:** Maya Dasa (Maya Dasa, 1720-1802) was born at Dafarwal; he was a *Krishnabhakta* who went to Vrindavana and learnt *Rasa lila*. On return to his state he became a preacher of *Krishna Lila* in Dogra countryside. This led to the development of a local Dogra variety of *Rasa lila*, and several troupes came into existence, who went from town to town and village to village for the performance of *Rasa lila*. Maya Dasa wrote more poems and devotional compositions in Braja-bhasha than in Dogri.

**1. A Devotional Song:** This Dogri *bhajan* of his describes the complaint of the milkmaids to Yashoda against Krishna.

Five or six milkmaids
went to Yashoda and complained:
Kahna teases us;
he doesn't allow us to pass,
when we go to sell milk.
Seeing us,
he snatches away the milk
and drinks it in front of us.

---

1. A tributary of river Chenab.

What's more, he scoffs at us.
Or, sitting in the court of Kansa,
O Maya Dasa,
He makes the entire Gokul ask for him

*Bhajan,* 18th century

**2. Twelve Months:** This is a string of short poems each beginning with the name of a month. Only eight of the twelve short poems are extent. Most of them are of eight lines, describing different incidnet of Ramayana.

**I** The month of Chaitra has commenced,
And Shurpanakha hastens to Lanka
To scream her plaint: "O you,
Who just sits here as the King, do you know
Two great warriors have come
And killed your *rakshasas,*
All the fourteen thousand of them?"
And says Maya Dasa, they have
With them, a beautiful woman.

**II** Then comes the month of Vaishakha,
Making Ravana ponder:
"Rama has appeared as an incarnation,
And I cannot hide myself for long.
Brahma has given me some boons,
And Narada has made some predictions".
Says Maya Dasa,
There lies the way to my salvation.
seek refuge at Rama's feet;

**III** In the month of Pausha, says Sita:
"Rama, my Lord, you have great prowess.
Go and kill that deer and bring it to me;
It has a gorgeous skin—yes, the skin."
Says Maya Dasa, Janaki takes no "no";
Janaki implores and begs and cries;
She frets and pesters and weeps.

**IV** In the month of Margashirsha, says Rama:
"Listen to me, Sita, you are crazy, yes.
It is no deer, but some magic form—
A *rakshasa* transformed as deer, yes,
Sent here by Ravana.
It seems to me to be Mareecha,
Roaming quietly, yes, roaming."
But Janaki doesn't agree, says Maya Dasa,
Rama picks up his bow and arrows—yes, bow and arrows.

V In the month of Phalgun, listen O sadhus:
Rama goes after the deer, yes, he does.
But the deer eludes him and jumps up into the sky.
Rama pursues and aims his arrows at him;
An arrow goes and hits the deer dead
Rama puts him to deep sleep.
Says Maya Dasa,
Though Rama he takes great pains to plead with her.
Janaki does not listen

VI The month of Jyeshtha comes, O sadhus:
A mendicant calls at the door;
Ravana comes in disguise;
He comes to beguile Sita.
With alms in her hands, Sita comes out.
The yogi announces his conditions.
Says Maya Dasa, Janaki does not agree.
There is deception in his mind.

VII It is the month of Ashad, says Sita;
"A great Yogi has come to my door".
She thinks and calculates in her mind,
And puts forward her toe to give alms.
Ravana catches her by the arm
And carries her on his shoulders.
Says Maya Dasa, Janaki did not pay heed.
And now she breaks into a wail.

VIII

Then comes Shravana and Sita weeps and wails,
Remembering Rama, calling his name:
"The king of Lanka has kidnapped me by deception;
come and get me released, O Rama!"
When Jatayu hears what she is saying
He challenges Ravana.
Says Maya Dasa, Ravana lets fly a fire-tipped arrow
And burns his wings.

From *Baramah*, 18th century *Tr.* by Shivanath

## A String of Kings

**Taihl Das**

Taihl Das (Taihl Das) was a writer and translator at the court of the Raja of Guler, a former Punjabi hill state now part of Himachal Pradesh.

Dhyan Singh, a relative of the Raja, was a very powerful minister between 1773 and 1785. In 1785, Dhyan Singh broke away from Guler and set himself up as an independent Raja of Kotla, which had till then been a part of Guler. Taihl Das, who wrote in Braja-bhasha and Dogri, remained loyal to Dhyan Singh and translated for him Bali Ram's Persian work *Rajavali* (A String of Kings) into Dogri with an introductory *Mangalacharanam* of seven couplets in Braja-bhasha praising Dhyan Singh.

*Rajavali* is a very important work in the history of the Dogri literature, being the first extant prose work. Found among the archival documents of former Guler state, it is in a language that is a beautiful mix of two dialects of Dogri, one spoken in Jammu and the other in Kangra. Besides giving the chronology of the rulers of Delhi from Mahabharata's Yudhishthira to the Moghul Shah Alam, it comments on the transience of worldly power and glory and wealth. These comments are the most beautiful parts of the work and some of them are reproduced below:

**The Poetry**

O kings, let me tell you about the "faithfulness" of this world. What is wealth, power and affluence. Your don't realise its transperce. This world looks like a pearl, but, in my way of perception, it is like the dew on the grass. When the wind blows, then pearls evaporate. I bow before the *maya* of Shri Thakur, the Divine. This world is undependable and false. But it appears to be real. The picture is drawn on water. But man, puffed up by his ego, driven by a variety of desires, gets engrossed in a play that has no firm base. This world is a game of dice and one is bound to be the loser in the end. Woe to the intelligence, a hundred woes to the thinking of those who are engrossed in the affairs of the world, drinking cups of pain and sorrow, intoxicated by the wine of forgetfulness! They are not content with what their destiny dispenses, but want more and still more from time and from destiny. It is written in the Puranas that the greedy suffer, and cry in helplessness in the end, when their desires are not fulfilled. What a stupidity that they go through such troubles and inconveniences. In such pursuits of the world, one never gets peace. There is always a lack of one thing or the other; if one gets wine, the cup is missing. No one ever got all his desires satisfied to his heart's content.

**Wordfull of Evils**

This world is like an old women, full of guiles, with a thousand sons-in-law and innumerable husbands. It is vile and hides within itself thousands of evils. White haired, it is always on the look out to ensnare and destroy people. Full of deception, it finishes off even men of valour. And it is also the beloved, the killer of her lovers. Such is this world. So many people have lived in this world and disappeared without leaving any trace behind. And there has been no one ever born, who has not got ensnared by its tresses. What stout heart has ever been able to resist its graces? And who is there that has not been felled by its tricks? This world is the other woman, the mistress endowed with a thousand magical charms—full of elegance and beauty. There have been many who have desired this object, in accordance with their respective religions. And there must be few indeed who have not desired it. Whatever grouses or words of condemnation we have for it are justified. We too have tasted its pleasures before we renounced it.

Why? Because we have seen with our own eyes all types of troubles and sufferings that our sages have described in the Puranas and in myths and legends of yore. One feels very sad and troubled to think of the end of emperors, *Chakravarti Rajas*. We should therefore bear in mind that when emperors and kings and leaders of men suffered what they did, "what hopes for better things should common mortals of this world cherish?

• • •

In days gone by, there was a kingdom known as Indraprastha. The rulers who passed orders and dispensed justice had people who were efficient in their work and ministers who were wise, and soldiers who were numerous and valorous, and treasuries that were impregnable. They were brave with puissance in their arms. They were greatly affluent and resplendent in their glory when they ruled. But today we do not find anything to remember them by, their whole world was lost, and there wasn't as much as the sound of footsteps. Rich merchants disappeared and nobody heard the sound of bells around the necks of merchandise-laden camels. They departed like bubbles of water, soundlessly, after enjoying pleasures and suffering sorrows according to their destinies.

**False and Faithless Word**

The details of these will be written in the pages that follow. But worldly people with wisdom should take what I say as the truth about this false and faithless world and should not get attached to it, should not fall in love with it, because it has not stood by any one. This story of the string of kings is not my creation. Those living in this world should learn from the facts about the lives of kings and princes. The visible beauty and enchanting colours of this world are in the eyes of Bali Ram—as seen by him. Those who have woken up from the sleep of Maya, illusion, have realised that this world is no more than a dream.

• • •

Yearning for affluence is an incurable disease—the more one tries to cure it, the more afflicted by it one becomes. Relations praise you outwardly but wish your death in their hearts. What treacheries and sorrows and regrets one doesn't come across in their ignorance. They indulge in wrong doing for happiness in life. They do not realise that life is dependent on breath. If breathing stops, that is the end of it all.

• • •

Bereft of breath, one cannot imagine the other world. If one were to think of what lies ahead, one would know what one is, where one is, and why one is what one is and where one is, and also what one should do. Captivated by the spell of Maya, one is a captive of one's own illusions. Just as a spider spins out threads from within itself and spreads them around itself, it cannot find a way out of the web. One who searches finds it within oneself. And one who does not search never finds the pure jewel. One who plants the tree of hatred in the soil of one's mind reaps its fruits, suffers and gets hurt by the thorns of the tree.

• • •

**The Mirage**

Pity indeed, a hundred pities that people in this world do not tread the path of justice. If you ponder, you will find that what appears to be a river full of waves is only a mirage. And the pleasure that you relish as nectar is death-dealing poison. But led by *Maya,* people do not understand what is good and what is bad for them. They are like the blind who cannot see anything.

• • •

He says that one rarely finds a person who ever came out of the whirlpool of *Maya* to reach the shore, like a peacock with a beautiful coat of feathers but snakes for its food. There is not one person to be seen who, remembering the name of God, attains mastery over his senses, which are the real enemies. There are very few such persons who think of the other world. On the other hand, there are many who sport the sacred thread around their necks, show the conch in their hands and worship some form of deity or take pride in worshipping the *Shivalingam.* Why do these fools do all this? To earn fame and reputation that so-and-so is a great observer of penance. They go to great lengths to take recourse to magic and deception like Samundrapal. It is said that he would cast a net and sit down with a rosary counting beads and ask now and then whether any bird had got caught in the net or not.

• • •

Bali Ram further asserts that there have been many sages who did not get worldly pleasures and therefore became *sanyasins* but carried in their hearts the desire for wealth and affluence and worldly things. Like vultures, they made loud noises that they had renounced the world, but actually they had their eyes on killing and eating up other living beings.

• • •

It is said that a man who is hungry and needs a whole loaf to satisfy his hunger is content with half a loaf, but a man who is fully satiated hungers for the whole world and still remains hungry. With him, it is not hunger but greed, lust.

• • •

One who is in search of the path to the other world needs to have a lot of courage and strength of will. Looking within, such a man takes to the straight path at the start itself, and reaches his goal.... All the *varnas,* communities and religions have shown their own paths and prescribed practices peculiar to them, and those born in them should follow the respective paths and not of others. Following one's own religion, one can cross over the ocean of this world easily and also do some good to the world. People in this world suffer due to their faults and misdeeds, otherwise God has made everything so natural and easy.

**The Refrain**

Kings and rulers in *kaliyuga* beginning with Yudhishthira, suffered sorrows and enjoyed pleasures during their reigns under the influence of the times and circumstances and due to attachment and weaknesses in their own character. I have described all these in this *Rajavali.* It is written in the Quran and the Puranas that each day is different from the other, and tomorrow cannot be today. Therefore this epoch of *kaliyuga* with its growing hold on people has made the whole world, particularly India, a place where there is increasing greed, false pride, deception and quarrels and bickerings in every home. Nobody loves anybody any more. Self-interest has become the ruling passion. And there are more and more sufferings, sorrows, regrets, fear of the powerful, hunger and troubles for the people.

• • •

I have written this *Rajavali* with the aim of telling people who find his world real that they should pass through it bearing in mind that it is unreal. They should take to the path of virtue, should be mindful of the future, should consider this body as a piece of wood that will burn to ashes, should steady the mind which is always hankering after pleasurable experiences,

These days I go to the well to fetch water,
In the company of other woman.
People of this place, Gangatha, are dirty-minded;
They deliberately put blame on the blameless.
How is one to talk and laugh with others?

How is one to open one's heart to someone?
Advise me, O Devi Ditta,
How to appease the mother-in-law and the sister-in-law.

From *Sikkh Deyan Mikki Devi Ditta,* 18th-19th century *Tr.* by Shivanath

**2. Campaign against the Raja of Kangra:** The two *kavittas* throw light on the history of the period when Raja Ranjit Dev of Jammu (1725-81) sent an expeditionary force under the command of his son Braja Raja Dev, to vanquish the Raja of Kangra. The Raja of Kangra had forubing occupied Pathyar a part of territory of Raja of Chamba. The Raja of Chamba had lodged a complaint about it to the Raja of Jammu.

**I** The first *kavitta,* in the dialect spoken in Kangra, describes the advance of the Jammu forces on Kangra.

When we learnt that Pathyar was annexed from Chamba,
We knew that it was an act of foolishness.
The forces of Jammu have crossed the river,
And already reached *Maachhi Bhawan.*
Some time between today and tomorrow
The Guler forces will join them.
They must have devised a strategy to get the troops from Dadwal;
Fighters from Sibba will also join in large numbers,
Tell me how Jaswals will retain their pride.

**II** The feelings of the women of Jammu, anxious to welcome back their husbands, returning from the campaign have been described in the second *kavitta* in the dialect spoken in Jammu.

How will they who have relished
the waters of the snow-fed streams,
Like the tepid waters of the Tawi?
How will they who have enjoyed the mangoes of Panjala
Find taste in the watermelons of Kandi now?
We are tired of writing letters, and our eyes are sore
With watching the path of their return.
Dattu, who would like to come back leaving new pleasures?
Rains have set in, kindling yearnings in our hearts,
Why shouldn't your thoughts turn towards us?

From *Kavittas,* 18th-19th century *Tr.* by Shivanath

## In Praise of the Goddess

### Shiv Ram

Shiv Ram (Shiv Ram, 1775-1830) was a nephew of the poet Devi Ditta (1723-1811). He was a poet who wrote in Braja-bhasha and Dogri.

He does not appear to have written much. The only Dogri poem of his that is extant is a prayer to the goddess.

Victory to you
O boon-giver,
be pleased with me!

Show kindness,
you with the effulgence
of a million suns.

Those who serve the Mother,
always get success
and prosperity.

They get the name
and fame of gods.
and the lord of gods.

Whenever someone remembers you,
you go to his help,
like the Supreme Lord

Who responded
to the cry of the king
among elephants.

Why do you worry your head, Shiv Ram?
Lord Shiva's beloved will relieve you of all troubles.

From *Deivi Maihma*, 18th-19th century *Tr.* by Shivanath

## Selections

### Lakkhu

Lakkhu (Lakkhu,1775-1840) was a Dogri poet who wrote in Braja-bhasha also. He is known for his riddles which were rhymed. He was born in the village Baguna, tehsil-Samba in Jammu. He was a carpenter and an ironsmith. Not well-educated, he was more a versifier than a poet, but his riddles, put together to please his wife who was fond of them, in rhyming verses of four, six or eight lines, form an important element of Dogri poetry.

### 1. Poems

**(i)** The following poem of his is a conglomeration of names—of places, fruits, musical instruments joined together and pinned together by the concluding couplet.

Lahore, Jhelum, Gujarat, Kashmir, Kabul,
Jammu, Kangra, Jhang, Multan I saw;
Poonch, Kargil, Gilgit, Kot Mittha
Yarkund, Ghazani, Khurasan I saw;
Lakkhu saw Balkh and Bukhara also;
But without the beloved, they looked deserted.

Grapes, sour and sweet, *batanks* and berries, *behis,*
Apples, pears, and *chotas* full of juice I saw.
Plums, pomegranates, walnuts and other dry fruits.
Innumerable fruits, plantains and bananas I saw.
Lakkhu walked through orchards also;
But without the beloved, they looked barren.
Singlestring *king,* bells, *sarang, sitar* and *dholak,*
*Veena,* flute, and the rhythm of cymbals I heard.
Drums, *damru, tabla, mridang*and *mainna,*
Brass plates and *kainsees* and *khaital* I heard.
Lakkhu heard and saw several musical instruments,
But without the beloved, they all sounded out of tune.

**(ii)** The second poem, given below, is a table of ten, composed with rhyming lines so that, it can be easily memorised.

One ten is ten,
Come in its infancy.

Two ten is twenty,
Come asking for sugar and *ghee.*

Three ten is thirty,
Tamed like a tiger.

Four ten is forty,
Becomes a pucca ploughman.

Five ten is fifty,
Asks for the way to pilgrim places.

Six ten is sixty
Places a cot inside.

Seven ten is seventy,
Tongue gets tied.

Eight ten is eighty,
Speaks out everything.

Nine ten is ninety,
Gnashes his teeth.

Ten ten is a hundred,
Lakkhu, there is no more fear.

18th-19th century *Tr.* by Shivanath

**2. Riddles**

Lakkhu has also written riddles, which are short pieces. Here in each riddle the poet also describes the situation in which he has created the riddle. His wife, Pakkho, who used to encourage him to create a new riddle before every meal, has been mentioned in riddles.

**(i)** It binds water
Holding body.
In *Thatti* village
It is grown.

Please dispatch us
A bit *campa*[1],
If you have it,
In your town.

Snatching health,
And beauty, wealth.
Casting this too,
A blot on you.

Lakkhu says that
*campa* is bad;
Get some other gift,
If you want.

[Ans. Opium]

**(ii)** They were alive,
And grass they ate.
When they died,
Started eating dates.

This is a riddle
Lakkhu made
When in *Kulli*
Pakkho went.

[Ans. Hides of dead animals]

**(iii)** A legged creature,
Is being tried,
By winged creature
In the sky.

1. A hut thatched with grass.

It is a riddle
Lakkhu made,
Sitting in the
Cooking place.

[Ans. A wasp carrying an insect]

**(vi)** In the Akkhani,
Hatching Makkhani.
Border merely,
Wheat 'nd barley.

Lakkhu says
this riddle comes
while sucking
sugarcane.

[Ans. A bird hatching eggs at the edge of a field]

**(v)** Rising cloud from
Southern country
Showering it on
Mountains high.

It has wetted
Higher places,
keeping dry
All lower places.

This is a riddle,
Lakkhu told,
My dear Pakkho,
You find out.

[Ans. A Chapati half-smeared with ghee]

**(vi)**

A water pit,
Dips in a pit,
And catches it,
A water pit.

Lovely riddle,
Lakkhu made,
Beating on the anvil,
Making ploughshare.

[Ans. A snake chasing a frog in the pit of water]

From *Bujhartan,* 18th-19th century *Tr.* by Desh Bandhu Dogra "Nutan"

# 8
# Medieval Nepali Literature

### Acharya Vishnupada

There had poets earlier too, but Acharya Visnupada (Acharya Vishnupada) or Vishnudasa (?-1393), a court chronologer of the Raskotian kings of Nepal is regarded as the first Nepali poet. His long prosaic chronicle of the Bamma (Varma) dynasty *Badai Raja Malaya Bamma* (Bada Raja Malaya Bamma) is a plain poetical piece on the achievements of Malaya Varma. Although an encomium in its nature, it helps to confirm the fact that Nepali poetry is laced with heroic rather than devotional sentiments.

The people's king Malaya Varma
Made his sword glitter in the air
Made his sword glitter on the land
The first king, the great king Malaya Varma
Enlightened the palace of Khadachakra.

The Manasarovara and Haridvara
He conjoined in his land.
There came the door-keepers,
There came the fort-keepers,
Made the Manasarovara flow through his land
And wiped his sword in the Alakananda,
And wiped his sword in the Bhagirathi,
The king Malaya Varma then sat on the throne.

Seated on the Delhi throne for one and a half day
He revised the rules,
Going to Jodhpur, the regime he changed
The King Malaya Varma then sat on the throne.

Then the king had a vision of Badri Narayana and Haridvara
Slaying seven hundred Suyals and seven hundred Budans
He made the long ridge a solid shield
And amassed a good fortune
The king Malaya Varma then sat on the throne.

Going to the east he defeated China
Going to the south he defeated Bengal
And flashed his sword in Sirmaura
The king Malaya Varma then sat on the throne.

Then the king conquered Ruhelkhanda,
Uttar Kasi and Kedarnath (?)
And gold in tributes came from Tibet
The king Malaya Varma then sat on the throne.

Then the great king Malaya Varma
Suffered a lot in the Liglig fort
And reaching there in Kathmandu
Offered a mace to Pashupati
And camped in a flower garden
Encircled by mace-carriers
The king Malaya Varma then sat on the throne.

Then the king invaded Dan
He slew the English, Moghals and Turks
And brought he changes in Doti Raj
Going to Garwal he revised the tithe
Going to Guguche he changed the rule
And summoned all the kings therein.
The Kumau king offered coconuts, the Doti king logs
The Sirali king presented fowls, the Chatyan king an·umbrella
The Salvan king tendered horses, the Bajhang king a gown
The Pokhar king preferred coins, the Dangal king a ladle
And along with his courtiers.
The Baijanathi king threw a feast
He wiped his sword in the Budiganga
The king Malaya Varma then sat on the throne.

Then the king Malaya Varma
Opened a market at Khadachakra
And raised a long boundary wall
And fenced the temple of Khocheranath
And the stewards and sentinels
The cavaliers and the charioteers
All attending from Dullu country
Kindled earthen-lamps in the temple
The worship went on for two and a half years
They lighted the lamps in the central place
Black pepper came from Maharashtra
And chillies from Ghodasain

Oil sufficed even for swimming
Thus *ashtami* was observed at Lamathada
The king Malaya Varma then sat on the throne
The king was thus coronated in the Khadachakra palace.

*Badai Raja Malaya Bamma,* c. 14th century *Tr.* by Gokul Sinha

**Blessing** *Raghunath Bhat*

The poem *Ashis* (As is, 1774) by the earliest Nepali heroic poem *Ashis* was written by Raghunath Bhat (18 century). Here the bard, first invokes the war-goddesses and then offers his benedictory wishes to his king, who is on his military campaign.

O horrible-mouthed one, roaring with a thundering sound,
Delirious with blood-thirst, sharp fleeting foremost,
O fair-haired one, having a triumphal garland in hand
And a wreath of headless trunks donning the breast,

Clapping for a fearful fighting, dancing out of tune
Begemmed with a goblin's eyes and raising greasy hands,
Bestower of fearlessness and defender of the devotee
May the mighty Mahakali give you a quarter for aye!

Kali, Gorakh, Vairavi and Mahishamardini ever more
May the blessings of these four be with you for your victory!

*Ashis,* 18th century *Tr.* by Gokul Sinha

**Selections** *Prithvinarayan Saha*

Prithvinarayan Saha (Prithvinarayan Saha, 1722-74), founder-king of neo-Nepal, was a shrewd politician as well as a good writer. Some maxims were dictated by him to a scribe in December 1774, just a month before his death, and long afterwards they were published under the title of *Divyopadesha* (Divyopades´a). It has two sections, the first deals with the historical narration of Gorkha campaigns, while the second consists of a series of policy pronouncements on a variety of topics, such as trade and commerce, internal and external policies, administration and so on. A number of letters, specially concerning political stratagems and addressed to various allies and contemporaries, and two poems in *Sadhukkadi* language are also there to his credit. The letters may be considered as an early form of political literature.

A few of his maxims and three of his letters are given below:

**1. Divine Precepts:** As it goes, the old man dies, the speech shifts. Told in front of you all, you may convey it to your progeny and they to theirs. This way this kingdom shall subsist...

Besides, this kingdom is like a yam between two boulders. Keep a close relation with the king of China. Also keep good relations with the king of the Southern Sea; he is very cunning. He has kept India suppressed. He is at present in the plains. Should the people of India unite, it may become difficult for him and he will surely come hither in search of forts.

**The Foresight**

Fortify the fragile tracts and keep the routes restricted. One day this may prove a power. Do not go to cut down, but cut down if one comes. So more can be cut at the Cure Pass, and treasures can be had too for five to seven generations. Shri Gangaji will be our boundary. Do not permit the traders of the plains to come up further than Godprasah. If they come into our kingdom, they will make paupers of our people. Wearing hand-woven clothes, we managed to control three cities of Nepal and nine lakh of Kirats and built a Hindu state. Ban the use of foreign cloth. Show some sample to those who know weaving within the kingdom, and train them to weave cloth. This saves the cash from going outside.

**Ways to Earn Money**

Export the indigenous herbs and earn foreign currency. Earn money, it makes the subjects healthy and thereby the palace strong. The royal treasure is but the subjects. Besides, I always apprehend one thing and that is the Munglan or Mogal land of India is nearby. There are fallen and fancy women. They mire the man inside a fretted room with their songs, beatings of drum and playing of sitar. Songs and music have a great attraction and wealth flows too. The secrecy of a country is also exposed by them and the enemy will betray. So nobody shall practise music, neither shall they be allowed to come up to the hills. And promptly say good-bye to *fagu,* so that it will not be able to understand the secret of the country. For one's recreation it is all the same to see the classical dances of the Newars starting from three cities of Nepal. If you pay something for it, it shall remain within the country. This way, one's country remains happy.

From *Divyopadesha,* 18th century *Tr.* by Gokul Sinha

(i) ***Letters to Ramakrishna Kuwar:*** Svastishri Sarvopamayogya Rajabharasamartha Shri Ramakrishna Kuwarkeshu Ashishpurvaka Patramidam. I'm well; hope you're in good health. Rest, the news is fine here. Further, when Kalu Pandey was slain in the Kirtipur war, I was disheartened that I shall never get victory over the three cities of Nepal. But you got it by your wisdom and by the strength of your sword. For this, giving an honorarium of half of the state even falls short. I grant you the surroundings of Simbhu and Dhulikhel as a usufruct to your descendants. I condole the loss of your brother in the war of Timam. Now, the trust is in you to march upon the Kirats. Iti miti Asvina vadi 5 roj 4 mukam Kantipur subham.

**(ii)** ***Letter to Svastishri:*** Besides, you have written that so many enemies coming from Majhuwa, Kulum, Mahadingla were slain, so many fled and so many wounded. It is fine to learn. We had sent you earlier 21 pots of gunpowder and five thousand bullets. This time we are sending 20 pots of gunpowder, 6825 bullets, 45 tolas steel, 750 pieces of stones, 900 sheets of paper. Dispense with it. Miti Magha vadi 5 roj 1 mukam Kantipur subham.

**(iii)** ***Letter to Svastishri:*** Besides, it is learnt from your letter that four to five hundred of Kirats were slain. You've done very well. I'm very much pleased with you. In the campaigns of Nepal and Kirats, your labour is superior to other generals. Felicitating you vigour, I'm happy to send you 22 pairs of raiments; wear them. Other officials are also supplied with them, distribute as per the name-list. 25 guns have been sent, hope it will do. Miti Phalguna vadi 9 roj (?) mukam Kantipur subham.

Ramakrishna Kuwarko *Nauma*
*Tin Patra,* 18th century *Tr.* by Gokul Sinha

**Friendly Advice and Winning of Friends** *Bhanudatta*

Nepali fiction-writing begins with Bhanudatta's (Bhanudatta 18th century) *Hitopadesha-Mitralabha* (Hitopadesa-Mitralabha). Hitopadesha is a trend-setter in Sanskrit itself and its follow-up in Nepali is quite natural. Appraising the common taste, what Bhanudatta gave in translation has become the historical base of Nepali fiction. His competence in prose-writing is evident from the fact that within a couple of centuries an elegant style of story-writing was evolved in Nepali.

Shri Ganesaya Namah: The task of all gentlemen be fulfilled by the blessing of gifts from Dhurjati or Maharudra. The crescent moon, like a white bubble of River Ganga, is being decorated over the hair of Maharudra and remains lustrous. By listening to this Hitopadesha one can understand Sanskrit speech, become smart to participate in debating, and acquire knowledge of ethics.

**Learning is Ageless**

Learned people of this world will never be old; thinking that, for everlasting value one should concentrate on learning, and try for earning wealth. Think that Death is over our head to kill us any time; so do good deeds at the earliest. The greatest wealth in this world is learning because one's learning cannot be taken away by the king; those who think of fixing the price cannot do it. It can never be destroyed. That is why no greater wealth is there than learning.

The way a river takes away all the wastages to the inaccessible ocean, learning leads a man to the king. Thereafter, the fruit of fortune may be achieved. Two kinds of learning are famous in this world, one is knowledge of scriptures or scientific treatise the other is military science. Between these two kinds of learning the heroism of the former may decrease in old age and may become ridiculous in the society. The second kind of learning people will adore for the whole life.

**Learning breeds Humility**

That is why the learning of scriptures or scientific treatise is the greatest. Learned people are known as humble men. Deserving people are known by their humble manners; deserving people earn wealth. Do good deeds with that wealth. With good deeds one can be happy here in this world and also in the other world. Anything that is kept in an earthen pot will never be impure as a boy being taught in boyhood will never be ignorant. Stories are best way to teach ethics to children.

Hitopadesha has been prepared with stories from many books including Panchatantra, like Mitralabha, Suhrudbheda, Vigraha, Sandhi, etc. The city of Patna is situated on the banks of river Bhagirathi, a tributary of the Ganga. A king, Sudarshana by name, full of royal grandeur and power was there in that city. The king happened to learn two *shlokas* while performing rituals "give up all doubts of the mind".

> Give up all doubts of the mind.
> Scriptures are the eyes of all who see unseen objects.
> Those who don't have such scriptures are called blind-folded.
> Pride of youth, boast of wealth
> Dirty politics and indiscretion:
> If any of these four is possessed by a person,
> That will be a calamity.
> Better not talk about a person
> Who possesses all the four.

When he learnt these two stanzas wisdom drawned on King Sudarshana. He thought that all his sons were fools and had not read the scriptures and wondered how to discipline them. He thought: "What is the use of such sons who are not learned and devout. Like an eye which has no use but is only a burden to a man. It is said: only the birth of those sons who bring glory to the lineage is a real birth in a real sense.

He who is not reborn in this world after death is like the cycling of the earthen pot by the potter, but if he is a learned son, he glorifies the whole of his lineage like moonlight on a dark night. Sudarshana, the king, after thinking thus, invited all the scholars in the assembly and said: "O learned persons! listen to me, you are all great scholars among the learned community, can anyone among you teach my sons the scriptures and make them live a decent life, like a rebirth to them? If you polish brass with gold dust, it will shine like jewels; likewise, in the company of learned people, foolish man can be a gentleman.

**Company one Must Keep**

It is said that in the company of lowborn people one's mind becomes mean, in the company of the middle class people one's mind becomes intermediatory, and in the company of great people one's mind becomes broad. That is why I thought that my sons would be disciplined persons in the company of all you learned people." After hearing such words from the king, Vishnu Sharma, the Pandit learned in all the scriptures such as Brhaspati, requested the king: "O king! why cannot a person of royal birth be taught? No fruits will come from the bad deeds done by an unworthy person because even with great efforts in teaching a crane never learns. Any deed, if we do it properly, never goes in vain. There are other reasons too, those sons of royal birth will never be unworthy because in the mine of emerald jewels, brass is never found. You have my word, Okay. I will make all your sons experts and masters in all scriptures within a month."

When heard such words from Vishnu Sharma the king became happy he humbly said: "Pandit Ji, if the learned people consecrate a stone, that will be an idol. Like the insect that sits on the flowers and on the heads of great people, the lowborn in the company of the great people become great. The metals in the eastern region become shining when the rays of the rising sun fall on them; in the same way in the company of decent people the low-born become great. Hence, I depend wholly upon you to give proper courses to all my sons."

After saying this the king called all his sons he introduced them to Vishnu Sharma. He ordered his sons to obey the sage Vishnu Sharma. Pandit Vishnu Sharma took all the princes to the top floor of the palace and started narrating interesting stories. He said to them: "O princes, the learned people pass their days by listening to poetics, the foolish people pass their days indulging in gambling, joking or by sleeping. Thereafter, to make you all happy I shall tell you wonderful stories of crows and tortoises."

From *Hitopadesha-Mitralabha,* 18th century *Tr.* by Haren Allay

**A Dialogue Between Lakshmi and Dharma**

*Lakshmi-Dharma Samvada* has been written in Sanskrit by Ramabhadra Padya Regmi is most probably translated into Nepali from his Sanskrit work of the same title. Even Bhanubhakta Acharya might have gone through this work and got inspiration to compose his *Badhushiksha,* an oft-discussed topic in modern women's circles.

> Where is truth there lives Lakshmi, the Goddess of Wealth.
> Where lives Goddess of Wealth, there lives Lord Vishnu.
> Where lives Lord Vishnu, there flourishes Dharma.
> Where there is Dharma, there is victory.

Dharma says: "O Goddess of Wealth, all people worship you in the world but why don't you go to every house? Some people are very rich, some people are very poor, what are the reasons for this? Why do you do this mistake? Why do you show this partiality?

The Goddess of Wealth says: "O Dharma! I shall tell you in detail, please listen to me. I live in the hands of womenfolk. I live with womenfolk. I shall tell you the bad habits of womenfolk. Listen, those women who are impolite, harsh, quarrelsome, insulting, over-sleepy and lazy are bad. Listen, those women who put spit and snot on the wall, who do not pick up spilt and fallen things, who do not care for pure and impure food, who mishandle utensils, who are without good conduct and who do not bathe, who keep clothes carelessly, who sit showing their hair in public, who go to bed with wet feet, are all of bad character. "Now, I shall tell you about bad eating habits; please listen. She who without serving food to her family and her husband eats secretly, who does not feel the taste while eating, the voracious eater, I never stay in the house of such a woman. Only devils live in such a house, they eat themselves. If such a woman earns property by working hard, day and night, all earnings of such a house will be taken away by the devils. As water in a copper pot evaporates, the property of such a house disappears, is taken away by the devils."

Dharma says: "O Goddess of Wealth, anything stolen by you in your previous birth, can be witnessed in this birth. Please listen! The curse of stealing gold and copper will be boils and skin diseases; by stealing brass one will be born as an ox; by stealing cotton, white-spotted leprosy will spread on one's body; by grabbing land one will be affected by waterphobia; by stealing books, one will be deaf and dumb; one who slanders gods and teachers will remain ever feeble; by stealing food one will be poor; by stealing metals, one will be childless. Ploughing land people of upper castes and warrior castes is probihited. If they do so, they will slaves for eight births and only then get salvation. . . ."

In the Saka year 1716 corresponding to Vikram Samvat 1851 on the 12th day, in the month of March and April at 4 p.m. at this auspicious hour, with a view to preparing a book I wrote what I found and viewed; learned people, please do not blame me. This written by Ramabhadraupadhyaya. Ram, Ram, Ram. . . . Here ends this gracefully.

From *Lakshmi-Dharma Samvada,* 18th century *Tr.* by Haren Allay

**A Bunch of Humour**

**Shaktiballava Aryal:** Shaktiballava Aryal (Saktiballava Aryal, 18th century) was a court scholar who chiefly concentrated on Sanskrit literature. His knowledge of Sanskrit poetics must have promoted classical metres in Nepali verse. But he himself wrote only two four-line verses in Nepali.

Nonetheless, he is most remembered for his play that earned him the title of "the first Nepali playwright". He wrote two Sanskrit plays *Jayaratnakar Nataka* (Jayaratnakar Nataka) and *Hasyakadamba* (Hasyakadamba). The latter was rendered into Nepali by the author himself.

A specimen from the first scene is given below:

The stage has been erected and draped properly. The artists get ready with necessary costumes and perfumes. After that, going to the stage the singers, dancers, actors and all collectively sing *nandi* chorus. There is no need for detail now. After *nandi,* one of the artists called Sutradhara (impresario) comes to front of the stage and addressing His Majesty Ranabahadur Saha, the king of Nepal, a country like a mark on the forehead of the world, who had graced the occasion with his princely presence, speaks: "Hail Your Highness!" and bows down.

**Sutradhara Speaks**

Then the Sutradhara, giving his ear to the sky, hears something and speaks:

"Aha! How to live here without my loving actress!" He looks at the screen from where the actors enter the stage and calls out:

"Today while giving ear to the sky I heard the nice story of a king named Pratapasena, O deer-eyed dancer! He is a leader among the kings of this earth. Therefore, on the basis of the same story, let us all have a play. Prepare the stage with curtains. All the artists with their instruments come on this stage. O lotus-eyed! O sweet ogler! Favourite of the love-god! embellished with sandal, musk and other perfumes, having two rounded breasts! O deer-eyed! O dear! Come over here, soon."

Hearing these words of the Sutradhara, a *nati* artiste named Kuranganayana enters the stage and speaks:

"O Aryaputra! Whose assembly is this?"

Sutradhara: It is the assembly of one who is full of fame and fortune, who is terrible to the kings of the world because of his tightened bows and mighty arrows, and he is none but the all-powerful king Ranabahadur Saha, the son of Pratap Saha, the son of Prithvinarayan Saha, the lord of Nepal.

Nati: O my lord! How is it! Why are you dragging a serf like me over here?

Sutradhara: (Laughing) What else does a woman know who is confined to the kitchen or lag in cosmetics! They only worry for what is and what is not in the household, crack a joke or play a prank with their husbands, that is all. They don't know who is miser or rich and who is foolish or wise. O deer-eyed woman! You need not feel ashamed. Why? Because, it is no shame for the pundits to read the Puranas, for the ideal kings to rule their state, for the noble wives to wash their husband's feet, for the merchants to sell their goods, for the beggars to beg and for the dancers and courtesans to sing and dance.

Nati: O Lord! You reminded me, I remember (moving around the Sutradhara and laughing) there is a town called Kinjalkpur, one hundred yojanas away from here, where there is a king named Dhaval Pratap Simha. My maternal home is also there. Once my father Jayapal used to describe the fame and valour of Nepalesvara Ranabahadur Saha to my mother Kaumudi. Now you too are describing the same. Ah! I am blessed! Blessed am I!

Sutradhara: O dear! How did your father come to know the good name of Nepalesvara Ranabahadur Saha?

Nati: O prudent one! Listen to me. The sound of cymbal is heard upto a distance of one yojana, the sound of a thunderbolt upto ten yojanas but the fame and name of a charitable person reach the three worlds. Lakshmi, the daughter of the ocean, sits by the side of a generous person. The uncommon deeds of such a person spread roaring all over.

Sutradhara: (Looking towards the green room) O tumtum-players! flute-players! Sarangi-players! Come to this august assembly. (They enter).

Nati: O thoroughbred! Which poet's play is being performed? Out of the nine *rasas,* which one does their play have?

Sutradhara: (Wondering) O weaker-vessel! Don't you know even this? Fie, shame on you. There are many respectable pundits in this city of Nepal. Among them there is one whose writings are far sweeter than those of others. Similarly, some are fine in poesy, some are physicians, some are astrologers who, like fowls, live just for food, some are logicians, some *tantrics.* O my better-half! But I don't like them. Therefore, we have to detail here the lusciousness of the learned poet Shaktiballava. What is the use of studying poetics and other ancillary literature? Poetry rejoices like a dancer in front of him whose base is Krishna. Among the nine *rasas, hasyarasa* or humour being the best, it is better to have an example of it. Over and above, it is the spring season. Women are now plucking the *shirish* blossoms. Trees are rife with flowers. Black bees are humming around the groves and cuckoos are cooing. Birds are fluttering in the sky. *Ashoka* trees are blooming. O deer-eyed lady! It is the spring festival!

From *Hasyakadamba,* 18th century *Tr.* by Gokul Sinha

**Rhymes on the Bull**

**Radhaballava Aryal:** *Sandhyako Kavitta* (Sandhyako Kavitta) is a poem by Radhaballava Aryal (Radhaballava Aryal, 18th century). Bull being the vehicle of Lord Shiva, a lot has been written on this subject in Nepali at all times, in all modes. One of the rulers, who was very fond of tauromachy, inspired a number of rhymesters to compose plucky verses.

Not less than six poems are found written by known and unknown bards. The one given below is the oldest known. It is a long poem of one hundred and seventy lines, of which only the first ten lines are reproduced here.

Shri Ganapatyaya namah
Swelling bodies, strong and hard
Bellowing sensually roving in the grove
Bully the brave is a terrible fight.
Hoary-haired, blustering aloud,
Like the rumbling cloud
Breaks the mounds, drifts the dirt
Covering stars and moon.
Dauntless sons of bovine fight so.
In such combat as waves do rise

Bound their bodies, looking so gruesome
Waging a war against the one
Who belongs to none but the same stock,
Fighting deadly with all trick and flam
Just to delight the assembled human folk
And to excite the love-god rife in them. . .

From *Sandhyako Kavitta*, 18th century *Tr.* by Gokul Sinha

**The Story of the Ten Princes**

*Dandi's Dashakumaracharita* is a famous work of fiction in Sanskrit. Writers in modern languages have not failed to admire it by rendering it in their respective tongues. The one who wrote it is not known. There are two translations in Nepali; both are anonymous. The first of the two extant Nepali renderings is partially given here which has well attempted to keep up the *Dandinah padalalityam* in Nepali as well. Like that of the original, its language is also sweet and simple, lucid and larkish. The piece is an exemplary prose work of the period.

One of the best cities in Magadh is the one called Pushpapur; all the other cities seem petty before its beauty. King Rajhansa, handsome like the god of love, as strong as the shining, mid-day sun, removing the miseries caused by enemies with his own power, eliminating the troubles of all the intellectual Brahmins with the gifts from the ritual of worship every day, ruling over the whole earth up to the oceans, spreading in all directions full praise for his good deeds, like the scent of jasmine flower, white like the moon, listening to the continuous singing of divine singers in the beautiful garden of Indra, the king of the gods, and having long limbs like the mountain Mandara at the churning of the ocean-like armies of the enemy. He had a wife named Basumati who was expert in all arts and was of an endearing manner. Staying in Pushpapur, the king of Magadh used to reign over the earth like his own wife.

**Like-minded**

The king was a traditionalist and had chosen his minister who could think the way he did. They were Dharmapala, Padmodbhava and Sitavarma. Among them Sitavarma had two sons, Sumati and Satyavarma; Padmodbhava had two sons, Susruta and Ratnodbhava; and Dharmapala had three sons, Sumantra, Sumitra and Kampala. Among them religious-minded Satyavarma, thinking that his world is meaningless set out for a distant province on pilgrimage. Worldly and materialistic, Kampala, ignoring the order of his father and his brothers, also decided to go out to distant provinces. Due to his skill in business, Ratnodbhava decided to cross the ocean for business. And the remaining four sons of the ministers decided to stay on at home obeying their fathers.

King Rajhama got into a conflict with Mansara, the king of Malwa. He set out from Pushpapur to fight with him taking with him the elephant-army, the cavalry, the animal carts and the big line of infantry soldiers. Mansara, the king, also taking with him many elephants and infantry soldiers, advanced towards him. While advancing this way, the entire area was overcast by dust and with the running of animal carts, cavalry and soldiers it seemed as if angels came from heaven and were sprinkling red powder on the newly-wed couples on the occasion. With the sounds of drum-beat all the directions became deaf. Many soldiers were killed with arms and weapons. It was a fierce battle that was between two armies.

Rajhansa, the king of Magadh, made Mansara, the king of Malwa, a prisoner of war, but king Rajhansa was benevolent, so he made Mansara king of the same country. Thereafter, king Rajhansa desirous of a son as the heir to the throne, started meditating and worshipping God, the Creator. After some time passed, the queen, Basumati, dreamt one dawn that God came before her to hand over the fruits of the tree of wishfulfilment. And in course of time she became pregnant. The king also, inviting all the courtiers, observed the first ceremony of the pregnancy.

One day, when the king with all the friends, ministers and the royal priests were sitting in all grandeur in the assembly hall, the watchman brought an ascetic before the king and stood with folded hands. The king asked the ascetic whether he came there from the distant place as a spy in disguise. The ascetic replied, "O Lord! visiting in disguise the cities of the kingdom of Mansara, I have come here knowing all the secrets of that country. You know what it is? The king Mansara after being defeated by you and in disgrace, despair, disheartened, worshipped Lord Shiva, and making Him satisfied by his worship he succeeded in getting a mace, the killer of the brave, and after getting it he thought that there was none more powerful and brave than him and he is thinking of using this mace against you. Know yourself the rest O Lord!"

His ministers beseeched with him that the battle should not be fought with king Mansara. King Mansara had become very powerful after he had got the mace, king Rajhansa decided to fight the battle, ignoring the words of his ministers, to fight he said was the duty of the warrior class. Having decided to fight the battle, King Mansara with the help of the mace gifted by Lord Shiva and keeping ahead of all the soldiers, entered Magadha Kingdom.

From *Dashakumaracharita,* 18th century *Tr.* by Haren Allay

**Panta Quintet**

**Gumani Panta:** *Lokraj Panta* (Lokraj Panta, 1790-1847), a native of Almora, Kumaun, and usually known by his pen-name Gumani, was a shooting star in the Nepali literary firmament. Once a subject of the Gorkha Kingdom, he has left a few short verses in Nepali to deserve a place in its history. The poems of Panta are usually regarded as heroic. But he is a harbinger of devotional poems also. Some Ramayana themes are found for the first time in his compositions. Both sorts of verses are given here.

**1.** Ever bearing the burden of taxes, O God,
Not a single hair is left on the scalp,
Even though none is leaving your kingdom
Thanks to the Gorkha king *iti badati Gumani.*

**2.** Hark, O king Dasaratha! I make a prayer
I bow down at your lotus feet for ever;
I'm greatly scared of this worldly river
Instruct me how to cross it over.

**3.** The daughter-in-law of the great king Dasaratha
The daughter of the all-wise King Janaka
Is grief-stricken in the confinement of Ravana
O Rama, O Lakshmana, O father and mother mine!

**4.** Let the people worship Shiva with cymbals and drums;
Let the others adore Ganesha with prayers and songs
Some others may offer their faith at Bhavani's feet
*Dhanyatmatuladhamaniha ramate rame Gumani kavih.*

**5.** I deserved the abode of Indra, albeit on earth laid me down
God made this highland for me raising it from below
Fathoming my feelings the *kafals* became red with wrath
Turned some other trees to blue, hoary grey with shame.

*Panta Panchaka,* 18th-19th century *Tr.* by Gokul Sinha

**Royal Duties**

**Lalitatripura Sundari:** (Lalitatripura Sundari, 1790-1830) appears to be a lone female writer in the literary scene of this period. She was a widow queen of Giranayuddha Vikram Saha, and the regent of the young prince, Rajendravikram. To train her son in the statecraft, she translated *Rajadharma,* the duties of a king. The language and style of Lalita is mediocre. She died in 1830 at the age of thirty-eight or forty.

Sage Vaishampayana says to King Janamejaya: "O Lord Janamejaya! after giving away gifts by their own hands to all the friends, the Pancha (Five) Pandavas, Bidur, Dhrtarashtra and all the women-folk of the Bharata dynasty, were observing the six months, camping on the banks of River Ganga for a month. During that time many great people came to see them, such as scholars, learned young people, Vyasji, Naradji, Devalarshi, Kanvarshi with their disciples and the learned scholars of Vedas, Brahmins, sages, hermits of repute in all the Vedas. Seeing them coming, king Yudhishthira offered worship and respect to all with all rituals and gave seats to them at the royal place. Those hermits and sages accepted the respect offered by King Yudhishthira and sat on the bank of River Ganga as per seniority. Seeing King Yudhishthira in grief all the hermits and sages consoled him.

Narada who had been consulted by Vyasadevji and other sages. He said to King Yudhishthira: "O Lord Yudhishthira with your own might and the grace of Lord Krishna, you won the whole world with noble actions. This war was dangerous for the whole world and you have survived it and you have performed the duty of a warrior; why are you not happy. You have destroyed all your enemies; have you made your friends happy or not? After achieving this glory, have you freed yourself from grief or not?" Hearing these words of Narada, King Yudhishthira told him: "O Lord! by the grace of Lord Krishna and the grace of the Brahmins and with the skill and power of Bhima and Arjuna, I have conquered this world; my kingdom now spreads over the whole world. Even then due to temptation I destroyed my whole dynasty, for which I am feeling very sad. After Abhimanyu, son of Subhadra, the five sons of Draupadi, and all such sons are killed, what for is it to reign in this world? O Lord! while remembering these sons, I thought in my mind that it would have been better to lose the war than win it. What use has been winning the war after losing every male member of the family."

From *Rajadharma*. 18th-19th century *Tr.* by Haren Allay

**Mahabharata: Gada Parva**

**Vijayananda:** A great many writers of the later period have tried their acumen in rewriting the classical epics. Among the earliest known, Vijayananda's *Gada Parva* has survived the moths. It is a bulky book, yet not fully published, containing more than two hundred leaves in MSS. Nothing is known about the author's life and his other works. The language of *Gada Parva* is more religious than literary. Quality wise, it is neither fine nor poor; at best it can be called mediocre.

*Shri Ganeshayanamah. Shri Saradayi namah. Shri Gurave namah. Shri Krishnaya namah. Shri Bhimasenaya namah.*

King Dhritarashtra, after having listened to all the details of the Shalya Parva, again orders Sanjaya to explain all the details of the Gada Parva. "O, Sanjaya! after all our army was killed by the sons of Pandu in the battlefield, what bravery was shown by the rest? What did Kritavarma, Kripacharya, Ashvatthama, the son of brave Dronacharya, and Duryodhana, the man of little knowledge, do at that time?

Listening to this question of King Dhritarashtra, Sanjay a said: "O King Dhritarashtra! the fort of the royal warriors, after the remaining women and children fled from there, became empty and the three great warriors became restless. Hearing the shouts of applause of the victorious Pandavas, seeing the broken articles in the tents and going to search for king Duryodhana in the evening, those three, Kritavarma, Ashvatthama and Kripacharya, did not desire to stay on in the battlefield. Those three left towards the pond where Duryodhana was hiding. King Yudhishthira also, accompanying all his devout brothers and desiring to kill Duryodhana, started searching for him, but could not locate him. King Duryodhana, taking his mace with him by the power of his learning, was seated underneath the water in water-meditation.

The Panava army was very tired. They were nursing their wounded. The Pandavas were in their tents. Knowing that the Pandavas, who had left the battlefield, were resting, Kripacharya and the other three reached that pond where Duryodhana was sitting. They told the king, who was sleeping in the pond, "Taking three of us, please fight with King Yudhishthira, this is not the sleeping time; please get up. If you achieve victory, you would be king; if not, you would be in heaven. You have killed many soldiers of the Pandavas, the rest of them are all wounded and injured. Your bravery and speed will be unbearable to them. Do not be disheartened; please get up."

We are here to do your bidding. Please do not feel discouraged. Hearing such words from all the three of them, King Duryodhana said: "O brave heroes! After all the brave persons have died on the battlefield, you are still alive; I am fortunate to see you all. Although many of them died in the battle of the Kauravas and the Pandavas, you are the best heroes alive; I feel very happy. I have my brave heroes with me.

We are tired; we need rest now let us not do anything now; only then we can win over the Pandavas. You are all tired now, and I am myself tired due to the wounds inflicted. O brave heroes! The armies of the Pandavas are rejoicing and excited, hence I have no desire to fight with them. You are all restless to fight with the Pandavas, it is no wonder. You have all tried hard to win the battle but no one can win over death and defeat. You take rest here tonight. I can fight on the battlefield accompanying you all tomorrow. There is no doubt." that. Please all of you rest arsured?

The detailed discussions that occurred among King Duryodhana, Kripacharya, Ashvatthama and Kritavarma were narrated to King Dhritarashtra by Sanjaya in this way: "After this was said by Duryodhana and listened to by the others, Ashvatthama told the frustrated King Duryodhana: O Duryodhana, please get up! Good fortune will be yours. We will win over our enemies on the battlefield. O Lord! all the fire worshippers, meditators, truthful ones, purified with the Vedas, hospitable ones, animal sacrificers, pond-builders, irrigators, temple-builders, food-givers, worshippers, I have vowed today to kill. If I do not kill the enemies on the battlefield, before the passing of tonight, before sunrise, may my respectable words and the good deeds of my sacrifice not remain. O Lord! I will tell you this truth, please listen to it." O Lord! without killing the Panchalas I will not put off my amulet.

From *Mahabharata: Gada Parva,* 19th century *Tr.* by Haren Alley

**The Song of Govinda**

**Hinavyakarani Vidyapati:** Nepali *Gita-Govinda* (Gita-Govinda) is a prose translation of the poetic work of Jayadeva by Hinavyakarani Vidyapati. There are a few other poetical works to the credit of Vidyapati. His writings install him in the forefront of *ritivadi* poets in Nepali. Unlike the original, the prose style of Nepali *Gita-Govinda* is circumlocutive and tough. Though tough, it retains the cadence of the original.

Offering greetings and salutations to Lord Krishna, sportive with Radha in rapt romantic mood somewhere in a lonesome place on the banks of River Yamuna, wishing all living beings be protected, love be to Krishna, the hearts of the devotees be delighted, all sins be absolved, the poet named Jayadeva composed the work called *Gita-Govinda* full of songs.

Radha is the chief among all the womenfolk of Gopinis. Madhava, Lord Krishna, is Narayana. With a desire to eliminate the sorrows of the world, both Lord Krishna and Radha are incarnated as human beings like Uma and Shankara. They roam about on the banks of the River Yamuna in a romantic mood. Groves and bushes along the avenue seem like apartments of a palace where lascivious people and pairs make merry. Having seen Krishna playing amorously here and there in the groves and bushes, Nandji, the chief among the cowherds, fearing for his son, told Radha: "O Radha! Balkrishna may be afraid of this darkness in the jungle. Take him home." Hearing Nandji's words, Radha said, wondering,

"Oh. what fear during the day time?" Hearing her Nandji said, "Oh, when the cloud covers the sun and darkness falls in and around the bushes of the forest or even if there is no darkness, the young child may get frightened, therefore take him to his mother Yashoda."

**Goddess Saraswati**

By the grace of Goddess Saraswati the book titled, *Gita-Govinda* was easily written by the poet Jayadeva because in his mind Goddess Saraswati herself has housed as tutelary deity with diverse feats. Or, he is like a *chakravarti* or emperor among the retainers of Lakshmi seated in the lotus. Or, like the king witnessing the art of dance performed by Padmawati. Again, Radha is Lakshmi, Vasudeva is the son of Vasudeva, the remover of the world's misery, the killer of demons like Kamsa and others, the saviour of the devout disciples, born as the eighth incarnation from the womb of Devaki in human form to protect the world and to love Radha, the performer of the *rasalila,* the actor of varieties of fun and frolic. All sorts of his activities are just a sport. O devoted ones! If you all feel happy hearing the sacred song of Jayadeva, please listen to it. Just remembering Hari absolves sins. Remembering Hari now like that, listen to the four-foot rhymed song, the best among the sixty-four fine arts, an esplanade of orgasm, that is very pleasant, very amorous, very supple, very decent, very fine.

No poet has been born ever since who has found fault with the lyrical verses of Jayadhar. He was the one criticise the lyrical verses blessed by Saraswati. Only for the use of soft ditties is Umpatidhara a poet. But he is wrong in the use of numbers. So Jayadeva is abler. Similarly, the poet called Sarana is shrewd in extempore reasoning only; Acharya Govardhan is an expert in romantic writing only. Likewise poets Dhoyi, Kshamapati, Lakshmana Sena, Shrutidhara and others are all fine only in particular fields. But the lyrical poems of Jayadeva are fair, fine, elegant, beautiful and pristine, which can easily be grasped just by hearing. Unable to find flaws in his style, all admire Jayadeva and marvel at his ability.

O piscine Keshava! assuming the body of fish you have delivered the Vedas from the bottom of the sea easily during the great deluge. You created Brahma out of your navel and handed over the Vedas for the creation, which is the basic text to decide what is to be done and what is not to be done. Therefore the Vedas are like a boat that helps people cross the worldly ocean. O Lord! You are all-powerful: You can do and undo: You are the supreme of all. Victory to You! O Lord! May You be able to liberate the people bonded in Your snare of Maya. O Lord!

O turtle bodied Kesava! Assuming the form of a tortoise you uplifted the world on Your back. Again on Your mighty back You are upholding mountains and forests, a chain of creatures of flesh and blood, this heavy world You are preserving. O turtle-bodied! among all You are the ablest! O God!

O You who have taken the boar's body! Assuming the form of a boar, You have freed this world. While upholding the earth on the white tusk, it looked like a spot on the moon, O Lord!

O Impersonator Narasimha! Your lotus-hands bore dreadful sharp nails in their fingers, peculiar and unknown, that tore the bee-black body of the demon Hiranyakashyipu.

O Narasimha Keshava! O Vamanarupa Keshava: In the disguise of a dwarf as a beggar you crushed the pride of mighty Baliraja. Brahma watered your foot when stretched to heaven. The very libation of water is the Ganga that makes the people burning in sin cool. O able Lord! . . .

From *Gita-Govinda,* 19th century *Tr.* by Haren Allay

**Hymns of the Milkmaids**

**Indiras:** Very little is known of Indiras (1827-?) save his date of birth and only surviving poem *Gopika-Stuti* (Gopika-Stuti). It is a translation of the first half of the X canto of *Shrimadbhagavata* and comes to nineteen verses. It retains the original Sanskrit metre but the vocabulary of the translation is often obscure. However, it is a nice melody with a good sense of rhythm and use of alliteration.

Braja has become glorious because of your birth;
Lakshmi does dwell here because of your love;
Behold! O Beloved one! All are longing for you ever;
We are yours, vainly roaming about in dim despair.

Lotuses in autumn bloom all fair and fine
But your charming eyes outdo their shine
O God of Love we are but at your sweet service
Would not our passions be slaked as yet?
The desire has become poison, cruel like a devil;
It's like fire and lightning and thunder dreadful;
It is as panicky as the brat of the monster Maya;
O Best of All! We are afflicted all the more.

You are not the son of the milk-maid, we perceive;
You are the Supreme Soul of one and all;
You have come to this world by Brahma's call;
And you took this birth in the clan of cowherds.

We got a quarter and got rid of mortality;
We were from our heart-seeking your holy feet.
Place your lotus hands on our bowing heads,
The hands that hold the hands of Goddess Lakshmi.

You are the destroyer of the distress of Braja;
Compose our tattered minds too, we Gopikas pray,

Our hearts insist on chanting your hymns divine,
Show us your comely face as sweet as a lotus bud.

Your feet alone absolve the sins of meek mortals;
The feet that take you to the grazier with the kine;
And they rest upon the hood of the serpent Kaliya
Put those feet on our breasts and calm our lust.

Your soft voice and your sweet speeches as well,
Your heart-stealing charming glances and all;
Have made the minds of ours sensual and impatient;
O Krishna! give us the bliss of the nectar of your lips.

From *Gopika-Stuti,* 19th century *Tr.* by Gokul Sinha

**Prayers of Draupadi**

**Vidyaranyakesari Aryai:** *Draupadi Stuti* (Draupadi Stuti) by Vidyaranyakesari Aryal (Vidyaranyakesari Aryal, 1806-45) is an original composition, though based on the Sabha Parva of Mahabharata. It is ten stanzas in *Svagata* metre. Despite its originality the purests of Hindi literature have always criticised it. Of course, its first stanza is totally in Hindi. Aryal's *Yugal-Cit* of twenty-eight verses in *Shardulvikridita* is but a metrical translation from the Bhagavat Purana. His third poem *Venu-Git* is also a translation, but has not yet been published.

Dushasana is taking off my cloth;
I do come to your refuge, O Lord!
Save me from shame amidst the Kurus;
I'll be your maid for ever and ever.

For three days I've been in my period;
Respectable persons are seated around;
What'll be my position in front of them;
I'm nearing my death, O Lord of mine!

Properly performing the Rajasuya Yajna,
And crushing the pride of all the kings,
You exalted the glory of King Dharmaraja,
Heed to my supplication too today, I pray,

I'm the queen consort of five Pandavas,
And the only sister of king Nrpasena,
I've been your votaress since my very birth;
Fulfill the prayer of this poor one, O Lord!

No ethics is there in Kuru's assembly,
Though Bhishma, Drona, et al are all there,

Shame and shyness all gone out of sight;
The act is open and known everywhere.

Sitting at the window, Suyodhan's wife
Is telling the tale of mine to her friends;
She's looking at me with a leer and jeer;
O Krishna! my heart is breaking asunder.

Putana, the nurse was redeemed from bondage
Who had come to you to feed her breast;
Sudama saw you with a handful of grains;
His house was filled with wealth and corn.

None is benign in this world, but you;
None else to think of in such distress;
Consider your devotee in this hard time;
And win your spurs in the world again.

Dushasana got tired of stripping the cloth;
And covered his face with hands ashamed;
Hearing the call Hari converged upon there
Where Dushasana was pulling off her cloth.

Seeing the plight of Draupadi there
He wrapped Himself around her figure;
All the people highly praised His glory;
Blessed! Blessed! be the miracle of Hari!

From *Draupadi Stuti,* 19th century *Tr.* by M.B. Rai

**Life of Krishna**

**Yadunath Pokhrel:** Yadunath Pokhrel (Yadunath Pokhrel, 1808-?) is an odd figure, wholly unrepresentative of his time. He is better known as a *virkal* poet for his patriotic poems, *Stuti Padya* I, II and III. Yet his Krishnacharitra (Krsnacaritra) is a short composition of twenty-one verses in *Bhujangaprayata* metre. He is reckoned as a devout poet of *Krishnabhakti* school. The first five verses are given below:

Lolling in the lap of mother Yashoda,
Smiling, sucking and looking about,
As the Lord enlightens on all around,
Hari makes my mind full of delight.

Rattling anklets on the lotus-feet,
And tinkling bracelet around the waist,
Donned in fineries and playing pranks;
When I muse, my heart fills with mirth.

Golden rings glitters in the ears,
Curly hairs hang about the rosy cheeks,
The crown on the head is gracefully bedecked,
A divine picture the mind does portray.

Olive-wear wraps the body black,
And the wild-beads reach down the knees
In silhouette he shines like a lightning,
The Lord's good looks captivate my mind.

Tender are the lips; milky are the teeth,
When laughing, they illuminate the atmosphere,
Still the Lord sports in the mother's lap;
It makes my mind confused oft and oft.

From *Krishnacharitra,* 19th century *Tr.* by Gokul Sinha

**Brahmayajnopanishad**

**Yogi Ambargira:** Yogi Ambargira (-1833) was more a *yogi* than a writer. Still he has written a large number of books. The details of his life are not known. He was primarily a prose writer, yet has composed some couplets in *Sadhukkadi* tongue. Seven books at least have been ascribed to him. *Gita-Govinda, Vedanta, Brahmayajnavedanta, Brahmayajnopanisad, Yogavasishtasar, Vairagyambara* or *Asamanako Bhasha Shrimadbhagavata Gita.* The first and the last are found in fragments. Yogi Ambargira was most probably a priest in the Rama-temple of Janakpur in his later days. From his works he looks a *vedanti* but *Gita-Govinda* shows him an upholder of *bhaktimarga* also. Though his language is languid, the subject matter he took up is quite substantial. Josmani,' a religious cult that flourished for quite some time in Nepal have taken to his works. This cult if all there may be scattered.

*Om Namobhagavatey Basudevaya.* Brahma is one pure consciousness. Extraordinary, super power unique. Maya is unique. What is Brahma? It is like a tree and its shadow. Tree and shadow are not separate objects. Without the tree, where is the shadow? Such is the relation. Brahma is pure and conscious. Maya is transitory and sensitive. Then Brahma is above Maya. No one is above Brahma. Brahma is complete, invisible, supreme. Brahma desired to be many, and so three divine powers were created, i.e. desire, action and knowledge. From Maya these three divine powers were created. Negative suspicion is false.

Brahma has got five names: Brahma, Being, Time, Action, and Nature. The meaning of this is that completeness is Brahma; knowing not of himself is Being; knowing not of himself, but being seen in time, is called Time. Seeing the body is Action, and the creator and the action within action, sweet and bitter, hot and cold, respect and disrespect, misery and luxury, forms Nature. The names of Maya are five: Maya, Sky, Ether, Space, Energy and Nature. The meaning of this is Brahma who is complete and able due to Maya to whom the Universe is like a body and there is the sky which being inanimate is called Ether. Conquering the whole world is called Energy; due to revolution it is called Nature. By the conjugation of two such objects creation is started: the five essential elements and the human being formed of these elements. The five elements are thus created separately.

From *Brahmayajnopanishad,* 19th century *Tr.* by Haren Allay

**Markandeya Purana**

**Bhavanidatta Pandey:** Bhavanidatta Pandey (Bhavariidatta Pandey, 1825-?) has translated a number of Puranic works like *Mahabharata Udyoga Parva, Markandeya Purana* (Markandeya Purana), *Atmabodh* besides *Mudraraksasa* and *Hitopadesh.* Pandey has an important place in Nepali prose literature. His language is refined and graceful. Even an arid subject like *Vedanta* is handled in an easy and comprehensible way to make it intelligible to the common people.

The following extract is from the sixteenth chapter:

*Sri Ganeshaya Namah.* A Brahmin once asked his intelligent son: "O son! tell me about those addicted to the system of the world which moves round like a circling wheel and have never been freed from it.

"I also know that all this world is false. But I do not know-how to get salvation from this world. Now, what shall I have to do? Tell me about it."

**Son's advice to Father**

Hearing such words from his father, the son said: "O father! if you respect my words and if you do not suspect them, please go to the forest leaving this domestic life and spend your life there; living with discipline in the forest, even leaving the worshipping of sacred fire, fully concentrating on God, giving up friends and worldly life, living alone, controlling mind and heart, live a hermit's life. But even in a hermit's life, give up all sensual pleasures and concentrate on meditations.

"With such a hermit's life you will be freed from the miseries of worldly life, and achieve salvation; and you will achieve excellent and spontaneous meditative contemplation. O father! with such achievement, you do not have to face misery; and then you will achieve salvation with super-human power."

Hearing such words from his son, the father said: "O son! now tell me which way meditation will lead me to salvation. With the control of five essential elements, i.e., earth, water, fire, air and other, tell me the way of meditation, O my son! I may not come again to this world and bear this trouble.

O son, with the addiction to supreme knowledge, one does not feel worldly pleasure; due to my innocence I feel for the state of the poor and the rich but I have a soul which may not be tied up. Tell me the path of meditation. My soul and body are with the rays of the sun. Spray upon me cold water which is full of words of the eternal spirit.

O son, being stung by innocence as if by a black snake and being dead by its poison, may I and my soul be given life again with your words full of nectar.

"He is my son, she is my wife, this is my house, this is my paddy-field: with all these things I have been surrounded and with worldly love. To place myself in a better state, please make me free and save me with the key of supreme knowledge."

Hearing such words from his father, the son said: "O father, once when Alarka asked Dattatraya, the great and intelligent one, he had explained what meditation was in detail; the same way of meditation I will tell you, please listen to me."

From *Markandeya Purana,* 19th century *Tr.* by Haren Allay

**Life of Shrikrishna**

**Basanta Sharma:** Basanta Sharma (Basanta Sarma, 1803-1890) also known as Basanta Kavi or Basanta Jaisi, is a pioneer Krishnamargi poet. His *Shri Krishnacharitra* (Srikrisnacaritra) is regarded as the first Nepali epic or *khandakavya* having 169 stanzas in classical metre. It is his independent work based on the *Bhagavat Purana* with some alterations in the story. The translation of *Mahabharata* is another of his major works. In his *Mahabharata* and *Shri Krishnacharitra* he has omitted the so-called vulgar scenes; this shows him as a less sensuous and more devotional poet. Another famous poem of his is *Samudralahari,* a Vedantic treatise containing 90 stanzas in a local metre. All critics agree that there is a genuine use of the vernacular in his works. Certainly, with him we discern the beginning of a breakthrough in the matter of shedding Hindi influence in favour of a more colloquial Nepali diction.

**15 stanzas from the poem are given below:**

**(1)** Shri Krishna, a divine incarnation, was born
in a certain city called Mathurapuri.
Wielded in his hands were the conch, the wheel,
the mace and the lotus;
His feet were as soft as the lotus itself.
A bejewelled crown he had on his head,
the wheel of *sudarshana* in his hand.
Shri Basudeva saw in him this form
the complete view of the four-armed one
which He revealed.

(2) Vigilant were the sentries
along with the elephants, the lions and the serpents.
But all swooned away in the night
under the spell of the illusion created by the Lord.
The door got unlocked, the enemies duped,
and so easy was the path
that he reached Gokul sprinkling the water of Kalindi,
Offering his prayers, the most devoted one in the night.

(3) Jasudaji, the worthiest one
whose house Basudeva stepped into
by opening the door,
and in a moment he stood before her.
Sleeplessness, anxiety and exhaustion:
because of the Jasumati was unconscious then.
Mayadevi, these new-born baby,
Basudeva took back to Mathurapuri.

(4) The day dawned, the night was gone,
it was bright everywhere.
The sentries came back to their senses;
they walked towards the gate.
The moan of the mother lightly heard,
the demons came flocking by,
The evil ones all went close to Kamsa
they reported that a son was born.

(5) Kamsa leaped, dreadful he became
with cruel eyes.
He drew close to Basudeva
and sat there for a while.
Brooding over something unknown;
he quickly dragged the baby away
from the lap of Devakiji,
and on an impulse took it into his arms.

(6) "Please do not kill it", Devakiji entreated thus.
His eyes were red, Kamsa was angry;
he did not care to reply.
Full of anger he caught the baby
desirous of killing it by all means.
Something miraculous did happen then
When the door was opened and
he brought the baby out.

**(7)** Mayadevi, Mother of the Universe, she was there
for a fraction of a second
The lock of the arms she broke and flew
up into the heaven with the speed of lightning.
A voice was heard, a revelation—
audible to each and every one,
that at Gokul his slayer was already born.

**(8)** On hearing this, King Kamsa returned
full of anxiety.
The future was fore-told;
his mind was in a fix
Back at the palace he called his ministers
and counselling did he take, to make sure
that, at Gokul, all new-born babies
were put to the sword, sparing not a single one.

**(9)** When the orders were passed thus,
everybody was alerted,
And those at the services of Kamsa
proceeded at the very next instance.
Hounding out day and night,
all became professed hunters.
But all the babies, in the kingdom,
were facing a great trial.

**(10)** The rays of the sun were manifest upon the earth
and Yashoda was awake;
Delighted very much the was
when she glanced at the baby's face
With supernatural sight she perceived
Bedecked with jewels the crown was there
over the forehead,
She smiled at once and planted a kiss
on the face of the Lord.

**(11)** A propagation of progeny she felt it was,
which amused her exceedingly.
To see such a countenance
but it was a matter of conjecture.
She went to Brahma, the sage, for an enquiry;
with folded hands she narrated all;
With devotion and concentration full
she told him all that had happened.

**(12)** Brahmaji reached Gokul, where he was received
with full paraphernalia
Going through the Shastras, the pros and cons,
He proclaimed the incarnation of Lord Krishna.
Saying this Brahmaji went out of sight;
which was followed by Krishna's naming
that took place in a gay ceremony.

**(13)** The *mrdanga,* the conch, the drum and the flute
the trumpet, the *damaru,* the cymbals, the *majira*
the *sitar,* the *veena* and the *khaijadi*
the *ektara* and other instruments all emitting strains,
of various kinds including the *dholak* too:
They were all played in tune with the set of nine
Exhilarating on the occasion of the naming day.
Extremely fickle was Kamsa's mind

**(14)** at this hour of the day;
worried he was, he spent in gloom the whole day;
scheming something once again, he called Putana
and told her all about his device.
Pleased he was for having heard
what Putana promised that day.

**(15)** Full of guile in her mind,
Putana thought for the second time.
She smeared poison on the nipples of her breast
and proceeded towards Gokul.
Finding Krishna alone she started
feeding Him at her breast.
But Krishna sucked her to death.

From *Shri Krishnacharitra,* 19th century *Tr.* by M.B. Rai

**The Book of Beauty**

**Raghunath Bhatta:** Raghunath Bhatta (Raghunath Bhatta, 1811-51) preceded Bhanubhakta in writing *Ramayana,* yet he lags behind in popularity when compared with him in language and style. But as an independent poet, we can ascribe to him a strong sensibility. His poems prove him an extempore poet, who could wield his pen with ease under every circumstance. He possessed a good knowledge of Sanskrit prosody and profusely used it in his writings. His *Sundarakanda* (Sundarakanda) is a treasure house of classical metres.

Exerting utmost strength,
And making the ocean a cow-hoof pond,
Setting ablaze the demons

Making his body as big as Mount Sumeru
He earned the name of a learned one
How fortunate! Hanuman came back again,
Kapipati, an appellation he got,
And gained the love of Shri Rama.

Doffing doubts with elation.
Hanuman leaped to cross the ocean
Which measured a hundred *yojanas* in length,
Abounding with sea-animals.

Adoring in mind the feet of Rama, he spoke:
"O monkeys! look at me now, in the sky do I go.
I'll have the sight of Sita; blessed am I,
And coming back I apprise Rama sure, I will.

"One who remembers the name of Rama
At the time of his death
Shall cross this endless earthly ocean,
And salvation he gets.
I am His messenger, whose gold ring
Is with me as a token.
It's nothing to cross this limited ocean,
Just keeping Him in mind".

Patiently this much Hanuman spoke
And with stretched hands and a straight neck
With lowered eyes and feet drawn up
Facing south he flew fast in the air.

Seeing his flight, gods in heaven
Talked to each other
Whether Hanuman could enter Lanka.
Eager to know, they were.
Turning to Mother-Serpent, they asked
Her to hasten to test
The intellect and strength of Hanuman
With some tricks.

Surasa went to hinder Hanuman;
She sat blocking his way and said:
"Knowing my hunger, gods gave me food,
Now enter my belly, come, if you could."

"I'm on Shri Rama's duty," said Hanuman,
Having heard her words.

"I am going to search for Sita,
It takes me no time.
After apprising Rama the news of Sita
I shall come back and enter
Your mouth; please be content at present
with just my salutations."

Even then Surasa said: "Get into my mouth;
Right now;
If you don't, I'll devour you up,
Since I am very hungry."

"Open your mouth, I get in and go;
I'm in a great hurry,"
Said Hanuman and made his body
A *yojana* big, dauntlessly.

At this Surasa opened her mouth
As wide as five *yojanas,*
Grew Hanuman upto ten *yojanas.*
She further widened it to twenty.
As Hanuman became thirty *yojanas,*
She widened her mouth to fifty.
Nimbly Hanuman, like a ring, got in
And out of her mouth, and said:

"I entered your mouth and came back too
Now let me proceed, my salutations to you."
As she heard this, she wondered at it.
Blessing the monkey, she admitted defeat.

"I had been sent by the gods to gauge
Your strength, so I hindered you.
Easily you can have the sight of Sita
And reach the refuge of Rama as well."

Saying this Surasa to heaven withdrew,
And flew in the sky Hanuman too,
With the agility of Garuda,
Keeping the work of Shri Rama in mind.

The Ocean in the meantime whispered to Mainaka:
"As Sagara nurtured me, the name *Sagara* I got;
Rama will be born in his lineage, and in his job
A monkey comes, for his repose you go as a hill-tip."

The golden peak of Mainaka took a human form
Coming close to Hanuman made a request to him:
"Have some fruits, O monkey! and for a while rest;
I've come up to host you at the ocean's behest."

"Since I'm on Rama's duty, improper it is to eat;
So the recess matters not; quickly I've to go
In search of Sita anon," said Hanuman and
Touching him with his hands, he soared like a bird.

As he went a little way
He met a dreadful Simhika;
When she slackened his speed
He eyed down and behold her.

She could grab the reflection
And eat the creature
He killed her with a kick.
And darted, facing Lanka.

Going south he saw on the land
A lot of fruits, birds and deer.
Then he saw on the top of Trikuta
Lanka, covered under sea-walls.

"By night I shall enter the city of Ravana,"
Thought Hanuman and bided all day long.
Assuming a small form as night fell
He entered the door of Lanka and was gay.

From *Ramayana,* 19th century *Tr.* by Gokul Sinha

**Poems**

**Bhanubhakta Acharya:** The role of Bhanubhakta Acharya (Bhanubhakta Acarya, 1814-1868) The short and long poems of Bhanubhakta Acharya, primarily *Ramayana,* are fundamental to the evolution of modern Nepali literature. His role in literary scene of Nepal is of great importance. He is an apex of the medieval period and an initiator of modern literature. He is a watershed between the old and new sensibilities and strides both the ages. Highly honoured by the Nepali speaking world, he is reverently regarded as the *Adi Kavi,* the Poet Premier. He wrote not only a complete epic but a number of other works as well. But to establish a chronology of his compositions is somewhat complicated. He wrote Ramayana piecemeal and his short poems are occasional pieces. However, it is known that his first two works of translations were *Prashnottari* and *Balakanda.*

**1. The Book of Boyhood:** In 1852-53 he completed the rest of the cantos, the *Bhanubhaktiya Ramayana* fully resting on *Adhyatma Ramayana.* He had however completed the first canto of Balakanda in 1941. But Nepali Ramayana has no *sargas*. The seven *sargas* and three hundred ninety-one *shlokas* of *Adhyatma Ramayana* have been condensed into one hundred and thirty-nine stanzas by Bhanubhakta.

Here the first six stanzas are taken from the renderings of K.M. Munshi.

One day Narada went to *satyaloka* with a view to do good to the world. Brahma was there and he fell at his feet; so he was pleased. As soon as Brahma permitted him to ask what he desired to ask, he said to him, knowing that Brahma was pleased:

"O Brahma, I have heard everything, auspicious and inauspicious. There is nothing left for me to hear, yet I have a desire. When the *kaliyuga* will come, human beings will be loose in morals and will commit sins of many kinds being impelled to do so by low desires.

"Some will not speak the truth, some will speak ill of others. Some will desire to possess the wealth of others thinking that is good. Some will be infatuated towards the wives of others and some will have a liking for violence. They will consider the body to be the soul like beastly atheists.

Slaves of passion, they will treat the wife as a god. Fathers and mothers will be like enemies in their eyes. Being Brahmins, they will sell the Vedas. Even if some study them, they will do so for earning wealth, thinking wealth to be a great object.

Kshatriyas will not observe the rules of the caste and those that are low-born such as Shudras will perform austerities like the Brahmins. Many women will be ruined by showing hostility to their husbands and fathers-in-law. How will such fallen people be able to attain salvation having crossed the ocean of the world?

This is the anxiety in my mind and I have come to ask for a way out. O Ocean of Kindness! how will these cross the ocean of the world easily? By telling me the way by which they can cross the ocean of the world easily, please satisfy me."

Out of compassion for the world, when Narada asked this, Brahma was very happy to tell him about it. "O Narada! there is no other major means than Ramayana to dissolve all sins. It is like nectar, favourable to all."

"Hearing all elements from Shambhu, Parvati sings it. She feels very happy knowing that the name of Rama is endless. Those who sing it will easily cross this world. Even death shall have no effect. Their every fear will easily pass over.

Among all the scriptures, this book that tells the tale of Rama is the greatest. Know it to be the major one among all the Puranas as well. Those who recite or even hear it shall get the fruit, the merit of which I cannot describe myself.

I had heard its glory from Shiva that if one reads even a single stanza with devotion, all the sins will be absolved. One who recites it everyday delightedly and attentively, is freed from the bondage of worldly life. He is like a god, though a human being.

If one just worships the book, he gets the fruits of an *ashvamedha* or horse sacrifice, his sins will be gone instantly. One who simply greets and salutes the book, he will enjoy the fruits that are earned by worshipping all the gods.

The fruits which are not attainable by reading all the four Vedas and expounding the scriptures, that are easily obtained by donating the book. If on the day of *ekadashi,*[1] going to some devotees house, one reads it with devoutness, one shall get the fruits of twenty-four times *gayatri*[2] recitals.

One who takes fasting on *Ramanavami* and wakefully spends the night either reciting or hearing this Ramayana with rapt attention, know all that he has made a *tulapurushadana* after a pilgrimage on the occasion of solar eclipse. He will be blissful, no doubt.

Even Indra will obey the person who recites Ramayana, admitting him as dear to, and a devotee of Rama. Reading it daily, one who performs good deeds, gains fruits a crore times more; decreases not a jiffy.

To absolve sin, Rama will reside in the heart of a Brahmin-killer even, if he reads for three days his soul will be pure. Rama bestows mercy on him. One who reads daily thrice, keeping Hanuman in front, shall enjoy all sorts of pleasures as he desires.

One who reads it going round a *tulsi* or a *pipal* tree, his sins of all births, whatsoever, shall be gone then and there. *Rama Gita* is greater still therein, the glory of which is known only to Shiva; none other knows about it.

Parvati knows half of it, I know only one-fourth. I deem to say there is no sin that cannot be destroyed by reading the Gita. Churning the Vedas Rama took out Gita as sweet as nectar. He gave it to Lakshmana, reading which one can cross this world.

Parashurama with the keen intention of positively killing Kartavirya used to read it daily with Shiva, bowing at His feet. Hearing the recitation of Rama Gita by Parvati, he began to read it. This made him Narayana.

If one reads the Rama Gita for a whole month, all his *brahmahatyas*[1] and other sins will be absolved, what more should I say. If one reads Rama Gita by the side of a *saligrama,* a *tulsi,* a *pipal* or a *sanyasi,* he is a great *mahatma.*

The fruits that cannot be expressed in words, they shall enjoy. If one reads in *Sraddha,*[2] their ancestors will cross over the bonds.

---

1. The eleventh day of lunar month.
2. One of the most important *mantras* chanted by devotees.

Following the austerities, on the days of *dashami* and *ekadashi* as well sitting under the *agasti* tree, one who solemnly decides to read Gita, and reverently reads Rama Gita, taking a fasting, he is not a man but as much as Rama. Those who perform no alms, no meditation and no pilgrimage but read this Rama Gita only, they will attain an everlasting refuge crossing over this world easily.

From *Ramayana: Balakanda,* 19th century *Tr.* by K.M. Munshi & Gokul Sinha

**2.** Bhanubhakta went to Varanasi with his grandfather Shri Krishna Acharya in connection with the latter's Kashivasa. There he used to listen to Shankaracharya's *Maniratnamala* recited by Shri Krishna every morning. Over time Bhanubhakta learnt to reute it and he could understand it too. Hence he translated it. The original text in Sanskrit consists of 32 stanzas, whereas the translation has 50 stanzas in the *upendravajra* metre.

These fifteen stanzas are given here:

**(1)** Like one sunk into the deep sea
I am put onto this wide world.
Tell me soon where I can take shelter:
Shri Krishna's feet are the main boat to cross

**(2)** Who is the person who is always in bondage?
The one who is always after worldly pleasures.
What is meant by the term salvation?
Apathy towards worldly interests is salvation.

**(3)** What is regarded as the worst hell?
This very human body is the worst hell.
What kind of nature is regarded as heavenliness?
When all kinds of nature are completely given up.

**(4)** What is the highest knowledge for which one should strive?
The knowledge of Vedanta will liberate all from misery.
How can a person gain salvation of the soul easily?
The realisation of the self or knowledge and no more.

**(5)** Which is the main entrance to hell?
The passion in a man drags him to hell.
And which act leads him to heaven?
The act of non-violence leads him to heaven.

**(6)** What kind of a man goes to sleep happily?
The one who becomes one with the Supreme Being.

---

1. The sin of killing a Brahmin.
2. Funeral ceremonies.

Who is the one to know-how to be awake?
The one who distinguishes right from.wrong.

**(7)** Whom should regard as an enemy?
Our ten senses are our worst enemies.
And whom would we know as our friend?
Those who could control ten senses, they are the friends.

**(8)** Who is the person to be known as poor?
The one who is after hankering is poor.
Then who is really a rich person?
The one who remains contented is rich.

**(9)** Who is to be known as a living corpse?
The one who remains inactive is a living corpse.
What is as joyful as nectar? Desirelessness.
What is meant by bondage? Undue attachment.

**(10)** Who plays the part of alcohol?
A woman who captivates the mind.
Whom do the learned treat as trifling?
One who is a slave of passions.

**(11)** What is meant by death, tell me today?
It is slander which is as good as death.
Whom do you call the *guru* of all?
One who gives good advice is a *guru.*

**(12)** Who is a disciple, a true disciple?
One who offers services to his *guru.*
What is meant by a chronic disease?
The world's cycle of birth and death.

**(13)** What is the cure of one's chronic disease?
To treat the world as transient is the cure.
What is regarded by noble persons as ornament?
One's modesty is regarded as the best ornament.

**(14)** Which is the best holy place for pilgrimage?
One's pure mind is the best holy place.
What is regarded as trifle by wise men?
Women and wealth are regarded as trifles.

**(15)** Which is the best teaching that one should listen to?
The teaching of Vedanta is to be heard from a guru.

What are the ways of realizing the Absolute One?

A good company, study of Vedanta, and contemplation.

From *Prashnottara,* 19th century *Tr.* by Gokul Sinha

**3. Song of Rama:** The *Rama Gita* is a philosophical treatise of Bhanubhakta Acharya, based on the *Adhyatma Ramayana.* It is an independent work of the poet later included in his magnum opus, the *Ramayana.*

(*i*) The Lord took a human form for the welfare of the common people and acted as the wise oldsters. He performed phenomenal feats so that mankind may hear or tell His divine sports and crush the worldly bonds.

(*ii*) Once Lakshmana sitting by the Lord's side asked him what was the deadly poison. Rama told him that it was the property of a Brahmin and he narrated the story of King Nriga in detail. Lakshmana was convinced; still he went on asking questions.

(*iii*) O Lord! You are the personified knowledge, soul of all corporeals, still you took this form and redeemed earthly burdens by every means. Only the devotees know that it is a divine drama of the Lord in soul-personation. They further say this divine sport is on account of your compassion.

(*iv*) O Lord! Considering you the Supreme, I seek refuge at your feet. Teach me the way how I may cross over the abysmal ocean of *samsara* or the birth-cycle and enjoying bliss I may reach heaven with ease.

(*v*) Having heard these words of Lakshmana, Rama with a smiling face, removing all sorts of anguish of His devout brother, imparted the knowledge of reality which is enjoined even by the Vedas, as a secure bridge for mankind to cross over.

(*vi*) First of all discharging all the duties of *varna* or caste and *ashrama* or stage of life and thereby having subdued ten senses and the mind, one should approach the *guru* and with incessant service of the *guru* should ask for divine knowledge. Attaining this knowledge many have crossed the *samsara.*

(*vii*) If one performs his actions with a craving, he shall be born accordingly. He enjoys the fruits concerned and again performs many other actions with his mind attached. Consequently being led by the force of his actions he is born again in this very world. Thus he revolves in this world like a wheel.

(*viii*) It is ignorance that like a foe causes all to revolve. Know what it is the knowledge of Self that puts an end to ignorance. There is no difference between ignorance and actions. Therefore actions cannot destroy ignorance. Nothing but wisdom destroys it.

(*ix*) Neither ignorance nor attachment is destroyed by the nescient actions. Such actions make one cycling in this world. So one has to realize the wisdom that has helped many to cross through. Forsaking wisdom who has reached the end by actions only?

(*x*) Some say that the Vedas also enjoin action as a firm supporter to knowledge; so performance of action is ordained for support. Let them say so. But not a bit support does knowledge need. Know it. How far should I tell?

(*xi*) Actions reside in body as an integral ego. If there is knowledge, bodied ego will vanish. Knowledge and actions are inconsistent; how can they become affable? It is only knowledge that is able to afford salvation. Know it everywhere.

(*xii*) The *shrutis,* like Vajasaneyi, Taittiriya, also maintain that knowledge needs not the help of any other. As such, realizing action as repugnant, one should renounce it altogether, and should aspire after knowledge whole heartedly.

(*xiii*) The meaning of this profound saying, *tattvamasi* or that thou art, should be properly understood. It consists of three words. Construe the import of these three words. *Tat* stands for Supreme Spirit, the word *twam* for individual self, and both are united by one word *asi.* One should contemplate on it day and night.

(*xiv*) The body is composed of *maya* or illusion; eventually it passes away. It consists of five gross elements. The body which experiences the weal and woe of this world is called *sthulopadhi* or the larger basis of the principles of one's soul.

(*xv*) Made up of ten senses, one mind and non-divisible five elements, sixteen in all, this astral body is known as *sukshmopadhi* or the subtle basis. It is the main organ that experiences. This subtle one is always within the gross disguise. When it is removed, the gross one shall dissolve. It does not stop a while.

(*xvi*) The sentient soul is free to disguise like a pure and clear crystal. When it comes in contact with a coloured object, the clear crystal also looks coloured. Out of these two delusions when the soul is singled out, it is liberated then and there. Otherwise there is no other way to attain the knowledge of Self.

(*xvii*) Crystal appears reddish in touch with red. Similarly the soul in touch with false representation seems false. But neither the crystal nor the soul has any red hue. This reflection is just a hallucination. This should be kept in mind.

(*xviii*) Wakefulness, dream and sound sleep are the threefold states of this intellect. But they too are false. Knowing that an eternal bliss is derived only from the Supreme soul, one should control these three qualities and realize the Self. The attributes within the Self are false; so renounce them.

(*xix*) The woeful world is not contained in the blissful Self. It is only due to ignorance that it reflects itself in the Self as true. Even a wise one mistakes a rope for a snake. In the same way the world of various attributes is seen in the Supreme Self.

(*xx*) Thus the wrong supposition is in the Supreme Self. Ego, desires, all the qualities of intellect; they have no essence. The Self is an onlooker. These attributes are extraneous, intruded for nothing, as heat enters iron.

(*xxi*) The Self should be recognized with the help of Vedas and from one's *guru*. By recognizing the Self one is released then and there. Therefore one should contemplate on the Self: What I am. No other way is there to destroy nescience.

(*xxii*) The Self can be realized thus: retiring to seclusion, restraining the ten senses and mind and meditation ever on Self-knowledge. Think that the manifested world is not other than the Self itself. By knowing this very becomes one with the Universal Self.

(*xxiii*) In the state of nescience *Omkara* is the verbal expression of the whole universe. When this expression is united with the Self, knowledge may go waxing. When *a, u, ma,* these three get merged in the Self in the presence of the Universe, then there remains nothing but the Self, devoid of all attributes.

(*xxiv*) When through knowledge one resolves that he is the very Self, he is said to be liberated, he falls not in misery. Controlling the ten senses and crushing the mighty passion when one practises *samadhi* or deep contemplation, Hari, the Supreme Lord, will appear before him.

(*xxv*) Ever meditate on the endless Supreme Being, endure pain or pleasure deeming it mere fate. Whiling away the days in this way, when one dies, he shall be merged with Me leaving the suffering of the world behind.

(*xxvi*) Being corporeal, one neither in the beginning nor in the middle, nor in the end, finds perfect happiness. It is a fact. Therefore leaving all other ways aside and meditating on the Self only, one shall be identical with me just as water reaching the ocean merges itself.

(*xxvii*) The Self, and only the Self is true; the rest is false. It seems true as in the case of rope and snake. Understand it; if not understood, serve Me and you shall understand. Otherwise it cannot be repelled.

(*xxviii*) I told you all the essence and the secrets of the Vedas. Those who ever muse on it; their sins of innumerable previous lives shall be expunged. Therefore, brother mine! the world you see is nothing but a false magic. By means of worshipping Me you live in the beatitude.

(*xxix*) Either blithely worship this manifested form of Mine or meditate on the unmanifested Supreme Self, it is all the same. Both are like Me, I am akin to both; analogously with Me they sanctify all the worlds touching with mere feet.

(*xxx*) Whoever, with faith and devotion in Me and in his preceptor, studies attentively this essence of *Srutis* as the fundamental principle, his ignorance will be annihilated, and becoming one with Me he shall easily cross the worldly ocean."

From *Rama Gita,* 19th century *Tr.* by Gokul Sinha

**4. Assorted Poems :-** Elements of medieval and modern poetry are perceptible in Bhanubhakta's short poems. They are purely mundane, written on various subjects ranging from rites and rituals, astrology and liturgy, health and hygiene to games and even gambling.

15 popular pieces are given below:

(*i*) Egrossed in grass his entire life
The money that he made
To keep the name hereafter also,
A well he caused to spade.

A grass-cutter, of a poor house:
But what a sense he has!
I, Bhanubhakta, being wealthy,
Am such today, alas!

To my credit neither have I wells
Nor have I any hospices
All are in my house shut up,
Whatever wealth and riches.

What a lesson the grass-cutter has
Taught me today in fact!
Fie upon me who am living,
Without a meritorious act!

(*ii*) There in Tanahu, the best of hills,
Shrikrishna Brahmin lived;
Owing to lofty Aryan strain,
To virtues he paid heed.
Being a savant, in sacred lores
He imparted me too well,
I am his grandson Bhanubhakta;
Know me that I tell.

(*iii*) Gajadhar's wife proved to be a bale;
She's taken adieu from all for hell,

Reaching their house, in porch I sat,
Drove she away an open night I had.

(*iv*) After long I behold Balaju today;
The heaven on earth, I deem to say.
Birds are roosting on creepers' arm;
Voice is vinous as soft notes charm.

Had I been blessed to poetize here,
What other delight would I look for
To make a damsel dance withal!
Along with Indra heaven would fall.

(*v*) Brisk belles in graceful gait
Tucking *gunakesari*[1] on their heads,
Wander about in cheery company
Kantipur city is Indra's heaven.

Millionaires myriad one can find;
Men are so happy in their mind;
It's thus a people's pleasure-ocean;
Kantipur city is the Kubera's heaven.

Like Bhot or London or a China city
Like those of Delhi the lanes are busy.
Like Lucknow, Patna, Madras somewhere
Kantipur city is the abode of Kubera.

Swords and sabres, *khukris,* rapiers,
Armed with pistols, guns and revolvers,
Bold and brave all swarm the city
Which is like this Kantipur city!

Where no malice and frauds are found,
Only there do the virtues abound;
The Lord of Beasts is seated for safety;
The abode of Shiva this Kantipur city.

(*vi*) None can count the gods who here dwell;
Shrines are here to consecrate all.
As holy as this there is no other land
*Ghat* is to redeem as Shiva doth stand
Maya of God, *Guhyakali,* the mother
Of cosmos, is seated, blessings to shower.

---

1. A Flower

(*vii*) This Girdhari has beset me, lord!
Much ado about nothing
But to entangle this intrigue
It is feasible that I think.
To humbly lay down before my lord
A few rhymes I make here;
Please peruse the poem I pray
The dispute will be soon over ...

[The poem is fragmented. A good number of verses seem lost.]

There are other materials too;
Paper, deeds and tokens;
Audience and evidence, all are there;
And converse that concerns.

I won't persuade further, Sire!
Please, if done, avert;
Gladly do I adduce these all,
Just to undo the knot.

True indeed the statements are,
That I mentioned above.
Records and proofs have been here
Produced for the probe.

If law-courts find not the facts,
This is for your decree:
I vouch to pay to the pie, my lord,
As law demands, from me.

(*viii*) Neither to ward off the death, Sire
Thus picking up a brawl;
Nor to become a millionaire,
Abounding with wherewithal.
The days but while away in vain
How to console the heart
Rule over it by any means.
Have mercy upon me, lord!

(*ix*) Just a few words of my mind
To vent I had been to you
Reporting my presence I go back,
As I could not see you.
Mute and dumb I proceed now
To my home today.

I shall come to your honour again,
My humble words to lay.

(*x*) How long should I supplicate
To judges and the jury;
They keep mum, and if they utter,
Just say morrow in perjury.

Why dilly-dally the more;
Just decide or dismiss avow
Know the morrow never comes.
I have become a pauper enow.

(*xi*) Ever I chance to see your honour
My heart is not in plight
The whole night free I enjoy the dance
I am in a great delight.

Mosquitoes, fleas, bedbugs are mates,
Sitting in their concert;
Mosquitoes sing and fleas do dance
I witness them in comfort.

(*xii*) Neither a service have I got
Nor a rich man am I;
By tillage I lived hard, did serve
To earn an honour high.

With a single mind I served;
So pleased was the lord
That over the honour an everlasting
Dishonour He conferred.

I aged, as old as forty years
And have a son of eight,
Time has neared for *bratabandha*,[1]
A moment that is great.

Helpless, I am lonesome here
In this tight corner;
How to perform this *bratabandha*
The world seems but sombre.

To teach *Gayatri* a father's right;
And mother's to give alms,
To read the Veda in early age,
To serve *gurus* and cows.

Time is such a momentous one.
A redeeming act it is;
How far should I implore the more;
Let me brief my pleas.

You are the masters of this earth
Even when, today
A Brahmin's rite is at stake.
I, therefore, beg to pray.

With humble request to your honour
Make this appeal here;
"To hell with your appeal": if so ruled
I have but to bear.

(*xiii*) The body is but a fleeting matter
Living by mere food, and grains
Much to account for, that this life,
Met with, in the long durance.
Suffered a lot falling to ailment,
The complaint was bout again,
Vainly was I caged at Kumaricok;
Wrecked, I came home from the den.

The ailment increased, troubled a lot,
But now feeling a bit fine,
Shall have the same fate if fettered again;
You are the only lord of mine.

(*xiv*) Let my love be undying, dear,
That I do conjure
Your heart a cage, a bird am I;
Let this act endure.

(*xv*) [In the anthology of short poems, the poet's Prologue to his *Badhushiksha* has also been assorted by the critics.]
Mind not, O my dear Tarapati!
One thing I should tell you;
The members of your family here
Are much brawler, I knew.

The wranglings of the house I heard
The brabble and the fight
I could not catch forty winks
Wakeful passed the night.
Nothing is wanting as I see

Riches, repute and fortune;
If the daughter-in-law is such a shrew
The house is how you run,
I composed here this *Bandhushiksha*
As I lost my temper,
May it help you to discipline
Your wife, daughter and other!

Albeit a guest am I Here,
It least concerns me,
I should say this, even though
You are a friend to me

*Fulkar Kavita,* 19th century *Tr.* by Gokul Sinha

# 9

# Modern Dogri Literature

## (SHIVANATH)

### Introduction: The Multilingual Pressures (1800-1900)

Multilingual literary tradition which had developed in Duggar during the previous century reached its Zeneth early nineteenth. It comprised serious writing on religion, philosophy, astrology and Hindu mythology in Sanskrit, kavya-style composition and *bhajana* (devotional songs) in Brajabhasha, and light literary diversion in the form of short poems, *geets* (songs) and *bhajans* in Dogri. The first two components appear to be pan-Indian, the third component was purely local and is represented in the extant works of poets like Shiv Ram (1755-1830), Raghbir Das (c. 1750-1820), Lakkhu (c. 1750-1840), Hakam Jatt (1807-1937), Ganga Ram (1823-93) and Rudra Dutt (c. 1860-90). Shiv Ram and his son Rudra Dutt carried on the literary tradition of the well-known court poet Devi Ditta. Raghbir Das was a disciple of the Vaishnava poet Maya Das. Both Devi Ditta and Maya Das belonged to the eighteenth century. Duggar Lakkhu was a carpenter who composed riddles for the pleasure of his wife the loss.

Hakam Jatt was an illiterate happy-go-lucky hermit who lived under a pipal tree on the bank of the river Tawi and loved to take the temple cows to graze in the nearby jungle. Ganga Ram was an erudite Sanskrit scholar, the author of a major work on astrology, written for the Jammu ruler Ranbir Singh.

Very little of what these poets (and there may have been many more like them) composed was committed to writing. It is presumed that much of what they composed may have been lost or appropriated by the flourishing folk literature. Shiv Ram was a temple priest and is known to have composed verses both in Brajabhasha and Dogri. An eight-line poem of his, 'Jai Ho Bar Dat' (Hail O Boon-giver), that has survived, is in praise of his patron deity Sukrala Devi.

### The Poet

The language of this poem is a mix of Dogri, Brajabhasha and Sanskrit adapted to Dogri phonetics, following Dogri syntax. A poem of Rudra

Dutt describes in simple rhyming lines the flourishing trade and commerce in Maharaja Ranbir Singh's Jammu. Raghbir Das was a Krishnabhakta, a devotional poet who wrote mainly bhajans, both in Brajabhasha and Dogri, expressing his devotion to Lord Krishna, praising Brajabhoomi (the land of Krishna's childhood days) and lamenting the transitory nature of life. A characteristic feature of these poems and of bhajana is their rhythm and music, embellished with alliteration and assonance, and their adaptation of Sanskrit and Brajabhasha words to Dogri pronunciation. Lakkhu started composing riddle verses in Dogri and then began to compose similar riddles in Brajabhasha. His Dogri poems show his capacity for stringing together words like names of places, fruits and musical instruments, to underline a sentiment like love.

Hakam Jutt was adept at composing extemporaneous verses called *luhanis* (dirges) in Dogri, and, through telling word-pictures, he commented on the contemporary social situation, on some typical characters and on himself, in a tone of ironic humour. Grinding grain, guarding the crops, warding off cattle and crows, carrying water over stony paths and so on that in how Ganga Ram that describes the harsh life of a woman of Kandi: The lot of woman was beng harsh in rural areas where every thing was scarce.

### *The Emergence of Dogri Prose*

A significant development of this period was the emergence of Dogri prose in three works of translation, namely *Rajavali* (A Chronicle of Kings), *Dharmapustaka* (The Book of Religion) and *Bachane Wala Koka Ai* (Who is it who saves?). *Rajavali* (c. 1810 or 1815) is a Dogri translation of a Persian work written by one Bali Ram for the Mughal prince, Dara Shikoh. The translation was done by Taihl Das for his patron Raja Dhyan Singh of Kotla, whose kingdom was annexed by the Sikhs around 1811. The theme and mood of the small book suggest that it was intended to provide philosophical consolation to the Raja. It is in part a chronology of the kings who sat on the throne of Delhi, from the Pandava king Yudhishtira to the Mughal emperor Shah Jahan, and in part a philosophical reflection on the transience of royal power and pelf. The language is a striking blend of Jammu Dogri and Kangra Dogri, the former dominating the diction and the latter the syntax, with a few Persian words adapted to the genius of Dogri thrown in.

### Dharampustaka

*Dharmapustaka* is the Dogri translation of the New Testament and was commissioned by the Serampore Mission. The manuscript, though ready for printing in 1818, was actually published in 1825. It is the first printed book in Dogri. Its language is rather quaint, both in diction and syntax, and it appears to have been prepared to cater to the entire *pahari* tract extending from Kumaon to Jammu. *Bachane Wala Koka Ai* is a Dogri translation of the Gospel of St Luke in a small booklet; its prose is very much the colloquial Dogri which is commonly use today in rural areas of Duggar. All three books used the Devanagari script.

## Takari Script

But during this period Dogri also had a script of its own tailed Takari, which was extensively used by the rajas of the Punjab hill states for official correspondence and by the general public for correspondence and writing. Maharaja Ranbir Singh of Jammu and Kashmir (1857-85) got the script reformed on the pattern of Devanagari, called it 'Name Dogri Akkhar' (the New Dogri Letters) and tried to popularize its use by causing a number of non-literary works to be printed in the script. Among these works were *Lilavati*, a translation of the Sanskrit text-book on mathematics by Bhaskaracharya, and *Vyavahara-gita,* a text book of sorts dealing with a variety of subjects. These give us an idea of the type of Dogri prose used at the time. With the death of the Maharaja and the adoption of Urdu as the school medium and official language by his successor, interest in Dogri script, language and literature declined.

## A Period of Decline: 1900-25

Being under feual rule, after the death of Maharaja the period for next fifty years was a period of great decline and near total darkness. The new Maharaja did not do much for the vernacular. Urdu and Punjabi made inroads into the multilingual literary situation and elbowed Dogri out of Duggar. Just about half-a-dozen men, who wrote some poems in Dogri as a diversion, kept the flickering light of Dogri literature alive. None of them published anything; their work has come down to us partly by word of mouth, and partly through manuscripts preserved by their families and friends.

Ram Dhan (c. 1853-1912), a goldsmith, who also made kites, was a poet who wrote in Brajabhasha, Punjabi and Dogri. His Dogri poem, 'Chandai Di Chandani' (Light of the Moon) is a beautiful lyric that appears in every anthology of early Dogri poetry. It describes the perilous course of love which is like 'Latakana Kachia Tanda Kane' (Hanging by an unspun thread), and depicts the daily chores and yearning of the beloved for the divine lover, the charmer with the flute, with whom she feels one, as moonlight does with the moon.

Mehta Mathara Das (1858-1926) was a government official who wrote poetry in Persian, Urdu, Hindi, Punjabi and Dogri. His Dogri poems are didactic in tone and deal with subjects like the achievements of Dogra rule and the exploits of Dogra soldiers, social reform, philosophic reflections on life and its changing and impermanent nature, and regret at the backwardness of the hill people compared to the *firangis* (foreigners) and the people from the plains.

Ram Prapanna Shastri, (1859-1937) and Sant Ram Shastri (1860-1945) were Sanskrit teachers who wrote poems in Sanskrit and Dogri. They appear to have felt more at home in Sanskrit, the language of their education, than in Dogri, their mother-tongue. They composed their poems first in Sanskrit and then translated them into Dogri. Thus Ram Prapanna wrote *Devika Lahari Stotra* (Paean to Devika) in praise of the sacred river Devika that is considered the local Ganga. Sant Ram wrote *Manasara Stuti* (Praise to Manasara) describing the beauty of Manasara Lake (a tourist spot in Jammu), whose waters are like 'mercury in a plate, sparkling like glass in the sun'. Sant Ram also wrote some poems directly in Dogri on the social vices prevalent among the Dogras, attacking old customs and superstitions while praising Duggar and Dogri.

Babu Kanshi Ram (1882-1943), well-known as 'Pahari Gandhi' (Gandhi of the Hills) was a political activist and social reformer who wrote poems in Dogri to reinforce his political and social preaching. His poetry is full of verve and exhortation, and was meant to awaken people to their social vices, superstitiousness, apathy, backwardness, lethargy, passive submission to poverty and injustice, and oppression of others, and to induce them to fight against their plight.

**The Period of Recovery**

The decline of Dogri was hurting intellectuals. They made efforts to stop the rot and succeeded to some extent. This period saw crucial developments both at the individual level and at the group or organization level, involving a conscious effort to create a significant corpus of Dogri literature. At the individual level, Prof. Gauri Shankar (b. 1900), a linguist and Sanskrit scholar who taught at the prestigious Government College in Lahore, brought out a Dogri prose translation of Shrimad Bhagavad Gita (1934); Pt. Har Dutt Shastri (1890-1956), a popular *kathavachak* of Jammu, published a collection of poems under the title *Dogri Bhajan Mala* (Dogri Devotional Songs, 1936); and Shri Gauri Shankar Bhadrawahi (1878-1947) published a verse translation of *Shrimad Bhagavad Gita* in the Bhadrawahi dialect. At the group level, the Dogri Sanstha Jammu, a literary and cultural organization, launched a programme for (a) the development of the Dogri language which was languishing as a mere spoken language, banished from educational institutions and government offices, and (b) the building up of Dogri literature which would capture all aspects of Dogra like. The Sanstha organized regular literary conventions and *kavi sammelans* (poets' gatherings) where the writers read their works, mostly poems and short stories.

Between 1944, the year of the founding of the Sanstha, and 1950, many Dogri poems, some Dogri short stories and a couple of plays in Dogri were written but very little of this material could be published. Only four slim books of poetry by Dinu Bhai Pant (b. 1918), a collection of short stories by B.P. Sathe (1910-73) and an anthology of selected poems by twelve poets were published under the auspices of the Dogri Sanstha. These works were of a pioneering nature in the sense that they built bridges between traditional, folk and rudimentary literary forms and modern literary tradition.

Dinu Bhai Pant's four books are *Guttulun* (Titillation, 1944), *Veer Gulab* (The Hero Gulab Singh, 1944), *Mangu di Chhabil* (The Water-serving Centre of Mangu, 1946) and *Sarha Bapu* (Our Bapu, 1948). *Guttulun* is a collection of poems on diverse themes of contemporary interest such as the naivete of a villager visiting the city for the first time, the valour of Dogra soldiers, the mendacity of the leaders, the awakening among peasants and workers, their impatience to win independence, the character of the community, and the natural beauty of the countryside. *Veer Gulab* is both a modern ballad in the tradition of Dogra bars of heroic, valorous action, and a mini-epic of *veer rasa* (the heroic mood) structured carefully in nine cantos. *Mangu di Chhabil* is a long narrative poem depicting the conflict between the haves and the have-nots, highlighting the problem of bonded labour. *Sarha Bapu* was written on Gandhiji's assassination.

B.P. Sathe's collection of nine short stories is called *Paihla Phull* (The First Flower, 1947). The stories are brief, crisp cameos of Dogra rural life, interspersed with pieces of folklore and legend, capturing succinctly some aspects of daily life and prevalent social mores, including the evil practice of reciprocal marriage called *dohri.*

Twelve poets who were most popular in the *kavi sammelans* in the second half of the 1940s came together and published Jago Duggar (Awake, the Land of Dogras, 1949-50). It contained their selected poems and geets. The poets included Har Dutt Shastri, the author of *Dogri Bhajan Mala* mentioned earlier, a doyen among Dogri poets, with his new poems forcefully lampooning social evils like mutual distrust, litigation and apathy. Dinu Bhai Pant was represented by songs bursting with patriotic fervour and zeal for social reform. Krishan Samailpuri (1900-80), an established Urdu poet, had two Dogri poems and two Dogri geets. Parmanand Almast (1901-78), popular for his romantic songs of love describing the beauty of the hills and the girls, had four poems, one of them being 'Moen Mullen Pandten Us Dangar Banaye De' (These Priests Have Turned us into Cattle), which attacked organized religion and its priests who exploited the common people. Then there were upcoming poets like Ramnath Shastri (b. 1914), Ved Pal Deep (b. 1929) and Yash Sharma (b. 1929), who made significant contributions to Dogri poetry later.

There were others, not represented in the anthology, who did not make any impact. Their subjects were purely topical and treatment superficial. The works of Shastri, Deep and Sharma were full of promise and showed serious concern for both their craft and their society. The general tone of their poems was exhortatory. Deep's poetry as seen in 'Holi' (The Festival of Colours) and 'Nami Azadi' (New Freedom) is rich in imagery, and rhythmic in flow. In 'Holi', the poet's creative imagination invests his progressive views with life and colour, when he calls on Holi to bring with it warmth and laughter for everybody:

Rain red rays like this
And come with bundles full of laughter.

In 'Nami Azadi' he calls on the New Freedom to leave the palaces and move into the fields of humble farmers, into the dark lanes of hungry workers and into the thatched huts of the poor. It says, *'Tun kache kothen ch bal'* (You should light lamps in the hovels of the poor). Ramnath Shastri's concern was with the rich past and tradition of the Dogras in contrast to their present apathetic state, while Yash Sharma's was with the peasants and workers.

Dogri poetry of this period was essentially audience-oriented, and it lacked the depth of individual experience and high quality craftsmanship. The tone was generally sentimental; the themes were limited to the sufferings of the poor, the beauty of the Dogra country, the simplicity, bravery and inertia of the Dogras, the exploitation by political leaders and agents of religion. The bulk of this writing is close to the folk tradition. Only it has shed some of the naturalness of expression of folk songs and acquired some sophistication in form as well as depth of emotional experience. The first short stories in Dogri show the same affinity to folk tales and legends, especially in their narrative skill, but very little else.

**Period of Development and Expansion: 1950-75**

Dogri literature had gained momentum. The third quarter of the century proved very crucial for the proved very important for growth the Dogri literature. During this period, the work started in the previous phase was carried forward by the Dogri Sanstha, now joining forces with other organizations like the Dogra Mandal, the Dogra Himachal Sanskriti Sangam, the Jammu and Kashmir Cultural Academy and a growing number of dedicated individuals. Some of these individuals contributed to more than one literary genre. Poetry and the short story came into their own, and new genres like drama, novel, general prose, essay and biography came to be cultivated. By 1969, when the Sahitya Akademi accorded official recognition to Dogri, a fairly steady multi-genre stream of Dogri literature had begun to flow.

***Poetry***

Poetry continued to be the most popular and prolific genre with the largest number of writers and publications involved in it. Dinu Bhai Pant added one more collection of poems entitled *Dadi Te Maa* (Grandmother and Mother, 1956) to his earlier output and then shifted his attention to playwriting. In fact, his last published play *Ayodhya* got him the Sahitya Akademi award. *Dadi Te Maa* contains some very powerful poems of social protest and a delicately etched pen-picture of a milk-maid in a poem of that name *Gurjari,* included in this selection.

Ramnath Shastri now wrote poems mostly inspired by some conscious concern or idea, working it out carefully and betraying greater deliberateness than spontaneity of expression. A selection of his poems, written over a period of twenty years, appeared under the title *Dharati Da Rin* (The Debt to Motherland, 1971). He also wrote a number of *ghazals,* later published in a collection called *Talakhivan* (Bitter Experiences, 1980). 'Eh Ratin Da Kheri Bela' (These Last Moments of the Night or Daybreak) included in this selection is from *Dharati Da Rin.* Ved Pal Deep wrote some very fine poems like 'Kala Mahnun' (The Black Man) and 'Badalai Nain Sijji Ri Sanyan' (Rain Soaked Evening). But later he concentrated on the ghazal and with the publication of his collection of ghazals, *Us Te An Banjare Lok* (We Are Nomadic People, 1968), he came to be called the Ghalib of Dogri poetry. This collection contains some of the finest Dogri ghazals. They are also notable for their rhythm, symbols and metaphors. Krishan Samailpuri also wrote ghazals in Dogri, collected in the volume, *Mariyan Dogri Ghazlan* (My Dogri Ghazals, 1972) but these seem anaemic compared to Deep's ghazals. However, Krishan Samailpuri, like Parmanand Almast and Yash Sharma, was essentially a writer of songs in a romantic strain and his geets, published under the title *Mere Dogri Geet* (My Dogri Songs, 1974), won him the Sahitya Akademi award. Almast's poems and songs were published in a collection called *Jhunak* (Jolt, 1961) in Persian script and *Ik Boondai Gi Tarasai Painchhi* (The cry of the bird for a drop of water, 1967) in Devanagari script. Yash Sharma has not published a book, although his poems and songs have appeared in journals and anthologies. 'Sanjan Ghirdeyan Chitt Kamhalavi Janda' (with the fall of dusk my heart withers) is a fine example of his work.

**The New Poets**

Dogri literary scene was in a flux. More than a hundred new poets emerged scene during this period. Here we can mention briefly the contributions of some of them—four seasoned poets who started writing only after fifty years of age, a dozen young poets from the Jammu region and five from Himachal Pradesh. The work of the older poets is particularly important, because they added bulk and respectability to the existing thin body of Dogri poetry at the beginning of the period. Swami Brahmanand Tirth (1897-1962) wrote six volumes of verses devoted to what he called Dogri Vedanta, a mixture of Hindu mythology, wandering ascetic-lore, the Bhagawata, the Puranas, the Gita and Persian Sufism. Raghunath Singh Samyal (1885-1963) contributed a number of poems full of patriotic fervour, religious devotion and social concern, as well as a verse translation of Shrimad Bhagawad Gita. Shambu Nath Sharma (1905-77) published a collection of poems portraying sensitively small and poignant characters from Dogra life—a poor girl, a clerk, a widow and her son—and Dogri Ramayana (1961), an epic of 330 pages. Ramlal Sharma (b. 1905) contributed four collections of poems and ghazals, his latest collection *Rattu Da Chanan* (Radiance of Blood, 1985) containing some very finely-wrought ghazals. Written in aphoristic and luminous couplets they capture the quintessence of his experience.

Among the dozen prominent many younger poets who have emerged from the Jammu region of Duggar, Kehari Singh Madhukar (b. 1929), Padma Sachdev (b. 1940) and Charan Singh (1941-69) have been trail-blazers. Narsingh Dev Jamwal (Narasimha Deva, b. 1931), Mohana Lai Sapolia (b. 1931), Tara Samailpuri (b. 1926), O.P. Sharma Sarathi (b. 1933), Jitendra Udhampuri (b. 1944), and Shiv Ram Deep (b. 1945) have also made important contributions. But Ashwini Mangotra (b. 1948), Santosh Khajuria (b. 1953), Kunwar Viyogi (1940) and Dhyan Singh (b. 1938) deserve mention as poets who have shown a lot of promise in their works.

Madhukar has published three collections—*Namiyan Minjaran* (New Shoots, 1955), *Dola Kun Thappeya* (The Bride's Palanquin, 1963) and *Mein Mele Ra Janun* (I have known the festival, 1975), the last winning him the Sahitya Akademi award.

### Madhukar's Poetry

Madhukar's poetry is characterized by great energy, a torrential flow of words and images, a deep concern for humanity, and irrepressible optimism. 'Kohlu' (The Oil Expelter) is one of his popular poems. Padma Sachdev has published four collections of poems—*Meri Kavita Mera Geet* (My Poetry, My Songs, 1969) which won her the Sahitya Akademi award and which has since been translated into Hindi, *Tawi Te Chanhan* (Rivers Tawi and Chenab, 1976), *Nheriyan Galiyan* (Dark Lanes, 1982) and *Pota Pota Nimbal* (Small Patches of Cloudless Sky, 1987). The bulk of her poetry reflects distinctively feminine emotions and feelings. They also demonstrate deep love for the motherland as well as commitment to Dogri, the Dogra land and the Dogra way of life. She has developed a considerable command over the subtle use of imagery and symbols but she is still best known for her first poem read at a *kavi sammelan* when she was in her teens, 'Raje Diyan Mandiyan' (Palaces of the Raja). Charan Singh has published just one collection of poems, *Jot* (Light, 1964), and it won him the Jammu and Kashmir Cultural Academy award. He is an experimentalist and an innovator and quite a few of his poems are full of personal anguish, captured with remarkable intensity and depth in memorable images, as may be seen in 'Daun Keengare' (Two Peaks).

**Emerging Poets**

Narsingh Dev Jamwal is a prolific writer. After two collections of ghazals, he found his rhythm and form in the poems of *Koraj* (Seepage,1971). 'Tashai Da Patta' is taken from this collection. He has since published one more collection, *Sogat* (Gift, 1987). Mohan Lal Sapolia's poetry is marked by a strong spirit of patriotic and spontaneous outpouring of verses, as may be seen in the poem 'Sutti Di Peed Jaga Karanan' (Kindling the latent love) taken from his collection *Sajare Phull* (Fresh Flowers, 1969). Tara Samailpuri's poetry is known for its forcefully realistic and rhymed descriptions of the life of a military pensioner ('Fauji Pensioner', 1956) and the cycle of seasons ('Baramah') describing twelve months in the water-starved Kandi area of Duggar. O.P. Sharma Sarathi's poetry as seen in his two books *Tandan* (Threads, 1971) and Partan (Layers, 1974) contains a strong intellectual and metaphysical streak, and attempts to grapple with basic questions of the human situation. The poem 'Mein Bi Bakhata Nayin' (I am not apart) from *Partan* is a good example of this.

Jitendra Udhampuri's poetry is also intensely personal, a web of memories, stained with pain and regret. He has to his credit six books of poetry, including a long, single-theme poem, *Chanani* (Moonlight, 1972) the first of its kind in Dogri, a collection of songs *(Geet-ganga,* 1986), an epic *(Bawa Jitto,* 1985), and his Sahitya Akademi award winning collection *Ik Shahar Yaden Da* (A city full of memories, 1979). Shiv Ram Deep has written both poems and ghazals with equal ease. Progressing steadily through *Ik Leekar Kavi Parchhame* (One line and many shadows, 1969) and *Mangmi Latten Di Daur* (Running with Borrowed Legs, 1974) he attained a style and sophistication of his own in the collection of Dogri ghazals called *Gamalen De Cactus* (Potted Cacti, 1981), which won him the Sahitya Akademi award.

There are Ashwini Mangotra's poems, 'Khubatiyan' (Cocoons, 1972), 'Lehran' (Waves, 1973) and 'Meri Basti, Mere Lok' (My Colony, My People, 1981) which are marked by a fine sense of rhythm, youthful vitality and natural spontaneity. Santosh Khajuria's poems collected in *Irichauli* (Rice with sesame seeds and jaggery, 1974) evoke an atmosphere and create word-pictures, concretizing fleeting emotions. Kunwar Viyogi has since published a long one-theme poem, *Ghar* (Home, 1979), which got the Sahitya Akademi award and a collection of sonnets entitled *Paihhiyan Bangan* (The First Cock Crows, 1987). Dhyan Singh's poems and experiments in verse, first published in journals and later collected in *Filhal* (For the time being, 1987), are characterized by fine imagery and leftist ideology. 'Akhnoorai Di Sani' (An Evening at Akhnoor) is a representative poem in this regard.

Prominent among the poets from the Himachal region are Dr Gautam Vyathit (b. 1938) with two volumes of poetry; Peeush Guleri (b. 1940) and

Onkar Singh Awara (b. 1928), with a volume each; and Sagar Palampuri (b. 1930) and Sudarshan Kaushal Nurpuri (Sudarsana Kausala Nurapuri, 1930-87) who have only been published in journals and anthologies. The poetry from this area, like most poetry from the Jammu region, makes either bald statements on the social situation or describes the beauties of nature. Sudarshan Nurpuri's poem 'Nikki Sari Jind' is typical of such poems.

### *Dogri Short Story*

The Dogri short story developed rapidly during this period and achieved some maturity and standard. B.P. Sathe published another collection, *Khali Gode* (Childless, 1970), which contains long stories with a strong autobiographical element. 'Masahni' (The Gift) is taken from this. Poets Ramnath Shastri, Narsingh Dev Jamwal and Ashwini Mangotra published a volume of short stories each, with Shastri bagging the Sahitya Akademi award for the collection, *Badanami Di Chhan* (Canopy of Ill-fame, 1973). Similarly, D.C. Prashant (b. 1915) and R.K. Abrol (b. 1930) who also wrote plays, and Chanchal Sharma (b. 1926) who wrote essays of literary criticism, published a volume of short stories each.

### The Best Writers

The Dogri short story came into its own and achieved artistic excellence in the hands of three writers who made an impact on the Dogri literary scene with their very first volumes towards the end of the 1950s. They are Narendra Khajuria (1933-70), Madan Mohan Sharma (b. 1934) and Ved Rahi (b. 1933). All three won Sahitya Akademi awards for their collections, Khajuria for his second volume *Neela Ambar, Kala Badal* (Blue Sky, Dark Clouds, 1967), Sharma for his fourth volume, *Dudh, Lahu Te Zehar* (Milk, Blood and Poison, 1971) and Rahi for his second collection, *Ale* (Calls, 1982). Their work is characterized by deep humanism, a keen observation of contemporary social reality, psychological insight into human character and behaviour, a high quality of craftsmanship, and creative and effective use of the Dogri language. While Khajuria draws his material and inspiration from rural Duggar, Sharma and Rahi cast their nets wider. All three show seriousness of purpose. 'Kastu Da Kala Tittar' (Kastu's Black Patridge), 'Ik Lamakadi Loth' (A Hanging Corpse) and 'Ale' (Calls) give some idea of their work.

The Dogri short story took another leap forward with the appearance, about a decade later, of four young short story writers who set the trend for realistic delineation of the social and human predicament in the context of urban and semi-urban life, deliberately eschewing sentimentalism and idealism. They are O.P. Sharma Sarathi (b. 1933), Om Goswami (b. 1947), Bandhu Sharma (b. 1934) and Chhatrapal (b. 1949). Sarathi published two collections, one of which, *Sukka Barud* (1971), won the Jammu and Kashmir

Cultural Academy award. He later concentrated on novels, producing five of them in quick succession. He won the Sahitya Akademi award for *Naga Rukh* (The Naked Tree), which is available in English translation as *Churning of the City.* Chhatrapal produced just one volume, *Tapu Da Admi* (Man of the Island, 1974), and then drifted into writing in Hindi. Om Goswami with four collections and Bandhu Sharma with two, have given to Dogri literature some of the finest short stories. The former won the Sahitya Akademi award for *Sunne Di Chidi* (The Bird of Gold, 1983). The stories of these two writers included in this volume are from their earlier works.

### *Dogri Novel*

Dogri novels which were published in early 1960, almost simultaneously. Were Narendra Khajuria's *Shano,* Ved Rahi's *Har, Bari Te Pattan* (The Flood, the Ferry and the Harbour) and Madan Mohan Sharma's *Dharan Te Dhuran* (Hills and Mists). They deliberately focus on the problems of Dogra rural-feudal society. They found technically amateurish and utopian. The women characters are idealized, and the solutions suggested simplistic. The fourth novel, *Phull Bina Dali* (Flowers Without a Stalk, 1970) by Shrivatsa Vikal (1939-70), though in the tradition and mould of the first three, is a fuller, more satisfying and appealing novel, with its beguiling Dogri prose. It won the Sahitya Akademi award (see Selection).

The Dogri novel attained maturity and sophistication after 1975 with the publication of works like N.D. Jawal's *Sanjhi Dharati Bakkale Lok* (Common Land, Estranged People, 1976) and Desh Bandhu Dogra Nutan's *Qaidi* (The Prisoner, 1980) both of which won the Sahitya Akademi award.

### *Dogri Prose*

The first book of essays and prose pieces in Dogri on different subjects was *Triveni* (Three Streams, 1961), a joint venture of Shyamlal Sharma (b. 1921) and Shakti Sharma (b. 1923). Two literary journals, viz., *Namichetana* (started in 1953) and *Shiraza Dogri* (started in 1964) and two small magazines *Rekha* and *Ambar,* published by D.C. Prashant and Om Goswami in the 1960s and 1970s respectively, gave considerable fillip to the development of Dogri prose. Many individual writers have contributed to this development but the three writers who played the most significant role in the development of the Dogri prose essay as a creative literary form are Vishwanath Khajuria (b. 1906) with his two volumes, *Duggar Da Jeevan Darshan* (The philosophy of life of Duggar, 1967) and *Saptak* (Seven Essays, 1968), Shakti Sharma with her one volume, *Syarhan* (Furrows, 1968), and Lakshmi Narayan (b. 1932) with his two books of essays full of wit and humour, *Kandyari De Phull* (Flowers of Kandyari, 1963) and

*Nikkimyan Nikkiyan Gallan* (Small Matters, 1973). The two essays and prose piece included here give an idea of the Dogri prose essay, one of them being from *Kandyari De Phull.*

Four books of literary appreciation in Dogri also appeared during this period. They were Lakshmi Narayan's *Sahitya Charcha* (Discussion on Literature, 1967), Champa Sharma's (b. 1914) *Kavya Charcha* (Discussion on Poetry, 1969), Chanchal Sharma's *Najar Apani Apani* (Points of View, 1972), and *Sahitya Darpan* (Mirror to Literature, 1969), a collection of papers read at a writer's conference. The first biography in Dogri, *Shere Duggar Lala Hans Raj* (1968) by Mulk Raj Saraf, was also published during this period.

**Dogri Drama**

Not much proper has been made in drama writing. Whatever has been written in this fold has been found wanting. *Nama Gran* (New Village, 1957), written jointly by Dinu Bhai Pant, Ramnath Shastri and R.K. Abrol is the first published Dogri play. Written with the objective of highlighting the need for village reform, it is marred by technical amateurishness and weak sentimentalism. The three other plays that followed suffer from the same flaws. Dinu Bhai Pant's *Sarpanch* (The Panchayat Chief, 1966) and Madan Mohan Sharma's *Janaur* (The Beast, 1970) are better structured plays and more satisfying, although the former suffers from didacticism, idealism and weak characterization. *Janaur* is a socio-psychological play. Dealing with the theme of spiritual emptiness and the frustration and lust of a crippled old man, it is bold in conception and interesting in its denouement. N.D. Jamwal's *Raja Mandalik* (1972) and *Allarh Goli Bir Sipahi* (The innocent maid and the brave soldier, 1975) are interesting experiments in translating folklore into a viable dramatic form. The play *Panch Parmeshwar* (Panch is God, 1968), based on a Premchand story is a very good effort at adaptation.

Dramatic literature in Dogri has been enriched by seventy one-act plays by different writers on diverse themes, published in journals and anthologies, besides two collections of radio plays by Madan Mohan Sharma, *Ik Janam Hor* (Another Birth, 1971) and *Yatru* (The Traveller, 1974), and two collections of one-act plays for children, *Us Bhag Jagane Ale An* (We are the masters of our own destinies, 1960) by Narendra Khajuria and *Dogri Bal Ekanki* (Dogri one-act plays for children, 1974) by Om Goswami.

Modernity has taken roots as an ongoing, vital element in the Dogri literary tradition.

## Milkmaid
## Dinu Bhai Pant

Dinu Bhai Pant (Dinu Bhai Pant, b. 1919) is one of the pioneers of modern Dogri poetry. A homespun wit, authentic Dogri diction, eloquent expression, intimate knowledge of Dogra life and its socio-political problems characterize his work. *Guttulun* (Titillation), *Mangu di Chabil* (Mangu's water kiosk), *Vir Gulab* (Hero Gulab Singh) and *Dadi Te Man* (Grandmother and Mother) are his four poetry collections. He has been honoured by the Jammu and Kashmir Akademy.

The poem *Gujari* (Milkmaid) taken from his collection *Dadi Te Man* is a lively portrait of a milkmaid, an uninhibited rustic, with a femininity which is charming and moving.

Vivacious, lovely and innocent,
Intoxicated with youth, that is Gujari.

She comes daily to vend milk;
Or to bring fodder and firewood.

With piles of pots on her head,
She walks swiftly as a deer,

Her features are winsome and perfect;
Smart, soft, strong and shapely,

Her sublime smiles resemble flowers;
She is fearless like flying doves.

Buxom and charming her face;
Encircled by curly locks.

Drops of perspiration on forehead,
Dazzling like pearls.

Arrow and bow, her eyebrows,
Shake many a stout heart

Intoxicated with youth, that is Gujari.

Winter's chill, or the *loo* or the sun,
Her laughter drives them away.

She climbs tough precipices
To scythe heaps of grass.

She reaches the tops of tall trees
To pluck leaves.

From high hills to deep waters
She roams like a tigress of the jungle.

She grapples with torrential waves,
To collect floating wood from flooded streams.

Reclining on grassy lands,
She sings tribal songs.

This daughter of mother earth
Sings as sweet as a nightingale,

Making all world inert or living
To stand still.

Spell-bound they hold their breath,
Hills listen in are, springs are entranced.

As if a nymph had lit
A divine flame on a river bank.

Intoxicated with youth, that is Gujari.

She knows no tiredness.
Her stone-like breast is as hard as her will.

The breast golden bulges,
Covered by silver beads.

Her shirt wears off
Too tight to keep its grip over her body.

Youth peeps out of her worn-off shirt
The care-free laughter of a *jogan*

This woman is a real woman,
Neither a slave nor a dependent,

Earns whatever she needs and consumes.

Gold cannot chain her,
None dare scandalize her;
Scandals do not touch her.
She is nourished by the food of work and is
Fresh like sprouts of a poplar tree.
Gentlefolk, moneylenders and traders,
Find excuses for calling on her
But she responds unabashed, and
Leaving them speechless.

Aware of their weak spots
She mocks at them, twisting her nose,
Points at the bulky belly of some,
Makes fun of the depressed nose of others;
Calls them by apt names;

Someone is a miser, other a mealy-mouthed toad
Another a cheater in weighing scales.

Intoxicated with youth, that is Gujari.

She shoulders her way through crowds,
Without seeking any support,

None dare molest her,
Who dare invite trouble?

She is no Sita who could be imprisoned,
She'd roar on the chest of a Ravan.

She is the first wave of Ganga's fall on the earth.
She is a fearless daughter of Adam;

Undaunted by fear or worry
Unused to deceit,
She makes light of every tough task.

She is a kinswoman of Radha,
And the youngest sister-in-law of Lord Krishna.

*Gujari*, 1958 *Tr*. by Balraj Puri
*loo* hot, desert winds
*jogan* wandering woman mendicant

**This Little Life**

*Sudarshan Kaushal 'Noorpuri'*

Sudarshan Kaushal 'Noorpuri' (Sudarsan Kausal Nurpuri, 1930-82), is a very popular Dogri poet from Himachal Pradesh, he started his literary career by composing verse in Urdu and was known for his *geets* (songs) and *ghazals*. His compositions were published mostly in journals. The which dominate themes, his poetry are love, sorrows and sufferings of common people.

*Nikki SariJind* (This Little Life) echoes in a very simple language the sorrows of a woman in the hills whose in-laws and neighbours taunt her because her husband has deserted her for another woman.

My life's so small a thing, and my troubles, so great, *Maa-e*!
People mock me when I talk about myself, *Maa-e*!

Separation from you has wasted me away
You, my enemy, have given your heart to another far away

See, my moon, the flower of my youth has wilted
my rival has her wish fulfilled
But here I pine and perish, and there is only mourning, *Maa-e*

If I sigh, my dear, your mother threatens me,
If I raise my voice, she instigates your father,
Your sisters are all ganged up against me,
Tell me, you sinner, where should I seek refuge?
Tears do not wash away what is fated, *Maa-e*

Neighbours are foes, they make up stories that torment me
Seeing me cry and languish, they taunt me
I am a *sohagan* but the}' call me a widow
People do not appreciate the sad ditties of my heart
They are snakes who sting without saying anything, *Maa-e*

*NikkiSariJind,* 1958 *Tr*. by Desh Bandhu Dogra 'Nutan'

*Maa-e'* painful! exclamation in Dogri, remembering the mother *Sohagan* a woman whose husband is alive

**Daybreak**

*R.N. Shastri*

R.N. Shastri (Ram Nath Sastri, b. 1914) is a distinguished poet, playwright and short story writer. He has been the most prominent among the pioneers of the Dogri literary movement led by the Dogri Samastha, Jammu. He has to his credit two collections of poetry—*Dharti Da Din* and *Talkhiyan,* some plays and prose essays, besides a collection of short stories, *Badanami di Chhan,* which won the Sahitya Akademi Award. He has also translated extensively from Sanskrit and Hindi into Dogri. His poetry is intellectually stimulating.

In *Eh Ratin Da Khiri Bela* (Daybreak) the poet evokes three beautiful images—the early morning symphony of sounds and sights, a bevy of girls and a young widow.

Breaks the day, light tip-toeing,
Sweet and seductive sounds arise,
Songs thus born the heart's chords pull,
Raising forms that no one knows.
I float on the waves of bliss,
Hands are mute and eyes are closed;
Ears feel a shower of pearls.
Clouds of rapture wrap the eyes.

Darkness tries in vain to hold
Curtains thin as strings of gauze
Woven by the artist just arisen.
Shines the texture of voices like dew
Tramping sounds of feet in streets
Strumming different strings do seem
Serenading a lullaby dull.

There goes a bevy of girls
Bearing golden dreams in heads
and hopes like twinkling stars
Out for splendours fair and new
Like birds soaring in the sky;
Swans, which feed on pure pearls.
Flying aloft, white and fair,
Filled with youthful glee, their sounds
Brighten streets with beams their own.
Pendant-lights, they march ahead
Striking darkness at its heart.
This, a group of Parbatis
Out to pray for Shiva's boon
And to welcome rising youth
Puts up arches numerous
Made of lucky leaves and blooms.
These are notes of Heaven's
Harmony of creation.
So does now the earth repay
Part of Time borrowed by it.

And there goes with hesitant steps
One bent low with pain unknown,
Under whose scalding feet there groans
Even the street she walks along.
Though the shock has subsided
The burden of sorrow weighs heavy still.

Widow'd she is, the *pant's* son's wife
Going to light lamps in the dark
As her daily wont to the tank
So as to cool her burning youth.
Trudging among the mounds and walls
She is tripped and her feet blister
Barricades and thorny fences
Countering her onward journey
Hardly can she hope to pursue
Dreams that beckon her from beyond.

Hold them in your vacant looks
Those illusions of guileful springs.
Hold the million burning embers
Encased in your silent lips.
Sighs of sorrow shake the beacon
Stunted desires beg and beseech

Storms and sufferings and frustrations
Lie hidden behind the silence.
The breeze that stole away the scent
Passes by clandestinely now.
The soil that had nurtured her once
Is nettled by her footsteps now
Earth and Heaven do never meet
All illusions and hopes are false.
Why are you scratching the soil there?
False hopes provide no props for peace.

*Eh Ratin Da Khiri Bela,* 1959 *Tr.* by Shivanath

**The Oil Press**

*Kehari Singh Madhukar*

Kehari Singh Madhukar (Kehari Sing Madhukar, b. 1929) is a prominent Dogri poet. He published three collections of poetry, with two of them, namely *Dola Kum Thapeya* and *Mein Mela Rajanun* bagging the State Akademy and Sahitya Akademi Awards respectively. As editor (Dogri) in the State Akademy, he edited its Dogri journals and publications for some years. His poetry covers a wide range of subjects—the socio-political scene, romantic love, march of history and humanity and touching vignettes of Dogra life. Optimism, rhythmic flow, rich imagery and humanism mark his work.

*Kohlu* (Oil Press) is a humanistic and progressive poem where the ox tied to the oil-press is symbolic of the toiling masses subjected to exploitation by the powerful.

The oil-press creaks as it works
the ox treads steady in its trail
destined to travel for life
without count of months and years
goes round and round
bells atinkle around its neck
pulling the pole, crushing the seeds
producing oil.

The lash strikes hard
bruising the body,
eyes covered, wits dulled
walks through all the seasons
scolded by the young and the old
to increase its speed,
bound to the wheel of helplessness
it can see no way out.

Thousands of-kos, it covers
still remaining at the same place
the oilman sells the oil
the ox is nowhere in the deal
one enjoys while the other
toils day in and day out
Why then this longing for life?
Why this keenness to live?

One earns, the other consumes
there it is that the hurt lies
the oil belongs to another
and so do the oilcakes
for him—only stale straw.
That's how the oil-press of this epoch moves
poor men turned into oxen
bludgeoned into blind grooves.

Helplessness weighs heavy on him
makes him thieve and do worse
blindfolded by faith
he begins to walk in reverse
caught in the cleft of frustration
he frets in vain in consternation.
The stick of unemployment forces him to toil
turning everything into oil
the hopes of the heart, the beauty of the body,
the lash of starvation pushes him hard
to increase his speed and blunt his mind,
he is seized at his wit's end.

Youth burns bit by bit
with no joy in living,
his master enjoys luxuries
while he bellows in pain
small children cry for food
he has to provide for his brood.
How long will the oil presses work
with people called oxen?
How long will helplessness force
them to mend their pace, to bend?
How long will they wear
the covers of blind faith, like oxen?

How long will they pull the yoke of unemployment?
How long will they crush their hopes into oil?
How long will they bear the lashes of oppression?
How long will they starve to feed the well-fed?

How long will the bell
    lull them into inaction?
How long will their hopes
    languish in cogitation?
Let them get together, none left,
    and resist becoming oil-seeds for the oil-press.
The shape of the world is changing
    just a jolt will do the trick
It's a matter of only moments
    All that's needed is a little push.

*Kohlu*, 1959 *Tr.* by Zahur-ud-din

*kos* measure of distance (approx. one and three fourth miles)

**A Song**

*Yash Sharma*

Yash Sharma (Yasa Sarma, b. 1929) is a poet highly esteemed for his sweet, soulful songs. He has also written plays and short stories, mostly found in anthologies and periodicals. His poetry shows a deep concern for the Dogra people. Particularly appealing is his romantic delineation of Dogra women in their lovelorn moods.

*Git* (Song) is a haunting, melancholy song of love, depicting die pangs of a woman separated from her husband.

As dusk swoops
my heart droops.
My tormentor, encamped in some distant land,
comes to mind to torture and rack,
memories of some things past and gone,
come and strike with a sharp sting.

As dusk swoops
my heart droops.
Left to the mercy of heartless relatives, I cannot speak
Will someone come and tell me how I should touch the moon?
Lost I feel, swindled by my love,
remorse gnaws me, day and night.

As dusk swoops
my heart droops.

My heart cries, how to console it?
Pray tell me, how to control it?
Eyes brim over when someone on yonder hill
passes singing a song of separation.

As dusk swoops
my heart droops.
I shed tears secretly, away from my relatives,
thus washing the stains left by your separation.
I light up lamps of memories
when darkness invades all corners.
As dusk swoops,
my heart droops.

*Git*, 1959 *Tr*. by Zahur-ud-din

**The Raja's Palaces**

*Padma Sachdev*

Padma Sachdev (Padma Sacdev, b. 1940) is known as the first modern Dogri poetess Her verse shows a happy blend of tradition and modernity, and gives voice to the pain and anguish of a woman's heart in a suffering world. It also expresses subtly the complex sensibility of the common man, in fresh, original imagery. Among her collections are *Meri Kavita, Mere Git* (My Poems, My Songs), *Tavi Te Chanale* (Rivers Tavi and Chenab), *Nheriyan Galiyan* (Dark Lanes) and *Pom Pota Nimbal* (Fingertipful of Cloudless Sky), the first of which won the Sahitya Akademi Award. *Raje Diyan Mandiyan* (The Raja's Palaces) voices the feelings of the oppressed and exploited poor, symbolized by an old woman, against the inhumanity and insensitivity of the powerful exploiters.

Do these Raja's palaces belong to you?
I am a wanderer without a home
My eyes lost their light years ago
They came, they plundered. They left me dazed
Uprooted the little plant of my garden
(The sapling was yet to flower)
My beloved had not yet gone very far
Before they severed the trembling branches from him
Do the raping and saw and sickle belong to you?
Do the Raja's palaces belong to you?

The morsel of food was snatched from my lips
The blood in the veins was sucked
The day of our sorrow and our tears, of our agony,
was just an unpleasant trifle for our lords.
They rained the lash on our trembling hands

And before our very eyes
Took away the last brass from our homes,
Emptying every box and iron trunk—
Do their load-mares belong to you
Do the Raja's palaces belong to you?

High walls kiss the sky
Entombed within are riches great
Bright red berets are a lovely sight
Remind us of our blood and plight
Here the boulders
Were unloaded from our shoulders
Here our sweat drenched the soil
These are the walls that arose from our toil
Do these edifices now belong to you?
Do the Raja's palaces belong to you?

Even today my deaf ears
Have heard the burst of the mid-day cannon
The hour of forced labour is over
'Tis time for my beloved to return
But there is not a sound in the lane
No longer my feet break into a run
To greet him walking down the lane
His voice echoes still in my ears
For me 'tis filled with fear and pain
Those that captured him midway—
Do those chains belong to you?
Do the Raja's palaces belong to you?

In whose lamps
Our blood burns as oil
Turning the dark night
Into full moonlight
These shining nights
mock us from afar
It is the night of the festival of lights
Their crackers explode in the sky
Our hearts splinter into little stars
Our children gaze at the fireworks in wonder
Do these lovely Diwalis belong to you?
Do the Raja's palaces belong to you?

It is we who dug the pits and filled them with compost
It is we who drank from the oozing mud

It is we who irrigated the seed beds in scorching heat
(My beloved saw my dried face and was angry)
The night of sapling brought joy to our hearts
When it came to flower, it was our festival of lights
But when we saw their growling eyes we asked—
Does this lovely vegetation belong to you?
Do the Raja's palaces belong to you?

When I was young in years
I entrusted myself to my beloved
A loving exchange it was
That gave him all the rights
His thoughts lit up my days
And followed me into my nights
A fleeting glimpse was a thing of joy
His name a tool of banter for my friends
Those wedded in pledges loving and solemn
Do those souls belong to you?
Do the Raja's palaces belong to you?

*Raje Diyan Mandiyan,* 1959 *Tr.* by Khushwant Singh

**An Evening in Akhnoor**

**Dhian Singh**

Dhian Singh (Dhyan Sing, b. 1938) is a well-known progressive poet in Dogri, but has published only one collection of poems entitled *Filhal.* A Marxist, he has experimented with poetic forms, both formal, like the *ghazal,* and folk, like *bhakh.*

*Akhanurai Di Ek Sanj* (An Evening in Akhnoor) captures the mood of an evening in the old town of Akhnoor, situated on the bank of the Chenab—the sights and the sounds of nature, as also the struggling labourers moving like waves. A cross-section of life is presented here.

The shadows come brooding
Over the undulating waves of the Chenab,
And with the stirring of the eastern wind
The sky of the mind is overcast with dusty mists
That begin to nurture sweet memories.

On the other side of the bank
workers and peasants rise,
Collect their tools and stride
Home like sinuous waves
Some birds parted since dawn
Hurry home to their nests
Absorbing die hues of the dying sun

The bands of waves begin to dance.
Under the canopy of hope
Thousands of lamps are aglow
Tides rise, beat against the banks
and return, wrestling, hoodwinking one another
Moons of gold and stars of silver
Start melting in the waves
Night descends with its hordes of darkness
And the roar of the Chenab echoes in its domes.

*Akhanurai Di Ek Sanj*, 1963 *Tr*. by Desh Bandhu Dogra 'Nutan'

**Two Peaks**

*Charak Singh*

Charak Singh (Caran Sing, 1941-69) was a gifted Dogra poet. Even in his short life, he gave Dogri poetry a new direction and depth with his experiments in poetic form, his intense personal, emotional expression, his fresh imagery, and his probing into the eternal questions of life and death and human anguish. His collection of poems *Jot* (1964) won the Jammu and Kashmir Cultural Academy Award.

*Daun KIngare* (Two Peaks) is a love poem, which depicts the rise, flow and ebb of the course of love, using symbolism drawn from nature.

Very softly, very subtly
Descend, and
Spread
Like unset, mad curls,
Thick silhouettes of Evening.

And under the shadow of the silhouettes,
taking cover for a while
with hearts beating,
bodies flinching,
eyes twitching,
arms around each other,

meet Day and Night
in a stolen hug.
And resting against the breast of the sky,
between two tall peaks,
rises from behind,
centimetre by centimetre,
quivering, and glowing,
the sweet moon.
On an evening like this

Like the emerging moon,
had risen and ripened
Love between us,
in hearts aquiver
in bodies aflutter
in eyes atwinkle.

Then this love of ours
blossomed like the moonlight,
flitted in the courtyards
of the palaces of our hearts,
on their terraces and towers
and bedecked platforms and squares,
now resting softly
now rising slowly.

But this love of ours
was the guest of an hour
Like moonlight of the full moon
Soon to set in the far western horizon.
It went down
along with the moon
behind two date palm trees,
quivering, swaying,
creating desolation
and anguish of separation.

And we, like the peaks,
two date palm trees
Lost in the dark,
stood like ghosts,
holding fire in our hearts,
smouldering silently
Like green firewood.
We continue to smoulder.

Burdened with pain
Lying heavy on the heart
We stand
Like the two banks of a river.
Very close,
Yet too far apart,
constrained by compulsions,
hedged in by custom and tradition,
we never meet.
In between,

the flux of time,
the waters of day and night
flow towards the banks,
on hollow foundations.

And into this water
Our salty tears drip,
trembling,
glittering,
whenever the moon comes up
between the two peaks
and goes down in the far west
behind the date palm trees.

*Daun Klngare,* 1965 *Tr.* by Desh Bandhu Dogra 'Nutan'

**The Black Man**

*Ved Pal eDeepi*

Ved Pal eDeepi (Ved Pal Dip, b. 1929), an eminent Dogri poet, first started composing verse in Hindi and later in Dogri. Fusing thought content with passion, his poetry covers a vast canwass of emotions—love, frustration, patriotism and commitment to social upliftment. Often called the Ghalib of Dogri for his masterful *ghazals,* he has also successfully tried other verse forms. Asa *Te An Banjare Lok* (We are nomadic people, 1968), a collection of ghazals, is his most famous work. He has been honoured by the Jammu and Kashmir Academy.

*Kala Mahnu* (The Black Man) has taken from the collection *Ajkani Dogri Kavita.* It is a powerful impeachment indictment of racial discrimination, inspired by the Black revolt in Congo against Belgian imperialism.

When I take a pen and a piece of paper
To collect the thoughts of my mind,
The picture of a black man
Rises before my eyes.
His blood is red—
The blood of all humanity.
His thick, tufted and rough locks are
Like an intertwined dense forest.
His muscles are as strong as trees.
His white teeth produce
Thunder and lightning;
At their very sight,
The glory of white civilization crumbles.
When I take up my pen to write verse,

It becomes a gun
Which a Negro of Congo
Hangs on his shoulder,
Somewhere in the deep dark wood,
Under the cover of a tree,
To fire at the Belgian army.
When I have put down a word
In ink
On a piece of paper,
It becomes
A bright piece of diamond;
Its dusty ores
Black hands sift out of deep earth,
Underneath rugged plains and rocks,
To deck the crowns
In foreign lands.
When I move my lips
To sing songs,
I feel
Tribes after tribes,
Countless families of mankind,
Like lions,
Move out,
Break their chains
Behind the barbed fences of
The zoo,
Built by their foreign masters.

*Kala Mahnu,* 1968 *Tr.* by Balraj Puri

**Kindling the Latent Love**

*Mohan Lal Sapolia*

Mohan Lal Sapolia (Mohan Lai Sapolia, b. 1934) is a popular Dogri poet. Eloquence, vigour, struggle and hope characterize his poetry, which is often concerned with the Duggar country, its people and heroes. His poems have gained wide spread popularity because of his lively recitation on public platforms. Among his notable collections are *Angare, Kacherian Da Naher, Bharat Sarha* and *Dholl Da Poll.* He has won the Jammu and Kashmir Academy prize.

In the poem *Sutti dit Pric Jaga Kama* (Kindling the Latent Love) taken from his collection *Sajre Phull* (Fresh Flowers, 1969), the poet identifies himself with a river flowing freely in total self-abandon. He offers a message of hope and love which he discovers in the environment around him from where he is watching he river flow majestically.

The colours revel for my sake,
The flowers blossom for me,
The moonlight smiles for me,
The music plays for me!

> The waves splash at me,
> Ecstasy sways me,
> From the tender limbs of earth
> I kindle its latent love!

I bank on every wave,
I rise with every tide.
When life is spent
Death comes to my rescue!

> I draw life out of death,
> Ecstasy sways me,
> From the tender limbs of earth
> I kindle its latent love!

How many-hued is the earth!
How bare the sky's chest,
Studded with twinking stars,
Every star, my companion!

> I embrace my companions,
> Ecstasy sways me,
> From the tender limbs of earth
> I kindle its latent love!

How lovely are the thorns,
Sharp and keen-edged!
They make the path come alive,
These thorns encourage me!

> I set my foe on the thorns!
> Ecstasy sways me,
> From the tender limbs of earth
> I kindle its latent love!

Jungles and wastelands in my embrace,
I play with torrents,
Rise with the tides,
I strike against the mountains!

> I renew life by staking it.
> Ecstasy sways me,

From the tender limbs of earth
I kindle its latent love!

Sorrows arrive, rest and stay,
After roaming the endless skies,
Broken, tired out and dejected,
They seek my lap's refuge!

I enrich them with beauty and lustre,
Ecstasy sways me,
From the tender limbs of earth
I kindle its latent love!

The fire of lust rages,
High hopes engage me,
The blisters on my palm smile,
Stones gall against my feet!

I turn stones into flowers,
Ecstasy sways me,
From the tender limbs of earth,
I kindle its latent love!

*SuttJ dl Pnt Jaga Karna,* 1969 *Tr.* by Balraj Puri

**A Playing Card**

*Narsingh Dev Jamwal*

Narsingh Dev Jamwal (Narsimha Deva Jamwal, b. 1931), a civil servant by profession, has contributed significantly to Dogri poetrv, Fiction and drama. He is also a painter and sculptor. For his poetry collections *Shama Jale Ki Dharki Dharki* and *Koraj*, he received the Jammu and Kashmir Cultural Academy awards. His other works include *Sanjhi Dharti Bakhle Manu* (novel) and *Dukhde Gotte* (short stories). Jamwal's writings disseminate his humanistic and idealistic approach to life and his reverence for the Creator.

*Tashai da Patta* (A Playing Card[1]) compares human beings and their behaviour to the movements of cards in a game of cards.

In this foursome sitting of the worldy crowd—
I am just a card in the game of cards.
One lifts me high to kiss with his eyes,
Another throws me gently in the court,
And still another dashes me with a bang.

Then mingled in a trick of cards,
I occupy the corner close to oblivion.
Sitting there like this I feel
That in this game I am not alone.

Men and women all over the world,
Are just cards, like me, in the game of cards.

From the Queens to the Kings and the Aces,
Down to Twos and Threes.
Fours and Fives, Sixes, Sevens and Eights
To Nines and over them Tens.

Some among them such as Jacks, are order bound,
And the Spades known as *Hukams* are given to ordering about.
Some among them such as Hearts are a lovely, throbbing red
And the Diamonds are of course nicely cut and cute.
And the Clubs known as *Chiriyas* are a lovely lot.
Some are young, plump and handsome,
And some are slim and dainty like a village belle.

Each of them has a distinct stance,
Each one his separate identity,
Each one has his pride and prestige.
Each one his value as occasion demands.
If three Twos get together
the Queen, the King and the Ace
Bend before them in submission.
All of them stage an act for a while—
Popping and plumbing,
Crossing and clashing,
Bidding for the trumps.

Gathered up in tricks, one after the other
They come together at one place,
Where all are equal—high and low,
Where Two and Three tarry,
There also repose the King and Queen and the Ace.
Each of them waits for the shuffle
That will give them a chance,
Once again to play their part.

Seated in the chariot of Time
The master player of the world
Has been at the game for ages.
As and when some colours fade,
A new set of cards He creates.

*Tashai da Patta, 1971* *Tr*. by H.R. Pandotra

**I Too Am Not Apart**

*Sarathi O.P. Sharma*

Sarathi O.P. Sharma (Om Prakas Sarma SarathI, b. 1933) of irish has to his Gredit three collections of poetry, two of stories and five novels.

His *Nanga Rukh* (novel) has received the Sahitya Akademi Award and *Resham de Keere* (novel) the Jammu and Kashmir Akademy award. He is a versatile write and a painter.

His fiction is characterized by a deep social commitment and ironic exposition of contemporary society. He is a metaphysical poet and his poetry is concerned with questions of Ultimate Reality and the human predicament.

*Mein Bi Bakhala Nayin* (I too am not apart) seeks to explore man's lot in the flux of time.

> Deep in the mouth of Time
> I seem to melt like a lump of candy,
> I am a lump of candy
> And yet I do not feel the melting
> And wonder if I have to merge
> With its flaming waves of heat.
> What is all this fun and frolic
> This simulation, this mask, this noise?
> I am told that some Being
> With large ears and eyes
> Is watching everything in a dream in his sleep.
> If he is fond of seeing dreams
> He should have made me a blade of grass
> Instead of a piece of candy
> So that He could feel me in his mouth
> And I could be saved from melting,
> worrying and being pulverized;
> I would then experience the softness of Time's mouth.
> But I do not know how ruthless, how great this Being is
> Swallowing, dissolving innumerable pieces
> Of whom I too am one.

Mein *Bi Bakhala Nayin,* 1974 — *Tr*. by Shivanath

# 10

# Modern Kashmiri Literature

P.N. PUSHP

## Footfalls of Modernity : The Nineteenth Century

Kashmir was feudal. There was no encouragement form Maharaja in any field. Modernity took a very long time to reach Kashmir, and longer still to touch the Kashmiri language. Not that it had to cover a considerable distance, but it had to cross a formidable barrier of political neglect and social atrophy.

The changing mood and modes in the neighbouring regions of the state infiltrated into the Valley through newspapers and periodicals, sometimes surreptitiously. Communication was not as it was in the neighbouring sates of Punjab and Himachal. Occasionally these happened to reach the Valley through personal contact and attracted attention in closed-door parleys; yet Kashmiri literature appears to have remained unruffled for long, waxing eloquent on the Sufi's indifference to temporal contours of social change. There was no newpaper in Kashmiri, not even a local one.

There though matel. It was resentment was, nevertheless, transmitted through doggerel, invective, lampoon and caricature by the folk theatre of Kashmir *(Banda-pathur)* and the folk ballad of ridicule *(Ladishah)*. The folk-artist often took resort to camouflaging the context unless his target was smaller fry like the peasant or the petty revenue official or priest. Since caricature has to be essentially topical within the parameters of the present, it can accommodate the element of modernity. And that is how modernity emerged in Kashmiri verse.1

### *Caricature and Invective in Poetry*

Maqbool Shah Kralavari (1820-75) caricatured the peasant as well as the revenue official in his 'Greestynama' (Peasant's Episode, 1865), while in his 'Mala-nama' and 'Peernama' he made fun of the covetous *mulla* and the conceited *peer*. Despite a surfeit of taunt and rebuke he reflected the socio-economic maladies of the times, and unwittingly took the reader into the arena of folk concerns, where vested interests clashed wildly.

Wahab Parey (1847-1914) evinced deep interest in the people's weal and woe through comments particularly on administrative indifference and civic apathy. His 'Darveshi' (Ways of the Darveshes, c. 1890), for instance, exposes the anti-peasant functionaries of the Revenue department, to which he had himself belonged in one capacity or the other. Some of these he aptly describes as *lootu-hakim* (official agents of loot).

The urge for social reform similarly appeared not only in the frequent improvization in the traditionally sung *vanavun* (ceremony song) but also in didactic verse written in defence of familial harmony and civic behaviour (including campaigns against social ills such as traffic in women). Daya Ram Ganju (c. 1925), in particular, directed his pointed jibes at a number of serious evils like unequal marriage fatalistically arranged by parents.

### *Echoes of Socio-Political Unrest*

Two outstanding events in the latter half of the nineteenth century seem to have left an indirect impact on Kashmiri verse of the period. These were the shawl weavers' strike in 1865 and the acute famine of 1878. The 'Aiiaz-e-Quran' (The Miracle of the Quran) of Mahdi Trali (c. 1880), for instance, wove fact and fancy into a verse narrative of protest and agitation that, in a way, indirectly anticipated the 1931 uprising. It invoked communal amity despite a mix-up of religion and politics, and highlighted the demonstrators' grim determination to see their grievances redressed.

### *Modernity Accerlerates Poetry* : 1900-47

(1887-1952) was the first Kashmiri poet to be exposed to the forces of change that swept over the Indo-Gangetic Basin. The hesitant steps of modernity, however, gained momentum owing to improvements in social mobility brought about by educational facilities and exposure to external impact. Ghulam Ahmed Mahjoor The Aligarh Movement, for instance, inspired the Kashmiri Muslims to set up an educational institution that could propagate the message of Sir Sayyed, a veteran of Islamic concepts. Mahjoor's earliest Kashmiri poem, read by him at an annual meet of the Society called Anjuman E Nusrat Ul Islam in 1908, acknowledges the impact of the Aligarh Movement on the Kashmiris. Dr Ikbal's timely advice to him to switch over completely to the Kashmiri language for his verse, emboldened Mahjoor to resist the compelling temptation of Persian and Urdu and also motivated him to steer clear of Sufi jargon. Mahjoor, therefore, started singing of love as a force integrating nature, man and society. He was drawn increasingly towards the scenic splendour of his native land which he depicted as a *gulshan* (flower garden), most probably as a befitting parallel to Ikbal's *gulsitan* (a key word in his *Sare jehan se accha yeh gulsitan hamara).* Mahjoor's poem is, however, qualitatively different: it articulates an open invitation to Kashmir's scenic bounties without invoking any historical nostalgia (to which he turned a decade later). Earlier he had, no doubt, versified a plea in support of the war effort (1918), but that was in response to an offer which he had accepted if he wrote favouring the government views on was he would he suitably rewarded. Whoever promised him went back on his word.

The upsurge of 1931 seems to have aroused his curiosity in the new developments. He was in fact a regular reader of quite a few newspapers and periodicals published in the Punjab and, naturally, he was aware of the local implications too. But, being a government employee, he had to keep away from political involvement and also to appear above suspicion. The romantic in him, therefore, preferred to harp 'fresh tunes on the lyre of love' till gradually he evolved a sort of flower[1] symbolism to camouflage his growing concern for his forlorn land so that he could unburden his heart without getting into trouble. Thus alone could he afford to sing:

Wake up early at dawn. O Garden-flow'r
Listen to the Nightingale's lament!

### *Romantic Nationalism*

Mahjoor's verse, accordingly, preoccupied itself with a deep love for the loveliness of the land of his birth and its folk. His depiction of the 'Greesty-Koor' (Country Lass, 1936) in this very setting proved to be a turning point in his literary career. It won him Tagore's warm appreciation which helped him further to get over a language dilemma that had often driven him towards Persian and Urdu in preference to Kashmiri. It also boosted his self-confidence so that his expression grew increasingly bolder even within the cautious bounds of a disarming ambiguity; while his growing commitment to the cause of freedom (1938 onwards) spoke through his flower-metaphored verse, invoking the gardener to resuscitate the flowers' and the nightingales. For instance, it pained him to see that

The garden is desolate, the dew is shedding tears;
Flowers tunic-torn are ill at ease.

He ardently echoed New Kashmiris concerns that had erupted into the Quit Kashmir Movement of 1946, and when the autocratic Bastille fell to heroic resistance, Mahjoor could not yet afford to breathe the romantic freshness of a long-awaited dawn. The Pakistan-abetted tribal raid hurled him into agony, which he shared with his readers, dubbing the uncouth marauders as 'man-eating wild vultures'.

Mahjoor thus not only mirrored the people's aspirations against the backdrop of the New Kashmir ideal, he also widened their enable them to think horizon and deepened their insight into the social implications of the new beyond their thoughts political change.

### *Other Voices of the Forties*

Other poets of the period may be discussed under the following broad categories:

**(1)** Narrative verse writers (in the *masnavi* style) like Shams-ud-Din Hairat Pandani (1890-1976) who persisted in telling or retelling in rhymed couplets titillating tales of love at first sight, separation and reunion.

**(2)** Traditional mystics like Samad Mir (1894-1959) and Ahad Zargar (1904-83), who flourished unaffected by the socio-political compulsions of the period.

***Modern Indian Literature***

**(1)** Humorists like Lala Lakshman (1893-1961) who lampooned sociallapses in conventional balladic drollery, sounding almost like anextension of the *Ladishah*.

**(2)** Partisans like Abdul Sattar Asi (d. 1951), Shams-ud Din Kafoor (1905-73), Ghulam Nabi Ariz (1916-65) and Pitambar Nath Dhar Fani (b. 1919) who enthusiastically espoused the cause of the peasant and the worker.

**(3)** Innovators like Abdul Ahad Azad (1906-48), Mirza Ghulam Hasan Beg Arif (b. 1910) and Zinda Kaul Masterji (1886-1966).

**(4)** Younger humanists like Dina Nath Wali Almast Kashmiri (b. 1910), Nand Lal Ambardar (1915-73) and Ghulam Ahmad Fazil Kashmiri (b.1914) who despite their predilection for the romantic occasionally also wrote on religious tolerance, communal amity and economic amelioration.

***Socialistic Humanism***

The dynamics of social change however was brought forward by Abdul Ahad Azad and some of his young contemporaries. He was, in fact, the first Kashmiri poet to adopt a positively socialistic outlook on life and literature. This was due to a congenial response to the new developments infiltrating into Kashmir, mostly through Urdu poetry. Despite the initial impact of Iqbal, the humanism espoused by Azad was considerably influenced by the radical humanism of M.N. Roy, avoiding any sort of religious rigmarole or communal commitment. Azad's verse, in fact, was a vigorous crusade against any sham or fad that had separated man from man. Denunciation of anti-social behaviour (sectional, national or international) became almost an obsession with the poet who appeared to be relaying the messages whispered into his ears by symbolic sources of eternal wisdom. Hence his poems on the candle, the moon, the stars, the cascade and the river. Had he lived beyond 1948, his poetry might have become richer in content and finer in form. Yet, even as it is, his socio-cultural perception of creativity has an authentic ring of urgency, as borne out by the poem 'Darya' (The River, 1945).

Azad's impact can be discerned not only on his younger associates like Arif, Ariz and Fani but also on some belonging to his own age group (like Asi and Kafoor), and even on his elders like Mahjoor and Masterji. Mahjoor in fact had in his 'Katsa-zoon' (The Autumn Moon) nominated Azad as his worthy successor. The poem itself is reminiscent of Azad's ardent muse.

### *Mystical Humanism*

Masterji (Master Zinda Kaul), a latecomer to Kashmiri verse, sang of eternal longing as well as perennial questioning, as for instance in his 'Lacariya Majburiya' (Helplessness, Ah Compulsion, 1942). His poetry is an appealing blend of traditional values and contemporary demands, in a substantially modern tone. His soul yearns passionately to be ferried across the river of time into a lovelier world, thriving on mutual reverence and all-round harmony—domestic, communal, national and international.

### *Peasants' and Workers' Woes*

Asi, a milkman by birth and a load-carrier by avocation of those who wrote mostly on the peasant and the labourer were; Kafoor, a farmer as well as a political worker; and Fani, then a young graduate, taking to Urdu journalism. Since no journals were available in the Kashmiri language in those days, their verse was published in *Vitasta* (an Urdu daily) and was avidly read. Basically journalistic verse, it had topical appeal and therefore facilitated the transition to contemporary writing.

### *The Saga of the Struggle*

Mirza Arif, however, initially wrote a number of short poems on various kinds of workers such as the craftsman, the load-carrier of the Banihal Range, the embroiderer, the shawl weaver, the woman shifting bricks and mortar, and so on. Later he turned his attention to the freedom struggle and its leader. His *Magar Karavan Soen Bronh Bronh Pankan Gav* (Yet our caravan dashed ahead, 1946) reverberates with the stirring saga of the struggle right from 1931 to the Quit Kashmir Movement of 1946. Naturally in 1947 he was gripped by the New Kashmir euphoria, which gradually petered out, allowing him time to re-order his literary strategy in the changed circumstances. Satire was no doubt his weapon earlier too, but in the fifties it became razor-sharp and turned Arif's *rubay* (quatrain) into a fascinating display of literary fireworks.

Decades later Mir Ghulam Rasool Nazki (b. 1909) also took to the quatrain and made creditable contributions to contemporary humour and satire, qualitatively different from the comic drollery of Khizr Maghribi (b. 1921) and Makhan Lal Mahav (b. 1926).

## Post-Independence Period: 1947-75

The tribal raid did a lot for the literary fermament of the valley. It was the later half of 1947. The raid proved to be a turning point in the literary development of Kashmir. The resistance organized by the National Cultural Front against the Pakistan-abetted tribal raid also brought writers together and opened up fresh vistas of literary endeavour. It threw up Dina Nath Nadim (1916-88) as a tireless organizer of the new movement. He poured out poem after poem in full-blooded youth, voicing the people's resistance to aggression and orchestrating their aspirations for peace. Peace for him was no idle gossip but a pre-requisite for the establishment of a new social order. His poetic sensitivity explored the creative potential for further experimentation in a number of genres like the labour chant, the lullaby, the free verse, the free-associational verse the opera and the sonnet. His verse patterns, accordingly, are strikingly fresh and scintillating, with dictional innovations that reflect a response to the momentous call to resist and restructure.

**Break from Tradition**

Quite a few of his poems of the early fifties like 'Vavan Vonanam' (The wind reported it to me), 'Vushun Vushun Vozul Vozul' (Warm and red, red and warm), 'Vothi Bagucy Kukili' (Arise, O Garden Dove) and *Ba Geva Na Az* (I will not sing today) register a startling break from the traditional technique of the *nazm* as perfected by Mahjoor and Azad. His 'Bombur Yembarzal' (The Bumble Bee and Narcissus, 1953), an operatic composition, depicts a tussle between the allies of spring and autumn, resulting in the ultimate victory of good over evil in an eternal struggle for survival.

The literary creations which occurred in that period fascinated many youngsters. They found Nadim's company quite rewarding and were, accordingly, attracted to new themes, in tune with the new awareness. Prominent among these were Noor Muhammad Roshan (b. 1919), Arjan Dev Majboor (b. 1922), Ghulam Nabi Firaq (b. 1922), Amin Kamil (b. 1924) and Rahman Rahi (b. 1925). In due course they were joined by a younger brand of promising newcomers like Vasudev Reh (b. 1926), G.R. Santosh (b. 1929), Musaffar Amin (b. 1934), Ghulam Nabi Khayal (b. 1935), Moti Lal Saqi (b. 1936) and Charrian Lal Chaman (b. 1937). They also hailed what they zestfully imagined to be the dawn of a New Kashmir. Accordingly they presented eloquent visions of utopian exuberance, though of course with occasional notes of caution and vigilance. Chaman, in particular, took delight in Freudian vagaries of the libido in the frustrating context of contemporary inhibitions.

These youngsters had a dream. Yet they had to face the grim realities of an uncertain transition, vitiated by the widening gap between political promise and administrative performance. Within a decade or so even Nadim's poetry registered a significant shift from rhetorical overstatement to ambiguous understatement, and by 1962 it became unbelievably simplified, merely penetrating into great trifles. He also unmasked pretension and debunked self-righteousness. His later poems (written after 1950) like 'Lakhci Chhu Lakcun' (Lakhci Has a Mole), 'Nabad ta Tethaven' (Candy and Artemesia), 'Harysat' (Vicissitudes), and 'Carykath' (Of Absurd Relevance) indicate that, despite his progressive outlook on literary activity, he moved gradually from slogan to symbol and beyond, to vision, particularly when some of his fellow-writers (Kamil and Rahi, for instance) got dispuntled and parted company.

Kamil and Rahi had both, like Nadim, switched over from Urdu to Kashmiri, carrying over the literary influence of Iqbal, Josh, Firaq and Faiz. Kamil, however, freed himself from Iqbalian rhetoric and experimented with the Kashmiri *ghazal,* as Firaq Gorakhpuri and Faiz Ahmed Faiz had done in Urdu. Both his (post-1960) collections, *Lava ta Prava* (Dew Drops and Sun Rays) and *Beyi Suy Pan* (My Own Self Again) bear the imprint of an experimental sensibility battled by what he terms *Nechanaty Mane* (Naked Meanings). Similarly, Rahi freed himself from the progressive dogma of socialist realism and grew more and more reflective. His *Nauroz-e-Saba* (Muse at Early Dawn) represents a watershed between his poetic work of the early fifties and his later fascination for the ambiguous and the obscure leading to serious literary experimentation. The positive outcome of this can be seen in his later poems like 'Qairi Darya Salsabu' (Heavenly is the surging sea), 'Jalva ta Zabur' (Vision and Word), and 'Takhliq' (Creativity), as uninhibited sensibility trying to evoke a suggestive image of the non-obvious.

Concerns like these are shared, more or less, by all contemporary poets among whom Firaq, Santosh, Rashid Nazki, Azim, Khayal, Saqi, Chaman, Marghub Banihali, Mashal Sultanpuri, Ghulam Ahmed Gash and Mohi-ud-Din Gauhar have occasionally succeeded in rising above the average.

A new generation of younger poets impressed by the changing perspectives in poetic articulation, are, however, making a laudable bid to keep abreast of the times. Among these standard-bearers of off beat verse, Rafiq Raz, Shafi Shauq, Gulshan Majid and Nasim Shifai have already made a significant start in the new direction, ensuring the emergence of a new poetic expressions. It is some cautions optimism which is egging them on.

***Prose***: The development of prose in Kashmiri is a post-independence phenomenon and the modern element in it appeared first, in fact, in the fifties like poetry prose in Kashmiri had become hackneyed. Prose hesiting had become stated almost state. The Kashmiri section of the S.P. College magazine, *Pratap* (1936 onwards), the only available medium then, could accommodate no more than undergraduate exercises in essay writing. Even the short lived weekly *Gash* (Daylight, 1940) could afford little scope for the development of prose other than that of news coverage. *Kongposh* (The Saffron Flower), the official organ of the Kashmir Cultural Congress, opened out opportunities for publication in the language. *Kongposh,* became a literary forum for the writers of the day and drew their attention to the need for Kashmiri prose. As long as it appeared (1949-56, though fitfully), it encouraged translation as well as original writing in a number of prose genres including reportage, the short story, the humorous skit, socio-cultural appraisal and literary appreciation. Among other journals that sought to promote the development of Kashmiri prose from time to time the following deserve mention: the Urdu *Gulrez* (Flower-Dropper), 1952-55, 1959-61; the multilingual *Pamposh* (Lotus), from 1951 for a few years; *Watan* (Nativeland), from 1965 for a couple of years; *Chaman* (Flowerbed), from 1965 for a few years; *Naeb* (Clue), for a number of years, and *Kashur Adab* (Kashmiri Literature) for a short period.

(Togetherness) The University Kashmiri Department's journal *Anahaar* (Configuration) The Jammu and Kashmir Cultural Academy journal *Sheeraza* have, however, vigorously persisted, coming to the rescue of Kashmiri prose. *Sheeraza,* incorporating its Annual entitled *Soen Adab* (Our Literature), ever since it first appeared in 1959-60, has commendably covered various areas as well as modes of writing in the Kashmiri language, such as language, literature, folklore, numismatics, historiography, travelogue, short story, drama, essay and special literary surveys, particularly during a centenary celebration year. *Anahaar* too has promoted similar objectives in a more selective and academic manner, and on a smaller scale, mostly as offshoots of seminar programmes. The fact, nevertheless, remains that the natural and sustained development of Kashmiri prose has been hampered by the lamentable absence of a daily or weekly in the Kashmiri language.

**Limited Incentive**

The few prose works that have appeared in print notwithstanding these serious handicaps, owe their publication either to the writer's personal dynamism or the incentive provided by the State Academy of Art, Culture and Languages that grants subsidies and award prizes. The Sahitya Akademy awards also have encouraged some enterprising writers (or their ambitious well-wishers) to see their work in print.

**Published Prose**

Some of the published prose works are as follows. Yavan *Nahaj* (Youthful Trends, 1951, edited by Kamil and Haroon) was the first anthology accommodating a small cross-section of Kashmiri prose written after 1947. *Kashiri Abduk Tarlkh* (History of Kashmiri Literature, Vol. I, 1965) by Avtar Krishen Rahbar was, in fact, the first work of its kind to appear on the development of Kashmiri language and early Kashmiri literature. *Kashiri Nasruc Kitab* (Book of Kashmiri Prose) by Mohi-ud-Din Hajini was the first collection of a single writer's prose, with a view to presenting a miscellany of plausible prose styles. *Maqalat* (Write-ups), also by Hajini, contained some maturer attempts at developing Kashmiri prose as a vehicle for reflective discourses, thematically as well as stylistically.

*Gashiry Munara* (Lighthouses) by Ghulam Nabi Khayal highlighted the literary peculiarities of world masterpieces in various languages, giving glimpses into the minds of masters (both eastern and western) such as Kalidas, Dante, Goethe and Shakespeare. *Sufi Shayiri* (Mystic Poetry, 1964-65) by Amin Kamil, initially written as introductions to anthologies of Sufi verse (in Kashmiri), despite a few howlers, presented a readable account of a scholarly dispensation. *Kashiri Abduk Tavarlkh* (History of Kashmiri Literature, 1976) by Naji Munawar and Shafi Shauq covered the whole gamut of literary development and devoted maximum attention to post-independence period, often with critical acumen. A few hang-overs of earlier writers (regarding the beginnings of Kashmiri writings, for instance), have, however, been quite uncritically allowed to persist. *Kahvat* (Touchstone, 1979) by Rahman Rahi is the most substantial anthology of a writer's profound writings on theoretical as well as practical criticism in a total perspective as applied to Kashmiri verse. *Zaban ta Adab* (Language and Literature) by Shafi Shauq, though not profound or austere, reveals a remarkable freshness of approach. *Jadid Kashir Shayiri* (Modern Kashmiri Poetry, 1982) by Hamidi Kashmiri is the first work wholly devoted to the study of modern Kashmiri verse, pinpointing the adequacy or inadequacy of the modern sensibility as understood by him.

**Modern Kashmiri Poetry**

Despite a lot of cliches employed in the criteria of evaluation prescribed in the work, its insistence on a new approach sounds quite authentic in terms of critical insights. *Slava Mir* (1960) by Akhtar Mohi-ud-Din is an absorbing travelogue on the author's trip to the Soviet Union, brimming with unique reminiscences of a variety of situations. *Safarnama-e-Chin* (Travelogue of China, 1978) by Mirza Arif also recaptures some memorable moments and impressions in a cultural-cum-technological setting.

*The Essay* (1986), a collection of essays by Dr Muhammad Zaman Azurdah, blazes a new trail in essay-writing, although a number of good essays had already been written and broadcast by other writers. Azurdah has a knack for weaving Joose sallies of the mind into charmingly personal utterances, though in a few cases contrived or even stereotyped endings spoil the charm. Besides the works referred to here, a number of good prose pieces have appeared either as seminar papers or as introductions to outstanding publications of the Cultural Academy. Yet, it has to be admitted that Kashmiri prose has still a long way to go.

***Short Story***: The short story in Kashmir appears to be quite impressive, qualitatively if not quantitatively. From the first story carried by *Kongposh* on the eve of the fifties to the stories of the eighties, there has been a sea-change. The early stories were more or less essayish, if not banal narratives, full of tendentiousness or wishful thinking and lacked the stamp of authenticity. Akhtar Mohi-ud-Din's *Sat Sangar* (Seven Cliffs, 1955), was the earliest collection to register high quality and contemporary freshness. These stories take the reader into the emotional recesses of essentially human characters whom he had known, right from his childhood, as lower class persons of no consequence. Nabir Shal and Bristy Vatul, for instance, in the stories 'Daryayi-hund Yezar' (Satin Pyjamas) and 'Danda-vazun' "(Bickering) respectively, strike us as significant tokens of lively assertion within their limited spheres of existence.

**Experimentation**

A lot of experimentation with a variety of fictional modes and moulds went on simultaneously covering the gamut from the Maupassant-type suspense or the O. Henry climax to Chekovian twists of the depth-psyche, and beyond, to the vagaries of the Existential Absurd. In between occurred attempts at varied possibilities of departure from the conventional norm. Before the sixties, the story woven around a single character was as popular as that woven around an incident of series OF incidents. 'Mai Ded' (of the early fifties) by Sufi Ghulam Muhammad, for instance, explored the inner personality of a vegetable vendor who had made a distinct impact through her affectionate nature on every one of her customers. Similarly, 'Khojabay' by Taj Begum Renzu depicted an aristocrat's maid-servant as a distinct personality in a specific setting.

Another young writer Bansi Nirdosh 'Bal Marayo' (I in youth shall pre-decease you) on the other hand, weaves a bewitching pattern out of a tantalizing criss-cross of expectation and exasperation. 'Kathi Manz Kath' (Story Within Story) by Amin Kamil underscores the relevance of the old devices to contemporary concerns, while his 'Aana' (Mirror) reflects the psychological undulations created in the human personality when facing a specific situation. Insistence on the situational rather than the event centred story, in fact, became the vogue after the sixties, particularly after the appearance (in 1967) of *Jadid Kashur* Afsana (Modern Kashmiri Short Story), a special number of *Sheeraza* featuring contemporary trends.

**Event to Situation**

The shift of emphasis from the *event* to the *situation* is borne out even by the titles of some of the short stories written during the period. We have, for instance, 'Mogli Gafara' and 'Shuny' (Vacuum) by Lone; 'Panun Marun' (Death of Self) and 'Treyum Arman' (Third Hankering) by Nirdosh; 'Vony Kahunz Chhe Vary' (Whose Turn Now?) by Shankar Raina; 'Sethah Momooli' (Quite Ordinary) and 'Narganad' (Infernal Rivulet) by Farooq Masudi; 'Hamzad' (The Double) and 'Tsakra-Vyooh' (Labyrinthian Formation) by Bharati; 'Nirvan' and 'Shithyomut Siryi' (Frozen Sun) by Rahbar; 'Taph' (Sunshine) and 'Halas Chhu Rotul' ('Tis Night

Yet) by Hari Krishna Kaul; and 'Curfew' and 'Tshayi Gity' (Quivering Shadow) by Ratan Lal Shant.

**Latest Trends**

The obsession with urban life is tending more and more towards the abstract, bordering on the absurd. Bharati's 'Dvan Aanan Darmiyan' (Between Two Mirrors), 'Anigatici Topaz-Khanji' (Topaz, Scrap of the Dark), and Bashir Akhtar's 'Sindabadun Aathim Safar' (Sindbad's Eighth Journey), and 'Yeti Ab Chhu Koluy' (Where Water is Taboo) may be cited as typical of the new concern to register a bold departure from the neo-conventional. The story writers of today are, by and large, taking care to see that they do not revert to the pre-1967 level of conventional craftsmanship. A number of stories written suffer from poor handling of language or want of experimental maturity. Yet a sizeable number have positively raised the quality of fictional treatment in Kashmiri.

***Novel: Early Attempts***

The Kashmiri novel has not made much progress. It is where it was fifty years ago. Whatever effort has been made has not proved to be of much substance. Of a dozen or so that have so far appeared in print, hardly any one can claim to be an excellent work by contemporary standards. The most lamentable cause for such a serious situation lies in the acute shortage of readers, aggravated by the absence of a daily or even a weekly that could serialize readable novels.

*Doed-Dag* (Pain and Anguish, 1956) by Akhtar Mohi-ud Din made a spectacular start as a neat social novelette on the theme of male high-handedness in marriage and divorce perpetrated on two loving sisters, one of whom the man had married, and the other whom he had illicitly used in bed. Though the work fails to rise above the average as a novel, in parts it is quite gripping.

Another novel written about the same time, *Gati Manz Gash* (Daylight in the Dark) by Amin Kamil, contrives an intriguing and even shocking possibility: a woman teacher born of Muslim parents and bred in orthodoxy falls in love with a Hindu youth to whom she has given refuge during the tumultuous tribal raid in northern Kashmir. The story as narrated, however, is sketchy and lacks substance. The next work (of the fifties), *Asy Ti Chi Insan* (We Too Are Human) by Ali Muhammad Lone, also lacks structural adequacy and grace of diction which differentiate a novel from a contrived travelogue. Intended to be about the Amarnath pilgrimage it fails to evolve as an integrated whole out of fragments of observation that sound like a running commentary.

The two novels by Ghulam Nabi Gauhar that followed (in the sixties) Possess solidity of detail, but they appear to have imitated outmoded models from average Urdu fiction. Gauhar's professional familiarity with the court (as a judicial magistrate) certainly gave his *Mujrim* (Criminal), a concrete story, a local colour, but his pompous language and formulaic treatment of the court scenes vitiate the work, while the irrepressible fondness for quoting his own verse irritates. *Myul* (Rapprochement), only a shade better, suffers from similar handicaps, particularly monotony of diction.

*Akh Daur* (An Epoch) by Bansi Nirdosh, though free from such excesses, fails because of its inability to provide an adequate structuring of the historical setting, even for the modest purpose of a novelette.

*Traesh Ta Tarpan* (Thirst and Water Oblation) by Amar Malmoohi is a sketchy narrative of superficial concerns precariously held together by sentimental outpourings.

*Pun Ta Pap* (Piety and Sin), a recent novel by Gauhar, has improved in structure through convincing sequences, but has not been able to integrate its florid descriptions with the contextual material, while its language strains after effect irrespective of relevance. *Sheen Ta Vatapady* (Snow and the Foot-track) by Prem Kishore deserves credit for exploring the nomadic life of the Gujar community (of the state). Yet it reads more like a synopsis of a potential novel than a novel proper. Some descriptions, however, stand out as pieces of attractive prose.

All told, a real contemporary novel, abreast of the latest in the craft of writing, has yet to appear in the Kashmiri language.

**Drama**

Kashmiri drama worthy of being labelled modern has appeared since independence. Attempts made in this direction before 1947 have, no doubt, a historical value as a prelude to modernity; but hardly any play worth the name had appeared by the time. Even *Greesty Sund Gara* (Peasant's Home) by Mohi-ud Din Hajini, serialized earlier (during the forties), in the magazine *Pratap* was no more than an account in dialogue form of a peasant's woes aggravated by the machinations of his exploiters as much as by his own imbecile docility.

Early fifties saw some effort in this direction when the drama wing of the Kashmir Cultural Congress initiated a vigorous programme of staging propaganda plays with a view to promoting socio-cultural awareness of the changing situation. Meanwhile, Radio Kashmir broadcast a number of innovative attempts at play-writing, and the Cultural Academy instituted drama festivals and competitions.

By a strange circumstance the first performance staged in 1953 was an opera *Bombur Yembarzal* (The Bumble Bee and Narcissus) by Dina Nath Nadim, about the symbolic triumph of spring over autumn (already referred to in the section on poetry). It was in 1956, however, that the first drama festival was celebrated and a demand arose for Kashmiri scripts. An operatic composition, *Himaal Naagraay* (co-authored by Nadim and

Roshan), was produced as a new experiment in combining shadow play with opera, but it proved abortive. Yet it sharpened the appetite for bold experimentation. Amin Kamil's *Haba Khatun* was powerfully scripted but it fell short of the demands of dramatic movement. Akhtar Mohi-ud-Din's *Nasti Hund Sawal* (Point of Prestige) adapted to stage requirements was effectively produced despite excessive intellectualization.

**Experimentation**

Meanwhile the availability of the Tagore Theatre, a gift of the Tagore Centenary Year (1961), gave a fillip to the drama festival for which the revival of the *Banda Jeshin,* the traditional folk theatre of Kashmir, was deemed a must in tune with the times. *Yahu!* (Hey Presto) by Radha Krishen Braru proved a wonderful catalyst in this respect, despite an inadequacy in production due to its urban performers' unfamiliarity with the subtle nuances of the rural idiom which they considered vulgar. *'Yahu,* incidentally, was the first Kashmiri play for which a chair on the stage was improvized as an invisible character.

On the other hand, the production of the Bhagat Theatre's first play, *Toz-Apuz* (True-cum-False) by Subhan Bhagat (assisted by Motilal Kemu) :in 1966, failed to sustain the *Banda-Pathur* tradition. It could not do so simply because it opted for a semblance of sophistication. Thematically, nevertheless, it registered a significant departure in caricaturing the neo-feudalism that was raising its head in Kashmir. Its sequel, *Taqdeer* (Destiny), presented an impressive satire on the precarious destiny of the common folk, of the peasant in particular.

Administrative incompetence of the establishment was there for every body to see. A forceful satire, emerged in Motilal Kemu's *Manzul-Nika* (Cradle Tot) and *Haram Khanuk Aana* (Mirror of the Harem). The latter play was the first to articulate the Absurd theme, but in terms of the *Banda-Pathur* tradition.

Ali Muhammad Lone's *Taqdir-saz* (Destiny-mender) prove quite innovative. It created a sensation with its vehement satire on the ruling class controlling the people's destiny. A funnier though less subtle play in the folk-style is Farooq Masudi's *College-Pathur,* mimicking the young collegian's hotheaded tantrums, while R.L. Shant's *Yali Pan Roey* (When the Thread Was Lost) is another impressive play on a similar theme, treated in a more sophisticated style.

The *Machama* plays of Pushkar Bhan are a class apart, quixotically burlesque, raising peals of laughter at every ludicrous turn of action or utterance. Equally delightful is the comic *Grand Rehearsal,* co-authored by S.L. Sadhu and Bhan.

A sizeable number of radio plays broadcast from Radio Kashmir would certainly merit publication as remarkable dramatic writing. *Fanda-baz* (Hoodwinker) by Sajood Sailani, for instance, depicts the underworld in a semi-serious yet convincing mix-up of frivolities, while *Ba Chhus Tsoor* (I'm the Thief) by Rahbar, *Chapath* (Slap) and *Yi Zahar Km Cheyi* (Who will sip this poison?) by Sadhu deal with social maladies in order to awaken the drowsy conscience of the audience to moral anguish.

As for historical themes, *Suyya* by Lone and *Tshay* (Shadow) by Kemu deal with the eventful times of two Kashmiri sovereigns, Avantivarman (ninth century) and Lalitaditya (eighth century) respectively. The treatment in both is too much like a documentary, with the result that the audience feels like listening to a narration of the action rather than witnessing the dramatic action itself.

*Birbal* by S.L. Sadhu, on the other hand, frames dialogues incorporating historical details of how Quda Gojwari sacrificed his life in order to provide refuge to a non-Muslim family in distress, by defying the fanatic fury of the Afghan oppressor.

Motilal Kemu's *Lal Bu Drnyas* (I, Lalla, am ori the march) embodies a unique experiment in playwriting by exploring the inner contradictions in human relations, particularly in the familial context vitiated by social evils like bride-burning. Kemu shows familiarity with stage techniques and possibilities; he has, however, yet to find an appropriate language. Kashmiri drama today is trying to come to times with modernity.

## Modern Nepali Poetry

### Beads of Devotion

*Bhanubhakta Acharya*

Bhanubhakta Acharya (Bhanubhakta Acarya, 1814-69) is a celebrated poet in Nepali, comparable to the great classical poets in other Indian languages. His *magnum opus* Ramayana has become the national epic of the Nepalis everywhere. Though he follows the Sanskrit prosody, his language and idiom are charming and easy for all to follow.

*Bhaktamala* (Beads of Devotion) best expresses Bhanubhakta's spiritual concerns. The poet depicts the anxiety of the prodigal son when he realizes the squandering of his life in mundane aspirations. He hopefully hastens to redeem the time past while his mind, untrained in spiritual pursuits, longs for the immediate vision of God.

Not that the benighted world
Is always without a sage
Whose wisdom-lamp can save
The erring human race;
Evil begets affliction
In the life to come—
Armed with this knowledge
The self-betraying man
Marches into the kingdom
Where oblivion reigns.
Let the Lord be glorified, O mankind!

Let the rampart of petty materialism
Not separate you from Him.
I have reached the dusk of a fleeting life,
How long, after all, could it last?
Repentant will I ever be
If I don't take heed still.
A moment of devotion can ferry me across
The temporal ocean, boundless and deep,
Or else, into the quagmire of disaster
Will I sink.

In the lingering modicum of time
What salvation can my devotion earn?
Indeed, only if the Celestial Monarch
Reveals Himself to me
As one emitting rays of benevolence
And comes forward to show a countenance

Beaming with paradisal smile
To shower upon me
The bounty of forgiveness and divine grace,
Shall I perhaps be redeemed.
A greater dunce than I
The world could not have ever seen,
Who for a sensual life
Frittered away the best.
What is the thing that most wickedly
Casts a spell on me
And turns me into its blind slave?

Fatuous were the worldly pursuits
That took away from me
What my starving soul needed most,
The timeless fruits of meditation
But meaningless are these lamentations now,
I raise within myself an image
Of a saffron-clad god
Adorned with a crown
And many an ornament,
But my feeble mind falters
And turns away from him.
How long shall I tread
The terrestrial path
In the thickening mist of despair
With longing for that beatific glimpse?

*Bhaktamala, c.* 1853 *Tr.* by Irshad Ahmed

**Two Poems**

*Virendra*

Virendra (Virendra, b. 1925) is a noted poet in Nepali. He represents the age of romanticism, free verse and prose-poetry, following the classical tradition of Nepali poetry. He has also authored stories and plays, and a novel. Along with Daniel Khaling, who ceased writing a long time ago, Virendra brought out a small volume of poems *Ekanta* (Solitude, 1950). These poems marked a sharp departure from both the classical and romantic moulds. The two major collections of his poems are *Meghmala* (1963) and *Swarnima* (1981), the latter being more experimental and complex. He is also a very good painter. An expressionist in his paintings, Virendra shows the same tendency in his poems. His poetry is replete with new colours, symbols and imagery. The poems *Mela* (The Fair) and *Chhorako Janma* (The Birth of My Son) exemplify this novelty.

**The Fair**

By different tones was the drowsy earth
defined by the furrows of flowers.
The sun and the moon were married at the moment
Chosen as auspicious by the blue sky.
To the nooks and corners fled
The venomous snakes.
Farming fields did divide the land
The banyan and the peepul shared shadows in their palms,
The village damsel changed her dress,
The goldsmith carved ornaments new,
The musician's performance touched the night,
The poet's lines breathed the spirit of enchanting fresh spring,
The night rinsed the stars,
The prostitute spoke and
In the main square a beggar became choosy
in opening his stall.
At every sour and bitter taste,
The lovers swore looking at the sun of desire,
The burly youths began to search
For the fallen stars with empty hands,
The moon lost the bait and paled,
The night covered earth's lap with gold,
The south-going Mechi,[1] having touched the feet,
Did not hesitate to begin the worship
For a few days,

1. *Mechi* name of a river

Only for holding the fair.

Mela, c. 1959 *Tr*. by Kumar Pradhan

**The Birth of My Son**

An embraceful of wealth I've,
I've sired a crying son,
Like the plant which bends when roses bloom
I have bent.
Tearing the greenish blue dream-surface of the lake,
His two bright eyes flashed like two fish,
Breaking the waves of eyelash waters in their swim
And stealing the gold of the sun with a morning song—
My world opens in a mother's embrace,
The sun rises,
In that I've grabbed life's simpleness,
I've sired a crying son.

Earlier it was dark within and bright without
Now the restlessness of all the brooks, streams and birds outside
Have been joined within,
The pleasant openness of the outside has now nested in the house
The outside has lost everything
The inside has got everything
Thus a veritable amount of the beauty of this world
Have I moved into my house
I've sired a crying son.

I forgot the music of the flowers outside
I can't remember the colour of the sky
Rather I've discovered
All meaning in the prattle of my son
I've sired a crying son.

My thick blood and
His thick blood
My oozing sweat and
His oozing sweat
Both have mingled
A knot of sorrow
Tinged with the hues of ire and revenge.
A bridge of power
Have I stolen from the gods

An embraceful of wealth I've got
I've sired a crying son.

*Chhorako Janma, c.* 1959 *Tr.* by Kumar Pradhan

**War and Warrior**

*Agam Singh Giri*

Agam Singh Giri (Agamsing Giri, 1928-71) is a noted Nepali poet who camr into prominence after Independence. His romantic temper, smooth musical idction and simple language made him quite popular. The very titles of this earlier words, Yad (Memory, 1955), Amsu (Tears, 1958), Atma-Vyatha (Pangs of the Soul, 1959), and Jivan Git (The Songh of Life, 1960) give ample evidence of his early moods.

After homicide,
And amid those revolting sells of carrion
Do not erect monuments
Of sublime Himalayan dreams;
Do not paint sacred memories
Your recollections are sullied and gory
Violence-ridden, blood-stained.
You had come leaving incomplete
The field you were tilling;
You had left home in haste
Without completing the roof you were thatching;
Cattle were bleating
As you had come without love;
You had come without pinning up on your breast
The flower that had blossomed in the prime of your youth,
The madonna of your heart
Has treasured thousand remembrances
With happy moments of love
She has now adorned her life;
The young, expectant eyes of her heart
Are cast on the trails that hear you back.
In the endless nurturing of hope of your return,
In the sweet act of your beloved's waiting;
With joyful expectations
She watches the ceaseless flow of time;
In her morning and evening ceremonial worship
She offers flowers and *prasad*,
Embodying her cherished tearful memories;
Unsettled by life's shattered moments
With the dismal solitude in her tender heart,
In all her tearful lamentations

She must be invoking gods for your long life.
Suppressing the silent pains of her heart
She articulates her soul's prayers;
With innumerable searing noons within
Numerous gorgeous evenings,
Many many expectant nights
Cherishing those hallucinations about you,
Clinging to the reminiscences of her florescent youth
She may sleep her life's last sleep
But the fond memories of your early days
May remain evergreen and pure
In that innocent highland heart
Wishes will not wither time immemorial;
The soul of love will continue to wait for rebirth.
It was a dedication not a dream,
It was relinquishment, not ambition;
War was not there
In your aspirations;
War was not painted
On your bright countenance;
Eager longings for war
Were not there in your eyes—
It was not a war of your own:
After slaying your own true self within,
You had to wake up on your own tomb;
You had murdered yourself
Before you unsheathed your *khukuri* for your adversaries.
The self-seeking tyrants had already sold off
Be the independence of your Himalaya;
O you were brought up!
Only to be sacrificed;
The prices had already been paid up
For your courage, strength,
Boldness and combative manhood.
It was not a war of your own and that is why
Your self-existence is crippled;
The blazing fire of an alien war
Had consumed your self-pride—
Dreams, aspirations, fondness of life
Were all shredded into pieces
And then, you had returned
With the ennui of a graveyard
Tired of war, with a wounded body.

Plaintive reverberations
Of the battle-ground,
Remorseful screams of rape victims
Frenzied tumult of the front
Terror-ridden crying of innocent children—
Concealing them all in your heart
You were returning alone by that narrow path
To your own beloved village
At a murky dusk
The horizon was overcast with gloom
Bearing in your heart the horrifying turmoil of the battle zone
The bitter shedding of tears
From their eyes;
You had returned towards that sacred thatched roof
Burdened with war-ridden memories
Of manslaughter and revengeful violence.
On the ethereal canopy,
In the eyes of the Himalaya
In the roar of the waterfalls
No expression of welcome was there:
The heart of your mountain was desolate
Joyful expectation was nowhere to be seen.

But, O brave warrior!
Do not stain the war-free tranquil present
With the inane glory
Of manhood, valour and hollow pride
That tamed a tyrannical, shattered warring past:
Keep away the harrowing memories,
Do not tell your melancholy tales:
Do not besmear with blood your present crystalline dreams;
Do not inflict the agonies of war
On the unfettered, uncontaminated realities of life;
Do not desecrate an age where there is no terror,
Where the screams of war have not yet reached.

*Yuddha Ra Yoddha*. 1970 *Tr.* by Irshad Ahmed

*prasad* offerings to the deity.
*khukuri* the long knife with a curved blade carried by the Gorkhas.

**What a Life!**

*Haribhakta Katuwal*

Among the most outstanding younger Nepali poets, Haribhakta Katuwal (Haribhakta Katuwal, 1935-80) proved his mettle through his collections of songs and poems that gained wide popularity. His poems embrace varied themes, which find lucid expression in lines that carry their own rhythm.

In *Yo Zindagi Khai Ke Zindagi* (This Life, O What a Life) he describes the vagaries and uncertainty of life.

This life, what a life!
Hallowed within but living outside
Sucked by the nuclear threat
Haunted by the ghost of matters difficult,
What a life, this life!

To rest the head on the barrel of gun to sleep
To walk on the edge of sword to live
Difficult to close eyes
Difficult to open eyes
This life, what a life!

Brittle glasses arranged in the showcase of a shop—
Like glass bangles, this life
While being put on the soft wrist by a lass
It may crack and break any time.
Like cheap rubber sandals,
While walking along the road
It may snap and break, this life!
What a life, this life!

*Yo Zindagi Khai Ke Zindagi*, 1970 *Tr.* by Kumar Pradhan

**The Earth, Flowers and Beasts**

*Girmee Sherpa*

One of the new poets who have made a mark in Indian Nepali literature Girmee Sherpa (Girmi Serpa, b. 1948). Born and brought up in Sikkim, educated in Darjeeling, he is an official of the Sikkim government. His generation, fed up with hypocrisy and deceit, is anxious for a new awakening.

The poem *Dharti, Phul Ra Taskarharu* (The Earth, Flowers and Beasts) reflects the angst and hope of his generation.

Say not that nothing grows
On this dusty earth!
This earth has conceived within it
Seeds of hundreds of colourful flowers,
Filled with beauty, fragrance and essence.

It behoves not
That this dusty earth thirsts for water
To grow something beauteous
On this dusty earth.

Deep within this earth
Its bosom is all seeped in water
And this earth does not cry for water.
Even at the last hour of death
As creatures in thirst pant for breath
This earth of ours does not feel restive
With the thirst of Adam's Wine.
It does not lose strength
Even at the height of the days of drought.

Dust may spiral up from the earth,
Mists and clouds may rise
From this earth—
But even in the trying hours
Her deeds of begetting,
Fostering and rearing
The young seedlings and buds
Do not miscarry.
It is upon this gracious earth
That our towering Himalayas,
Our Alps
Stand majestically erect,
And men look up to them
As their own personified glory
They devoutly worship them
As Nature's sacred imageries
Again upon the breast of this very earth,
The Ganges and the Yamuna
Run their infinite rippling courses,
And our other sacred rivers
The Amazon and the Mississippi
Meander along its expansive breast.

These rivers are ours
The largest and the longest,
And are our rich legacies,
All these sacred treasures
And glories of ours
Are again like living legends
On the same breast of our earth,
They take life and run natural courses
Being fondled again
At the same loving breast
Of the earth.

We are the sons and daughters
And descendants of this earth.
Be it our duty
With devotion and love
To plant young seedlings of flowers and fruits.
Should we need water any hour
We shall be taking different directions, each,
Treading the chosen path, each
Move to fetch water
From the bountiful
Ganges and Yamuna and Mississippi,
The Amazon and the Volga
And other such benevolent rivers.
And again we may be together thus water-borne
And we may sprinkle it
Over the budding flowers in the same garden of ours
And then over our own deep wishes and ideals.

The need of the hour behoves
That watch-huts be raised upon the high mountains
Like the Himalayas and the Alps
Just so to enfold with protective care
The planted seedlings
From the ravages of both beasts and pests,
Scarecrows to be posted
In every nook and corner of the garden
To keep eternal vigil.
The blossoms are fragile and delicate
As by nature they are born thus
To be protected with fondling care
Against the blast of torrents
And the violence of the beasts.

While treading along the chosen path
Of my lonely course of life
I chanced to see
A delicate young seedling
Aspiring to bloom in full youth
Strangled to death and torn off;
A heart-rending scene—
And another I found
Callously uprooted and thrown away
To dry and die in dire distress!
It is sure

The crying misdeeds are perpetrated
By none but the heartless brutes and beasts.

And in tears heavy with grief
The loving earth did cover
The dead flowers with shrouds,
Lo! she has lain the shrouded dead flowers
Upon her own lap!

We did imagine in profound thought
To post scarecrows
In every nook and corner of the garden,
Walls and fences raise all around it,
And watch-huts erect
On the hills and around brooks
To give watchful protection
To the young flowers against the fears and dangers
From brutes and beasts
And thus drive them away
From the scene,
And save the young plant uprooted,
The infant bud strangled to death.
Be that as it may,
The vast earth
Cannot be slain in blood.

The earth has enough
Strength and fertility
To grow as many seedlings,
Buds and blossom as possible
Hence, never is the earth
An arid desert,
A dead and dusty mass,
Nor lost in sterility.

*Dharti, Phul Ra Taskarharu,* 1974 — *Tr.* by Jas Yonjan 'Pyasi'

Tweaking our ears you bid us stand
To account for every paisa that we spend.
He who is left with strength to crawl
Even after your clarion call
To march ahead is indeed the blessed one.

You come, the real mother, at the very end,
A barking dog harping on the dreams
Before dreams. Even as I walk the earth

And mock at the three skyward trails
I'm perturbed and sick to the core.
Those that had conquered Death have fled
The battlefield and my taut nerves
And tensed muscles ask: is it
Victory or defeat?
Strength in my arms but none in the guts,
The bow wills but the arm betrays.
Coward flesh ignores the counsel of the mind
And the ladder raised against the sky falls

Will the eye ever spot the trap
Set by loving flesh?
Will man ever transcend the limits
Fixed by womb and birth?
He who divines this song will seek
Yet another face of the Mother.

*Mayiya Mum Mukhagalu,* 1970 *Tr.* by B.C. Ramachandra Sharma

## The River

**Abdul Ahad Azad**

He unveiled the stark reality of life in his compositions, which stressed the commonness of human aspirations and universal brotherhood. He brought a revolutionary freshness and fervour to kashmiri poetry. He gave a new turn to the couplet-form, *nazm.* His poems first appeared in a series of booklets under the title of *Kalam-i-Azad* and were brought out in a single volume, long after his death. Azad's three-volume history of Kashmiri literature, *Kashmiri Zaban Aur Sain,* written in Urdu, is considered a landmark in Kashmiri literary criticism.

The poem *Daryav* (River) eloquently brings out the turmoil of the human spirit and man's unending quest for truth, change and progress.

My yearnings find expression
In bubbles, commotion, tumult;
It's in wandering to distant goals
That I find the music of life.

I move on day and night
Through rocks, ravines and creeks;
I do not pause for praise,
I do not pause for play;
I am at home with the bats
As I am with the bulbuls.

Flatter cannot tickle me
Nor disparagement make me falter;
A purpose brought me here
And I live to see it through;
I am not fettered, as men are,
By the fear of disapprobation.

Forever faring forward,
I know no turning back;
I don't adorn myself like flowers,
Nor build nests like the bulbuls:
My delight is in swift eddies,
Revolutions and earthquakes.

I cleave the sides of the banks and bunds,
And level the high ground with the low;
Leaping o'er proud, strong obstructions,
I scare their wits away.
I do not seek a fight.
But meeting it, I do not quail.

I hurl myself against stone ramparts
And other mortal barriers;
Then collecting once again the fragments
Of my scattered self,
I hurl down rocks, wear down hills
And roam in the forests free.

I give wings to the cloud
And the gift of mercy to the rain,
And it's I who dress the firmament
In blue and purple robes;
Mine is the voice of thunder,
Mine the flame in the lightning.

I spread green velvet carpets
On my banks for friends,
For tired limbs of hard-worked labour
And for lovers of pleasure;
They come and sit and bathe and drink
In freedom and in joy.

But I do not wait on any one!
Hindus, Muslims, men of wealth.
Rajas, nawabs come and rest.
Seeking balm for bruised spirits.

But to me they are all suppliants
Among the many who come to me.

I shall not rest till the world is rid
Of the embankments that divide,
Of ditch and hollow that deform
Its smooth and lovely face.
This passion, like a consuming fire,
Burns me even though I'm water.

Coming and going, birth and death
Are all the same to me.
I don't wonder who will come,
Nor grieve at the fine men gone—
Futile fears and anxieties,
Which trouble the weak of heart.

Big mountains know my might,
For I split their hearts asunder;
But with gentle caressing hands I bathe
The bodies of beautiful girls.
My flowing stream and waves and eddies
Are bursting with truth and love.

I play soft tunes on my santoor
To flowers and the bulbuls,
But the thunder of the drums of revolution
Is my music for hard-hearted rocks;
My gurgling sound is sweet indeed,
But it hides a potent fire.

Puppets of Time, however great,
Quail at the wrath of my waves;
But I play the nurse to flower shrubs
And feed them with my milk;
To the cedar, pine and cypress
I've given my life without stint.

I love to be gentle, I love to play
In the midst of loveliness;
I carry drink to the thirsty iris
In gracefully moving streams,
And I stop to obtain the image
Of the lotus in bloom in the lake.

*Daryav*, 1940 *Tr.* by T.N. Raina

*Santoor* a stringed instrument, indigenous to Kashmir played by tapping the strings with two mallets

**Freedom**

*Ghulam Ahmed Mahjoor*

The part played by him in enriching the Kashmiri language and awakening the poor masses during the freedom struggle is unparallelled. He is acclaimed as the poet of New Kashmir. Ghulam Ahmed Mahjoor (Ghulam Ahmad Mahjur, 1888-1952). The crooning songs and melodies gathered in twenty tiny collections of poems, have made him immortal. The delineation of nature in its chaste flavour is his forte.

In the poem *Azadi* (Freedom) the poet, while depicting the poignant scene of Partition, grieves over the fact that the fruits of freedom have not been shared by the common man.

God be praised that Freedom
has dawned, though after centuries,
And our homes and hearths
feel its glowing warmth.

Before the four corners of India
bathed in the sunshine of
Independence, lots of people were pushed
into the cauldron of hatred.

Freedom showers benevolence and prosperity
on the West,
But in our land it makes
only a hollow thunder.

Alas! Freedom brought in its wake
nothing but a long shadow of
Anarchy, poverty and oppression
and sad, divided households.

Independence is like the wonder hen
that lays a golden egg or two
But this queen-rooster has
taken too long to hatch them.

Freedom is like a coquettish
fairy from the high heavens,
Who condescends to stroll
into the houses of a chosen few

Freedom was supposed to end
capitalism, but instead it is
Now amassing capital
favouring only the near and dear.

The masses find freedom's burden
heavy as the Hari Parbat

Just a fortunate few find it
light as a flower petal.

Peasants and landlords are now
engaged in bloody feuds,
Freedom secretly silent,
is watching from afar.

Rulers frolic like bridegrooms
while the people are in mourning!
Freedom has blessed them with
ivory castles of amorous privacy.

Ministers are busy riding
their newly-acquired cars.
How can they find time to
heal the wounds of the poor!

People are stunned with sorrow
and their hearts are restless;
They dare not relate their woes
lest the cops should beat them up

*Azadi,* 1949 *Tr*. by T.N. Kaul

Hari Parbat a hill situated in Srinagar city.

**Six Rubaiyaats**

*Mirza Arif*

Mirza Arif (Mirza Ghulam Hassan Beg Arif, b. 1910) started with moraliste mysticism in the early forties but soon switched over to socio-political concerns. During the Quit Kashmir Movement (1946) he reflected the people's aspiration for freedom. In the mid-fifties, however, he ventilated his anguish at the disturbing gap between promise and performance in three small volumes of quatrains entitled *Rubaiyat-e-Arif* (Rubaiyaat of Arif, 1954). He has also to his credit two earlier collections of verse and a Kashmiri translation of Omar Khayyam. His recent collection of quatrains *Lole Vetsar* (Reflections on Love) won the Sahitya Akademi Award for 1985,

The six quatrains rendered here from *Rubaiyat-e-Arif* articulate the poet's sense of disillusionment and bristle with bitter irony in these rubaiyat, he has commented on the persisting vestiges of the old order.

If an old tree-trunk sends out a tender sprout,
Will one who knows give it a different name?
The old order has just been pruned, no more,
An idiot may, perhaps, call it democracy.

Bullets chase a poor fellow; bread eludes his grasp.
Even in freedom helpless, hapless he
Sheeplike must submit to one who kills.
Butcher alone has changed; the cut is as it used to be.

Will 'Hail, hail' and public audiences aught avail?
Will mere bits of raw thread ever darn the wounds?
As long as the knife-blade reaches not the abscess-root
Will the commissions remedy the nation's cancer, ah?

The minister's doggie frolics up the sofa sets,
Some kiss it; some others embrace it.
Behold the labourer, ah, still with the rope on his
shoulder, furrows on his brow,
Belly sunk in, heart aburn, liver heating up.

A cool capitalist you, O Chinar!
Green you look in spring, turn bloody in autumn.
The empty-bellied poor you lull to sleep.
What fire, then, is it that consumes you within?

This, the Hindu's day; that, the Afghan's. O!
Different are the days of Bhagavan and Rahman,
Blessed indeed the day when people say
'our own day has come.'
Arif aspires to see the day of Man adawn.

*Rubaiyat-e-Arif,* 1954 *Tr.* by P.N. Pushp

Chinar the world famous shady tree of Kashmir resembling oak.
Bhagavan Lord God.
Rahman the Compassionate One.

**To the Bulbul**

*Ghulam Nabi Firaq*

G.N. Firaq (Ghulam Nabi Firaq, b. 1922) is a notable poet. Initially he was influenced by socialism and his writings reflect his concern for the poor and the downtrodden. A mature portrayal of life and nature is his forte. He has to his credit two volumes of poetry, *Yim SamMay* (in collaboration with Rahman Rahi) and *Nav Shar Sombran,* and two books on literary criticism. He is a poet who has brought new ideas and a new style into kashmiri poetry.

The poem *Bulbulas Kun* (To the Bulbul) tells how a single mellifluous note of a songthrush, even in dreary midwinter, can lift a person on the wings of imagination, into the forgotten world of youthful spring days.

O bulbul, strange bird!
Your loud call was so very sudden

That my sad heart gave one wild leap,
For in a flash my world was quite transformed—
Full of roses, bulbuls and spring verdure.

I had been reading a Greek play,
My mind absorbed, my fancy feeding
On a King's story, so true to life,
Where new strife treads on the heels of the old.

Though silver lay on the trees and around,
When you struck your harp, blossoms came
And my winged fancy soared to heaven—
Spring often does bewitch one's eyes.

The sun shone bright in an azure sky;
A snowwhite cloud sailed, not very far,
We stood, enraptured, gazing at the lake,
My love and I, in an island bower.

Suddenly someone knocked at the door,
Fled was the dream and I was awake.
A cold gust rushed in like a raider,
And back I was where I had been.

I have fastened doors and windows;
Icicles on all sides sparkle like grass;
A black cloud blanket wraps up the sky;
A chill wind pierces the marrow of my bones.

The last chinar leaf on the branch
Hangs withered and lifeless like a corpse.
Drunk with power, Midwinter has his day.
Even the fire-pot we cling to is cold.

You are a strange bird, O bulbul!
How can I forget that in dreary midwinter
You made me roam in flowering meadows?

*Bulbulas Kun*, 1954 — *Tr.* by T.N. Raina

**Helplessness**

*Zinda Kaul*

Zinda Kaul (Zirida Kaul 1886-1966), popularly known as 'Masterji', was the first Kashmiri poet to win the Sahitya Akademi Award for his collection *Sumran* (Rosary) in 1956. He mostly sang of eternal longing and perpetual interrogation in the contemporary context, and exposed religious sham. In the bewildering aspirations of today he discerned the authentic urgency for ensuring a lovelier tomorrow harmonizing the national and universal demands of the time. The poem *Lacariya, Majbunya* (Helplessness) articulates a deep concern with the varying parameters of the eternal quest. The diction registers an admirable blend of form and content, matching sound to sense, without succumbing to cant and cliche.

Man would wail; he would not swallow his tears.
But could it avail him aught?
Why then should he allow his eyes to shower blood?
Why then should he toss his head against rocks?
Knowing no one pays any heed to him
Why then his itch for abject complaining?
Why then shoot arrows in empty space?
  Helplessness, O, compulsion!

His physical frame slowly, but surely, wears away.
Hunger, thirst and cold shrivel him up.
Sickness, crises, wife, kids, grief and
Worries stupefy him.
Even if he tides over such misfortunes,
Hankerings galore still embarrass him.
His heart rests on no object.
He goes on craving for he knows not what:

For the 'Good' he has never seen?
For the 'Good' he has never known?
Yet he pursues something that he thinks is lost.
Has he received a heady dose in slumber deep?
  Misery, ah, because of want and longing!

Someone in the distant past somehow, indeed,
From far away did see His back profile.
That hearsay then reached our ears too.
That then sunk deep into our hearts.
He, we are afraid, isn't on speaking terms with us;
As if, in unknown retreats, He sullenly keeps aloof.
  Love's ailment, perchance, is self-imposed!

He stays far away from us, in hiding as it were,
Having plugged His ears with cotton pads.
Does He ever show concern for our welfare?
Does He bear us in mind and care to think,
'What must have befallen those whom I had
Cast into the darkness of death
And set them asearch for Me o'er hills
And woods, ravines and dales?'

Beauty knows no compassion, no, none!

Well may we counselled be, 'Should one expect
A pear from a willow tree? Should we?
Should we expect a warm response from One
Whom affection leaves untouched?
Whose whereabouts we do not know,
How then reach out to Him?'
Could yet our hearts retreat or desist?
And can we chain the wind?
But should we blame the heart for the predicament?
Is love an idle flirtation?

The deer would hear, in fact, his own echo;
Within himself does lie the musk concealed.
Nevertheless, he must run on and on
Over the wilderness in search of it.
Likewise, the human heart gambols and frisks about
Inexorably, blindly and heedlessly.
The scent of the Beloved draws it out in endless search.
If the search ends in one object
It must surely start elsewhere afresh.
Would the moth pretend indifference and keep off
When from far away the candle invites it?
Would it not hurl itself in mad delight
Tearing off the seven sheaths of intellect?
Well may the candle lie awhile beyond the naked eye.
Is Beauty mere sorcery?

Helplessness, O, compulsion!
Misery, ah, because of want and longing!
Love's ailment, perchance, is self-imposed!
Beauty knows no compassion, no, none!
Is love an idle flirtation?
Is Beauty mere sorcery?

*Lacarlya, Majburlya,* 1955 *Tr.* by P.N. Pushp

**Six Quatrains**

*G.R. Nazki*

G.R. Nazki (Mir Ghulam Rasul Nazki, b. 1910) had already established his reputation as an Urdu poet before he tried his hands at *Qata* (four-line poem) in Kashmiri. Mostly akin to the *Rubai,* this form enjoys the freedom to employ metres and measures traditionally denied to the latter. His first collection of 200 *Qatat* appeared under the title of *Namrudnama* (Ways of Namrud, 1965). The second collection of quatrains, *Awaz-i-*

*Dost* (The Friend's Call, 1986) got the Sahitya Akademi Award for 1987. Shakespeare gave many new words to the English language. Likewise the quatrains that Nazki has written have became a part of daily conversation in Kashmiri.

The six quatrains rendered here from *Namrudnama* evince not only a freshness of approach to life but also a remarkable appropriateness of diction, sharpening the poet's running commentary on the times.

Beauty was atrip in waterscapes,
Greenlands' ears captured the fairy chants.
Cascades dashed ahead hurriedly washing their faces,
Spring, they say, had cast its sidelong glances all the way,

Frost has run away; the snow-clad mountain slopes are shivering;
The winter's tresses are a tangled mess.
Peach blossoms have absorbed the beloved's hue,
O, the terrible briskness of the almond grove!

The high-handed one twisted the poor man's neck,
Compelled him to sell his spouse, dismantled his hovel,
Rushing to the religious head, they lodged a plaint with him.
Said he to them, 'Go, say the *Khutma* prayers; ask for the
master's well-being.'

Land, wealth, orchards and houses,
Comforts, vicissitudes, miseries, woes and misfortunes,
Horses, cattle, wife, children and brethren—
Before these eighteen thousand gods have I to bend my head.

Philosophy and knowledge, nowadays, are empty terms;
No warmth is found in them, no ardour, no fervour.
Only the frost of doubt, the icicles of make-believe,
The snow of existence, and icy winds of guess-making.

Today's civilization is a veiled carcass;
Time shall come when secrets will be uncovered.
All the white and black tissues will show up at once,
Let the darkness vanish, let the mountain-tips enjoy the glow.

From *Namrudnama,* 1965 *Tr.* by P.N. Pushp

Rubai quatrain
Khutma thanksgiving prayers

**Naked Thoughts**

*Amin Kamil*

Amin Kamil (Muhammad Amin Kamil, b. 1924) is a major voice in Kashmiri poetry and one of the chief exponents of modern *ghazal* in the language. His verse is at once original, innovative and colloquial. *Laveh*

*Te Praveh*, which received the Sahitya Akademi Award, is a significant contribution to the *ghazal*.

The poem *Nethanani Man!* (Naked Thoughts) laments the lack of appropriate means for free expression of thought and craves for a new form of poetical experimentation unfettered by traditional patterns.

My love provides this desert with
Your lovely hair's luxuriant shade.
Time and again your memory
Knocks wildly at the door of my heart,
Who would for ages live alone?—
It's not with that wish we were born.

When the wind had idle sport with the lamp,
Trembling seized the lights of heaven,
Being helpless, for the mind lives close,
The heart put a lid on its agony.
Hate never will know softened lips;
Love is blest with streams of tears.

Old goblets are now too small for thought—
I wish some better forms were found,
Else I might sell, not sing love's yearnings,
And follow only in others' wake.
Who says man can't be found here now?
Then what are these? Only ghosts?
The brocade of words is not to be had,
And naked thoughts just waste away.

The dog wears a collar of gold—
O how your barking thrills my heart!
In this city of sad decay
Even a fluttering heart is a treasure.

*Nethanani ManI,* 1965 *Tr*. by T.N. Raina

Old goblets poetic diction and forms.

**Creation**

*Rahman Rahi*

He is the most eloquent advocate of obliquity in Kashmiri verse. kashmiri switched over to it Rahman Rahi (Abdul Rahman Mir, b. 1925) from Urdu. His Kashmiri *ghazal* and *nazm* bear the impact of the new Urdu verse (of Firaq and Faiz in particular). His *Navroz-e-Saba* (Muse at Early Dawn) won the Sahitya Akademi Award (1958) and represents a literary watershed between neo-traditional modernity and non-traditional contemporaneity. It also explores the lyrical potential of the monologue in the Kashmiri *nazm*. From the sixties, his poetry has blazed a new trail of indirect articulation.

The poem *Takhllq* (Creation, 1965) offers a significant insight into the creative possibilities of his new experiment and expresses an interpersonally shared–experience of the ecstatic moment beyond the moment.

Your gentle touch has turned my door ajar,
Come in, come in. Here I am, indeed.

You, the imperceptible whiff of the spring breeze,
I, the backwood's eyeful ripplet, in your perennial quest.

Somewhere have I visioned someone, the like of you:
Sort of trinklets jingling somehow in the void;
Sort of beating of the wings at dead of night.
A restless serpent vanishing, as if, into a heap of hay.
What a predicament!
I consecrate my life to you.
Won't you tarry just a while?
Fain would I see you entire.

No, shut not the door;
I feel breathless.
Charms are throbbing restive on your lips.
What madness this!
I'm all alone.
Your eyes are uncannily magnetic.
Could I relax a while?
Narrow's this dungeon.
Thirsty, O, I feel;
Your breath is all ablaze.

What wizard this, O Lord, bewitching me?
His arms are soft like a hyacinth.
His movement spieder-like on cobweb track.
Frisking for a while, a roe.
Panting next, a tiger, O.
Awful high-handedness, this.
Not for a sale, O Tempter, I,
Illusions shouldn't make fun of me.
Disclose your identity;
I'll see.

Ah me! Every hair of mine's aflame.
Whither has winged away my restless heart?

How's it no limb of mine does touch the ground?
My eardrums bibrate, as if, with some flutter of the wings.
How deep and dark a cave is this!
Where, O, where am I?
Have I to sip this fiery fount?

Darling, you've entered my interior;
Have I not embraced you?
No god are you now;
No Eve am I.
In every glance you have grape juice adrip.
In every pulse you have a star astir.
Under your eyelashes oozes an earthy sap.
My fingers feel a cool comfort within the lighting flash.

Last evening this window was shut,
Shouldn't I, otherwise, have woven a dream?
The mountain-tops are dawn-ablush;
Today, the breeze is tiptoe
Behold the early chinar bough; 'tis all asprout.
Every leaf of it enjoys a sappy hue.
Every fragrant touch of it inebriates.
Every turn of it unfolds fresh youthfulness.
O my heart, distract no more the bees,
I feel fatigued today.

*Takhllq,* 1965 *Tr.* by P.N. Pusnp

Chinar the world famous shady tree of Kashmir, resembling oak.
nazm poem (Urdu).
ghazal a popular poetic form in Urdu.

**Night Watchman**

*Vasudev Reh*

Vasudev Reh (Vasudev Reh, b. 1926) is a well-known progressive poet in Kashmiri. Blind since infancy, his handicap has not dampened his zealous passion for the Muse. His visual images are faultless. He is well-versed in Urdu, Hindi and English, besides his mother-tongue. Both his *ghazals* and *nazms* reflect a soaring imagination and deep understanding of life. His poetry collection, *Sabgard,* won the Jammu and Kashmir Cultural Academy Award.

The poem *Sabgard* (Night Watchman) gives a clarion call to his compatriots to beware of the forces of degeneration and advises them not to lose hope and not to justify means by ends.

My cry every evening is 'Beware!'
And when I say 'Beware!' I mean what I say,
It's my caution to you all, young and old,
When every evening I cry out 'Beware!'

My vigils, O my friends, are not enough to see you through,
If you yield to careless slumber, no thief will hesitate,
But with the slightest chance will take whatever you have saved;
And there's no dearth of knaves, beware!

I only cry, 'O brothers, wake up and beware!
In this uneven world, you've to struggle to your end.
If you'd secure your peace, surely now's not the time for rest!
Do not let go the skirt of courage, beware!

Do not take it lightly when you hear my call.
You shouldn't let others plan your present and your future.
Have no faith in robbers' oaths, their duty and their creed.
In short, think of what may happen, beware!

When you hear my cry, don't say, 'What's it to me?'
Don't treat it as an alien voice and say, 'What's it to me?'
When someone starts a fire, don't say, 'What's it to me?'
That's what I shout in town and village, beware!

The time is slightly out of joint; how can one set it right?
Though this can't remain for ever, it's a phase one cannot change.
Brigandage will slowly cease, but God knows what'll be left.
Beware, O brother, these times, beware!

O friends, save the toy houses you as children built in play.
Hold fast to the present time; to let it slip is folly.
Don't rest when the pipe calls the snake; it's not a foreign
sound.
See that the flame doesn't burn the bride's dreams, beware!

*Sabgard,* 1965 *Tr.* by T.N. Raina

**Daybreak**

*Moti Lal Saqi*

Moti Lal Saqi (b. 1936) won the Sahitya Akademi Award for his collection of poems *Monsar*. He has written five operas and some short stories, and compiled the works of several old masters like Nund Rishi and Parmanand. He has edited five volumes of folk songs and two volumes of Sufi poetry. Among his publications are *Modri Khwab* (poetry), *Ankvan* (research papers) and *Samad Mir* (monograph). He has been honoured with the Jammu and Kashmir Cultural Academy Award, as well as the Padma Shri in 1989.

The poem *Sahra Petha Subah Tam* (Daybreak) describes how Nature changes its hues and moods from early dawn to daybreak. Allegorically, darkness yields place to light to enable *ghazal*-king Rasoon Mir's beloved, Kongi, to find her path in the inebriated atmosphere while the hill streams are singing with abandon.

As the tired night sank behind the mountain,
Young dawn put radiance on his face;
The morning breeze played soft tunes on forest trees;
Boulders bathed in Kaunsar waters;
The streams sang softly morning songs
Like mothers singing lullabies
To tender infants in their arms.

The night beheld its death draw near;
The stars in a row packed up their goods
As light chased darkness from the sky,
A flame appeared on the eastern hill;
The morning star bent low his head
And departed, like someone in grief.

As I looked at the lakes of pearls,
My heart bloomed, hope radiating light
Seeing the morning's spendour, I felt
That Zuval Maal had come by stealth
To keep her tryst with Rasul Mir.
The east was the prophet of the coming light,
And gentle nature seemed to say
That life would be like the flowering dawn.

*Sahra Petha Subah Tam,* 1966 *Tr.* by T.N. Raina

Kaunsar waters: The Kaunsar Nag is a mountain lake on the northern side of the Baniha) range. Zuval Maal one of the names given by the poet Rasul Mir to his beloved.

**Candy and Artemesia**

*Dina Nath Nadim*

Dina Nath Nadim (Dina Nath Nadim, 1916-88) was an important progressive poet in Kashmiri. Influenced by Marx, Iqbal and Chakbast in the thirties, he started writing in Urdu and Hindi. Shri Rabindra Nath Tagore always exhausted poets to write in this own Mother-tongue. He also haded Tagore's advice and started writing in Kashmiri. He introduced new forms into Kashmiri poetry such as blank verse, sonnets and operas. A progressive to the core he wrote mostly about the common man. His opera *Bombur Yamberzal* received the Soviet Land Nehru Award in 1970 and it was also staged in the USSR. In 1976 he was awarded the Honorary Fellowship of the Jammu and Kashmir Cultural Academy. His poetry collection, *Shihil Kul,* won the Sahitya Akademy Award.

The poem *Nabad Te Tethavyan* (Candy and Artemesia) dexterously depicts the rovings of the restless soul of man for communion with nature, transcending the barriers of race, religion, time and clime.

Two moths gyrating round a lamp.
Bride and bridegroom of the *vyog.*
What compulsion brought her to that tree's shade?
Having swabbed the kitchen, Teka Batany'
Has just appeared at the ventilator.
Some belle, perspiring under her shawl,
Fear and fire consuming her,
As hyacinth fragrance pushes the window.
In Manzgam the sandal tree has blossomed.
The blue curtain is all a-flutter—
Perhaps Cleopatra's moving towards her bath,
Twin buds in a flower vase
Poised to strike like hooded snakes.
Sheshanag in his ocean home.
Brahma born of a lotus flower.
Sound of bangles and whispered speech
Behind that curtain in that room.
I think it's now the middle of the night.
A pair of eyes behind the window panes—
O how big and how passionate!
Devouring gaze, hungry lips, toss of the head!
Smooth silk with softness irresistible—
An avalanche is sliding down that slope!
How big and cool the bulging chinar
And how straight and lofty the cypress!
The *monal* shot upwards with winged speed
And, like a fawn, leapt into the glen.
Convulsed with rage, Karna shouting at Kunti!
In that manger, a child is born!
Frowning look into the pictures on the wall!
The worker's wife talks to her husband
Breaking ten days' ice.
After the setting of the moon, in pitch dark,
Where has Mary, draped in white, with soft

And furtive gait, gone round that hill?
The face of the dawn is hectic red,
The clouds blushing to the lobes of the ears,
The winds with dishevelled hair
And all grass in the garden soaked with sweat.
The tender, graceful jasmine plant
Is slightly bulging in the middle.
The bitter and the sweet are woven fine.
Shakuntala moves again to her father's home.

*Nabad Te Tethavyan*, 1968 *Tr.* by T.N. Raina

*vyog* a circle, gaily decorated with pastel mud colours on which the bride joins the bridegroom at a Kashmiri Pandit wedding.
Tekca *Batany* name of a Kashmiri Pandit girl. It may not refer to any specific person.
*monal* a magnificent Nepali pheasant.
*Karna shouting at Kunti* die rage of Kana at the revelation of the truth about his birth by his mother who had abandoned him when he was born before her marriage. She now wanted him to desert the Kauravas and fight against them.

**Craving**

*Ghulam Rasul Santosh*

Ghulam Rasul Santosh (Ghulam Rasul Santos, b. 1929) he started composing poetry at the relatively late age of 27. Lyricist for the first Kashmiri movie *Man Zi Rat*, he has won awards from the Jammu and Kashmirs. Cultural Academy for his opera *Gulrez*, and play *Butt Te Buldozer.* His verse collection *Be 'Sokh Ruh* (The Restless Soul) received the Sahitya Akademi Award. He has also published a novel in Urdu, *Samandar Pyasa Hai*. A prominent exponent of Tantric Art, he has thrice won the Lalit Kala Akademy Award and been honoured with the Padma Shri. He is a renowned poet of kashmir.

Santosh's poetry is characterized by simple diction and a quest for unravelling the mysteries of nature. The poem *Tresna* (Craving) is a portrayal of a restless, roving mind, anxiously in search of an anchor.

Adjure the twinkling stars upon the firmament,
So they put up their blinds early tonight.
The extent of my roving eyes they thwart,
And tilt the balance of my endless thoughts.

Something unknown betokens me tonight,
Moaning of dogs since dusk a pointer is.
Could it presage that death is prowling around?
My left eye has been throbbing since the morn.

Take heed, someone has banged at the shutter!
Down there, away went someone whizzing past.
My neck is strained, unbolt the shutter,
I wish to fold the moonbeams in my arms.

Ask the *Kartik* moon studded in the sky:
How can she fail to remember her murky nights
When darkened is her lustrous destiny,
And with the stars she hide and seek does play?
Beaten through and through it is an endless
Age since I, a hermit's fire, set ablaze.

Ask the night-watchman of roadside shops:
Whose shop guards he, the slow-witted man?
His life's mart insolvent has become,
He puffs his baccy at the shop carefree
As though a child of fortune sits enthroned.
At dawn when all bestir for daily tasks,
With grounded snout he, bitch-like, sprawling lies.

Pull down the shutters please and bolt the door,
Someone, behold, upset the roosted birds.
To me, it seems, the babe is screaming shrill,
Who's there hiding behind the lamp-post?
Let be, what are you mopping at this hour?
Without a coverlet I frozen feel.

Cover not my face with the blanket, please,
Someone unknown hallooes me from below.
Look up if he be death's messenger true:
Someone stumbled and down the steps rolled.
Where have you gone? Come here please, one of you,
My parched throat a sip of water needs.
Would one of you narrate a kingly tale,
A tale that ends not till the day of doom!

*Tresna,* 1973 *Tr.* by S.L. Sadhu

*Kartik* The month of October/November in the Samvat calendar

**Dreams**

*Muzaffar Aazim*

Muzaffar Aazim (Muhammad Muzaffar Mir, b.1934), Every poet who writes poetry does it in lyrical form. But no one had done it in kashmiri. Aazim was the first poet in kashmir. He started *vatsun* form of kashmiri poetry. His collection *Zolanna* (Fetters) established him as a poet of love and beauty, who combined verbal melody with sensuous suggestion, but without any special message. This work, together with his poems *Mani Kaman* (Heart's Desire) has received awards from the Jammu and Kashmir Cultural Academy. He is also the recipient of the Soviet Land Nehru Award.

The poem *Hawsos* (Dreams) affirms the poet's faith in love as the harbinger of a brighter and happier tomorrow. It is full of evocative nuances expressive of the changing seasons in Kashmir. The period of forty days around *Magh* is the season of snow and frost, the coldest part of the year. Then comes the thaw at the end of the bitter winter. And as the spring warmth comes, the soil loosens and attains a 'relaxed' state. It can now be 'responsive' to nature's eternal scheme and nurse the seeds through affection.

Relaxed, responsive and expectant,
A black patch of land
Nurses within its breast, cold and dark,
A few seeds dry as sand,
Benumbed and lifeless in early *Magh*

Under nature's rimy hand.
Dreams:
Fresh and vibrant,
Gorgeous and fragrant.
O mighty Sun God:
When will thy beams kiss them awake?

*Hamsos*, 1974 *Tr*. by S.L. Sadhu

*Magh*: December end/January.

# 11
# Modern Kashmiri Fiction: A Selection

## The Bride's Pyjamas

**Akhtar Mohi-ud-Din**

Any writer whose very first collection of short stories won him was Akhtar Mohi-ud-Din. His real name is Ghulam Mohi-ud-Din Wani (b.1928). He is acclaimed as a leading writers of fiction in kashmiri the Sahitya Akademi Award in 1958. He has also published another collection of short stories, *Sonzal,* a novel *Dod-Dag* and some plays. His early writings were in Urdu. A deep understanding of human nature and skilful handling of emotional subjects are the main characteristics of his work. Mohi-ud-Din was honoured with the title of Padmashri.

*Daryayi Hund Yaezar* (The Bride's Pyjamas) describes with rare charm the rejuvenated feelings of an old couple who accidentally discover the woman's bridal dress which had been lying in disuse for ages in a forgotten nook of their house.

Nabir Shalla, the darner, was already three-score-and-ten. He owned a ramshackle, two-windowed wooden house on the banks of the Jhelum. He sat on the verandah of their house engaged in his work, his thick glasses mounted tight on his nose, and crooned his favourite rhymes with a childlike lisp:

She brought me a goblet of wine,
And took my breath away.

Nabir Shalla had passed most of his years sitting on the verandah and all the time had remembered only two songs which he recited in season and out of season. The second song was:

Her skin is smooth as a ripened peach,
Oh God! Keep her safe from the world's gaze.

From early childhood there had been a curious lisp in his speech. With the loss of teeth it had become more pronounced. The little swath of grey beard shone like snowflakes on his face as if small tufts of cotton scattered over the garment of Dame Shalla had been glued to his cheeks. In spite of a distant tremor in his hands, he was able to make a living; indeed, customers flocked to him for he was an expert at the job, many times better than most.

Nabir Shalla loved his and of coruse his ramshackle house wife Khotan Didi more than anything else in the world. Every evening she would gently press his back and caress away his day's fatigue, fetch him platefuls of hot rice, and fill his hookah *chilim*. Whenever he sat on the verandah crooning his rhymes and running his darning needle through a patch of *rafal* cloth, she would sit in front of him, sifting cotton or spinning at her wheel. Nabir Shalla would make a sly comment, 'You be the prentice and I the master.' Pricked by his remark Khotan Didi would retort, 'Why should I be the 'prentice? Why not you?'

Khotan Didi had only one tooth left in the front of her upper jaw; and since her lower lip had caved in, this tooth hung out like a nail. Her face was wrinkled like a shrunken turnip and her hair matted like a piece of dirty white cloth. It was twenty years now that she had had her last baby, but in her life she had been confined with pregnancy about ten times. Unfortunately, none of her children had survived except two daughters. Both of them were now married, settled in their homes and had relations of their own. In their wooden shack Nabir Shalla and his wife lived reasonably well without ever encountering a serious misfortune; they had to take loans for their daughters' marriages but had gradually paid off to the last penny. Khotan Didi had only one regret that none of her sons had lived. It was rumoured among their relatives and their social circle that they, the Shallas, possessed a large fortune worth a thousand or two. Heaven alone knew their real position. They lived off their meagre earnings and that was all.

His thick glasses mounted on his nose, Nabir Shalla worked on a piece of rafal cloth today crooning his favourite rhyme with the same childlike lisp:

> She brought me a goblet of wine,
> And took my breath away.

By his side sat Khotan Didi at her spinning wheel humming in time to the music of the wheel. It had rained, though not for long, yet the waters of the Jhelum were muddy and the heat was oppressive. He would have preferred not to work in this heat but then he was the sole earner. Whether he liked it or not, work he must. He had begun to realize that it was his sweat and blood that went into the mending of others' clothes. He was all in a sweat and the rafal cloth on his bare knee gave him much trouble. But work he must, and in order to forget his discomfort he hummed his rhymes while he worked. He finished darning a patch, and in order to cut the cord, cast about in search of his scissors.

'I put them on the shelf, Khotan Didi said.

'Bring them here, I need them.'

Khotan Didi had rheumatism in her legs. She could not move about and found it difficult to stand up. If she could have her way she would not move about at all for the rest of her life. Yet she could not turn down her husband's request. She moved in considerable pain and began searching for the scissors. She looked on the shelf, looked into the small tin-box, but the scissors were nowhere to be found. Nabir Shalla grew impatient. He wanted to finish his work and stretch his limbs and rest. 'Look sharp, will you?' he cried. Khotan Didi pulled a bag from the shelf. It was full of worn-out children's garments and old clothes. 'How very sad!' thought Khotan Didi wistfully. 'The children all dead, but the clothes are still intact.'

And one by one she remembered her children and the tears suddenly sprang to her eyes. Her flat breasts began to tingle. As she was throwing the old clothes about, she chanced upon a pair of rose red pyjamas. Those were the pyjamas she had worn on her marriage day; a long, long time ago, but they were still there—the only thing left of her dowry. Her heart gave a sudden throb as she plunged into the memories of her youth.

Khotan Didi blished. She tried to hide the pyjamas so that her husband would not see them but the glaring red colour of the garment screamed for attention. She blushed all over again, her heart beating like that of a virgin and tongues of flame licking her entire body. Images floated before her eyes of her godmother leaving her nuptial room and of Nabir Shalla approaching. She was the newly-wedded bride and Nabir Shalla her youthful groom. For a moment Nabir Shalla appeared before her once more as a young man. She looked sideways at her husband, who gave a chuckle and hummed his usual melody, 'Her skin is smooth as a ripened peach. . . .' Nabir Shalla appeared to her really young in his *pheran* and *pashmina chaddar* while a turban of the finest brand of muslin crowned his head. Here was his groom fresh from the marriage ceremonial; here was she, weaving a net of silly ideas and anticipating the advances of Nabir Shalla with trepidation.

With persuasive softness, Nabir Shalla wheedled her, 'Why don't you put on those pyjamas?' Khotan Didi blushed again. She said nothing. Nabir Shalla continued, 'Come on, why not?' He let his patch of cloth drop and came near his wife, speaking with feeling, 'Why do you hesitate? Put on the pyjamas. You are a nice woman.'

'You're a big fool', said his wife irritably.

'But why?' asked Nabir Shalla.

Khotan Didi sat quiet and motionless. It was not easy for her to make free movements of her body.

'Alright', growled Nabir Shalla, and went down the stairs. Khotan Didi felt relieved. She gathered up the clothes and put them in a bundle, but she did have a last look at the rose red pyjamas before hiding them under a pile of rags and tossing the bundle into the shelf. She looked around for her husband. Where could he have gone, she reflected. But in her heart she felt a twinge of regret; why had he not forced her to wear the garment? She was sad.

It was some time before Nabir Shalla came back humming his rhymes. Khotan Didi now felt embarrassed and she blushed every time she remembered her bridal pyjamas; it was difficult for her to live down the memories of her youth. All of a sudden she found Nabir Shalla was in a gay mood. He was ascending ascended the stairs singing softly. Now he stood before her holding a pound of mutton in his hands and handing it over to her asked, 'Did you put those pyjamas on?' Then, after a pause, 'What an obstinate woman you are!'

'Aren't you ashamed of yourself? At your age, behaving like a monkey', his wife remonstrated.

'Ashamed?' cried Shalla. 'Aren't we man and wife?'

Khotan Didi tried to change the conversation, 'What's this mutton for?' she asked.

'To cook, what else?'

Khotan Didi at once realized that she had a lone tooth and Nabir Shalla none to do justice to the mutton. But Nabir Shalla was no fool. He said, 'Boil it until it is soft. It won't be too hard to chew. But why, you still haven't put those pyjamas on?' He tugged at her and pouted like a baby and would not let her go. At last she agreed that Nabir Shalla should leave her alone to change into the red pair of pyjamas.

Nabir Shalla left the room and went down the stairs holding the pound of mutton in his hand. Khotan Didi shut and bolted the door. She untied the bundle quietly, passed the string through the pyjamas and changed into them. She was all aflutter. She forgot her rheumatism for the moment and went down, looking forward nervously to her encounter with her husband. Suppose someone saw them! O my God! Whatever was he up to at this age? Oh, God, what a prospect! With her thoughts all ajumble, she entered the kitchen noiselessly.

Nabir Shalla had mounted a pot on the hearth to boil the mutton and was sitting, now singing and now blowing into the fire. Khotan Didi would have preferred to sit down without her husband noticing her, but her foot caught in a mat string and down she came with a thud. Nabir Shalla gave a start. He saw Khotan Didi lying flat on the floor and uttered a long frightened cry. But in a moment Khotan Didi lifted her chin and smiled at her husband. Nabir Shalla held her arm and helped her to get up. 'You aren't hurt, I hope', Nabir Shalla spoke anxiously. Khotan Didi shook her head in reply, now thoroughly abashed. 'Well, get-up then',

Nabir Shalla pleaded. Again the same shake of the head in reply. He insisted that Khotan Didi should stand up in her pyjamas. She tried to resist but he was on the war-path. He seized her and pulled her up like one possessed and began to tease her amorously like a newly-wed. Khotan Didi forgot that she was an aged woman and had grandchildren; Nabir Shalla forgot that all his teeth had fallen out and that his son-in-law was already an old man. It was a marvellous sight to see Khotan Didi holding her ground and Nabir Shalla tugging at her sleeve, shoulder, or whatever he could lay his hands upon.

Suddenly there was a knock at the door. Somebody coughed. Nabir Shalla ran back to his place and sat as if nothing had happened. Khotan Didi was bathed in a sweat. The newcomer was none other than their elder son-in-law who had been watching their amorous antics with a puckered brow.

'*Salam-alaikum*' said Nabir Shalla. 'Please come in.'

But the son-in-law retraced his steps without saying a word, his face flushed like a red-hot flame. Khotan Didi was covered in shame like one caught red-handed. She looked guiltily at her husband, but he suddenly got up saying. 'Why do you look so guilty? But why? Isn't this our home? And a man is a prince in his own home, isn't he?'

*Daryayi Hund Yaezdr,* 1955 *Tr*. by Motilal Raina

*chilim* a clay bowl for holding tobacco and coal fixed to the hookah.
*rafal* a warm cloth of soft fibre.
*pheran* a long loose garment.
*pashmina chaddar* a kind of woollen shawl.
*saldm-alaikum* Muslim form of greeting.

**Faata's Divorce**

*Akhtar Mohi-ud-Din :* This excerpt has been taken form the Novel Dod-Dag sickness and pain. Where there is poverty and lack of daily necessities, seamg side of life becomes glaring. Disease sets in and there is no money for doctors and medicines. Other socio-economics disabilities raise their head. Dod-dag takes a deep look at the malady.

*Synopsis:* Faata and Raja are two orphan girls living with their maternal uncle, Qadir Wani, a poor darner. His wife wants to get rid of the nieces and appropriate whatever little patrimony they have. Faata is accordingly married to Sha'ma Saheb, a dealer in *namda* rugs. Once Faata leaves, the house becomes a veritable hell for Raja. One day she slips out and seeks refuge in her sister's house where both Faata and Sha'ma Saheb welcome her.

In her sister's home, Raja is free from the oppression of her aunt. Sha'ma Saheb treats her as his own daughter. She herself feels a stake in the well-being of this house and takes the initiative in cleaning and brightening it up. Meanwhile, Faata's health starts deteriorating. She has inherited tuberculosis from her mother. His husband who has no faith in physicians, advises prayers and amulets. However, his advice is not taken seriously by Faata who wants to die in peace after solemnizing Raja's marriage.

When Raja attains adulthood and blossoms into a lovely young lady, she attracts the attention of Abdul Ghani, a clerk in the business house of Sha'ma Saheb. Ghani is young, strong-built and handsome, with a glib tongue and a stubborn urge for enticing women. Sometimes Raja casts a glance at him and does not feel any guilt about it. He develops a passion for her and once gets an opportunity to convey his love to her. Raja does not take the incident as an affront; rather, it enables her to see herself in a new light.

Ghani soon realizes that Raja is a somewhat distant goal. His objective is an immediate marriage which can yield both monetary gain and carnal pleasure. He involves his employer Sha'ma Saheb in raising his stock in the matrimonial market with the double purpose of securing unhindered attachment to a woman and to come socially closer to Raja. Sha'ma Saheb, Faata and Raja participate in Ghani's marriage. Raja lends a hand in the singing and minstrelsy without being self-conscious. She is present among the close relatives when *henna* is applied to Ghani. She finds him casting meaningful glances at her but does not feel alarmed or upset and, in fact, draws some satisfaction from the experience.

A few months later Ghani discards his wife, who belongs to a family of blacksmiths, but he does not want a legal divorce. Meanwhile, Sha'ma Saheb sides with the blacksmiths and on the strength of his evidence the court awards a decree of divorce. This infuriates Ghani who decides to take revenge on Sha'ma Saheb whose business is already on the decline. Shortly afterwards, Ghani takes another wife from an indigent family, but divorces her in a few months.

Faata's health deteriorates further and as a result of her persuasion Sha'ma Saheb gets Raja married to a dealer in walnut-wood articles. He is a widower with three children and fifteen years older than her. Though Raja has not got for a life companion the sort of robust and handsome youth that a woman of her age longs for, she makes the best of the situation and attends to her wifely duties with devotion. Her visits to her sister being restricted, she feels deeply worried about Faata's health. Once she visits her after a long interval. Events move so fast there on that day, that in a few hurried hours Raja arranges the divorce of Faata from Sha'ma Saheb and takes her to her own house.

After divorcing his second wife, Ghani had been watching closely the affairs of Raja. He makes a strategic move; he offers to marry Faata. When Faata moves into his house, Raja looks her up off and on. During one of her visits, Ghani requests Raja to stay for the night. He arranges matters so cleverly that Raja cannot turn down the request. She sleeps in a bed next to her sister. Late in the night she is taken aback on finding that Ghani has slipped into her bed. He has been using faata as a decoy to ensnare Raja Ghani overawes Faata so much that she cannot even protest. Shortly thereafter, Faata dies leaving Raja to her fate.

Ultimately Raja is divorced by her husband and with nowhere to go, she marries Ghani for whom she continues to be no more than an instrument for satisfying his carnal desires. Dreading the expected birth of a baby, he plans an abortion, without her consent. The acute suffering through which she passes on this account later brings about a qualitative change in Ghani's behaviour, who is now chastened.

The following excerpt describes the tension-laden events leading to Faata's divorce from Sha'ma Saheb.

*Excerpt:* The more Raja felt worried about Faata, the more did her love and affection for her intensify. Once, in a dream, she saw her going to the shrine of Dastgir Saheb along with their mother and, on awakening, felt very upset when she realized that it betokened Faata's death. Raja wished for a miracle to cure Faata.

After a few days she went to her sister's house where she found Faata lying sprawled on the dusty floor, almost sinking. Faata's husband, Sha'ma Saheb, was not present. Faata lay in a sleeping posture as though unaware of her existence. The whole house was bathed in melancholy. The shutters of the showroom were closed. They had remained so over a long period. Who would open them when all business had ground to a halt? Sha'ma Saheb shuddered even to cast a glance at it. Only dogs bestirred themselves in the factory and no one cared to shoo them off. Raja felt no distress on seeing the condition of the showroom but the emaciated form of Faata moved her to tears. She had no relations except Faata who, she felt, was the only memento of her deceased parents.

Raja was whirling in this very ocean when Sha'ma Saheb came in. He was panting for breath as though he had been running ahead of someone chasing him. He felt embarrassed to see Raja who was dear to him even then.

'When did you come?' he asked Raja. 'Why didn't you wake up your sister? Oh! What a sight to see her sprawling thus like a buffalo!'

On finding Sha'ma Saheb using derogatory remarks against her sister, Raja could not restrain herself. She would not have spoken at all to him had he not referred to Faata in such words. With an expression entirely unexpected, 'Talking of her in such terms, you have driven her to the present sorry state!'

Sha'ma Saheb did not pay sufficient attention to Faata, as warranted by her illness, but he had no aversion to her either. Around that time he was overwhelmed by worries and occasionally displayed annoyance while talking to Faata. At the moment he had only tried to be witty and was taken by utter surprise when Raja placed an entirely different connotation on his remark. He was annoyed by her wisecrack.

'What is it you said?' he questioned her.

Raja retorted, 'I call a spade a spade. Did you ever care to arrange medical treatment for her?'

Sha'ma Saheb had not imagined that Raja could grow so rhetorical. But Raja started sobbing and Faata woke up.

'What's the matter, dear? Did he say anything harsh to you?' she asked Raja. Till that moment she did not know that Raja had come to see her, nor what Sha'ma Saheb had done. When she heard Raja sob and saw her husband there, she gathered, as though told by some invisible spirit, that they had had a tiff.

'Stop, dear, stop crying,' she told Raja, 'it is I whom misfortune has been dogging all along!'

Sha'ma Saheb was non-plussed. He failed to make out which of his words could have provoked Raja to break into sobs. He felt enraged and shouted, 'What makes you shed such feigned tears?'

He felt that, all said and done, Raja was under some obligation to him. But the latter burst out like a provoked she-bear, 'Truly is it being said that you are an idiot.'

Her rattling words opened his eyes. Here was Raja whom he had brought up like a daughter. The jibe was a blow he could not stand and he said in a roar of rage, 'Am I an idiot? Is that so? You have been brought up on my crumbs and now you choose to place me at the receiving end! You have been able to secure a husband merely through the dirt of my (grass) slippers and now you talk to me of wisdom. . .!'

These insinuations set Raja's blood boiling. She turned crimson with rage, as though she would catch hold of Sha'ma Saheb by the lapel of his garment and drag him on to the bare ground.

She cried thoughtlessly, 'Ho! The penurious beggar scraped together a few *paise* during the German war and has overweening vanity!'

Raja had heard these words from her husband and uttered them when her anger reached bursting point. Sha'ma Saheb felt as though hit by a bullet in the side. Rage unhinged his mental balance. Faata too was dumbfounded at this verbal cudgelling and could not speak a word to either of them. Her heart started palpitating. When Sha'ma Saheb could do nothing to stem Raja's outburst, he turned to his wife and gave her a thrashing to his heart's content, though he had never raised his hand against Faata earlier. Her illness having left only the skin on her bones, she fainted as a consequence.

Raja could not stand Faata being subjected to thrashing. She was mad with indignation and Sha'ma Saheb appeared to her to be an unmitigated lunatic. She cried desperately every time he hit Faata. Springing up she caught hold of Sha'ma Saheb, rent his turban asunder and tore his garments. This further fanned the anger of Sha'ma Saheb and he started a 'renewed spree of spanking Faata. Had the neighbours not rushed to intervene on hearing the tumult he might have beaten her even to death.

The neighbours set about pushing water down Faata's throat to bring her round while Raja went to bring her husband. The latter was averse to getting involved in this tangle and felt really bewildered when Raja insistently proposed that Faata should seek a divorce from Sha'ma Saheb. He did not know where he would shift Faata after she was divorced and he did not want her to stay in his house. 'Why be bothered by others' troubles? She is a TB patient to boot, and one has to attend to her whims and fancies.' Despite that, he came running to the scene of trouble for two reasons: one, because his youthful wife implored him to and secondly, because this was a godsent opportunity to square up a grouse he had been nursing in his heart against Sha'ma Saheb.

Raja next went to call a few prominent men living in the neighbourhood. Prominence is attained in a locality by only such people who are wealthy. Accordingly, Raja brought all the moneyed neighbours to the house of Sha'ma Saheb. She sent word also to Abdul Ghani who had formerly worked as a clerk in the firm then owned by Sha'ma Saheb. He was now slandering Sha'ma Saheb for having collaborated with his in-laws (a family of blacksmiths) in a suit for obtaining a decree of divorce for their daughter. Additionally, he wanted to please Raja after whom he still hankered. Cancelling all other engagements he came to Sha'ma Saheb's house in high spirits.

Well-to-do people always tend to develop an aversion for a neighbour who might once have been financially better placed than themselves, but who is now down and out. On such occasions they grab the opportunity to demonstrate their supreme wisdom and to cut him down to size. When the elite gathered at Sha'ma Saheb's house and took up the matter, they asked the defendant to present his case. He felt fully demoralized as though he had committed an unpardonable sin. He could not muster courage to look the jury in their eyes. Till the other day all of them were awe-struck by his affluence. Today, when these very people came to sit in judgement over him, Sha'ma Saheb felt humiliated but could not give vent to his injured feelings. The elite grasped the opportunity: they smirked over trivialities and repeatedly uttered '*Masha Allah*' which hurt his sensibilities all the more.

Raja's husband, being the nearest of kin, set the ball rolling, though much against his will.

'You have ruined her health,' he charged, 'and rough-hewn her even otherwise and, you beat her black-and-blue to boot. . . .'

'*Subhan Allah!*' orchestrated the elders, fondling their beards as though the act of the greatest injustice had taken place in the house of Sha'ma Saheb. Abdul Ghani also ejaculated *'Subhan Allah!'* Sha'ma Saheb heard it clearly, but made no response. His limbs began to shiver with rage.

'If you cannot support her,' continued Raja's husband, 'divorce her. The poor woman will work for her living by husking paddy.' The elite were pleased—and, in fact, he himself felt pleased—at the utterance. He repeated, 'The poor woman will work for her living. . . .'

Raja was in the adjacent room preparing a cup of cordial for Faata. A few women of the locality were also there. Raja told them, 'How dare Sha'ma Saheb utter such unbecoming words to insult my sister! I shall have him taken to task. . . . Look at his effrontery in spanking her! Would that his arm fell apart. . .!'

Faata had come round but not fully. She could not make out what all this was about. She did not recollect the thrashing she had received. She was bewildered to see the neighbouring women around her and to hear the shouts of the men in the adjacent room. When she could not make head or tail of it, she closed her eyes and once more dropped asleep against the breast of Raja.

When Raja's ears caught the words of her husband, she retorted, 'Why should she take to husking paddy? Has she no one to look after her? She has nothing to worry about as long as I am alive.'

Raja's loud utterance jolted Faata awake. This single retort revived her memory and tears streamed down her face. In a low voice she said to Raja, 'Of late he has grown somewhat peevish, otherwise he looks after me well. Don't know what incensed him.'

Raja replied, 'If he is not in a proper frame of mind, let him take it out on someone other than my sister. Let him say goodbye to such notions. Does he imagine you are a helpless orphan and nobody will make a protest on your behalf?'

Sha'ma Saheb had never entertained such feelings and Faata knew it. Raja was also aware of this. But then at the height of her indignation she shouted, 'We shall seek instant divorce. My sister will not be left in misery. I may go to the extent of plying the spinning wheel to help her make both ends meet.'

Raja's husband, a dealer in walnut-wood articles, felt terribly upset to hear Raja harangue in this manner. First, being his wife, she should not have plunged headlong into the fray, and secondly, after Faata's divorce he would have to carry home a permanent source of endemic worry and irritation. But he dared not say anything to Raja and, in the company of other men, continued to run down Sha'ma Saheb.

Faata entreated Raja not to be carried away by emotion and said that she craved to breathe her last while lying by Sha'ma Saheb's side.

'Don't overshoot the mark', she implored. But Raja was adamant, riding the crest of fury. She was out to show Sha'ma Saheb low. 'How dare he assault Faata in my presence?'

Turning down Faata's importunities, she secured divorce for her in a matter of minutes. Sha'ma Saheb's creditors had already got hold of the ornaments, valuables and trousseau belonging to Faata. The question of his ability to pay *mehar* did not at all arise. As a consequence, Faata stepped out of her husband's house empty-handed. She was shedding copious tears, for she had spent eight years in this house as Sha'ma Saheb's life-partner.

If a husband and wife are torn apart owing to poverty, indigence or sickness, resentment against each other is only a passing phase. Once formal divorce is effected, the embers of resentment cool down and the original affection starts burgeoning again. Tears roll down their cheeks almost the moment they part company. Both are remorseful and forgive each other in their heart of hearts. Each wants to satiate the eyes for the last time with a look at the other so that the impress of the face and form does not get blurred for the rest of their lives. Each wants to ventilate his/her heart's sickness and pain to the other, but this becomes impossible. They cannot talk to each other: even looking at each other is taboo. Mrs Grundy is likely to comment that the man lacks 'manliness' and that the woman is bereft of 'modesty'. If anyone sees them looking at each other, they will carry the appellations 'pimp' and 'harlot' for the rest of their lives.

Faata was averse to leaving Sha'ma Saheb's house. But why should she not leave? What was Sha'ma Saheb to her at that hour? If she stayed there even for a moment, she would expose herself to the charge of immodesty and defiance of the elders. She wanted to have a glimpse of Sha'ma Saheb, but Raja put the veil over her head and led her out to her own house. Sha'ma Saheb heaved a sigh after their departure, as though he had lost heavily in the gamble of life. Youth, honour, wealth and social relationship had already gone and, on that particular day, even the last stake failed him. He, so to speak, turned hollow from inside.

While Raja was going down the steps her ears caught the words, 'Madam, am I to meet death prematurely?'

Raja knew the speaker to be Abdul Ghani. Having secured a divorce for Faata she was feeling elated, as though she had taken a fortress by assault. She was displeased with what Abdul Ghani said, which implied that he had ignored the leadership of Raja and the words of wisdom she had uttered during the crisis. She got enraged and but for the fear of ignominy she would have peppered his pate with her slippers. Despite that she remarked, 'Do you have no one at home?' To which Ghani replied, 'No, madam, no one. That's why I approach you.'

His untoward reply pumped up Raja's indignation further and she shot back, 'You have your sisters. Why don't you approach your sisters?'

Abdul Ghani giggled: 'Who has ever done so? What I mean is that I have no wife.'

To exchange words with a philanderer like him was like hurling a stone into muck. Realizing this, Raja lapsed into silence and went her way. Abdul Ghani also became quiet and left in glee.

From *Dod-Dag,* 1957 *Tr*. by S.L. Sadhu

*namda* a Kashmiri rug made of raw unspun wool and then embroidered.
*Masha Allah* : God's will.
*Subhan Allah* : My Immaculate God, an exclamation.

**Omens**

*A.K. Rahbar*

A.K. Rahbar (Autar Krisen Rahbar, b. 1933) is one of the pioneers of Kashmiri fiction. His first collection of short stories, *Tobruk* (1958), is well known. Since then his stories have been appearing regularly in various literary journals. The distinctive features of his style are effective dialogues, an objective stance and a subtle satirical strain. He has also written a history of Kashmiri literature covering the period up to A.D. 1800.

In the story *Sig* (Omens) the author shows how baneful belief in omens can be. The absurdity of such blind belief is highlighted with the victim meeting with disaster just when the omen seems to him to be most propitious.

Nath's head emerged from the quilt as the clock struck eight. Rubbing his eyes, he said (God knows why), 'O, the day is far advanced!' But as he was struggling into his shirt, his handsome face turned ashen pale. Soon his earlobes were red. Obviously his eyes had alighted on something that gave him a premonition of disaster. 'How awful!' he said, 'God knows what is coming! The walls may collapse—or anything! She has no bloody sense! She has never been careful!' Biting his lips, he got up in a fit of towering rage and rushed into the kitchen pounding his feet only to discover that his wife wasn't there.

'Damn it! Whenever I look for her, she is never here, but always hanging about there at the water tap!' His eyes flaming with anger, he went to give her hell. But he got stuck at the threshold for two or three women of the locality were also there. They were all drawing water, chatting away happily and laughing.

'O, how wayward these women have become now, having neither fear nor modesty!. . . Just watch that white turnip!. . . Go on! Wave your arms in gay abandon, you devil! Behaving as if this were your father's estate!. . . Now look at the other woman! Rahim Miskeeni!. . . Go on with your unbridled coquetry! Proud of your new blue cotton dress, aren't you? Go on!'

He went on talking to himself thus, mimicking and nicknaming them. Their presence, however, did act as a deterrent, and he went inside. Not that his anger had cooled down. On the contrary, biting his lips and gnashing his teeth, he was pacing up and down the room adjacent to the kitchen.

The truth is that his wife, Chanda—let us be fair to her—had not noticed him. If she had, she would have sensed from the first glimpse that trouble was brewing for her, that perhaps she had slipped up somewhere, and would have devised some means or other to make his anger dissolve.

Chanda—pet name, Chandi—was indeed the purest silver *(chandi)* without even a grain of copper. She was originally from Tula Mula village and though she had spent almost her entire life in the city, the moulding effect of her early environment had been a permanent gift. She remained pure and serene, though she understood the changing colours of the times. Like the Tula Mula spring, her sensitivity revealed to her the goodness and wickedness in others and the forces operating around her.

Chanda knew every nerve and fibre of Nath. She felt his every pulse. If he sometimes went beyond limits in abusing her, she wouldn't open her mouth. With someone else in her place, the home would have been a perpetual battlefield, with angry tongues pouring venom. The food cooked in the house would have provided a daily feast for the local cats and dogs. Whenever he flew into a foolish temper, Chanda remembered the advice of her wise father, which had helped reconcile warring members in many a family. 'You can't clap with one hand; the sound comes when two hands meet. Just as heat is generated by rubbing your hands, anger too is generated and aggravated by two tongues lashing at each other. So you should never be angry. If somebody is angry with you, just keep quiet. Remember that silence is golden: it sweetens a person just as steam gives flavour to meat.'

That is why Chanda never let even a word slip through her lips, whatever the provocation. Otherwise, the situation would have developed thus:

The husband's anger and abuse would make the wife retort: 'O, you lean scarecrow! Go and munch water chestnuts somewhere! Leave me alone, will you?'

Husband: 'You bundle of rags. Go and eat dried fish in shade somewhere!'

Wife: 'Your mother is a bundle of rags. Yes, she is! Your sister is a bundle of rags!'

She would then go through the customary ritual—tear her hair, tear her shirt, bare her breasts and scream, 'O, I'm being killed! Is there no one anywhere?'

The quarrel would naturally grow fierce. Arms would swing into action. The 'Quit Home!' movement would be born, like 'Quit Kashmir!' in the recent past. All the neighbours would assemble, and the couple would become a laughing stock, the butt of everyone's ridicule and taunts. And sure as hell the home would be destroyed.

Chanda was filling her pot when a loud thud and a child's cry came simultaneously. What had happened was that Nath's child, Bota, had crawled up to him, and he had picked him up and flung him down.

'O God! Bota has had a fall!' Chanda beat her chest, rushed in like the wind and picked up the child. 'O what a calamity,' she said, 'to be alone and helpless! Wish there were someone here to hold him and fondle him! Just see! He is still asleep, so much in love with his quilt!'

*'Chi! Chi! Chi!'* shouted Nath. 'Don't you see anyone here? Why not issue more orders to your slave, so that he could at least go and massage that Rama Khasu?'

Chanda was absolutely non-plussed and unnerved with his unexpected shouting. She couldn't understand what on earth had happened. Coming from the bright light outside into the dark room, she couldn't make out anything at first. Hearing her father's name taken so lightly and with such disrespect for no reason at all struck her dumb.

'Why don't you say something?. . . I could at least buy some snuff for that snuff addict! After all, am I not a slave of the great Arakh Zeb Begum?'

Chanda remained silent even after this volley had been fired. She was only wondering where she had slipped up.

'O, how you stand there,' he continued shouting, 'gazing like a demon, eager to eat me up! Why on earth didn't you tell your mother that you didn't want to marry? On the contrary you were delighted at the prospect of wearing a nose-ring and sitting in an exalted position with your youthful airs and whims and all the rest of it! When this brief bloody facade is over, you women start addressing yourselves to your real mission in life—ruining other people's homes!'

'After all what have I ...

'What have you done? (speaking with a child's lisp) Nothing my child! You know nothing! (shouting again) Look, let me tell you this: I'm not going to be swayed by the rolling of your almond eyes! Yes, I know you are hell-bent on destroying me!'

'What are you saying? What is my . . .

'What is your fault, eh? I tell you the cat polishing off the ghee is not half as exasperating as the rascal wagging its tail afterwards. O, I wish my mother were alive! She would have grabbed you by the shoulder and flung you out of the door. Would you ever have dared to place an oil-lamp like that?'

'Oil-lamp! O, was it visible?'

'Yes! Yes!' he shouted. 'It was! Wasn't it?'

Chanda was plunged into thought, wondering what to do. After a few moments of quick thinking, tossing her snaky curls from her face and rolling her almond eyes, she said, 'O, how obsessed with omens you are! I am amazed at your wisdom! When this same lamp dissipates darkness, bringing basketfuls of light and illuminating everything, when it fondles the butterfly, the thief of youth, and helps you fulfil all hidden desires, you call it the lamp of longing! And now ...'

'I must say that you have learnt a lot of philosophy today!' shouted Nath. 'That white turnip obviously has taught you all this. Did you ask her if the beans came out well?'

This oblique thrust put her out quite a bit. She had hoped her strategy would work, but it had failed. His anger still blazed. Another idea flashed across her mind. 'Okay,' she said, 'tell me, didn't your aunt, who has instructed you on the significance of various omens, also tell you that every bad omen loses its effect if you tell others what you have seen?'

'Yes, she did,' he said, 'but how does it help?' His colour brightened a little, because his aunt had once taught him how to escape disaster.

'Just go out there and tell everybody that you saw an oil-lamp early in the morning, that you don't know what will happen, that walls will collapse, etc. The omen will lose all its force.'

'Really?'

Believe it or not, this jackass came out into the street dressed like Wasa the Mad, in a long loose woollen *kurta,* with his thick locks of hair dangling from his top! Chanda valued her dignity, and was quite shocked seeing her husband's abnormal behaviour, but what could she do? If a disease is incurable, you've got to bear the pain. It is destined agony. How could she fight against the antediluvian beliefs of that half-mad fellow?

After this propitiatory ritual to thwart the evil designs of the ill-omen, Nath ate well, and was in the upper room getting ready for his office, when Chanda's younger brother, Nika, dropped in as usual to look them up. After some conversation he looked around for Bota. The kid had fallen asleep with blue patches all over his body, and Chanda had to relate the whole story to Nika.

Nath was perhaps coming down the stairs when Chanda sneezed violently. 'Now, who the hell sneezed?' he shouted. 'It's nothing, sir', said Nika, a little curt. 'I sneezed.' 'Nothing?' said Nath. 'A sneeze doesn't spare anyone. It is not partial like a brother or a sister!'

'Are you well, sir?' Nika asked.

'O yes, very well!' he answered. He was seething with anger, and wanted to bash in Nika's nose. But he didn't say anything, because after their father's death Nika was the darling of his brothers and sisters. They were intensely attached to him.

However, he left in a dismal mood. Emerging from his narrow lane, he took the Gankhan lane to his office. He stopped at the Khanakah gate, where he mumbled a prayer with his head bowed and hands folded above; he moved briskly ahead past Fateh Kadal and Habba Kadal, crossed over the bridge and proceeded via Tankipora.

He was employed in the silk factory. He reached his office ten minutes late, went straight to his room and started pricking holes in paper with his pen, just as the sneeze was pricking his heart and loomed large all over his mind.

Observing his agitation, his colleague Ghulam Nabi said to him, 'Nathji, what makes you sad today? At the crossroads?'

'O, no!' Nath threw a sidelong look at him and started pricking the paper again.

'Come, Nathji, something seems to be wrong!'

'O, how shall I tell you? I had just woken up when I saw an oil-lamp; I had hardly got out of the house when a wretched youngster sneezed. Well, anything can happen!'

'Ha! ha! ha!' Swinging his white *salwar*-clad leg, Ghulam Nabi said to another clerk, 'Do you hear, Makhan Lal? Nathji saw an oil-lamp first thing in the morning, and then someone sneezed. He says that a storm can break!'

'But it did, didn't it, just a while ago?. . .' He was about to elaborate on it when Ghulam Nabi cautioned him with his tongue, and he kept quiet.

'Nathji,' said Ghulam Nabi, 'don't be so superstitious. These old thoughts and beliefs are gone now. They are out of date—I mean beliefs like, "If he crosses your path, you'll be stung by *bhang*" or "If she casts an evil eye on you, you'll die within a fortnight", or similar nonsense.'

There was loud laughter from one corner. It was the senior clerk, Ghulam Rasool, who had been listening to the conversation. He took off his spectacles and started blowing on the lenses to clean them.

'Just listen', he said. 'We've got an old lady in our house—my grandmother, I mean. She, always upbraids me for moving about in clean, well-pressed clothes. "Don't you see Fatah the Idiot," she says, "always at the window, with her evil eye—O may these eyes of hers fall out!" One day I asked her, "O mother, what has all that to do with me?" She answered, "What happened to Gula the driver? What a Rustam he was in both strength and beauty! How did he disappear? You see what I mean?" I retorted with anger, "What rubbish! You people know nothing, but keep on nursing stupid beliefs—that person cast an evil eye on him, this person something else, etc. Granny, no one will ever give you even a bullet, let alone an eye!"

Everybody burst into laughter. Ghulam Rasool continued, 'I told her that it was liquor that had killed Gula. He would drink two or three bottles neat; what on earth could be the consequence but death? But she would not be convinced. Her mind remained forever wedded to her stupid belief in omens. The same seems to be Nathji's condition too! But while you can understand this kink in an uneducated person like my grandmother, I am baffled how Nathji can subscribe to this belief.'

Makhan Lal butted in, unable to control himself, 'But I tell you everything that happens is preordained to the minutest detail. All of us have to accept this truth despite our brave show of initial disbelief. ..."

Ghulam Nabi cut him short, 'O no! Look, he will go to pieces this way.'

'But tell me,' said Makhan Lal, 'didn't it happen this morning?'

'What happened?' asked Nath, fearing the worst.

Ghulam Nabi pulled out a paper and showed it to him. 'Here you are, see for yourself. Both of them have got promotion.'

Nath collapsed, though he could understand nothing.

Gradually the day wore on and it was four o'clock. Closing time. The clerks made a beeline for the gate. Nath left with Ghulam Nabi who, while they were walking along, repeated to him what he had said earlier.

Nath reached home. The night came and ended. A new day dawned. Nath left again for his office. He was in high spirits today, like a bird on the wing, as it were—because his right eye was throbbing!

Four o'clock, and the clerks sprinted away again. Nath stuck to Ghulam Nabi. Not that they had the same route, for Ghulam Nabi did not live at Gankhan. Not that he had taken Ghulam Nabi's advice seriously: in fact it was completely lost on him. On the contrary Nath's logic was this: Ghulam Nabi's company had brought him luck yesterday because the sneeze had its evil effect. 'If I leave with him today, maybe I'll gain a fortune. The suspicious throbbing of my right eye combined with his favourable company can work miracles!'

At Maharaj Bazaar, Ghulam Nabi bought some toys. 'My child won't allow me to enter,' he said, 'if I go empty-handed.' Nath remembered Bota. 'Why not I also buy something for him? Yesterday's fall had made him hostile; he doesn't come to me at all.' He bought a rubber doll and a rattle for eight annas.

As they moved on talking about things in general, Ghulam Nabi said, 'Now Nathji, have a look at your shoes. Why can't you have them repaired? The sole is completely gone. If you have a fall, you'll blame it on this or that person's evil eye!'

'O don't worry! I'll have it repaired tomorrow. Today I am not afraid of anything, not even monsters. The devil himself will be powerless, because inly right eye is throbbing!'

'O God! Have I only wasted my breath!' said Ghulam Nabi to himself, wondering how irredeemable this slave of omens was. But what could he tell him? It was like sowing paddy in the wilderness.

As they were moving from Hari Singh High Street towards Sher Garhi, Nath's shoe heel got dislodged and twisted. He fell down and was crushed under the wheels of a speeding vehicle.

'O Ghulam Nabi!' he screamed, 'I'm killed. See, my right eye was throbbing! I'll never believe in omens again!'

The road was a pool of blood. The rubber doll with its dishevelled hair lay on one side and the rattle on the other. Ghulam Nabi turned white, with tears welling up in his eyes. He felt a cold sweat. Then in a flash he burst into laughter like a mad man. 'Ha! Ha! No one can harm me! Not even Satan! You have left an example! A memorable example, because your right eye was throbbing when you got killed!'

*Sig,* 1958 *Tr.* by Trilokinath Raina

**The Mirror**

*Amin Kamil*

Amin Kamil (Mohammad Amin Kamil, b. 1924) started as an Urdu poet and switched over to Kashmiri in 1952. Besides being a notable poet, he is a dramatist, novelist and short story writer in Kashmiri. His collection of short stories, *Kathi Manz Kath,* and a novel, *Ghati Manz Gaash,* have won awards from the State Cultural Academy, Srinagar. He speaks the commonman's language in non-traditional diction choosing every word with meticulous care. He has translated two plays of Tagore into Kashmiri.

The short story *Aina* (The Mirror, 1966), relates to an ageing wood craftsman who has lost all zest for work as well as for life in general but who experiences a fleeting revival of interest in his craft when he has a tender romance with his neighbour's wife, carried on through her reflection in a mirror on his wall.

'Master, behold the mirror.' That was Ghulama, with bowed head, apprising the master craftsman Ghafoora of some fact.

The master craftsman would look into the mirror after muttering to himself, 'That is as it should be.' The mirror was hanging on the wall in such a manner that it reflected the house standing opposite. On the balcony of this house, Zeba, the one-eyed wife of Gula the painter, used to saunter forth and Ghafoora used to make amorous gestures to her reflection in the mirror.

● ● ●

Master craftsman Ghafoora was about sixty years old. According to an old saying, a man shows signs of dementia when he approaches sixty, but Ghafoora evinced no such decline. However, worldly sorrows and vicissitudes had literally beaten him up. That was why his face always wore a sad, lugubrious look, and everything around him, including his craft and the people, repelled him. He had practically lost interest in everything, so much so that whenever he took up a block of walnut wood he would chisel a somewhat crude and ungainly design on it and thus spoil it. That was why, perhaps, he came to be nicknamed 'the woodhead'. Time was when he had earned renown as a master craftsman in woodwork and his workmanship was so unique that it came to be referred to as the Ghafoora style. Even now, when an old-time British customer went shopping for woodcraft, the shopkeeper would, while offering him a walnut-wood box, beguile him by saying, 'Sir, this is Ghafoora-made. See how wonderful the craft is.' That was because Ghafoora's artistry needed no critical examination. But now the masterly touch was lacking and he had literally become a woodhead. He used to wonder why, with the same tools and the same blocks of wood, he could no longer carve the old, artistic designs. On the other hand, those who had once worked as apprentices and assistants to him, had graduated to master craftsmen. Whenever he saw specimens of their craftsmanship, he would admire them with wide-eyed wonder. Since he knew their antecedents, he would mutter to himself, 'These artistic creations need young blood. They have not gone grey like me.'

He would often relate stories of his younger days to Ghulama and Wahaba, both of whom were apprentices in his workshop. In fact, when a man loses grip on the present and when his future becomes misty and nebulous, he starts attributing his plight to adversities. Ghafoora also nostalgically recounted how delicate and artistic his workmanship used to be and how foreigners came all the way to his workshop to photograph him. He also recalled that articles designed and fabricated by him used to sell like hot cakes. Again, how once when a block of wood cracked at three places, he joined it so dexterously that even the acknowledged connoisseur, Khwaja Subhan, could not detect the defect. When Ghafoora told him about it, Subhan gave him a reward of Rs. 20 and exclaimed, 'Today I accept defeat; you are the real master of this craft.'

But whenever in such pensive moments Ghulama and Wahaba asked him why he no longer displayed such mastery, his face would wrinkle up and a strange sadness would engulf his countenance. He was now accustomed to taking the block of wood close to his eyes to figure out where he should impress the design. Apparently, his eyesight had deteriorated.

Ever since he had started making amorous gestures to the mirrored reflection of the one-eyed Zeba, he appeared to be getting the fleeting world back into his grasp as if he had shed thirty years of his age at one stroke. He seemed to feel so young that he would dye his hair; he replaced his skull-cap with a fur cap and started wearing a jacket of sunproof cloth which he had purchased at an auction. The exhaustion that he used to experience while carving wood somehow vanished and he felt fresh blood coursing through his veins. He gave up coarse work and reverted to delicate workmanship with new designs. He appeared to be recovering his lost artistry and this drew the admiration of his apprentices Ghulama and Wahaba. They felt proud of him because his workmanship was unparalleled. In fact, Ghulama once asked him, 'Master, why have you reverted to your old delicate craftsmanship?' The truth of the matter was that Ghafoora was himself wondering how his old mastery had returned to him. Ghulama said, 'I asked you this question because the Englishmen who were admirers of your fine work are no longer there; the Indian businessman is satisfied even with rough-and-ready workmanship.'

Ghafoora retorted, 'Fool! Money is not the be-all and end-all of everything. You wait and see what wonders I shall produce. I have still many years to go.'

The truth was that Ghafoora had experienced a tremendous rejuvenation of his faculties ever since he started his love affair with the image in the mirror. He used to work with such delicacy and artistry on wooden blocks that he seemed to be doing so to impress his lady love—Gula painter's wife.

● ● ●

Gula the painter belonged to some distant *mohalla.* He had come to live for a month or two in a rented house for his own house had caught fire and all his possessions had been reduced to ashes. Gula used to go out to do his professional work and his wife would be left alone in the house. Colours being available at home, she would appear every day in a differently hued headscarf. Actually she did not have dozens of scarves; she must have had hardly two or three. But due to the facility for dyeing the scarves in the house she gave the impression of possessing a large number of them.

Ghafoora, however, was not captivated by Zeba's multicoloured scarves; he loved her for her good looks. To hide her blind eye, she would let a lock of hair fall over it with a deliberate touch of insouciance. This lent a further romantic air to her beauty. Anyone would have fallen for her. Ghafoora also had been bewitched by this style of her hair-do, though he was aware of the defect in one of her eyes.

In the beginning, Zeba was ignorant of the goings-on in Ghafoora's workshop. She used to come to the balcony casually to survey the bazaar below or to dress vegetables in a basket. Once she happened to catch a glimpse of Ghafoora. He was looking at the wall like a simpleton and making strange gestures. She wondered why he was doing so. Clever as she was, she pondered over the matter and ultimately came to know that he was ogling at her through the mirror. This set her aflame and she could not fathom why this old fool was not mortified at his behaviour. But doubts assailed her as to whether he was actually looking at her or if she was unjustly suspecting him. After putting him to the test on a few occasions she was convinced that he was casting amorous glances at her through the mirror. Following this discovery, she would saunter on the balcony whenever she was free and reciprocate Ghafoora's love-making. The old man would convey his sentiments to her mirrored image in his own odd ways and she would acknowledge just one out of a hundred gestures. Ghafoora would, however, avoid looking at her directly. For him the mirrored image was but a mundane shadow of the truth, as is the case with godmen who regard the world as a reflection of the Ultimate Reality. This image had become for him a divine inspiration, a symbolic persuasion and an irresistible attraction.

It was Ghulama who would first behold Zeba on the balcony. While at work, he would unwittingly or otherwise keep a watch on her movements. Whenever she emerged he would, without raising his head, whisper to Ghafoora, 'Master, the mirror is there.' Upon this Ghafoora would stealthily look into the mirror and see Zeba's face reflected like the moon in a pond of water. He would smile first and then, with the block of wood still in his hand, touch his forehead as if to say *salaam* to her. In the sheer joy of love-making he would forget his surroundings and make juvenile gestures, so much so that anyone seeing him would split his sides with laughter. The consolation, however, was that only Ghulama and Wahaba were there to watch his antics and they did so on the sly.

● ● ●

Ever since Ghafoora started his game of love, he would open the workshop early in the morning, mop the mirror clean and survey his face in it for some time. He would dress the hair of his eyebrows and then moisten his lips in such a manner that the corners of his mouth almost touched his ears. This he did ostensibly to make full-fledged love which helped him overcome the weight of his sorrows. It smoothened out the creases of his brow and made his face look buoyant. He had purchased toothpowder from a wayside quack and would shine his teeth with it in the morning, although only a few were left in his mouth and those that were, had developed large cracks.

Meanwhile, his apprentices would arrive and he would allot them work for the day. They would gather their chisels, hammers and other tools and set to work.

Ghulama observed his master's love-making with suspicion and curiosity. Ghafoora used to touch his eye with his fingers to convey to Zeba that he was charmed by her lock of hair. At this Zeba would moisten her lips and deliberately touch this very lock in a coquettish manner. When Ghafoora saw her do that, he would gesture as if he was sniffing the scent of the lock. He imagined that Zeba, the one-eyed, had applied a lot of perfume to her tresses and the smell was wafting across to his workshop. For sheer effect, he would keep his fur cap aslant on his head and light a Red Lamp cigarette, all the while beholding the reflected image in the mirror.

Ghulama used to watch all this with amusement. He would see his master blowing kisses into the mirror and Zeba promptly offering her cheek. On such occasions, Ghulama would shout in an undertone, 'Master, what about doling out a few coins for a cup of tea?'

Ghafoora did not like this interruption in his reverie. He would shout back, 'Ghulama, have you gone crazy? Why don't you take the money from my pocket?' While saying this, he would become so ecstatic at Zeba's response that God alone could fathom the depth of his feelings. Ghulama would hint to Wahaba who in turn would dip his hand into the pocket of the master's waistcoat which used to be hung up on the wall. Ghulama knew that this delicate moment of love-making was the most opportune for extracting a favour from the master. He himself used to feel relaxed at such times.

On seeing Ghafoora in this state, Zeba would also have a hearty laugh and glide back into her room. As she disappeared from view, Ghafoora would again pick up his chisel and hammer and resume work with such alacrity that it would leave his apprentices dumbfounded.

● ● ●

One day Ghafoora and his apprentices were working as usual in their workshop. Ghulama was expectantly waiting for Zeba to emerge while. Ghafoora was looking forward to a hint from the former. However, when Zeba's usual time of coming on to the balcony had passed and Ghafoora received no hint from Ghulama, his heart started sinking. At that time he was working on a cosmetic box and had chiselled an exquisite design on it. His heart began to palpitate furiously and forebodings gripped him. He wondered if Zeba had fallen ill. Or maybe Gula the painter had got suspicious and forbidden her to come on to the balcony. As time kept passing, Ghafoora's hand became shaky. This reflected itself in the leaves being carved on the wood getting detached from their stems and the grapes already carved cracking up.

Ghulama also felt something was amiss with himself, he could not reduce his itch even after smoking lots of cigarettes. Once in this mood he perhaps had a glimpse of a bird fluttering its wings on the balcony and involuntarily he shouted, 'Master . . .!'

At this exclamation, Ghafoora looked towards the mirror, but did not find Zeba's reflection in it. The hammer slipped out of his hand and he closed his eyes, holding his head against his palm. He experienced a reeling sensation. Ghulama felt mortified at having given a false hint to his master.

The following day, being a Friday, was a holiday for the workshop. On Saturday morning, when Ghulama and Wahaba jovially walked up to the workshop to start their work, they were taken aback to see Ghafoora's condition. He had again put on his skull-cap and donned an old, tattered *pheran.* He was sitting in front of the workshop, executing rather crude and unrefined designs. He wore a sepulchral look and it looked as if everything around was repelling him. Ghulama and Wahaba began exchanging curious glances. They were dumbfounded and could not guess anything. They walked in and, after offering the usual salutation to the master, started their work.

While they were busy working, they also kept thinking why the master was looking so haggard and woe-begone. They felt a strange change in their own behaviour and tried to find reason for the gloom on their master's face, the slow movement of his hands and the unusual blinking of his eyes. By chance, Ghulama looked towards the painter's house, only to find it wearing a desolate look, with all the windows on the first floor shut. This had never happened before. Ghulama concluded that Gula and his wife must have left this house and moved to some other locality. Then he looked towards the wall but found the mirror missing. He said almost involuntarily, 'Master—the mirror?'

'It has got smashed', Master Ghafoora replied in a guttural, broken voice.

*Aina,* 1966 *Tr.* by D.N. Kaul

pheran a loose Kashmiri gown.

**Sunshine**

*Harikrishna Kaul*

Harikrishna Kaul (Harikrsna Kaul, b.1934) is an outstanding short story writer and playwright in Kashmiri. He switched over to Kashmiri after he had carved out a place for himself in Hindi with the publication of three collections of short stories in that language. He has published three plays and two collections of short stories in Kashmiri and won several awards for his works.

The short story *Taph* (Sunshine) ably depicts the dilemma of an old Kashmiri woman who moves to Delhi to spend the winter months with her son and daughter-in-law but is not able to adjust to the sudden and marked environmental change. At the time of her journey back home she yearns, in vain, to carry basketfuls of sunshine from the plains as a possible solution to her problem.

In Delhi, Poshikuj felt herself in a new world. She breathed a sigh of intense relief. 'Above everything else, there are no Muslims here. You see only Hindu brothers everywhere. The milkman is a Hindu brother, the greengrocer is a Hindu brother, the barber is a Hindu brother. . . . And God has delivered me from that vile woman!' This was the greatest relief for Poshikuj, the 'vile woman' being her eldest daughter-in-law, the very thought of whom sent an involuntary shudder down her spine. 'O, how that shrew would find fault with me at every step. Earlier, we were not talked about in the neighbourhood, but this bawling woman made the neighbours talk and brought me disgrace. However, God is just and has given her what she richly deserves, but her wretched luck has also involved her husband. Poor Gaasha has been reduced to destitution. He and Saaba are from the same womb, and see what power and position Saaba enjoys here!' Musing thus, Poshikuj made up her mind never to go back to Kashmir, not even in summer.

It was about ten. Poshikuj came out into the yard to bask in the sun. One half of this enclosure was a well-kept lawn with flowerbeds all around. The other half was paved with bricks, with many flowerpots on it. There were also some flowering creepers clinging to the walls of the house. Saaba, Poshikuj's younger son, Surendra Nath, was allotted this good 'D' type accommodation in Sarojini Nagar. On the ground floor a drawing room, a store, a kitchen and an open space in front of the kitchen which they had furnished with a table and chairs and converted into a dining room. On the first floor was a bathroom, a lavatory and two bedrooms. One was used by the couple and in the other a bed had been installed the other day for Poshikuj. Then there was the flat roof with a rain shelter. Surendra Nath had returned three years ago from England, where he had gone on a government scholarship for advanced studies, after completing which he started his career in the Indian High Commission there and returned to India on being posted as an, officer in the External Affairs Ministry. His salary was about a thousand rupees a month. He had got married before leaving for England—a thing which filled Poshikuj with terrible regret. Had he been a bachelor still, she mused, any millionaire would have now been on his knees at her feet, begging to have Saaba as a son-in-law. But she never communicated this personal grief to anybody.

She sat in the chair on the lawn, basking in the warm sun, the nerves and veins on her shoulders and back thawing and the rheumatism that plagued her in Kashmir disappearing. She looked up and liked the azure sky very much. From the first-floor verandah hung clothes spread by Chhoti, her younger daughter-in-law, for drying. She found them radiant. 'I tell you, a foreign machine is really a great thing, it did not take Chhoti five minutes to wash these clothes, and see how white they are.' While she was admiring the washing, she spied Chhoti's brassieres among the clothes. This made her blush for shame. 'O God, I hope the neighbours haven't seen this. What would they say?' She left her chair and started pacing up and down on the lawn. Suddenly an idea struck her and she started plucking flowers, gathering them in the hem of her sari. She planned to take Chhoti to a temple. 'They say Birla Mandir is worth seeing here. It will not take long, say at the most half-an-hour, and we can have food on our return.' She went inside, put the flowers on the dining table, and sat in a chair. 'I don't know when Chhoti is coming down. She has been in the bathroom for more than an hour. God alone knows what she is rubbing on her body! I must say she has become rather bold after coming to Delhi. Anyway, she is a thousand times better than that slut.'

After some time there was the sound of the bathroom door opening and Chhoti's sandaled feet pattering down the stairs. She had changed her blouse and sari. The hair was not plaited, but Poshikuj felt that she looked much better now than earlier in that horrid gown.

'O *Mataji,* what have you done?' said Chhoti on seeing the flowers on the table. Poshikuj stood dumbfounded, feeling she had done something wrong. Chhoti continued, 'Why did you pluck flowers in the garden, particularly the hollyhocks?' She was partly sad, partly angry.

This display of temper on the part of her daughter-in-law was worse than death for Poshikuj. She said to herself, 'It is only a matter of flowers, and see what delicacy she exhibits! There I was called *kaakanya* and here I have become Mataji. Mataji be damned!' But swallowing her anger she answered calmly, 'I thought we could go to the temple.'

'You should have asked me first. There is no temple in this locality or nearby. The only places near here are Ashoka Hotel and Chanakyapuri.'

'What is that?'

'You won't understand that. Come, let us sit in the sun outside.'

Poshikuj was aflame from top to toe. 'This daughter of Govinda the Idiot can understand and I cannot. No, it is necessary to shut her up right now, else I won't have any right to speak tomorrow.' She said, 'What do you take me for? Don't I know that Birla Mandir, which people come to see from various countries, is here in Delhi?'

'Mataji, Birla Mandir is very far from her. We've first to go to Connaught Place, then to Gole Market, and Birla Mandir is beyond Gole Market.'

A downright lie Poshikuj was sure. The day before yesterday she had seen from the roof something like a temple in the direction of the setting sun. It had a bluish dome, and her mind had told her that if at all Birla Mandir existed, here it was. Bent on calling the bluff and with her feet firmly planted on the ground, she said to her daughter-in-law, 'Then what temple is that which has a blue dome, the one that can be seen from our roof? *Mai* also said that it is Birla Mandir.'

'Mataji, what does *mai* know? That building is neither a mosque nor a temple. It is the Pakistan Embassy, that is, the office of Pakistan in India.'

Poshikuj could not swallow this any more than unwholesome rice. 'What an idiot she is taking me for! But a lie has never any roots. . . . No one dare mention the name of Pakistan in Kashmir where there are Muslims everywhere. And she wants me to believe, I suppose, that there is a Pakistan office in Delhi! What fantasies this daughter-in-law of mine is feeding me on! But, as they say, you can do nothing to a person who abuses you from the other bank of the river or to one who is excited and talks irrational nonsense to your face. . . . But if I argue with her, she might start shouting at me like the other shameless woman does. Then, where do I hide myself ? Silence is golden, my soul!'

It was now about midday. Chhoti lit the stove and made *chapatis*. She had already cooked vegetables in the pressure cooker in the morning. Now she put it on the stove to heat it up. She placed two glasses on the table, sliced onions on one plate, and, taking a lemon from the fridge, squeezed it on the onions. Poshikuj realized she was making arrangements for a meal. She said, 'See, I am telling you I shall not eat anything for lunch today.'

'But why, you are not going to fast today?'

'No, why should I fast? But I am telling you I am not going to eat off a plate any more. Give me food in that small metal basin. I shall eat sitting on the floor.' Saying this, she went to her room upstairs. There was a torn carpet she had brought with her from Kashmir with her bedding wrapped up in it. She took this down to the dining room and spread it on the floor. Chhoti gazed at her for a long time. She was in a fix, but being helpless, brought her a few *chapatis* in the small basin and the vegetables in a *katori*. Poshikuj took a hand-towel out of her petticoat pocket, put the *katori* on it and holding the basin in her lap, started eating with relish.

After lunch, Chhoti went upstairs and came down after about an hour, having changed her clothes and combed and plaited her hair. 'I am going to Miss Kapur,' she said, 'and shall be back by 3 o'clock.'

Poshikuj did not say anything to this announcement. However, her silence did not prevent Chhoti from going out. She had a quick look at her watch, and left. Poshikuj felt very hurt, but at the same time said to herself, 'Who am I to stop her from going anywhere? Let her do what she likes!'

She went out into the sun again. Its caressing warmth revived her. 'O, my life for this warm sunshine! If you think of it, this is the only blessing here.' She pulled her sari up and started scratching her right leg and gazed at her feet which were roughened, cracked and fissured with cold. 'A plague on the winter of that place which destroys one's hands and feet!' Thinking of the cold reminded her of Bitta. 'The poor fellow's feet with the bursting chilblain and pus oozing all over! I had warned that hag, that witch, a hundred times. Your son's feet will be ruined, I told her. He needs socks and fur boots. But would she listen?. . . How costly fur boots also have become! And how much salary does poor Gaasha get? Barely enough for the month! Can never make both ends meet. He is without an overcoat himself and shivers with the cold. . . . Fate, and nothing else!'

Poshikuj looked at the various houses around. There was silence every where. 'As if no one exists anywhere! As if they were all dead! Isn't there such a thing as a neighbour here? A little chat with each other now and then? But no one seems to know anyone here. . . . Anyway, what would I make of their language, the *tee-tee-tee* of the women here?. . . And what amusing and strange names they all have here! One is Mrs. Joan, another is Mrs Sundaram, another is Mrs. Prakash, another is Mrs. Someone. Look at this Sikh woman in this very house. Her daughters and daughter-in-law may be my age, but her name is also Mrs. Kem Singh. Wonder why they all have the same name "Mrs." Delhi seems to be a good place, but it is nothing.'

The sound of a scooter broke her reverie. She guessed Saaba must have returned. Yes, it was Saaba. Pushing the scooter inside, he said, 'How are you mother? Spent the day well, I hope?' 'Yes, well', she said. 'May God bless you.'

Saaba went upstairs and came down immediately. 'Where is she gone?' he asked.

'She has gone to Mrs. Kapur.'

'Which Mrs. Kapur?'

'The one who comes here with her hair blown up in various shapes. Fair and slender.'

'Who? Was it Miss Kapur, by any chance?'

'Yes, that's what I told you.'

Saaba burst out laughing. 'Mother, you didn't. This is Miss Kapur, Kapur Sahib's daughter. You said Mrs. Kapur, which would mean Kapur Sahib's wife.'

'I would say, may calamity seize such .things! How do I know these nice distinctions?'

'Being here, mother, you will. I'm afraid, you have to know these nice distinctions.' Clinching the conversation thus, Saaba got up and was going to his room when Poshikuj said, 'How is Chhoti so friendly with this Kapur? I don't like her ways.'

'No, mother, she is very good. Anyway, whatever she may be is of no consequence to us. We are concerned with our own interest in her.'

'Your interest in her? What does that mean?'

'That means her father is a very high official in All India Radio, and Chhoti is trying for a job there.'

Poshikuj was aghast at this revelation. 'What are you telling me? Do you mean that you will now be making your wife also work outside the house? Do you find it difficult to manage even with your high salary?'

'It isn't for money, mother. You see, she feels very lonely at home. This would give her some occupation. . . . And then, if our income goes up, what is wrong with it? We've a lot of expenses. And then we have a radio but not a television, a scooter but not a car.'

'I can only say that this is greed!' That's what Poshikuj understood, and she told him this to his face.

Saaba only smiled at this, and bent his head. Noticing what was on the floor, he said, 'Who has spread this wretched *satranji* here?'

Poshikuj could see that he was angry. She said quietly, 'I did. Why?. . . I can't eat food sitting on a chair at the table.'

He kept quiet. After some time Chhoti returned and he had a private consultation with her. When they had finished tea, they engaged a taxi and took Poshikuj to Chandni Chowk, where they bought for her a steel *thali,* a low wooden table, a sari with checks and an image of Shiva. Returning home, they served her food in the steel thali.

Poshikuj couldn't get a wink of sleep that night. Her mind was assailed by a thousand random thoughts. 'So they are going to purchase a car. How lucky this daughter of Govinda the Idiot is! Anyway, let me say she has brought good luck to her husband. On the contrary, look at that wretched creature who has brought nothing but penury to her husband. . . I wonder if poor Gaasha has been able to buy a cycle. He said he would if payment by instalments was possible. Walking every day from Rainawari to office and back wears out the poor fellow's limbs.'

'If you think of it, a quilt is too heavy for the Delhi winter. ... It will be freezing cold in Kashmir. I will ask Saaba to write to Gaasha that he shouldn't stay out late. A plague on that Jawahar Nagar girl's tuition! God forbid, if something happens to him, we'll all be destroyed.'

'What millions of varied things are on sale at Chandni Chowk! How many shorts and bush-shirts that Bitta would like! I would have bought one for him if I had my own money with me. Anyway, I shall go there one day and buy him a bush-shirt, shorts and a hockey ball. I shall also have to buy bangles for the girls in the other house and a sari of sorts for that wretched woman.'

'I know very well that if I continue staying here with Saaba, I will have all the comfort in the world. He was telling me that he would take me to Hardwar next month. . . . How *he* also longed to go to Hardwar all his life, but even his ashes could be immersed only at Shadipur! How on earth was it possible for Gaasha to raise five or six hundred rupees'. Had Saaba been here, things would have been different.'

'I say there are Muslims here too! How those *burqa* women were walking in Chandni Chowk! Aren't they shrunk with fear here as we are there? Fear destroys us there because we feel these would be killed here. But who can govern irrational fears?'

A sound of the bedroom door opening and someone moving briskly over the cement floor was heard. Poshikuj could make out whose steps they were. A few minutes later there was the loud ringing sound of the flush being pulled. 'A plague on her stomach!' said Poshikuj to herself. 'Another ... no wonder with the tons of *sookhi dal* she ate last evening.

She has woken up the whole world with that ringing noise. Better she had announced it from the radio station where she is going to get a job.'

The day was dawning when she got up. After moving her bowels, she had a bath and was back in her room again. She wrapped herself up in a blanket. Kept the image of Lord Shiva in front of her and started reciting *bhajans.* She remembered a bit of *Mahimna Param,* which also she recited. After the prayer, she went up to the roof and started basking in the sun. She felt that the sky was vast and big here, not like in Kashmir with mountains on all sides leaving only a bit of the sky in between. 'Perhaps it is the vast sky that broadens the vision and enlarges the horizon of these people here and brings them prosperity. One likes to remain neat and clean here.'

While she was absorbed in these thoughts, Saaba called her. She went downstairs. There on the table were cups and saucers, bread, eggs and other things for tea, neatly arranged. He was sitting in a chair, reading the newspaper. He was wearing a dressing-gown. Chhoti emerged from the kitchen with a teapot. She was also wearing a dressing-gown with her hair tied up with a piece of red ribbon. Placing the teapot on the table, she took out of the fridge butter and strawberry jam which she spread on the slices of bread. Poshikuj ate a couple of these slices with tea. Husband and wife had some eggs in addition. Seeing them eat eggs, particularly Chhoti, Poshikuj was reminded of Bitta. 'How lean the poor boy is! But he doesn't get even a cup of milk. If his mother had sent him here along with me, he would have put on some flesh.'

After breakfast Saaba went up to his room and Chhoti followed him after keeping the used things in a basin for *mai.* A little later, both husband and wife came down, having changed their dress. Poshikuj looked them up and down.

'I am leaving for office, mother, and she is coming with me to the market. I shall help her to buy meat.' Saying this, he started the scooter. She sat behind him, placing her right hand on his shoulder. The scooter started racing along the road making a *thup-thup* sound.

She remained gazing at the road after they had left. 'I have fifty or sixty rupees. Perhaps I shall send this amount to Gaasha. It might help him to purchase a cycle. . . .' She was thinking this when Miss Kapur made her appearance. *'Namaskar,'* she said, *'Mrs Bhan ghar main hain?'* Poshikuj could make out what she had asked and answered. *'Market gay! Meat lane.'* Miss Kapur nodded with a smile.

Poshikuj did not like this smile. She said in a cold manner, *'Baitho, baitho, abhi ati.'*

But Miss Kapur did not sit with her. She entered the drawing room as if it belonged to her and settled down on a sofa.

'What arrogance you have, you wretched widow!' said Poshikuj with a toss of her head, and went out into the garden. After some time

Chhoti returned with the purchases. Poshikuj said, 'Mrs Kapur inside. She is waiting for you.'

'Mataji, say Miss Kapur, not Mrs Kapur!'

'Alright, I will say Miss Kapur. I talked to her nicely, and she started grinning at me.'

'You must have got the wrong impression. This poor girl is not like that', with these words, Chhoti also went into the drawing room.

That the daughter-in-law did not believe her, hurt Poshikuj very much. 'First, it is my own stupidity. Both husband and wife think no end of this hag. And why shouldn't they? They need her father's help. Miss Kapur! Hunh! God knows how many men she must have had, and still she calls herself "Miss!"'

The warmth of the sun was making Poshikuj feel drowsy, when there were peals of laughter in the drawing room. She suspected that both Chhoti and Miss Kapur were having a laugh at her expense. . . . She felt that it would be wrong to continue staying here very long. If only there were someone to accompany her, she would go back to Kashmir in three or four days. . . . And if she only could—if it were possible—she would carry with her basketfuls of this sunshine.

*Tdph*, 1967 *Tr*. by Trilokinath Raina

*kaakanya* sister-in-law; *mai* old maidservant, *satranji* thin cotton carpet

**Where Love is Scarce**

*Bashir Akhtar*

Bashir Akhtar (Basir Akhtar, b. 1944), one of the torch-bearers of the younger generation of Kashmiri writers, is essentially progressive in his outlook and art. In his delectable short stories he has identified himself with the cause of the downtrodden and presented a realistic picture of the social order in his native land. His work is marked by a rare sense of humour and sarcasm.

*Yati Ab Chu Koluy* (Where Love is Scarce) deftly portrays the helplessness of the unsophisticated rural folk who suffer at the hands of an arrogant and corrupt police officer.

As the jeep reached the police station, the driver changed gears. The engine roared and a long blast of smoke gushed out through the silencer. The driver was ready to shift from the clutch to the accelerator so as to drive in through the gate when Deputy Superintendent Sarbuland Khan asked him to halt in a loud voice.

The driver was caught unawares. His right foot went mechanically to the brake instead of the accelerator. The jeep obeyed the order and stood still.

Khan Sahib reached his hand to the dashboard and picked up his cane. He then came out of the jeep, removed his cap and, depositing it in his left armpit, marched in through the main gate.

The sentry posted at the gate saluted him as usual with such a loud tapping of his boot that the birds perched on the nearby pomegranate tree were scared away. Even then it seemed that Khan Sahib either did not hear the loud report or ignored it and went ahead. The cops sitting in the corridor got alerted and a silence as of the graveyard overtook the whole police station.

Khan Sahib went into the room banging the door behind him. After sitting in the chair he pressed the call-bell which, however, did not ring. He pressed the button again but with no result.

'Bastards', he muttered. It was not clear whether he was referring to his orderly or to the electricity department, because when he looked up at the wall the light was off while the orderly was standing at the door as motionless as a statue.

'Call the *havildar*', he said fretfully. The orderly did a right-about turn and was ready to step out when another command came, 'And listen.'

The orderly turned back, brought his hands down and stood like a log.

'Have you brought the thing I wanted?' asked Khan Sahib with his eyes cast down. The orderly, on hearing this, stood at-ease and walked up to the table. Picking a pin from the pincushion he cleaned his right ear with it. Then he smiled and said, 'That has been lying here for long, sir.'

'Good, very good', said Khan Sahib and nodded too. 'In the whole establishment, you are the only useful hand.'

'So kind of you, sir', grinned the orderly baring his dirty teeth and gums.

'It is alright', said Khan Sahib, meaning that the orderly should leave the room.

When the orderly had left, Khan Sahib picked up the papers lying in the tray on his right. He had a cursory look at them and then put them back in the tray. Blinking his eyes he spanned the whole of the tabletop. Everything was in order, pen-stand, paper-weight, pincushion, blotter and glass. Under the glass lay a group photograph which bore this caption in clear letters.

'Lest we forget. On the occasion of the transfer of DSP Raja S.B. Khan.'

Inexplicably, Khan Sahib heaved a sigh. The glass covering the photograph had a round blot in one corner resembling a circle drawn by a child with the compass, which he later fills with colours. He passed his finger slowly over the blotted portion. He felt that the spot was rough. He remembered that only the other day he had placed a hot cup of tea at that very place when he had to entertain three guests at his own cost.

'A useless beggarly village!' he bemoaned with anger and turned the chair round with a jerk. Then he looked again at the glass only to find that the blot had vanished.

Khan Sahib was astonished. He bent down and looked at the tabletop from a different angle. Lo! The blot was still there, shining brightly in the light coming from the window. Inadvertently, he lifted the paper-weight and rubbed the glass with it. The rubbing produced some scratches on the glass around the blotted spot. Khan Sahib caught hold of the paper-weight with three fingers and using the full force of his hand spun it into a whirl. The paper-weight revolved like a top on the smooth surface of the glass. While rotating it took a few somersaults over the caption of the group photograph and then raced down to land on the planked floor with a bang.

Khan Sahib reclined, lit a cigarette and taking a long puff closed his eyes.

Before his transfer to this place, he has spent eight years in the city. Fortune had smiled on him. Even earlier, he had always got prize postings. In the city, motor vehicles plied all the day, shops remained open until midnight and people thronged cinema houses. There were noisy crowds in front of the vendors selling roasted meat sticks, jostling and pushing passing women and cracking dirty jokes at them. In short, one tumult surpassed another and cases were registered at the police station in quick succession. Khan Sahib remained occupied round the clock with complainants flocking to his office as well as to his residence.

'What a poor substitute this accursed village is!' he heaved a sigh. 'If a filthy rural woman goes round the village with a basketful of cowdung on her head who will dare to molest her and whom can we haul up?'

Khan Sahib's children studied in a public school and were used to a high style of living. They could have anything for the asking. They lived in a spacious bungalow situated in a posh colony. Guests dropped in throughout the day and a contingent of servants remained in attendance.

The DSP again picked up the papers kept in the tray, examined them one by one and finding them of no use twisted them with the hand and threw them down saying, 'All trash. There is nothing in them.'

Meanwhile, the havildar appeared at the door and sought permission to come in.

'Where were you all this time?' Khan Sahib asked in an angry tone.

'Sir . . .' the havildar tried to explain but the DSP cut him short saying, 'Shut up!'

Khan Sahib got up and took a few steps around the table. Then he picked up the twisted paper bundle from the floor and threw it at the havildar's face. Displaying his clenched fists, he roared, 'Have you called me here for these trivial matters? How many years have you been in service?'

The havildar replied, 'Eight years, sir.'

'Stand erect.'

The havildar obeyed. He stiffened his neck, centred his gaze at one point and stood motionless like a snowman. Then he submitted, 'Sir, this is a small village and very few crimes are committed here. Then the residents of the village. ..."

Khan Sahib again interrupted him. 'There is no need for any explanation.' He then walked to the window on the west, had a look at the distant landscape and turning round asked the havildar, 'Is this a habitat of the dead? Can't anyone here lose even a rooster?'

The havildar drew a long face and then looked out of the window. The sky was still overcast. The plateau was filled all over with grass made luxuriant by last night's rain. It was lush green, fresh and clean.

The cattle owned by the villagers grazed in this pasture. On one side under the shade of a tree, stood a snow white mare. It was as beautiful as an Arabian steed, tall and robust. Its front legs had been tied together to restrict its movements. For picking blades of grass it had first to hop forward on its front legs and then move its hind legs. It was evident that the mare was accustomed to walking with its front legs tied together. Despite this, the havildar felt that such 'cruelty' constituted a cognizable offence warranting interference by the police.

When Khan Sahib enquired a second time whether no one in the village could lose even a hen, the havildar said in a subdued tone, 'Yes sir, this can definitely happen.' Then he saluted Khan Sahib and walked away.

What ensued can be summed up as follows:

Rasool Dar was a horse-owner. He somehow managed to make both ends meet. He would bring a horseload of firewood from the nearby forest and sell it to keep the wolf away from his door.

This occupation he had been following for years. He possessed a mare which he loved dearly.

After finishing the day's chores, he used to set the mare free to graze in the pasture. He would, of course, tie its front legs to prevent it from straying into anyone's vegetable garden. There were vast expanses of common grazing land. The mare would have its fill and return home by nightfall.

Last night, when the mare did not come home until past midnight, Rasool Das got worried. Accompanied by his wife and children and with a lantern in hand he went round the plateau barefooted. Then the family returned and searched the cattle-sheds of all the villagers. He even enquired of the passers-by but there was no trace of the animal.

In the morning, Rasool Dar, after careful consultation with members of his family, proceeded to the police station to lodge a complaint. When the uniformed clerk heard his plea, he laughed in his sleeves. Picking up his pen he said, 'Have you a cigarette?'

Being a poor rustic, Rasool Dar was not used to smoking cigarettes. Of course, he puffed at the *hookah* at home. So he replied that he didn't have any.

The clerk stared at him with disgust and his mood underwent a sudden change. 'Why did you come here with your tale of woe? Are we your father's servants?' Rasool Dar got flabbergasted and was about to cry when another constable lambasted him with, 'Who told to sit in the chair? Go and squat near the door.'

Rasool Dar got up quietly, walked out and sat on the cemented staircase.

Meanwhile, a third policeman rushed in, gasping for breath. Rubbing his hands he said to the clerk, 'Sir, there is no trace of both wire and holder.'

The clerk cast a glance at Rasool Dar, then hinted something to the cop and said with the assumed air of an SHO, using abusive language, 'Search the pockets of that son-of-an-ass. He has come here with an innocent look. It is he who must have stolen the electric bulb at night.'

He had hardly uttered these words when the two constables pounced on Rasool Dar as vultures sweep down on a corpse. They tore his clothes to shreds, slapped him till his face bled and then threw him out of the gate as if he was a dead dog.

The man who accosted Rasool Dar outside the police station was apparently a godsend. After hearing about his plight, he advised, 'Have policemen ever been moved by tears? You do one thing. . . .' But without suggesting the way out, he posed a question, 'Have you got any money?'

Rasool Dar said, 'No.' The man moistened his lips and whispered in his ear. 'Do you know Satar Janda who runs a tea-stall in that corner?' Rasool Dar was intrigued and replied, 'Yes, I know him very well. His sister is married to me', he added shyly.

'In that case, you have nothing to worry. Our boss is his close friend. You might have occasionally seen him in his shop.'

'No, sir. I did not have any idea of this. Many thanks for telling me', said Rasool Dar with folded hands. He felt happy that his prospective saviour happened to be his own man. Brushing his beard with his hand, he walked back home gleefully. His wife was beside herself with joy when she learnt about the influence wielded by her brother. She filled a brand new *kangri* with sweets and made straight for her parental home.

The tea-shop of Satar Janda being in close vicinity to the police station, cops used to frequent it throughout the day. The village bumpkins too visited the shop. Satar and the havildar were so friendly that they often jestingly pushed and punched each other.

Early morning on the following day, Satar Janda and Rasool Dar went to Khan Sahib's official residence. Satar walked straight into his drawing room, leaving Rasool Dar outside.

Rasool Dar was by now convinced that things were going smooth by the grace of God. He said to himself, 'The police might show mercy on me and make a search for the mare.' But when he saw Satar coming out of the house haggard and woebegone, his heart sank.

Satar Janda heaved a deep sigh and said, 'Don't you know a policeman does not spare even his father? He can rob even his sister's husband of his pyjamas. The DSP was demanding a sum of Rs 1600 for starting investigations.' Explaining the point further, he continued, 'The fact remains that we don't know who stole the mare. Had we any suspicion we could cite the names of a few persons. In that case, we have to pay only Rs. 500.'

A word of advice followed, 'Now you do one thing. In your statement you mention at least three persons as probable culprits. If you do that, then you will have to pay only Rs 800 in all. The police will themselves search for the mare and we will be spared the trouble of going from pillar to post.'

Rasool Dar got his statement recorded just as the police ordered him to. In fact, the clerk himself drafted it. Rasool merely affixed his thumb impression on the paper.

A carpenter named Rahim was Rasool Dar's neighbour. While he himself was a gentleman of sorts, his son was a man of the world, who donned the attire of a city youth and applied perfume to his hair. In the evening when the members of the family sat chatting in their house there was sudden call from outside. Rahim's wife was the first to come out. Her womanly intuition led her to suspect that her son must have committed some misdeed. On seeing the policeman in her courtyard she turned pable with fear. She beat her breast and began cursing her son. The boy swore by God pleading his innocence, but his entreaties fell on deaf ears.

At last the carpenter went to the police station and paid a sum of Rs. 500 to ensure the son's freedom and safety. The matter was closed but he never forgot the manner in which Rasool Dar had stabbed him in the back.

The second person implicated by Rasool Dar was named Samad Munna. When he returned home after depositing the hush money at the police station, his wife raised hell. Pulling down her muslin headgear she prayed to God to inflict some calamity on Rasool Dar.

When the third man, Samad Garatal, was also summoned by the police for no fault of his, he did not take it lying down. Instead, he called a meeting of the village panchayat at which Rasool Dar was censured and served with an ultimatum that if he persisted in involving the children of innocent people in false cases, the villagers would be forced to think of ex-communicating him.

Rasool Dar was in an unenviable position. He had lost his mare and money. He had become a pauper due to lack of work. To top it all, he had to face the reprimand of the villagers and the ignominy. The poor man felt like committing suicide. He shed tears of blood and begged the pardon of the village elders by laying his cap down and kissing the soles of their feet. He publicly vowed not to visit the police station again even if he had to face starvation. He could work as a day labourer to earn his food but where would he find shelter for his family in case he was asked to leave the village for good.

Rasool Dar not only made this solemn promise but also kept it to the last word. He swallowed the pain of the loss of the mare and started work as a daily wage-earner.

There is the famous story of an old man clasped by a bear. The man wanted to free himself but the bear would not loosen its grip. Though Rasool Dar wanted to detach himself from the clutches of the police, the latter would not let go of him so easily.

After a fortnight, a constable came to his house at noon when Rasool Dar was sitting near the window ruminating over his sad plight. The cop called out his name in a very loud voice and said, 'Come to the police station. They have found your mare!' In a jiffy, all the village elders and urchins gathered at the police station. The onlookers saw the snowwhite mare actually standing in the police station compound. But it did not look as healthy as it used to. It lacked all vigour. Rasool Dar went near it but could not believe that it was his mare. However, when the mare saw its master it furiously pulled at the rope which fastened it to the tether. Khan Sahib was convinced that the mare belonged to Rasool Dar.

A villager queried of the DSP, 'Sir, where did you find it?'

Khan Sahib shouted back, 'What have you to do with that? Your purpose is served. Isn't that enough?'

'Yes, it is', another villager said cutting short the matter. Rasool Dar placed his cap at the feet of the DSP.

Intriguingly, Khan Sahib in a show of anger turned back with a jerk and walked into his office. The villagers felt small and regretted their behaviour. They made entreaties to him to forgive them for having questioned him. It was ultimately decided that all the village elders would sign the following press release thanking the police:

We, the residents of the village, heartily thank Raja Sarbuland Khan and all concerned functionaries of the police station for the help ungrudgingly rendered by them to us in times of trial and tribulation. They never gave us a chance to grumble.

Sd/—Residents of the Village through the lambardar.

The following Monday, Haji Aziz Wani, the headman of a neighbouring village, visited the police station to demand payment of the expenditure incurred by him for feeding the mare during the period it was supposed to be missing. Raja Sarbuland Khan flew into a rage and showered abuse on him. The lambardar was trembling with fear.

With blood-red eyes, the DSP said to him, 'How dare you come to me to ask for such expenses? Don't you know it is a crime to keep someone else's horse in wrongful and hidden custody for such a long period?'

The lambardar argued, 'But, sir may God's wrath fall on me if I hid the mare! It was brought to my house at midnight by your own man who said you have ordered me to tie the animal in the cattle-shed and keep a strict watch over it. Reimbursed to the last penny.'

After saying this, he took out a piece of paper from his pocket, 'This is the full account. The total comes to Rs 88. Please tell me what sin I have committed.'

Khan Sahib swallowed the bitter pill. He pulled at the lambardar's blanket and said to him. 'Get up and identify the constable who went to your house.'

'Sir, I could not see his face as it was pitch dark', was the lambardar's reply.

'You might have been blind but we are not', said Khan Sahib taunting the lambardar. He then turned towards his staff and gave the following order:

'Let all policemen, one by one, pull out the hair of this old rogue's beard.'

*Yati Ab Chu Koluv*, 1975 *Tr.* by T.N. Kaul

*lambardar* headman.

## Modern Konkani Fiction: A Selection

### Sign of Sirdars

*V.J.P. Saldanha*

V.J.P. Saldanha (Vincent John Peter Saldanha, b. 1925) is a distinguished novelist, dramatist and poet in Konkani. He is also an acknowledged journalist in Konkani and Kannada. However his forte is the historical novel in Konkani and he is fondly referred to by his pseudonym 'Khadap' meaning rock (i.e. Peter). He has written 35 novels, 60 dramatic works, two operas, more than 1500 poems and songs and numerous articles. He has won several awards for his significant contribution to Konkani language, literature, art and culture.

***Synopsis***: *Sardaranchi Sinol* (Sign of Sirdars, 1966), though fiction, depicts faithfully a number of historical events and figures during the tragic period of the captivity of Canara (Konkani) Christians (1784–89) during the reign of Tipu Sultan, known as the Tiger of Mysore. As a consequence of that 'politically motivated' policy, the Christian community faced total extinction in Canara.

The events narrated in the novel take place around 1785—roughly during the second year of the captivity. By that time most of the community had either perished or gone underground. Very few families had survived—exempted by the Sultan's concession. A few others had escaped arrest, and hence were compelled to live miserably in forests or other such hideouts. And some others, having had to abandon their homes and farms, disguised themselves as Muslims or Hindus and carried on precariously.

From the religious point of view, the position was more tragic. The religious leaders were absent from the scene, as they had fled to Goa at the outset.

The well-known Christian households in or around Mangalore were perforce deserted. The famed churches were either wholly or partially demolished, burnt and razed to the ground.

Despite the calamity, it was not a total blackout. For some inexplicable or unavoidable reason some influential families were spared and along with them some other powerful families partially, if not fully, escaped the rigours of captivity. A few stalwarts from such families were holding enviable positions in Tipu's administration or army, and some of them were Sumi was married off soon, and that left only two of them. At Sumi's wedding, everyone bustled about with joy. Mother too. If, some time, I saw her laughing aloud in company, I wanted to ask her—and what about Mani's dying?

Yet, when Mani died, I didn't write home at all. I kept receiving letter after letter from mother, so I wrote back: Stop writing to me.

In answer, mother wrote me a very long letter.

Then the college people planned a trip to the caves at Ajanta. I said, the caves might help me feel better. So I went to Ajanta.

*Kosla*, 1963 *Tr*. by Vilas Sarang

*smallpox* refers to the superstition that to mention a disease or misfortune is to cause it to happen.

*bhakari* coarse flat bread made of rice, maize or millet, eaten all over Maharashtra, especially in the villages.

## Modern Nepali Fiction: A Selection

### Ravaged Life

*Rupnarayan Sinha*

Rupnarayan Sinha (Rupnarayan Sinha, 1907-55) was a pioneer in the field of the modern Nepali short story. His prose was elegant as seen in his novels, articles and editorials in *Khoji* and *Bharati* and in his stories in the collection *Katha Nava Ratna* (Stories: Nine Gems, 1950). An idealist and romantic by temperament Sinha preaches without being moralistic and satirizes without acrimony. He treats his characters, particularly the female characters, with sympathy and compassion. The story *Bidhwasta Jiwan* (Ravaged Life) exemplifies this point.

**1.** With the rays of the sun that was about to set, the waters of the sea and the grains of sand on the beach resembled a mass of pink, multicoloured flowers. I lay on the beach gazing at the waves constantly hitting the shore and receding. At a short distance from me was sitting a woman trying to read something. A boy aged four or five years came running and embraced her and then said, 'Mother! Do you like the sand house that I have made?'

As she tried to embrace him her sari slipped down her shoulder. The left arm of the woman was amputated from the elbow. I was overjoyed to hear the Nepali language at a far-off place like Puri but at the same time the sight of her maimed arm made me feel wretched. Covering her left shoulder with a red velvet cape, she moved forward leading the child with her right hand. After having walked a few steps the child said, 'See, the house I have made is like Toria-Moria.' His mother laughed aloud and said, 'You silly boy, say Victoria Memorial.'

Mother and son sat on the sand and were soon engrossed in the amusing act of house-building. I returned to the hotel.

The Second World War had just ended. Having bidden farewell to my military career I had gone to Puri for a month's rest.

I had sat down for my evening meal in a corner of the dining hall of the B.N.R. Hotel. The dining hall of this hotel is worth seeing. The immediate impression one gets on entering the hall is of refined taste for interior decoration. People of different nationalities assemble there. The Nepali woman entered with a Sikh man, their arms round each other's shoulders. She was dressed in a black sari and had applied thick make-up on her face to make herself pretty.

The two of them sat a few tables away from mine and started chatting.

Of course I could not hear what they were talking, but one thing was quite obvious. The Sikh was requesting her for something and the woman was shaking her head in refusal. After a while the Sikh seemed to be changing the subject: he would say something and the woman would laugh.

The following morning I was lying down at my usual place on the beach in swimming costume. The Nepali woman came and sat nearby along with her son and the Sikh. As I was looking at her, suddenly we caught each other's eyes. She continued to gaze at me for some time blankly. After that she turned her eyes slowly towards the sea.

The Sikh and the little boy started talking in English. The child knew a little bit of English.

'When will you return to Calcutta?' the Sikh asked.

'Never.'

'Why?'

'Because there isn't any sand to play in.'

I had just started learning swimming. I entered the sea with the Nulia.

About seven days passed. Sometimes I would see the woman sitting alone on the shore immersed in reflection. Sometimes I would find her totally engrossed in a joyous sport with her child. At times I used to see her walking by the sea hand-in-hand with the Sikh.

One day I saw her in the temple of Jagannath bowing down before the deity in reverential self-oblivion. I have always been an agnostic; I am neither aware of God's existence nor do I think that there is any such possibility. I had gone to the temple only for fun.

I came out of the temple and while strolling on the main road to the left of the temple I happened to bump into a woman. Immediately I said, 'Sorry.'

The woman looked at me and said in Hindi, 'It's entirely my fault.' Again she smiled and said, 'I think you are also staying in B.N.R. Hotel, aren't you?'

I asked her in Nepali, 'Aren't you Nepali?'

Without saying anything in response she greeted me with folded hands and entered a shop.

After returning to the hotel I was relaxing on the green lawn. I moved to the upper side of the ground when I heard the boy, whom I had seen with the woman, cry. He was insisting on being allowed to play with the watering kettle in the garden. 'No, I won't give you this: your clothes will get wet and Memsaheb will get angry', said the gardener.

On seeing me the boy said in English, 'Wicked gardener.'

I said in Nepali, 'Pooh, you shouldn't play with water or mud. You should play football.'

The boy looked at me slightly confused and then started crying loudly.

Comforting him saying that I would buy him a football, I carried him to the place where I was sitting.

After a while he became friendly with me. When we were talking his mother called him all of a sudden, 'Tito!'

Turning his face towards his mother he said, 'Mother, why don't you come here?'

'Hurry up. It's time for tea', said his mother.

Obstinately the child refused to go and insisted that she should join him. The woman did accordingly.

'Has the boy introduced himself to you? He is very naughty.'

'I really don't think so; he is a pleasant child. Tito, go to your mother', I said.

The boy asked, 'What about my football?'

'I will definitely get one for you', I said.

His mother scolded him saying, 'You imp! Whosoever comes your way, you ask for a football, don't you? I will teach you a lesson!'

**2.** The sea and the beach of a moonlit night; the grains of sand are transformed into fine grains of silver, the rhythmical breaking of the waves on the shore produces the sound *dhudum-dhudum*.

I came out of the hotel and went towards the seashore, a solitary confused traveller. I felt as though there was an incessant call from the sea, 'Come, come into my bottomless bosom. Here there is peace, here there is contentment. This breast is as generous as it is vast.'

I started wandering on the shore aimlessly. My bare feet sank into the sand. The cool breezes of the sea instilled in me a new kind of freshness, an unusual experience. A few men and women were lying on the beach relishing the captivating scenic beauty of nature.

All of a sudden my attention was drawn by somebody's melodious song towards which I slowly moved.

The singer was the same Nepali woman who had literally cast a spell with her song on her Sikh friend who was accompanied by another person. For a long time I quietly listened to her song, spellbound.

The next evening the Sikh was not seen there at dinner. There was somebody else. The woman came to the dining hall dressed in the same way. The man accompanying her was in a dinner suit of the English type. The two were talking. I could not quite make out what they were saying but I clearly : understood one thing; he was making requests with folded hands. The woman was nodding her head again and again in refusal. Once or twice he tried to caress her cheeks which put her off and she pushed his hands away.

The next morning she was entertaining the child on the shore. This time she had not applied make-up on her face. She was simply attired—a vivid image of motherhood. Her mind, her life seemed to be far, far away from the problems of the world. She appeared to be emptying her bosom by pouring all the love that bubbled up within her, on the child.

When the boy saw me he shouted, 'Where is my football?' The woman greeted me with folded hands and said, 'Don't listen to what this boy says. This is how he gets on everybody's nerves.'

'I have promised him. So I must buy him a football', I said.

She requested me to sit down. For a long time the three of us sat there and talked. The child was busy making, unmaking, remaking sand houses. He asked for my help and threw a handful of sand on his mother's lap.

Three days later in the evening when I was lying on the beach, ruminating over my bygone military career, all of a sudden I heard someone sobbing near me and I looked back. It was the same woman. She was crying bitterly and tears were streaming down her cheeks.

I quietly got up and stood near her which perhaps she did not notice, because she was constantly looking into the sky and crying.

I inquired in a low voice, 'What is the matter?' Why are you crying?'

She looked at me in a pitiable way and without saying a word turned her eyes, filled with tears, to the other side.

I didn't know what to say or what to do, and in a state of indecision, I sat down there. Slowly darkness engulfed the sun in the western horizon. The people on the beach had dispersed.

With unexpressed sympathy I was sitting by her. Who could comprehend the heart-rending affliction of the past that was tormenting her?

After a short silence I once again expressed my desire to know what had happened to her.

The woman composed herself. Wiping her tears with the edge of her sari, she said with a long sigh, 'How long are you going to stay here?'

'I will be here for another seven days', I replied.

'Where will you go from here?'

'I have yet to decide that.'

'What is your occupation?'

'I was a major in the army. The war ended, I bade farewell to my military career for ever. I don't know what I will do in future.'

As we were talking Tito came. Deliberately trying to digress, I asked, 'What sort of name is Tito? Why do you call him Tito?'

The woman replied with a smile, 'When he was a little boy trying to speak he could not pronounce *"chha"*, he would say *"tito"* instead of *"chhito"*. It became a habit with him to say, *"Tito amma tito"* and this is how he got his name.'

I went towards the town with Tito to buy him a football. The woman kept waiting for us on the beach.

In a short while I returned with Tito and joined her again. Leaving the child in the hotel we again returned to the shore.

**3.** 'How lustrous are your eyes but behind them I see a dormant sea of tears.'

'Don't look into my eyes.'

'Why?'

'There lies concealed the story of my ravaged life.'

'How can you say that yours is a ravaged life when you are so beautiful, young and blessed with a loving son.'

'I am an amputee, a widow, a bird in a storm, a withered flower.'

'You must derive comfort from the fact that there are innumerable people in this world whose plight is much worse and whose suffering much more intense.'

'Who can read the contents of my heart; who knows how it was shattered. We sit on the beach of this deep blue sea, ignorant of what lies in its vortex.'

For a while quietly we watched the thickening darkness. The woman broke the silence by saying, 'Are all soldiers cruel?'

'Why should they be cruel? The only motto adopted in war is kill or be killed. I should kill the enemy before he kills me.'

'But conscience?'

I replied with a smile. 'The question of conscience and reason arises only when you live in a civilized society, not on the battlefield.'

'Cruelty runs through each and every vein of a soldier', she said in dissent.

'Absolutely wrong', I protested.

'It was the same kind of brutality that ravaged my life', her voice trembled in plaintive remonstrance.

'Did some heartless soldier kill your husband?'

'My husband made me half-dead, murdered an innocent youth and Tito and I were deserted, steeped to the lips in misery.'

'Was it jealousy?' I asked hesitatingly.

'God knows', replied the woman, heaving a sigh.

'Please tell me, what happened?'

'Do you believe in God?' She asked, trying to change the subject.

'I am neither a theist nor an atheist. I have not seen God. I can neither prove that God exists nor do I have evidence to refute it', I said.

'Is there any element of truth in the laws of the universe and the idea of the irrevocable nature of fate?'

'Not at all'

'I believe in God, but my faith in him has been almost shattered. Indeed fate is inexorable.'

Slowly she narrated the story of her life in a controlled voice.

Tito was only two years old. Friday was his birthday. Only the previous year my husband had returned to his battalion after celebrating Tito's birthday on a grand scale.

There was a letter from my husband to the effect that he was reaching home on that auspicious day which also happened to be Tito's birthday. I considered myself to be the luckiest.

The two preceding days were spent by me cleaning our little cottage. I had adorned the pictures of Tito and my husband with garlands and kept them on the table near the bed.

I kept my husband's clothes carefully folded on the bed so that he could change when he reached home and I made Tito wear new clothes.

My simple but beautiful arrangement amazed Tito who would sometimes Vturn to me and say with a smile,' *Tito amma tito.'*

I would put him on my lap and say, 'Okay son, your father will come soon.'

I was anxiously waiting for my husband with a heart overflowing with love.

There was a knock at the door and I rushed out with Tito.

A lame soldier shivering with malaria suddenly sat down near the door. He could not be more than eighteen years old. War had consumed his energy, his vitality, his youthful vigour to which his debilitated body bore eloquent testimony.

'I have only one grandmother who has returned from Burma. When I went to see her I got an attack of malaria', said the soldier.

I took him inside. His body was hot as though it were burning.

I made a bed for him on the floor. I was sponging his forehead with a towel. Tito was watching curiously from the bed.

Suddenly I saw somebody' shadow on the door: I got up and went towards it. It was my husband who had returned from war after an year. I was overjoyed and being unable to control myself I went to embrace him.

'You whore! I have seen your filthy deed with my own eyes. Again you are trying to deceive me?' he walked back two steps and thundered.

I said, 'You are misunderstanding me; first listen to me.' But he didn't. I was the first victim of his bullet. The only thing I remember is the dreadful sound that came out of his pistol and Tito's scream.

After a week when I gained consciousness I found myself in hospital. My left arm that sustained the bullet injury was amputated from the elbow. Tito, who was lying near my mutilated arm, was again and again saying, 'Hurry up, mother, hurry up.'

*Bidhwasta Jtwan* *Tr.* by Irshad Ahmed

*chhito* hurry up; quickly.
*Nulia* a tribe of Puri whose main occupation is to teach swimming.

**The Price of the Fish**

*Shiv Kumar Rai*

Shiv Kumar Rai (Siv Kumar Rai, b. 1919) is a well-known short story writer in Nepali. An active politician and social worker, he was the first Nepali to be included in the West Bengal ministry of Dr. B.C. Roy. He has also been associated with the All India Radio and has worked with the Nepali daily *Himalchuli.* Rai has written one novel, four collections of short stories and a book of poetical tales. His story collection titled

*Khahare* (The Hill Stream, 1976) was given the Sahitya Akademi Award in 1978.

*Mdchhdko Mol* (The Price of the Fish) tells the story of the poor fisherman Ranay who catches the fish in the hill-streams for his livelihood, and one day pays the price of the fish with his own life.

**1.** The torrential rains had just stopped. The swift winds blowing from the south had scattered the cloudlets which were just turning white. At places where the clouds had been washed away the blue sky could be seen. There was no sign of remorse. After losing balance for a while nature was silent again. Only die stream filled with the tears of the sky was roaring down. The din of the mountain stream was echoing through every nook and corner of the hills around.

After coming out of his hut, the fisherman Ranay stretched his palms over his eyebrows and looked at the sky. He also looked intently at the roaring stream. He was a man of short stature but strong constitution. He wore a very old *dowra-swiwal* of cheap quality fit only to be called rags, sewn at several places and a checked black waistcoat adorned width a line of white buttons. A colourless cap of cheap quality was on his head. His swiwals were folded up to his calves. He looked a typical man of the village.

Ranay looked at the roaring stream once or twice and then, carrying a small fishing net, went towards it. Everything looked alright except the small bridge down there which had been washed away by the rains. This filled him with despair. Though a man of short stature, he covered quite a distance jumping with quick movements. Studying the depth of the water and the white foam circling there, Ranay threw his net into the water and then pulled it out with the full force of his hands. About a dozen fish which had come out along with the sand and the leaves started to struggle and leap by the side of the stream.

**2.** This was Ranay's occupation to earn a living. Ranay's father too had been a fisherman like him. He had died ten years ago having been caught in the roaring currents of the stream during *sawan.* How his memory was buried under the sands of time. The common folk feared the evil spirits. They believed the it was not wise to walk after dark as the eyes of the evil spirits would fall upon them if they did so. For Ranay all these beliefs had no meaning. He himself was a man possessed by a spirit. He was himself reaching this stage of an evil spirit. When the men of the world were in deep sleep and their consciousness walked through a dreamland and a deep silence pervaded everywhere, Ranay carrying a bamboo torch light in his hand and taking advantage of this darkness, sought the presence'of the fishes in their resting places. In the dancing light of the torch his weather-beaten face looked fearsome. The white sunken eyes in his fearsome ugly face pierced through the stream and die mountains around. Perhaps the evil spirits of the Stream too were afraid of this living devil. With a circular movement Ranay, once again threw his net into the deep black waters. All the fish which had been caught in the whirlpool of the current fell into the folds of the net. Ranay's face beamed with joy. His eyes gleamed with delight. He began to assemble all the fish on a bamboo string.

His mother had died when he was a child and he was left all alone in this changing world. He must have dreamed of a life partner in his own way—a small family by the side of the stream. His small son who has just learnt to walk comes staggering to him while he is catching fish and says stammering, 'Father, I will also catch fish.' Getting annoyed he tells his wife, 'O mother of Goray! Please take the child from here!' Or on returning home from the market after selling fish, the mother of his son Goray offers him a cup of tea flavoured with pepper, with a smile on her face. He experienced such joy of a family life in his imagination.

**3.** Carrying the fish on a bamboo pole Ranay went towards the market. He was wet up to his knees. There were wounds which had turned blue due to the body knocking against the pointed stones of the stream. Blood was oozing from some places. Although it was very cold owing to the rains, he was experiencing the warmth of hot fire in him.

At the marketplace a man asked 'O brother! What is the price of your fish?'

'Eight annas!'he replied.

'Isn't the price too high for the fish of a stream?' Looking at the blue injuries of his limbs he said, 'The price is not too high considering the trouble taken.' Ranay had felt that the price of the fish should have been much more than this, but he had no idea of what the fish would really fetch.

He had finished selling all the fish by five. Ranay counted the money and found that he had earned ten full rupees. Desire took deep root in him. He thought if business went on like this, then he would be able to earn not less than one hundred and fifty rupees a month. He could meet the expenses of taking a wife after building a small hut, by investing the labour of only two months. This desire took firm root in his mind. His attention was drawn by a new shopkeeper by the side of the road as he was thinking about all these things. A woman about twenty-five to thirty years of age was standing in front of the door. She did not seem to possess the destructive fire of youth, but the fading colour of youth was still there.

'O brother fisherman! Why not have tea sometimes in our shop also?' The youthful Ranay did not think it wise to let go this opportunity of having a chat with the woman. He said, 'Why not! What do you have to offer me?' After placing the *shelvoli* potato curry and tea on the table in front of Ranay the woman asked him if she should bring fish also.

Ranay looked at the brown pieces of fried fish looking delicious, making his mouth water.

He asked, 'How much?'

'Two annas per piece', she replied.

'O my God! So much for a piece?'

He was puzzled as his imagination failed to see the point.

'Do you know that this piece would cost eight annas when it reaches a hotel? How, then, can two annas be too much?' Ranay thought, the price of his fish should have been higher. He was really selling very cheap. Yet these two people had not been able to understand the exact price of the fish. Again the same desire arose in him—'a small hut by the side of the stream and a partner for life'. He looked straight at the face of the woman. He felt as if his heart stopped beating for a while and started beating again with great force. He seemed to have lost his senses for a while.

He asked, 'Where is your husband?' The woman gave a straight reply, 'O! My husband? He went away before me. My in-laws are in the bazaar. My father-in-law loves me but mother-in-law is good for nothing. She hates me. So I have separated from them to live alone.'

The last sentence awakened his inner desire. He mused, 'There is no harm in being a widow. She is still young and being a widow she may love me.' Now he must save some money to build a hut. As he was about to walk back home, the widow told him, 'Brother! Please do not forget to come again.' Ranay was surprised and his heart filled with joy. He said, 'Certainly yes, if death does not take me away.'

**4.** It was already seven when he reached the stream. He felt very light of body that evening and his heart was filled with joy. His youthful emotions were surging up. It was again the same dark night of *sawan;* the stars had disappeared and gone away to some other region. The sky was covered with clouds. The rains were about to come down. The clouds thundered. The sound reached the surrounding mountain chains and echoed all over the place. The stream was flowing with the same gurgling sound. Ranay went towards the stream with a lighted bamboo torch in his hand. The clouds thundered again. A sudden fear arose in his fearless heart. In the flash of the lightning he had a glimpse of the face of his dead father and he felt as if his memory was deceiving him. The clouds were thundering as though to warn him not to go to the stream but he was adamant and did not pay any heed to this. He had only one thought in his mind: that by doubling his earnings he would fulfil the desire of his heart. Ranay once again threw his net into the whirling pool with all his might. The fish had lost their sense of alertness due to the light of the bamboo torch. About twenty-five to thirty fish of different varieties were caught in the net. He reached his hands into the den of the fish and felt their presence everywhere. He took out the fish-catching basket from the running water and found plenty of fish entangled in it also. Ranay had neither sleep nor hunger. His hopes were flying high on the wings of imagination. He was not aware of his physical exertion. Black foamy clouds arose from the west and all of a sudden from the top of the mountain roaring water came gushing down. Ranay did not know that his death too would

'No, you fool, we didn't take away your homestead. I bought oxen for you, so you could work for a living. I gave you a field, and you went berserk and killed the buffalo. So what are you saying? If you sell your house and land, you'll get some extra for the road. If you go towards the plains, you will find a means to make a living or will you go towards Mungloon?'

'We'll find out after we start moving; we'll go where God takes us.'

Nande wanted Dhane to move. He wanted to acquire Dhane's house and yard, as his sister's son was in need of a house, and Nande wanted to put him there. He said, 'If you want to set the price of your property, come tomorrow. Tomorrow I will get everyone together. And tomorrow we will calculate how much will be left over after you pay. Even if you are not here to register the land at the district office, I'll do it for you.'

The next day, the important men from the village were gathered in Nande's yard to make a decision about Dhane's fate. Dhane, with a long face, was sitting in a corner. He was troubled over one thing: 'How much will the property fetch? When the moneylender settles the account will there be anything left over for the journey, or will I lose that too?' A price was set for the house and yard, and all the cooking implements, cattle and other things. An agreement was prepared. After the moneylender's cut, there was seventy-five rupees left over for Dhane. But since Nande wanted to show generosity towards a person leaving the village for ever, he didn't take two months' interest, and he placed eighty-five rupees in Dhane's hand.

### *Chapter 29*

As Dhane went up the hill to Terse Lemachane's house, the sun had reached the ridge in the west. Dhane had come out to pay Terse the five rupees he owed. Terse was sitting outside on the seat by the door. Dhane took five rupees out of his belt and said, 'Hey brother, I borrowed this a few days ago. Also last year I took some meat from you and didn't pay for it. What can I do? All my property has been taken, and tomorrow or the next day, I'll probably be going.'

Terse understood, and asked, 'Will you be taking your family too?'

'Yes I have to take them with me—how could I leave them? Our stay in this village is over. Who can say if we'll meet again?' Dhane wiped his tears.

Tears came to Terse's eyes also. He wouldn't take the money Dhane offered him. He said, 'Use it to get the child something to eat on the road, brother, I don't need it. We are going to be in the same situation ourselves soon; how long does it take to lose all our property ? If I had three or four hundred rupees, I could help, and you wouldn't have to leave the place of your grandfathers, but what can be done?' Even though Dhane stubbornly insisted, Terse would not take *the* money. Putting it in his belt he took leave.

When Dhane reached his house, night had fallen. Maina had been looking him out as she stood in the yard. Dhane went inside and sat at the edge of the fireplace, and Maina sat by his side. After some time, Dhane related everything to Maina. 'Tie up all the baggage. Tomorrow, as soon as it is light, we have to leave. I don't want to stay in this sinful place any more.'

'We have to leave this place that has been the family residence for ages! The sweat of my father-in-law's family fell on this house and land, and it's not yet dried! Now we'll leave it.' Covering her face with her palm, Maina began to cry.

Dhane, stroking her head, said, 'What can we do? If the laws of fate are written like this, why cry?' He consoled her as he wiped her tears. But who would wipe his own tears which fell on Maina's head?

Dhane was there to give consolation to Maina. As long as he existed, Maina was not burdened with responsibility, but who could help Dhane? The Creator was his only hope, but even the Creator at this time sat somewhere apart and laughed loudly.

### *Chapter30*

At the call of the rooster, the three went out by the front door. First Dhane with a bundle of homespun wrapped in two blankets on his back. Another small bundle swung from his hand. Behind him, Maina was carrying the baby on her back, and had attached a small bundle to her hand. She was sobbing quietly. Dhane wiped his tears so that no one would know he was crying. The small baby was crying because his sleep had been disturbed.

The two came into the front yard and looked fixedly at the empty house. Maina's eyes rested on the *tulsi* grass at the edge of the yard. She set the bundle on top of the wall and went inside and returned with a small earthen pot of water. As she watered the tulsi grass, she murmured, 'After tomorrow, you may dry up and die. Who will come and sprinkle water on you? When will I get the chance to sprinkle water on your bed again?'

Inside, in the inner room, the sweet cooing voices of pigeons sounded. Maina went inside again. The baby was crying in full force, but she was not conscious of it. Inside, she began to search for a small earthen pot by feeling around in the dark. At last she found it and put her hand inside the pot—had even the broken rice grains come to an end? Gathering the bits together, she took a fistful and went to the side of the room to put it down among the pigeons, startling them.

'After tomorrow, who will give you food? How will you manage? Maybe someone will fill his stomach with you!' Leaving the cooing pigeons, she rested her head on the wall of the inner room and began to cry.

Dhane again called from outside, 'It's late. What are you doing?'

Maina suddenly remembered the animals, and hastily went towards the shed. When the cattle saw her, they began to bellow. Maina put some straw in their beds and began to stroke them. The words came of themselves:

'After today, your new master will come. He'll give you good hay and food. Don't kick anyone, do your work honestly. If you don't, they will beat you. . . .' Filled with strong feeling, she began to cry as if mad, and a stream of tears came from her eyes.

After some time she regained her composure and went to the front yard. She went into the storehouse at the front of the yard. She looked around inside carefully. All her life she would cry when she remembered the hand- ; mill, the rice-husking machine, the beams, pillars, roof, tree—each thing. On ... one side an old ewe was tied up, and alongside her two lambs were wetting in the litter, filling up their stomach. Maina went to her and stroked her and the ewe began to bleat. She lifted up the lambs and held them in her lap, and pressed her cheek to theirs. The animals seemed to whisper to her. Dhane, impatient, called from outside and Maina got up, wiped her tears and went out. Dhane was already on the main road. She took her parcel and followed.

The journey of these three beings was a picture of compassion. Father, mother and baby looked back from time to time and then headed forward again. It is hard to think of a precise literary prototype for their journey. If someone had seen them at that time, it would certainly have reminded him of Ramachandra's going to live in the wilderness. Rama lived in the wilderness for fourteen years and then returned. But these three beings had locked the door and were leaving for ever. There was no hope in their hearts of some day returning to this place.

Their journey was not for the purpose of practising austerity in the wilderness, nor was it for finding a homestead. This journey was not a planned one; they didn't know where they were going. Where would they end up? Where would they find a real dwelling place?

House, storehouse, garden, shed—all were quiet; life had gone out of them. Always, Maina and Dhane used to bathe each morning and view the sun from the kitchen garden. Maina would take the small vessel in hand and worship the sun conscientiously by sprinkling water in that garden. But there would be no one in the garden to make the offering of water.

From today, with the first rays of the sun, Dhane and Maina would begin a new life. It is possible that this new life would be better than the last, but it could also be worse. But whatever was destined to happen—as the sun gave them his blessings—from this house, kitchen garden, hearth, wherever they spent a great part of their lives, they will be very far away.. . very far.

*Basdin*, 1957 *Tr*. by Larry Hartsell

## Verily Like Us Is She—Maina's Mother

*Indra Bahadur Rai*

Indra Bahadur Rai (Indra Bahadur Rai, b. 1927), renowned as a writer of short stories in Nepali, is equally successful in the essay, literary criticism and the novel. He was the principal architect of the *Ayamith Lekhan* or Dimensional Writing movement was launched in 1963. Deriving inspiration from various aspects of modern thought including discoveries in physics and psychology, and also from new art movements like Cubism, Rai attempts in his new stories the presentation of reality in a novel fastion *Hami Jaitai* (Verily Like Us Is She—Maina's Mother) is an abstract with layers of meaning. Maina's mother is here viewed from the perspective of time ever present, as an archetype. The woman sells leafy vegetables in a market but is seen centuries before the market square came into being. The archety- extends beyond the recent past to a primitive, nomadic period. The woman lives in the ever present time and the woman, as the title suggests, is like all of us.

Lifting a bound bunch of vegetable leaves the prospective buyer asks, 'How much is this?'

But that would be merely reporting the incident, not presenting it in the raw. What he actually did was: He woke up the bound leaves, bid them to be combative with him, domineered over them. Pleased, he said, 'How much is this?

'That one, a rupee'.

An enraged sense of irrelation reverberates through him, his interest being impaled. Maybe he still harbours the jungle possibility of getting things for nothing.

'Sered and withered,' he said, clearly an effort to find something wrong with the greens that would really lead him to let go the bunch and clear away.

Maina's mother waits for the next bayer to come.

Get moving, we'll move along the foothill of the Himalayas. Take a north-easterly direction.

Those who stumble to this place later on may exclaim: It seems that ages ago a branch of the Nepalis had inhabited this region founding a settlement by the name of Darjeeling. Many a remnant of theirs have been found. Evidences are extant that they just beguiled their time—a century and more—amusing themselves with the toy town of theirs. Tiny roads, houses and workshops too have been unearthed. Lacking adequate means of subsistence here they perforce had to move out and fan throughout the continent. But the days of colonizing virgin lands had long been past.

'No longer should we stay in Darjeeling,' shouted the man. 'No jobs here. Education and qualifications are of no consequence. There's not enough grass and fodder for the cattle. The rainfall has diminished over the years. We must migrate. We'll make the move by sunrise tomorrow. Put all our womenfolk and children and belongings on the carts. Post strong-armed youths at the front to lead the line and equally lusty youths at the rear to protect it. We shall halt beside a stream by sundown. After faring a hundred leagues we'll finally decide where to head for.

Come whatever may, we must move out.

Maina's mother sprinkled water over the bunches of *rdyo* leaves. The leaves when felt, would all be alive and fresh if they could be taken to a water-place like that of her village. She felt that everything could be saved here and kept alive. Only, there is not enough water.

'Oh, you've come already?' asked she seeing a woman come. 'Haven't you sold any?' asked the woman eyeing the half-awake bunches. 'Didn't you sell any?' Maina's mother remained mute and silent. 'Oh, I should have sold them myself, carped the woman.

'Give me something, just what you have', she begged. 'My husband, he is on his deathbed.' She was visibly nervous and panicky.

Circles, watery circles, around every fallen raindrop. Raindrops in their multitude descending on the lake. The spattering rain has made the whole forest noisy, further enhancing our awareness of it. A strip of a path runs around the right-hand curve of the lake and one sees three hasty bodies racing along it. One of them, a large-limbed one, comes up to the tent and rushes in. Takes a breather and, under that great downpour, smiles familiarly as though to say, it did rain hard after all, didn't it?

To run like that he had rolled the trousers up to the knees and now the massive calves of his legs could be seen.

'They say you're building a new house, this time a *pucca* one, up there on the spur', said her mother and could not help looking again at those bulging hind parts of the legs. Maina's mother for her part had hit upon such hints when her mother talked ramblingly of her past which was not often. Her mother, who kept a tent-shop at this very spot where now the daughter hopes against hope to make a fair living by selling vegetables of sorts.

'I hear Darjeeling will grow fast to become a really big town,' said he. 'That suits us all, doesn't it?'

'Stop talking', bade the torrential rain that cried them down. Inside the tent here the fireplace was sending up faithful flames and much smoke which seemed to be encased within the tent by the rain. The man had found a low wooden stool to sit on. Almost immediately he stood up to point out, 'See the rainwater. It's flowing into the tent.'

'Have you got anything to dig a ditch with?' asked he.

'No. Nothing whatever.'

The man picked up a stick, just a length of a dry branch, and started digging a not-too-shallow trench around the tent. The woman saw fresh earth being dug up, saw herself encircled all around by it, saw the rainwater had now stopped flowing in. 'The flowing-in has stopped', spoke she. But that robust body and soul of a man went on working, making the trench look fine too.

Maina's mother ducked and a boulder ('Man goes to the moon') hurtled past her. A missile ('Live like a man') aimed at her struck her in the chest and she crumpled down. Well, all the sorrows were her familiars that never ceased regularly visiting her while haughty happiness disdained ever to drop in at her place. Any one of the worldly big news could come down rolling upon her and pulverize her. She tended to burrow underground and escape it. The heavy weight of hope could bury her a full fathom deep. She made a bid to resist burial by raising herself up as the mountain does.

Whence can one get the best view of the Himalayas? Ever on the look-out for that spot and moving on we came to this part and halted. Now we don't feel like going further anywhere else. A house that throws its windows open early every morning and views the Himalayas—such a house should each one of us build and possess here.

Man, we fear, is never in perfect health. He soon grows weary of everything. Surely an invalid's taste of things. But we never do grow weary of the Himalayas.

If ever we leave or are made to leave this place we will carry away with us this land, carrying the entire soil with us. We will ask even our five-year-old ones to carry this wealth or property of theirs in small packs on their shoulders.

Casting off their slumber, the bunches stood up. They unbound themselves straight. They yawned long and deep. There came a small gust of warm afternoon breeze. The rayo plants dotted all over with yellow flowers leaned back against it and swayed. She yearned to weed out the grasses and felt their moist touch. She felt a longing to pick up the rusted tin can and water the plants. She breathes happiness of having planted something or other in the terraced field. Stumps of bamboos keep standing in her ken. Her very existence suspended the while, she watches a single twirling leaf come down. She returns home climbing up the many terraces.

Why at all did you come here?
Why at all did you come here?

Why at all did you come here?
Why at all did you come here?
Why at all did you come here?

A grindstone in the bazaar. Nepali bronze plates too.

Yes, the honour and self-respect of a thousand homes is for sale in the bazaar. This grindstone should have remained planted to the earthen floor of a home, clasping the earth and becoming one with it. Why should it have to turn vagrant and be here in the bazaar? And those medicinal herbs? Their place too is at home, inside closed tin cans and cane baskets. The bazaar is a thousand homes rendered asunder. She wanted to pick up the home-parts, disembodied as they were, and reconstruct them into wholes. Yes, all our household wares are displayed here for sale or bidding as are ourselves too. First men left the hearth and home and the household things followed them—to the bazaar. Yes, they have taken a firm stand and want men to return home.

Maina's mother suddenly wants to go home. She is as suddenly scared of the broad daylight and this bazaar.

Sita seeing Ravana the evil one nearby cast a gloomy look. Contemplated in the innermost of her mind the lotus feet of Sri Ram.

She casts nervous glances in an effort to retain her sense and consciousness. Black dots of men climb up the steps and talk. Unending talk. All sights are sounds now here. The gray flap of a tent and a canvas bag—they swing and strike each other. The faint shadow of a flag flies past her and the sound from a microphone whirrs in her ears. My stand is this: I was born here and I'll always live here. This small stack of vegetables is all that I have or can ever manage to have. Honest possession this, by selling this much alone I should get a decent living. Yes, this is my stand. The bazaar unquiet and restless and scabbed all over keeps on scratching itself with its paws.

The sun is placed atop the high column. Why at all did you come?—someone who kept himself unseen asked her. Why did you?—a roving voice of the bazaar asked her. A passer-by turned back and asked her the same question. Men ranged in a line moved towards her demanding her answer to the same question. Windows sprang open for gaping mouths, transfixing gazes and shrill voices to bid her answer the question. Stricken with fright she covered her head with the tattered piece of an old shawl and spied through a window-peephole in it. The fear that she felt was the self-same, ages-old fear.

Some might trample upon the vegetables. She flung herself on them to hold them in her embrace.

By the evening, with an enthusiasm greater than ever she was selling the vegetables. When the evening was pitched as a tent in the sky she placed a wooden box and a Nepali basket over the spot, a daily ritual of

Maina's mother's to keep it under her certain occupation for a tomorrow.

*Hamli Jastai Mainaki Ama,* 1964 *Tr.* by the author

## Modern Oriya Fiction: A Selection

### Six Acres and Eight Gunthas

*Fakir Mohan Senapati*

FakirMohan Senapati (Fakir Mohan Senapati, 1843-1918), father of the Oriya novel and short story, had little formal education and took to writing late in his life. As Diwan of several feudal states in Orissa, he gained first-hand experience of the lives and manners of the common folk, which found vivid expression in his works. With his four novels, *Lachama, Cha Mana Atha Guntha, Mamu* and *Prayascitta,* two volumes of short stories and autobiography, he brought a new dimension to the Oriya language which would favourably compare with the sister language Bengali. The four novels together, in fact, present a picture of two centuries of the social history of Orissa. Marked by an earthy realism, rich in irony and humour, they also have a religious strain, with the wicked being punished in the end.

*Cha Mana Atha Guntha* (Six Acres and Eight Gunthas) is a vivid account of the exploitation of the poor village folk by the zamindars.

**SYNOPSIS:-** Ramachandra Mangaraj magically changes his legacy of penury into one of plentifulness through an act of treachery and dissimulation when he literally robs the zamindari off its decadent owner. Mangaraj, now grown overtly ambitious and fearfully amoral, has a singular mission in life: the acquisition of wealth. He is amply aided and abetted in this by his mistress Champa, a vile woman with an undesirable past. In the Mangaraj household Champa, by her mercurial presence and impetuous manipulations, practically drives Santani, Ramachandra's wife, into a world of self-imposed passivity as it were, where she is condemned to live as a recluse, surviving only by her superior faith in divinity, until her death on a very auspicious day.

Champa, devious and deceitful, traps the hapless Saria and Bhagia, a childless and poor weaver couple of the village, into mortgaging their *chha mana atha guntha* (literally a plot of land measuring six acres and eight gunthas) to Mangaraj. Mangaraj makes the couple, pining for a child, believe that they will have one if they build a temple for the village goddess. They mortgage their land for money to build this temple. But Mangaraj cleverly gets a court decree in his favour. The loss of land ultimately proves to be their undoing and doom. Unable to release their only means of livelihood and reduced to a life of misery, humiliation and acute deprivation, Saria dies a heart-rending death at the doorstep of Mangaraj and Bhagia goes stark mad.

# Index

## M



## N

**O**



**P**

## S